THE CONSCIENTIOUS JUSTICE

US Supreme Court justices make decisions that have a profound impact on American society. Empirical legal scholars have portrayed justices as either single-minded or strategic seekers of policy, and there is little room in these theories for things like law, reputation, or personality. This book offers a fresh perspective that will jar Supreme Court scholarship out of complacency. It argues that justices' personalities influence their behavior, which in turn influences legal development and the US Constitution. This impressive group of authors exhaustively examine every part of the Court's decision-making process, and focus on the trait of conscientiousness and how it influences justices over nine different empirical contexts, from agenda setting to writing the Court's opinions. The Conscientious Justice is an important and comprehensive account of judging that restructures existing approaches to analyzing the High Court.

Ryan C. Black is Professor of Political Science at Michigan State University and a faculty affiliate with the MSU College of Law. He has published three books and more than fifty articles or chapters in a variety of peer-reviewed political science journals, peer-reviewed interdisciplinary journals, and law reviews.

Ryan J. Owens is the George C. and Carmella P. Edwards Professor of American Politics at the University of Wisconsin-Madison.

Justin Wedeking is Professor of Political Science at the University of Kentucky. He has co-authored three previous books and many articles in a variety of peer-reviewed journals and academic outlets. His work primarily analyzes the US Supreme Court.

Patrick C. Wohlfarth is Associate Professor in the Department of Government and Politics at the University of Maryland, College Park. His previous research has been published by Cambridge University Press and various peer-reviewed journals. His work focuses on judicial behavior and legal institutions in the United States, including executive branch litigation, the impact of public opinion, and opinion writing.

The Conscientious Justice

HOW SUPREME COURT JUSTICES' PERSONALITIES INFLUENCE THE LAW, THE HIGH COURT, AND THE CONSTITUTION

RYAN C. BLACK
Michigan State University

RYAN J. OWENS
University of Wisconsin-Madison

JUSTIN WEDEKING
University of Kentucky

PATRICK C. WOHLFARTH
University of Maryland, College Park

CAMBRIDGE
UNIVERSITY PRESS

CAMBRIDGE
UNIVERSITY PRESS

University Printing House, Cambridge CB2 8BS, United Kingdom

One Liberty Plaza, 20th Floor, New York, NY 10006, USA

477 Williamstown Road, Port Melbourne, VIC 3207, Australia

314-321, 3rd Floor, Plot 3, Splendor Forum, Jasola District Centre, New Delhi - 110025, India

103 Penang Road, #05-06/07, Visioncrest Commercial, Singapore 238467

Cambridge University Press is part of the University of Cambridge.

It furthers the University's mission by disseminating knowledge in the pursuit of education, learning and research at the highest international levels of excellence.

www.cambridge.org
Information on this title: www.cambridge.org/9781316618004
DOI: 10.1017/9781316717554

First published 2020
First paperback edition 2021

A catalogue record for this publication is available from the British Library

Library of Congress Cataloging in Publication data
NAMES: Black, Ryan C., 1982– author. | Owens, Ryan J., 1976– author. |
Wedeking, Justin, author. | Wohlfarth, Patrick C., author.
TITLE: The conscientious justice : how Supreme Court justices'
personalities influence the law, the high court, and the Constitution /
Ryan C. Black, Michigan State University; Ryan J. Owens, University of
Wisconsin; Justin Wedeking, University of Kentucky; Patrick C.
Wohlfarth, University of Maryland.
DESCRIPTION: New York : Cambridge University Press, 2019. | Includes
bibliographical references and index.
IDENTIFIERS: LCCN 2019031648 (print) | LCCN 2019031649 (ebook) | ISBN
9781107168718 (hardback) | ISBN 9781316717554 (epub)
SUBJECTS: LCSH: United States. Supreme Court. | Judicial process – United
States.
CLASSIFICATION: LCC KF8748 .B53 2019 (print) | LCC KF8748 (ebook) | DDC
347.73/26–dc23
LC record available at https://lccn.loc.gov/2019031648
LC ebook record available at https://lccn.loc.gov/2019031649

ISBN 978-1-107-16871-8 Hardback
ISBN 978-1-316-61800-4 Paperback

Contents

Acknowledgments   *page* x

1 **Introduction**   1
   1.1 Conscientiousness and Supreme Court Justices   3
   1.2 Why Care about Conscientiousness and Supreme Court
        Justices?   5
   1.3 A Roadmap for This Book   6

2 **A Theory about Justices and Conscientiousness**   11
   2.1 The Evolution of Scholarship on Judicial Behavior   12
   2.2 Scholarship on Personality and the Court   16
   2.3 Conscientiousness: A (Judicial) Trait Worth Examining   20
   2.4 Conclusion   27

3 **Measuring Justices' Conscientiousness**   29
   3.1 Step One: Identifying and Collecting Texts   30
   3.2 Step Two: Translating Texts into Traits Using IBM
        Watson Personality Insights   34
   3.3 Step Three: Standardizing the Measure across Document
        Types   38
   3.4 Measurement Validity   46
   3.5 The Multiple Hazards of Using Concurring Opinions to
        Estimate Personality   58
   3.6 Conclusion   67
   3.7 Appendix   69

4 **Conscientiousness and Supreme Court Agenda Setting**   78
   4.1 The Agenda-Setting Process   82
   4.2 A Theory of Conscientiousness and Agenda Setting   89
   4.3 Data, Measurement, and Analysis   93
   4.4 Conclusion   110

5   **Conscientiousness and Legal Persuasion**   112
     5.1   Persuasion: The Roles of Credibility, Emotion, and Logic   113
     5.2   A Theory of Conscientiousness and Brief Writing   114
     5.3   A Theory of Conscientiousness and Oral Arguments   118
     5.4   Data and Measures   121
     5.5   Methods and Results   126
     5.6   Conclusion   135

6   **Conscientiousness and the US Solicitor General**   137
     6.1   The Role of the Solicitor General   139
     6.2   A Theory of Conscientiousness and Support for the OSG   142
     6.3   Data and Measures: Support for the OSG at the Merits Stage   144
     6.4   Methods and Results: Support for the OSG at the Merits
           Stage   148
     6.5   Data and Measures: Support for the OSG at the
           Agenda-Setting Stage   152
     6.6   Methods and Results: Support for the OSG at the
           Agenda-Setting Stage   157
     6.7   Conclusion   160

7   **Conscientiousness and Majority Opinion Assignments**   161
     7.1   The Opinion Assignment Process   162
     7.2   Factors Leading to Opinion Assignment   164
     7.3   A Theory of Conscientiousness and Opinion Assignment   171
     7.4   Data and Measures   172
     7.5   Methods and Results   175
     7.6   Conclusion   180
     7.7   Appendix   181

8   **Conscientiousness and Opinion Bargaining**   183
     8.1   Bargaining Over Supreme Court Opinion Content   184
     8.2   A Theory of Conscientiousness and Opinion Bargaining   190
     8.3   Data and Measures   193
     8.4   Methods and Results   197
     8.5   Conclusion   213
     8.6   Appendix   215

9   **Conscientiousness and Supreme Court Opinion Content**   222
     9.1   Opinion Language and the Supreme Court   224
     9.2   A Theory of Conscientiousness and Opinion Writing   226
     9.3   Data and Measures   227

9.4	Methods and Results	234
9.5	Conclusion	243
10	**Conscientiousness and the Treatment of Precedent**	**245**
10.1	The Court's Treatment of Precedent	247
10.2	A Theory of Conscientiousness and the Interpretation of Precedent	250
10.3	Data and Measures	251
10.4	Methods and Results	256
10.5	Conclusion	268
11	**Conscientiousness and Public Opinion**	**270**
11.1	Public Opinion and the Court	272
11.2	A Theory of Conscientiousness and Public Opinion	275
11.3	Data and Measures	277
11.4	Methods and Results	280
11.5	Conclusion	284
12	**Conscientiousness and Recusal**	**286**
12.1	Federal Recusal Law	287
12.2	The Evolution of Federal Recusal Law	288
12.3	Current Recusal Practice	291
12.4	A Theory of Conscientiousness and Recusal	294
12.5	Data and Measures	296
12.6	Methods and Results	300
12.7	Conclusion	313
12.8	Appendix	316
13	**Conclusion**	**319**
13.1	The Importance of Conscientiousness to Judging	320
13.2	The Payoff for Understanding Judicial Conscientiousness	323
13.3	Where Do We (and You) Go from Here?	324
References		327
Index		348

Acknowledgments

This book required more time to write than any of our previous works. But it was a labor of love. Along this lengthy (and sometimes meandering) journey, we accumulated a number of debts. First, we thank John Berger, our editor at Cambridge, for sticking with us through delays and significant revisions we ending up making as we went from book prospectus to final manuscript. We couldn't ask for a better editor.

We also thank the several anonymous reviewers who provided feedback on our proposal and the semi-final draft of the manuscript. Your insight strengthened this book more than you know.

In the pages that follow we examine virtually every stage of the Supreme Court's decision making process. This wouldn't be possible but for a number of researchers who made their replication data available to us and helped us with questions as we sought to add our personality measures to them. For being exemplars of scientific transparency, we thank: Tim Johnson, Paul Wahlbeck, and Jim Spriggs (chapter 5); Forest Maltzman, Jim Spriggs, and Paul Wahlbeck (chapters 7- 8); Tom Hansford and Jim Spriggs (chapter 10); and Bob Hume (chapter 12).

In a similar vein, we gratefully acknowledge both Ezra Brooks and Alec Gilbert, two programming ninjas, who used their superpowers for good (we hope) to make our computers work with the software programs that we used to estimate justices' personality traits. This assistance saved us months of time that it would have taken to do the work on our own and they (mostly!) withheld harsh judgment about our sometimes-kludgy programming skills.

We presented various components of this book at a number of conferences and workshops dating back to as early as the 2016 Midwest Political Science Association. Subsequent conferences include the European Political Science Association (2016), the Midwest Political Science Association (2017, 2018), the

Western Political Science Association (2017), the Conference on Elite Personality and Political Institutions at the University of Notre Dame (2017), the American Political Science Association (2017), the Southwestern Political Science Association (2018), the Michigan Political Science Association (2018), the Northeastern Political Science Association (2018), and the Southern Political Science Association (2019). As you can tell, this project, much like Johnny Cash, has been everywhere, man. As for workshops and seminars, we thank their participants and the University of Wisconsin-Madison, Duke University School of Law, the University of Kentucky, University of Maryland's American Politics Workshop, University of Minnesota, and the University of Illinois at Urbana-Champaign for providing us with the opportunity to present our work.

As you can see, we have received advice and suggestions from a great many people and places. Conference discussants, seminar participants, colleagues, and friends also helped us along the way by providing comments and advice. They are, of course, absolved of any responsibility for any errors and views we set forth in the ensuing pages. At the risk of omitting someone (we apologize if we have), we count (and thank): Scott Ainsworth, Jason Anastasopoulos, Miles Armaly, Ryan Bakker, Tiffany Barnes, Horace Bartilow, Emily Beaulieu, Christy Boyd, Marcus Brody, Barry Burden, Adam Candeub, David Canon, Alex Denison, Bryce Dietrich, Keith Dougherty, Luzmarina Garcia, Matt Hall, Tonja Jacobi, Jesse Johnson, Tim Johnson, Devin Judge-Lord, Eric Juenke, Steve Kautz, Jonathan King, Chris Krewson, Elizabeth Lane, Owen Lars, Michael Lynch, Pete Lynch, Tony Madonna, Wayne McIntosh, Jamie Monogan, Mark Peffley, Ellie Powell, Alan Schaefer, Rachel Schutte, Jessica Schoenherr, Shane Singh, Kyla Stepp, Alex Tahk, Travis Taylor, Richard Vining, Steve Voss, and Mike Zilis.

We owe a particular debt of gratitude to Chuck Ostrom, who provided generous support for a multi-day writing retreat which focused our efforts and pushed this book over the finish line. It would have taken months to achieve what that four day retreat accomplished. Everyone should be so lucky as to have such departmental support.

Wedeking dedicates this book to three of his coaches who have had a lasting impact on his life and career, more so than they perhaps realize. Coach Warren Bolin taught the importance of working hard every day at basketball practice- not just some days. He assured him that someday future employers would highly value employees who came ready to work hard. He was right. Coach Craig Hansen repeatedly stressed, even when circumstances might suggest otherwise, that "It's a great day to be alive and play football." It is, as Coach Hansen knows, not only a great attitude to approach football with, but also a great one for life too. And to Coach Matt Pawlowski- who excelled at teaching the finer points of being fundamentally sound- that to be unsound for even one play can have a larger impact on the outcome of a game (as well as in life).

Finally, to our spouses and children: thank you for understanding when we retreated to offices, coffee shops, hotel and pool lobbies, and Charlotte, North Carolina to work on this project. You make all of this possible and worthwhile.

1

Introduction

All human beings have personalities that influence their behavior. Though it may surprise some to hear, US Supreme Court justices are human beings. What this means, of course, is that justices have personalities that influence their behavior and, in turn, legal development and the US Constitution. If Court watchers want to understand the Court, they must understand how justices' personalities shape their behavior. *The goal of this book is to establish that justices' personalities – and, more specifically, their conscientiousness – influence judicial decision-making.*

A few brief examples should prompt you to believe that personalities matter on the Court. Consider Justice James McReynolds, who served on the Court from 1914 to 1941. He appeared to hate everyone and everything around him (Knox 2002). Once, when Justice Harlan Stone remarked that an attorney's brief was "the dullest argument" he ever heard, McReynolds responded, "the only thing duller I can think of is to hear you read one of your opinions" (Abraham 1999, 134). An anti-Semite, McReynolds refused to sit for Court pictures with Justice Brandeis, telling his colleagues, "As you know, I am not always to be found when there is a Hebrew around" (Mason 1964, 216–217). One book says he was "the rudest man in Washington, with unspeakable manners – sarcastic, peremptory, and antagonistic" (Knox 2002, xix). Not surprisingly, his colleagues refused to send him "the customary letter of appreciation" when he retired. Not a single justice attended his funeral (Cushman 2003, 749).

Think, next, of Justice Harry Blackmun, who served on the Court from 1970 to 1994. Blackmun notoriously lacked self-confidence. He told prospective clerks "that his was the least desirable clerkship at the Court, in part because his colleagues were more intelligent and better teachers than he" (Lazarus 2005, 23). His own oral argument notes drip with self-deprecating remarks (Johnson 2009). In *NLRB* v. *Food Store Employees Union*

(73–370),[1] he wrote to himself, "What am I doing here on the U.S. Supreme Court!" In *Hadley* v. *U.S.* (91–646), he wrote, "What really am I doing here?" Woodward and Armstrong (1979, 143) note that "Blackmun often seemed paralyzed by indecision" and that "[t]he problem was greatest on cases where he was the swing vote." His indecision was so palpable that Justice Black once remarked, "If he [Blackmun] doesn't learn to make up his mind, he's going to jump off a bridge some day" (143–144).

Finally, think of Justice Antonin Scalia, who served from 1986 to 2016. Scalia was perhaps the most aggressive and acerbic opinion writer (and questioner) on the Court. Dissenting in *King* v. *Burwell* (2014), he shook a giant admonitory finger at the majority, calling the majority opinion "pure applesauce."[2] Dissenting in *Obergefell* v. *Hodges*, he declared that he would "hide [his] head in a bag" before he signed on to Justice Kennedy's opinion.[3] And his concurring opinion in *Webster* v. *Reproductive Health Services* (1998) ripped Justice O'Connor, saying that her views "cannot be taken seriously."[4] His pugnacious personality was not limited to opinion writing. During oral arguments, he regularly interrupted attorneys and his colleagues. Justice Alito (2017, 1605) remarked that Scalia turned oral argument into "a contact sport." Indeed, in *Pennsylvania* v. *Ritchie* (85–1347) – only two months after Scalia took his seat at the Court – Blackmun wrote in his personal papers, "Too much questioning and arguing by Scalia again!" (Johnson 2009).

These are but brief examples, yet they should make the point. Justices have distinct personalities, and it seems eminently reasonable to believe these personalities influence their behavior on the Court. McReynolds's attitude surely influenced how he interacted with his colleagues when they discussed the content of the opinions they wrote. Blackmun's hesitancy almost assuredly influenced how he voted to set the Court's agenda. And it does not require much to believe that Scalia's aggressiveness affected not only oral argument but also the Court's treatment of precedent, his relationships with his colleagues, and other actions. Stated simply, justices' personalities must

---

[1] Throughout this book, we will refer to the docket number of cases when we discuss them in the agenda-setting or oral-argument context. Doing so makes it easier to search for them at http://epstein.wustl.edu/blackmun.php?p=3 and https://sites .google.com/a/umn.edu/trj/harry-a-blackmun-oral-argument-notes. When we discuss cases the Supreme Court heard and decided, we will refer to the full United States Reports citation or, when necessary, the Supreme Court Reporter.

[2] *See King* v. *Burwell*, 135 S.Ct. 2480, 2501 (2014) (Scalia, J., dissenting).

[3] *See Obergefell* v. *Hodges*, 135 S.Ct. 2584, 2630 (2015) (Scalia, J., dissenting).

[4] *See Webster* v. *Reproductive Health Services*, 492 U.S. 490, 532 (1989).

influence their behavior on the Court. To think otherwise would be "a fiction of Jack-and-the-Beanstalk proportions."[5]

To read empirical legal scholarship over the last fifty years, though, one would hardly see any mention of justices' personalities. With some important exceptions (Hall 2018; Collins 2011; Klein and Mitchell 2010; Baum 2006; Wrightsman 2006; Baum 1997; Gruenfeld 1995; Aliotta 1988; Tetlock, Bernzweig, and Gallant 1985), scholarship has ignored the role of personality in judicial decision-making. Instead, studies portray justices as either single-minded (Segal and Spaeth 2002) or strategic (Epstein and Knight 1998) seekers of *legal policy*. Scholars largely treat justices as fungible, with only their ideological differences worth examining. We agree, then, with Schauer (2000, 617), who bemoaned that political scientists do not "even pause to examine the possibility" that things other than ideology determine judicial behavior (see also Epstein and Knight 2013; Posner 2008). There has been almost a singular focus on ideology.

Put simply, empirical legal scholarship has remained in "the clean and well-lit prison of one idea" (Chesterton 1908, 22). That idea has been that justices seek policy goals above all else. It's time to break out. Empirical legal scholarship must grow beyond its existing boundaries. It must recognize how justices' *personalities* influence judicial behavior.

This book seeks to help in that regard. It focuses on how conscientiousness influences justices' behavior. We set our sights squarely on conscientiousness. We exhaustively examine its effects on justices throughout the decision-making process. And while so doing, we employ the most sound measure of personality to date.

1.1 CONSCIENTIOUSNESS AND SUPREME COURT JUSTICES

Personality is a difficult concept to define. Indeed, even psychologists are "unable to arrive at a commonly accepted definition" of it (Greenstein 1969, 2–3). One definition calls personality, "the set of psychological traits and mechanisms within the individual that are organized and relatively enduring and that influence his or her interactions with, and adaptations to, the intrapsychic, physical, and social environments" (Larsen and Buss 2014, 4). Another distinguishes the study of personality into two parts: "the fundamental goal of understanding the structure of personality and also the fundamental

---

5   *Bank One Chicago v. Midwest Bank and Trust Co.*, 516 U.S. 264, 279 (1996) (Scalia, J., concurring).

goal of understanding the functions of personality," where "understanding the functions of personality concerns how personality works to guide and direct human functioning in diverse life domains" (Snyder 1994, 163). These definitions seem, at least to us, full of jargon and not particularly helpful to most readers. Thankfully, we can turn to the concept of traits to help define and understand personality. The scholarship on traits has a more recent scholarly pedigree and tends to be cleaner and clearer. As a consequence, most personality scholars today focus on traits. And so do we.

Most scholars argue that a trait is a fairly stable feature of someone's behavior. It is a behavior that is "typical of the person in question" (Mondak 2010, 5). One could think of traits as central tendencies. As McCrae and Costa Jr. (2003, 7) note, traits are "dimensions of individuals' differences in tendencies to show consistent patterns of thoughts, feelings, and actions." Thus, when we say someone is agreeable, we mean that she *usually* is agreeable. She could, of course, be uncooperative and disagreeable from time-to-time, but her typical behavior tends to be agreeable (Mondak 2010). In other words, a trait is different than a state of being. Someone who is angry right now is in a state of anger; someone who is prone to anger across many situations would have the trait of disagreeableness.

Scholars have identified five major traits possessed by all humans. These "Big Five" traits are conscientiousness, agreeableness, neuroticism, openness, and extraversion. Conscientiousness bespeaks dependability (Mondak 2010, 53). It captures whether a person is loyal and hardworking. People who score high on the conscientious "dimension" tend to be hard workers, perform well at their jobs, and are academically successful. Perhaps a bit of an overstatement (but not much), one could think of an intelligent Boy Scout as the image of conscientiousness. Agreeableness focuses on interpersonal relations, with an emphasis primarily on the degree to which a person interacts positively with others. Neuroticism touches on emotional instability. Openness to experience touches on a person's sensitivity toward change and routine. Extraversion is a trait that relates to an individual's tendency to be outgoing or demure.

While all of these traits combine to create a personality profile, we focus on the trait of conscientiousness throughout this book. We do so for two primary reasons. First, we believe that focusing on one trait is theoretically more precise and informative than examining every trait. Trying to write a careful and coherent theory about how five different traits interact with one another and influence justices in numerous judicial activities would devolve quickly into cherry-picked hypotheses and post hoc rationalizations. Rather than trying to theorize about all traits (probably unconvincingly), we opted to focus on one trait and examine it exhaustively over nine different contexts. By focusing on one trait, we can follow it through the entire judicial decision-making process, from agenda setting to the published opinion and more, an enterprise which begets focus and clarity.

That explains why we focus on one trait, but it does not explain why we focus specifically on conscientiousness. We focus on conscientiousness because it is the trait most directly relevant to judging. Meticulousness and academic rigor – concepts tied to conscientiousness – are necessary to become a judge. Consider the requirements established by the American Bar Association's Standing Committee on the Federal Judiciary.[6] The ABA demands that Supreme Court nominees "possess exceptional professional qualifications," such as "industry and diligence…intellectual capacity, judgment, writing and analytical abilities, knowledge of the law," and other related characteristics.[7] Furthermore, the ABA's Canons of Judicial Ethics explicitly demand that judges be conscientious.[8] Specifically, item 34, titled "A Summary of Judicial Obligation," declares that "[i]n every particular [a judge's] conduct should be above reproach. [A judge] should be *conscientious*, studious, thorough, courteous, patient, punctual" (emphasis added). Simply stated, of the Big Five traits, conscientiousness seems to us the most relevant to judging. (The reader interested in the other traits will note, however, that we control for the other four traits in every one of our models.)

1.2 WHY CARE ABOUT CONSCIENTIOUSNESS AND SUPREME COURT JUSTICES?

Readers should care about conscientiousness and the Court for at least three reasons. First, knowing how conscientiousness influences justices can answer a number of current mysteries about justices and the Court. We sometimes observe justices behave in ways that existing scholarship cannot explain. For example, why might a conservative justice like Clarence Thomas vote to grant review to a case when other conservative justices do not? Why do some justices vote to overrule precedent when their ideologically similar colleagues do not?

---

6 https://www.americanbar.org/content/dam/aba/uncategorized/GAO/Backgrounder.authcheckdam.pdf.

7 To be sure, "judicial temperament" touches on agreeableness and openness, but those features appear not nearly as important to observers as the analytical features related to conscientiousness.

8 https://www.americanbar.org/content/dam/aba/administrative/professional_responsibility/pic_migrated/1924_canons.authcheckdam.pdf.

Why are some justices more susceptible to legal persuasion than their ideo-logically similar colleagues? Existing theories cannot answer these questions. Their predominant focus on ideology leaves them mute. A focus on conscientiousness, however, can answer these questions. And our analyses reveal that conscientiousness plays a strong role in all of these behaviors.

Second, readers should care about conscientiousness and the Court because conscientiousness influences every aspect of judicial behavior. As we show in every empirical chapter throughout this book, Court action and the evolution of law are functions of conscientiousness. Sometimes, conscientiousness plays a stronger role than the factors we currently believe influence justices; sometimes it plays a more subtle, supplemental role. But always, it matters. Conscientiousness influences whether a justice votes to hear cases, receives opinion assignments, upholds precedent, recuses, follows public opinion or the Solicitor General, and many other factors.

Third, the importance of conscientiousness – and how it shapes judicial decision-making – matters to policy makers. Presidents who seek to influence the Court ought to pay attention to the conscientiousness of those whom they select. After all, conscientiousness may make a justice more (or less) effective on the Court. Presidents seeking effective appointees should take the time to understand their nominees' personalities and how they expect them to interact with the justices with whom they must work (e.g., Rosen 2007). Because conscientiousness influences how justices behave, those who select justices must understand it. In other words, there are both academic and policy-based reasons to understand justices' conscientiousness.

To be clear, we do not argue that conscientiousness – or personality more broadly – is the *sole* factor that explains judicial behavior. We simply argue that conscientiousness is another factor – an important one, to be sure – that explains judicial behavior. We agree with Atkins and Ziller (1980, 190), who argue "the issue is not really whether personality, in and of itself, explains the policy outputs of courts . . . On the contrary, the conceptual utility of personality theory . . . lies in the extent to which it provides [additional] explanations" to known behavioral patterns. Understanding conscientiousness can provide a fuller understanding of the Court's behavior.

1.3 A ROADMAP FOR THIS BOOK

This book unfolds as follows: Chapter 2 explicates our theory and provides important background information for readers. We discuss existing theories of judicial behavior, including their strengths and their weaknesses. We then provide an extended discussion about psychology scholarship and the role of conscientiousness in explaining human behavior. Throughout the book, each hypothesis we proffer draws from this chapter and its theory.

Chapter 3 discusses how we measure conscientiousness. We measure conscientiousness by examining justices' pre-nomination speeches and writings. We employ IBM's Watson Personality Insights program to derive empirical estimates of their traits.[9] We follow the path set out by Winter, who broke ground in measuring the personality components of political actors by using their written (and recorded) words (Winter 2003). Winter used this method to determine the personalities of presidents, other world leaders, and even individuals in the business world. Others have verified the use of language to assess leaders' traits (see, e.g., Keller and Foster 2012). After an extensive discussion of our measurement methodology, we provide an exhaustive series of analyses to establish the criterion validity of our measures. We then compare our measures of justices' personalities to a similar, recently published study (Hall 2018). The comparison reveals our measurement approach to be substantively and empirically stronger. We urge scholars to employ our estimates of justices' personality traits.

Chapter 4 examines how justices' conscientiousness influences their behavior at the Court's agenda-setting stage. Justices enjoy the legal authority to select which cases the Court will hear and decide each year. And while scholars know quite a bit about the conditions under which justices set their agenda (see, e.g., Black and Owens 2009a), they know next to nothing about how personality influences those decisions. Using the private archival data of Justice Harry Blackmun, we scrutinize how conscientiousness influences justices' agenda setting votes. The data uncover three important results. First, highly conscientious justices are more likely to seek to resolve legal conflict than justices who are less conscientious. Second, highly conscientious justices are less likely to cast tentative "Join-3" votes. Third, highly conscientious justices are less likely to pursue forward-looking policy goals than less conscientious justices.

Chapter 5 focuses on whether conscientious justices are more likely to be persuaded by strong and credible legal arguments than less conscientious justices. After the Court grants review to a case, it receives written briefs from the attorneys and then holds oral argument. The attorneys provide justices with information about the case and try to persuade them to vote for their position. Existing scholarship suggests that justices respond to strong legal arguments (Black, Hall, Owens, and Ringsmuth 2016; Johnson, Wahlbeck, and Spriggs

---

9 https://www.ibm.com/watson/services/personality-insights/.

2006). They are less likely to vote for the party that employs emotional language in its briefs (i.e., the less credible attorney), and they are more likely to side with the attorney who makes a stronger oral argument. We seek to understand why. More specifically, we analyze whether those findings apply to *all* justices similarly, or whether, as we expect, those results obtain primarily among the most conscientious justices. Our analyses reveal that conscientious justices are most amenable to strong legal arguments.

Chapter 6 analyzes whether conscientious justices are more or less likely to support the US Solicitor General. The SG's office is highly successful before the Supreme Court. Recent scholarship ties that success to the SG's practice of making professional and objective arguments to the Court (Black and Owens 2012*b*; Wohlfarth 2009). We go beyond these findings, however, and argue that particular justices – the highly conscientious ones – are more likely to put a premium on that high quality information. Our results concur. Conscientious justices are more likely to support the SG's position than less conscientious justices. And these results hold whether the SG is a party to the case or participates as a "friend of the Court." The conscientious justice appears to value the SG's high quality information more than less conscientious justices.

Chapter 7 investigates the conditions under which Chief Justices assign majority opinions to some justices but not others. When the Chief is in the majority coalition in a case, Court norms empower him to assign the opinion, either to himself or to another justice in the majority coalition. The question we seek to answer is whether the Chief is more likely to assign opinions to increasingly conscientious justices. The results show that Chiefs are, in fact, significantly more likely to assign opinions to conscientious justices. Because of the strong norm of equitable opinion assignment – everyone receives about the same number of opinions these days – the Chief's powers are somewhat constrained. But some cases are more important than others, and in those cases, Chiefs favor conscientious justices.

Chapter 8 analyzes whether conscientiousness influences how justices bargain and negotiate with each other over the content of opinions. After the majority opinion author circulates his or her draft opinion, other justices in the majority coalition can (among other things) join the opinion, ask for changes, make threats, or refuse to join. We analyze whether a justice's conscientiousness influences the duration of time it takes her to write a majority opinion. We also examine whether an increasingly conscientious justice is more likely to bargain with opinion writers, and whether conscientiousness influences the types of bargaining tactics justices employ. Our results suggest that conscientious justices take longer to draft opinions than less conscientious justices. They take their time in an effort to write more thorough opinions. Contrary to our expectations, increasingly conscientious justices are, on average, less likely to bargain with opinion writers. Nevertheless, they are more likely to bargain in salient cases. And when they do bargain, they are more likely to make suggestions than less conscientious justices.

Chapter 9 examines whether justices' conscientiousness influences the content of the opinions they write. The chapter investigates how justices' conscientiousness influences the legal breadth, cognitive complexity, length, and rhetorical clarity of the opinions they write. Rooted in the theory that conscientious justices will be more likely to seek out as much information as possible to resolve a legal dispute, the results suggest that conscientious justices write opinions with greater breadth, opinions that are more cognitively complex, longer opinions, and (contrary to our expectations) slightly less readable opinions.

Chapter 10 examines whether increasingly conscientious justices are more likely to overrule precedent. Our theory is simple. Conscientious people believe they must fulfill their roles and obligations. The role of a justice, at least according to most people in the public and in the legal community, is to follow rather than circumvent precedent. Therefore, conscientious justices should be more supportive of precedent. Our analyses concur. Conscientious justices are more likely to treat precedent positively than their less conscientious colleagues. Further, to the extent that conscientious justices must circumvent precedent, they do so in a limited manner, and appropriately within the realm of legal treatment. They are less likely to overrule or criticize a precedent than their less conscientious colleagues. Instead, they distinguish those precedents.

Chapter 11 investigates whether conscientious justices are more likely to follow public opinion than less conscientious justices. We believe conscientious justices seek out information about the Court's external environment. Why? Conscientious people tend to value their professions and protect existing norms. The Court needs public support in order to survive. As such, we suspect that conscientious justices will pay attention to public opinion when reaching decisions. The results agree. The most conscientious justices in the modern era exhibited considerable concern for public opinion when making decisions. By contrast, the least conscientious justices exhibited no responsiveness to public opinion at all.

Chapter 12 probes judicial recusal, a normative topic that has become newsworthy in recent years. We analyze whether conscientious justices are more likely to recuse themselves from cases than less conscientious justices.

Because conscientious individuals tend to be more dutiful than less conscientious people, we believe conscientious justices will be more likely to recuse. They are. Whereas less conscientious justices stay involved with cases to accomplish their policy goals, conscientious justices remove themselves to avoid the appearance of impropriety.

Chapter 13 offers our concluding thoughts. We lay out the implications of our findings and discuss the future study of judicial behavior. We theorize what a Court full of conscientious justices might look like and discuss what our examination of conscientiousness can tell us more broadly. It is our hope that other scholars begin to examine personality more carefully and how it interacts with existing theories about the Court and justices, all in an effort to gather a more realistic understanding of judging on the High Court.

We should note one thing for the reader. In most of the empirical chapters, we replicate existing studies (either our own or those of others) while adding conscientiousness and the other four personality traits. Because those models contain different variables, some chapters include some covariates not found in other chapters. While this approach allows us to examine numerous empirical questions across a multitude of judicial actions, it does come at the (very slight) cost of employing different covariates in different chapters.

* * *

When Chief Justice Fred Vinson passed away, Justice Frankfurter stated, "This is the first indication that I ever had that there is a God" (Cooper 1995, 31). Writing to Frankfurter, then-Solicitor General Philip Elman remarked:

> What a mean little despot he [Vinson] is. Has there ever been a member of the Court who was deficient in so many respects as a man and as a judge[?] Even that s.o.b. McReynolds, despite his defects of character, stands by comparison as a towering figure and powerful intellect... This man is a pygmy, morally and mentally. And so uncouth. (Cooper 1995, 31)

Does personality influence judicial behavior? It sure seems as though it must. And our goal is to find the answer.

2

A Theory about Justices and Conscientiousness

When it comes to determining what Americans want from their judges, abstract ideals collide with contemporary expectations. Many of us claim to desire judges who will decide cases based on nothing more than law and logic. Aristotle also echoed this thought more than two thousand years ago when he wrote that "law is reason unaffected by desire"(Aristotle, translated by Benjamin Jowett, 350 BCE).[1] This idealistic conception of law and judging lives on today. Chief Justice Roberts underscored it when he told the Senate Judiciary Committee that judges are merely umpires who call balls and strikes. Indeed, Supreme Court nominees in the modern era have largely fallen over themselves declaring their fidelity to this general principle (Wedeking and Farganis 2014).

And yet we also want judges with the "right" personalities. Ask yourself: what characteristics should the ideal judge have? Surely most everyone would agree that a judge should be fair and impartial. To that list, most would add intelligent, qualified, honest, trustworthy, efficient, organized, and dependable. Further, most everyone would want that judge to be careful, watchful, thorough, and diligent. The Code of Conduct for US judges insists that they perform their duties diligently.[2] What are these adjectives, if not descriptions of judges' personalities? Put simply, when we say we want judges who are tabula rasa, we really want judges with, among other things, certain personalities.

---

[1] Translation by Benjamin Jowett, Book 3, Part XVI, http://classics.mit.edu/Aristotle/politics.3.three.html.

[2] . In many ways, the Code of Conduct for United States Judges has codified these traits to an extent. This is not more plainly evident than in its requirement that judges remain impartial. In other words, judges need to, at least *initially*, keep an open mind. The same thing can be said for the traits that are closely tied to conscientiousness. More specifically, a key pillar of the Code of Conduct insists that judges perform their duties *diligently*, which is an adjective often used to define *conscientiousness*.

Of course, everyone knows that judging is not *really* purely objective. And we've known it for some time (Gibson and Caldeira 2011). Frank (1936, 120) wrote that "the law is not a machine and the judges not machine-tenders." In fact, much of the last eighty years of empirical legal scholarship has focused on understanding how justices' ideologies influence their behavior. And on this score, scholars have amassed a great deal of evidence. Knocking down that straw man really was not so hard.[3]

Yet even this empirical work suffers from a huge blind spot (Epstein and Knight 2013). It ignores the importance of personality. Existing scholarship fails to explicate how justices' personalities influence their behavior, even as scholars have become numb to the importance of other extralegal considerations.

In this chapter, we describe the evolution of scholarship on Supreme Court justices' behavior. This scholarship has gone through three major periods: the mechanical jurisprudence (or legal theory) period, the attitudinal period, and the rational choice period. We discuss each and then offer our theory of personality, focusing specifically on conscientiousness. At the conclusion of the chapter, we will have traveled over a hundred years, provided an overview of judicial and personality scholarship, and theorized how to merge the two.

2.1 THE EVOLUTION OF SCHOLARSHIP ON JUDICIAL BEHAVIOR

During his senate confirmation hearing to become Chief Justice, John Roberts stressed the importance of judges following precedent. He noted:

> Hamilton, in Federalist No. 78, said that, "To avoid an arbitrary discretion in the judges, they need to be bound down by rules and precedents." So even that far back, the Founders appreciated the role of precedent in promoting evenhandedness, predictability, stability, the appearance of integrity in the judicial process. (Roberts 2005, 142)

He went on to say: "Judges and justices are servants of the law, not the other way around. Judges are like umpires. Umpires don't make the rules; they apply them" (Roberts 2005, 55).

Roberts's comments represent the dominant view of judicial behavior for decades, if not centuries, in America. It is a view which holds that justices decide cases based on "the law" without regard to their personal policy

---

3   Though the ease through which this happened may reflect our own hindsight bias.

preferences or other extralegal considerations. By applying legal principles to the facts of cases, judges arrive at sound decisions without injecting their personal beliefs into them. It is a mechanical process: Examine the facts of the case. Find existing case(s) with similar facts. Apply the law from previous case(s). Repeat. Such is the objective case method approach to judging.

Harvard Law Professor Christopher Columbus Langdell more formally introduced this case-method approach in 1870 (Kimball 2006). Langdell believed that "law, considered as a science, consists of certain principles or doctrines. To have such a mastery of these as to be able to apply them with constant facility and certainty to the ever-tangled skein of human affairs, is what constitutes a true lawyer" (Langdell 1871, iv). A case-method approach to studying law, he argued, would allow students of law, and judges, to discover legal doctrines by tracing their slowly revealed truths over a series of cases (where a series of cases, in many instances, spanned centuries). Soon, most law schools in the country taught the case-method approach, and many scholars believed it was how judges and justices actually decided cases.

Not everyone agreed, however, that judges and justices applied the law so mechanically and objectively. A collection of scholars called "legal realists" denied that the common law had a fundamental structure discernible by objective behavior and neutral legal principles. Instead, the legal realists insisted that legal doctrine was the product of social conflict and political compromise (Ackerman 1974, 121). Fictional was the notion that judges mechanically applied fundamental legal rules to resolve disputes. Legal realists began to collect data to examine whether justices in fact ruled according to law or whether, as they believed, justices injected their own policy preferences into their rulings.

Cracks showed in the mechanical jurisprudence façade at least as early as the 1930s. Perhaps the most notable crack came from the events surrounding the "switch in time that saved nine" (Ho and Quinn 2010). During the Great Depression, Congress passed President Roosevelt's New Deal legislation in an effort to improve economic conditions. Some of these laws were radical. The Court struck down several such laws, particularly in the 1934–1935 terms. In response, FDR proposed a plan that would add new members to the Supreme Court, increasing its ranks from nine to fifteen, to give him a robust majority that would, instead, uphold New Deal legislation. This Court-packing plan put the Court in the crosshairs, and it made some justices nervous. The public's support for FDR and the New Deal was a rising river, threatening to flood and overtake the Court. So, in *West Coast Hotel* v. *Parrish* (1937),

Justice Owen Roberts abruptly departed from his usual voting tendencies and cast his vote to uphold New Deal legislation.[4] His switch did two things: First, it signaled that FDR's Court packing plan was unnecessary (thus preserving the number of justices at nine). Second, it signaled to scholars that legalistic explanations of judicial behavior were, at best, incomplete.

Shortly thereafter, in 1941, C. Herman Pritchett sparked a revolution in legal scholarship when he argued that "it is the private attitudes of the majority of the Court which become public law" (Pritchett 1941, 890). In other words, the mechanical legal theory was empirically wrong. Pritchett did not merely state his proposition, though. He also supported it with data. He examined the cases in which justices dissented. He observed, first, that justices were dissenting more than ever and, second, that the same groups of justices tended to dissent with each other. Fault lines between the majority and dissenters seemed clear. He wondered: If the law dictated justices' votes, as many of his time argued, why did justices dissent? And why did they dissent together in blocs? Pritchett's answer: justices were driven by ideological goals that influenced how they voted. And his data seemed to concur.

Scholars after Pritchett followed suit. They raced to collect and analyze data on justices' votes. Like Pritchett, they argued that justices' policy preferences influenced their behavior. Soon, a new theory of judicial decision-making dominated. This model argued that justices decided cases solely to further their policy goals. As Segal and Spaeth (2002) argued, justices with liberal attitudes over criminal law, for example, voted liberally in such cases. Justices with conservative beliefs voted conservatively. This "attitudinal model" argued that (1) when a judge lacks political or electoral accountability, (2) has no ambition for higher office, and (3) serves on a court of last resort that controls its own agenda, the judge could – and would – decide cases purely on policy grounds.

Beginning in the 1990s, however, a new approach took hold. This new "strategic model" agreed that justices seek to effectuate their policy goals, but argued that they are constrained in their pursuit of those goals by their need to work with other actors and institutions (Epstein and Knight 1998). To maximize their policy preferences, they argued, justices act strategically by taking into account the choices they expect other relevant actors to make. For example, justices who want to vote liberally might need to moderate when faced with a conservative president and Congress. They might need to moderate when faced with colleagues who are centrist or conservative. And they might need to moderate when they face a conservative public.

---

4 See *West Coast Hotel v. Parrish*, 300 U.S. 379 (1937).

The strategic approach was a step in the right direction. It moved scholarship away from a myopic and unrealistically narrow focus on ideology. But even today it still requires improvement. It's time for a new theory of judging, or at least one that incorporates additional factors. Indeed, Epstein and Knight (2013, 13) – the architects of the strategic model—have made similar comments, imploring scholars to go beyond their existing work. They have called for "a restructuring of the very foundation of the (political science) study of judging," moving away from a nearly singular focus on ideological goals. As they put it:

> [I]t is impossible to deny that political scientists have offered an extremely unrealistic conception of judicial behavior for far too many years. It's time to move toward a more realistic understanding … If the process of judicial decision making is best characterized as a complicated mix of motivations, then the motivational framework should allow us to accommodate this complexity and, perhaps, to distinguish the conditions under which different types of motivations apply. (24)

Their call follows repeated entreaties by Baum and Posner for scholars to think about how other goals motivate judges (Baum 2006; Posner 1993). For example, in *How Judges Think*, Posner (2008) argues that justices are not legalists but neither are they influenced only by policy preferences. He argues that factors such as leisure, income, job satisfaction, popularity, prestige, reputation, and avoiding reversal may influence judicial decisions. He goes so far as to say that these factors may account for outcomes we generally attribute to ideology. Similarly, in a number of studies, Baum has asked scholars to think more carefully about judicial motivations (Baum 2010, 2006, 1997). In particular, he has pointed out the need for greater research into personality and judging.

To be sure, some scholarship has answered the call. Some empirical studies have focused on how precedent may actually constrain justices, showing that precedent is a norm (Knight and Epstein 1996) that corrals justices. Other work shows how early judicial treatments of precedent influence subsequent treatments (Spriggs and Hansford 2002). Moreover, research shows that precedent conformance varies depending on a justice's length of tenure on the Court (Hurwitz and Stefko 2004). Going further, many scholars argue that the force of precedent works as a constraint through justice-created institutional constructs, such as jurisprudential regimes that serve to identify relevant case facts or a particular level of scrutiny for the justices to use (Richards and Kritzer 2002; Scott 2006; Pang et al. 2012; Bartels and O'Geen 2015). Along similar lines, other research has argued for the importance of precedent as one of the key "legal" factors that influences justices' decision-making (Bailey and Maltzman 2011). Other recent work reinforces the importance of precedent's legal impact within the legal hierarchy (Masood, Kassow, and Songer 2017).

We have, in a sense, come back to the starting point where Pritchett made his mark. What *does* explain judicial behavior on the High Court? It has to be more than policy alone. Indeed, even Pritchett came to lament the work of his successors, stating: "[P]olitical scientists, who have done so much to put the 'political' in 'political jurisprudence' need to emphasize that it is still 'jurisprudence.' It is judging in a political context, but it is still judging" (Pritchett 1969, 42). To this comment, we add that it is still judging – but by humans with personalities.

2.2 SCHOLARSHIP ON PERSONALITY AND THE COURT

Despite the fact that a link between personality and judicial behavior seems intuitive, scholars have largely ignored it.[5] Some studies simply tip their hats to the importance of personality. For example, Goldman (1966, 377) documented the rates of dissension and unanimous reversals across federal circuits, writing, "Personality characteristics ... may be relevant [to this behavior]." Yet there was no further inquiry or follow-up. Other studies discuss the importance of personality (and psychology) but do so without empirical tests (see, e.g., Wrightsman 2006).

One area where scholars have examined personality and judging is in explorations of how cognitive aspects of personality might influence justices. Some of this early work was done by psychologists. For example, Tetlock, Bernzweig, and Gallant (1985) discovered that judicial ideology is related to a justice's integrative complexity, a cognitive structural variable that assesses the degree of differentiation and integration through which a justice interprets events in the world. In other words, it examines whether justices see the world in black and white or in shades of gray. Gruenfeld (1995) later found, however, that

---

[5] Some research advocating the importance of personality has been put forth to explain aspects of mass behavior (e.g., Mondak and Halperin 2008; Mondak 2010; Mondak et al. 2010). For example, we know that people with certain personalities are more likely to seek out political information, to be exposed to disagreement, to hold certain attitudes, and to participate in politics (Mondak 2010). Other research has focused on personality and presidents (e.g., Laswell 1930; George and George 1964; Hermann 1984; Winter 1987; Barber 1992; Rubenzer, Faschingbauer, and Ones 2000) and legislative behavior (Barber 1965; Hermann 1977; Crichlow 2002; Ramey, Klinger, and Hollibaugh 2017). These studies all show that personality influences the choices political actors make. But similar scholarship on the Supreme Court is hard to find.

this result was conditional on the status of being in the majority or minority coalition.

Not until much later did political scientists and empirical legal scholars analyze the effects of personality on decision-making.[6] For example, Collins (2011) examined whether cognitive dissonance theory explains justices' decisions to write concurring opinions. Moyer (2012) studied whether conservative judges have a cognitive need to simplify the world. Braman examined motivated reasoning and the Court (Braman 2009; Braman and Nelson 2007). Owens and Wedeking (2012) analyzed how cognitive rigidity can lead to ideological drift on the High Court. But even these studies, while clearly useful, do not answer our questions. They do not directly address the connections between justices' traits and their behavior.

Two studies more directly address how personality influences justices. First, Aliotta (1988) examines how justices' personal *motives* influence their decisions to write majority and separate opinions. She conceived of personality as three personal "motives" (the achievement motive, the affiliation motive, and the power motive) that influenced justices. While the study was an important first step, it was hampered by serious limitations. First, it examined personality through the lens of personal motives. On its own, this is not a limitation. Motives are clearly important to personality (Winter et al. 1998), and traits scholars acknowledge this (Roberts et al. 2014, 1324–1325). Indeed, as we began work on this book project, we sought to define personality as an interactive effect between traits and motives. The problem, however, is that the scholarship on motives is not nearly as extensive as the scholarship on traits. Traits have become the dominant aspect of personality that scholars study. As a consequence, there is simply less agreement on what motives are and, more concretely, how to measure them.[7] What is more, Aliotta measured these personal motives by coding the justices' statements during their confirmation hearings. But these remarks are unlikely to be good samples from which to draw because nominees make them under conditions where they have strong incentives to mask their true beliefs and motives. In addition, much of the

---

6 One early exception was Gibson (1981), who explored the impact that self-esteem has on behavioral activism in judicial decision-making. By interviewing a sample of California judges, Gibson was able to test a theory about how self-esteem had an indirect impact on the behavior of judges, working to influence the judges' role expectations (see also Atkins and Ziller 1980).

7 The debate about motives has many aspects. Part of the debate stems from disagreement on what motives are central. Other key aspects of the debate stem from the methods used to measure motives, whether implicit and explicit motives are being assessed, and the relationship between explicit and implicit motives, as well as their relationship with traits (Roberts et al. 2014, 1324–1325).

nominees' language comes in response to topics that *senators* want to address. So, while this work was advanced for its time, it did not spur much follow-up.

More recently, Hall (2018) sought to examine the role of the "Big Five" personality traits on five areas of judicial behavior: (1) agenda setting, (2) opinion assignment, (3) intra-Court bargaining, (4) voting on the merits, and (5) separate opinion writing. Hall proposes a "psychoeconomic" model of decision-making in which justices purportedly engage in utility maximization such that their personality traits structure how they derive utility from decisions. While we agree with the fundamental sentiment of Hall's (2018) study – that justices' personality traits matter – we are compelled to point out some of the study's limitations.

The first limitation is theoretical. Hall applies personality through the lens of economic utility maximization. But, utility maximization quickly becomes troublesome when integrated with personality traits, at least in terms of studying the Court. After all, utility maximization is a volitional and strategic effort. Personality, on the other hand, is largely involuntary. It operates "in the background," often without conscious control, like the human pulmonary, circulatory, or nervous systems.

If, alternatively, the argument is that utility is a product of everyone's trait profile, that is easier to understand conceptually. Nevertheless, the theorizing quickly becomes intractable. There are so many trait profiles it would take a Herculean effort to theorize about all of them. As Figure 1 reveals, even if we simplify things, where each of the five traits have only a high or low level, there are approximately thirty-two different trait profiles, each with a different utility. As this shows, the enterprise of identifying and sorting trait profiles quickly becomes complicated with five traits and rank ordering the many possible combinations of utility. Suffice it to say, deriving utility from a range of personality traits is an extremely challenging task. A full explication of the interaction between economic utility maximization and personality must, absolutely, contend with these different variations – and theorize them all. The study, however, does not do that. It really cannot, given the large number of possible trait profiles.

The second limitation with Hall's study is methodological – and it cuts to the heart of the matter. As we discuss more fully in our measurement chapter, Hall derives his indicators of justices' personalities using the text of their concurring opinions written while on the Court. This is problematic — very problematic. Concurrences are endogenous to decision-making and behavior on the Court, thereby creating a serious circularity problem. Justices write concurrences for a variety of reasons. It is analytically inappropriate to use case and vote driven information written by the justices while on the Court to

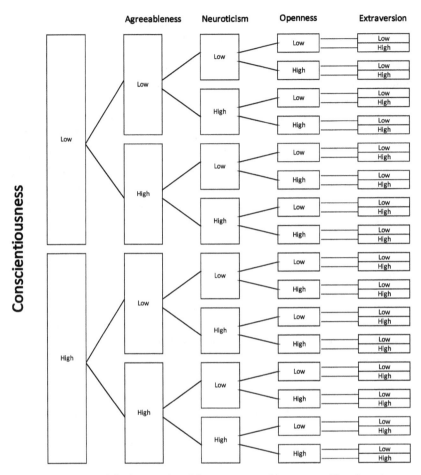

FIGURE 1: A simplified example of the many possible trait profiles, focusing on conscientiousness.

generate scores that then predict those justices' votes and behavior … while on the Court.

To summarize, scholarship started with an aspirational and noble view of judging. But with the systematic collection and analysis of data, scholars came to identify a host of extralegal influences on judicial behavior that challenged that view. Scholars soon identified policy preferences as the main drivers of judicial behavior. The recipe for judicial behavior, however, surely calls for more than a cup of policy preferences. It must include other ingredients. We argue that personality is one such element.

2.3 CONSCIENTIOUSNESS: A (JUDICIAL) TRAIT WORTH EXAMINING

Personality is "the set of psychological traits and mechanisms within the individual that are organized and relatively enduring and that influence his or her interactions with, and adaptations to, the intrapsychic, physical, and social environments" (Larsen and Buss 2014, 4). We focus here on the core *structure* of personality, the "Big Five" personality traits (McCrae and Costa 1987; McCrae and Costa Jr. 1997).[8] Traits have a long history in personality psychology. In recent years, trait scholarship has become one of the leading approaches to understanding personality (John and Srivastava 1999).

Roberts, Jackson, Fayard, Edmonds, and Meints (2009, 369) define a trait "as a tendency to respond in certain ways under certain circumstances . . . [(Tellegen 1988)], or, more generally speaking, [a] tendency to think, feel, and behave in a relatively enduring and consistent fashion across time." A trait is "big" (e.g., Big Five) in the sense that it contains several lower order facets or dimensions of that trait. This means that most personality scholars conceptualize traits in a hierarchical manner, where a main trait is the higher order trait, but also has lower order dimensions or "facets." For example, some common subdomains of conscientiousness include reliability, orderliness, impulse control, decisiveness, punctuality, formalness, industriousness, and conventionality (Roberts et al. 2004). While personality researchers agree on the Big Five, they have yet to agree on the number and exact dimensions of the lower order facets. As such, we focus our efforts on the higher-order traits.

Conventional wisdom suggests that personality traits are heritable, largely stable, and immutable over time. Much of this thinking, however, has evolved in recent years, with evidence showing that the environment plays more of a role than heritability, and that trait change does take place. The heritability of traits is a common misconception that persists. As Roberts et al. (2014, 1316) summarize, the best estimates suggest only between 40 percent and 50 percent is heritable, citing Krueger and Johnson (2008). This suggests, they argue, that the majority of the variance in traits are due to environmental influences.[9]

---

[8] While we only use traits here, we also acknowledge that there is more to personality research that future research should explore. For example, future work should look to explore the boundaries and connections between traits and motives and their potential interaction (Winter et al. 1998; Roberts et al. 2014) and also do more to address the critique of traits as descriptions versus traits as explanations (e.g., Pervin 1994).

[9] Regarding the stability of traits, this line of thinking appears to have originated with an early psychologist named William James, who wrote, "Already at the age of twenty-five you see the professional mannerism settling down on the young commercial traveller, on the young

There is a growing line of research showing that personality traits do change over a person's life. While the changes are not large, there is no longer support for the "personality is made of plaster" argument (Bleidorn et al. 2009; Helson, Jones, and Kwan 2002; Roberts and Mroczek 2008; Scollon and Diener 2006). Recent research suggests that this debate can be explained by personality scholars emphasizing different aspects of trait models.[10] We are agnostic on this debate, but we think it helpful to think of personality as made of clay – something that can be molded and shaped. Personality traits are likely to be relatively stable at predicting relevant behaviors, yet may also lead to different outcomes under different states or situations.

While some scholars still debate the correct number of traits, they largely have settled on the Big Five (McCrae and Costa 1987; John and Srivastava 1999).[11] The Big Five traits consist of conscientiousness, agreeableness, neuroticism, openness to experience, and extraversion.

---

doctor, on the young minister, on the young counselor-at-law . . . It is well for the world that in most of us, by the age of thirty, the character has set like plaster and will never soften again" (James 1890, 121). This belief, however, appears to be dated.

[10] Jackson and Roberts (2017) argue that traditional trait models (e.g., Five Factor Model) "emphasize stability across time and context, whereas social cognitive models of personality . . . emphasize change across situations and time" (Jackson and Roberts 2017, 134). This means that they are different levels of personality analysis, the "broad trait level that exists across multiple contexts and time, whereas [social cognitive models] focuses on the state level manifestations" (Jackson and Roberts 2017, 134). The key is that both of these describe the same system, but emphasize different components. This can perhaps be best understood, Jackson and Roberts (2017) argue, by the idea that if an individual displays one instance of unconscientiousness, it does not mean the person is not highly conscientiousness. Roberts et al. (2014, 1316) write: "The assumption that traits are immutable is clearly wrong. Empirical evidence has repeatedly shown that conscientiousness, and the related constructs that fall within the conscientiousness spectrum, such as impulse control, are both changeable and continue to develop and change well into adulthood [(Jackson et al. 2009; Roberts, Walton, and Viechtbauer 2006)]. Though changeability should not be taken as meaning inconsistency."

[11] Pervin (1994) discusses the debate about the proper number of factors in a way that one could describe it as the "five plus or minus two" critique. Some research supports the idea that there are traits outside the Big Five. Waller and Zavala (1993) present evidence that there may a "Big Seven." Spain, Harms and LeBreton (2014) discuss "dark" traits such as Machiavellianism, narcissism, and psychopathy, as opposed to the "bright" traits like the Big Five. Cheung et al. (2001) found some differences with the five-factor structure when examining cross-cultural populations, finding stronger evidence for a six-factor model. And six factors were also found among early childhood subjects (Soto 2015). In terms of the debate about what exactly the five factors are, McCrae and Costa (1987) point out that initially several variations of the five factor model emerged. For example, in his critical appraisal of the five factor model, McAdams (1992) describes one variation of the factors as: "(I) Surgency (Extraversion), (II) Agreeableness (Warmth), (III) Conscientiousness (Will), (IV) Emotional Stability (Neuroticism), and (V) Culture (Intellectance, Openness to Experience)" (McAdams 1992, 331). At present, however, most trait scholars have settled on the Big Five traits.

- *Conscientiousness* is a person's tendency to act in an organized or thoughtful way. It captures whether a person is dutiful, deliberate, driven, persistent, self-assured, or hardworking. In surveys, people who score low on conscientiousness, in contrast, tend to be carefree, unstructured, self-doubting, and content.
- *Agreeableness* is a person's tendency to be compassionate and cooperative toward others. An agreeable person dislikes confrontation, is unassuming and humble, and tends to be altruistic in the sense that helping others is genuinely rewarding. Highly agreeable people are seen as warm, sympathetic, kind, and cooperative (Mondak 2010). People who are highly agreeable work well in groups (Barrick and Mount 1991), are risk averse, and seek out good relationships with others.
- *Neuroticism* is the extent to which a person's emotions are sensitive to the individual's environment. Neurotic people tend to be sensitive to what others think of them, are vulnerable to stress, have a fiery temper, are prone to worry, and focus on things that they are unhappy about. In contrast, the opposite end of the trait is typically labeled emotional stability.
- *Openness* is the extent to which a person is open to experiencing a variety of activities. For example, a person high in openness is adventurous and likes to experience new things, will seek out creative experiences, is intrigued by new ideas, and will challenge authority and traditional values.
- *Extraversion* is a trait that describes a person's tendency to seek stimulation in the company of others. People high in extraversion are outgoing, sociable, experience a range of positive feelings, like to take charge of activities of others, and like fast-paced environments. Extraversion is probably the single most commonly studied personality trait. In contrast, individuals who are on the opposite end of the trait are introverted.

We turn our attention, now, to conscientiousness. What is it? We've already offered a brief description. More specifically, Roberts et al. (2014, 1315) define it as "a spectrum of constructs that describe individual differences in the propensity to be self-controlled, responsible to others, hardworking, orderly, and rule abiding." Along these lines, John and Srivastava (1999, 121) argue that conscientiousness "describes *socially prescribed impulse control* that facilitates task- and goal-directed behavior, such as thinking before acting, delaying gratification, following norms and rules, and planning, organizing, and prioritizing tasks" (emphasis in original).[12] Conversely, those who are less conscientious tend to be careless (McCrae and John 1992) and display disinhibition, with an orientation toward immediate gratification and impulsive behavior (Krueger and Markon 2014). Numerous other descriptions of highly conscientious people suggest they are deliberate, self-disciplined, well-organized, competent, dutiful, orderly, responsible, goal directed, and thorough. A host of studies contextualize these definitions and clarify what they mean, and the next several paragraphs discuss them.

Scholarship indicates that conscientiousness correlates positively with job performance. Witt et al. (2002, 164) argue that "[w]orkers high in conscientiousness are predisposed to be organized, exacting, disciplined, diligent, dependable, methodical, and purposeful. Thus, they are more likely than low-conscientious workers to thoroughly and correctly perform work tasks, to take initiative in solving problems, to remain committed to work performance, to comply with policies, and to stay focused on work tasks." Research has shown that conscientiousness is one of the best predictors of job performance across many different criteria and occupational groups (Mount and Barrick 1998; Salgado 1997). Barrick and Mount (1991) find that increased conscientiousness correlates with better job performance among professionals, police, managers, salespeople, and skilled and semi-skilled workers.

Furthermore, highly conscientious people are dependable, orderly, self-disciplined, hardworking, and achievement striving. Barrick, Mount, and Strauss (1993) find that sales representatives high in conscientiousness set higher goals and are more committed to those goals than less conscientious sales representatives. On a similar note, conscientious people tend to work well on teams because they are more dependable, thorough, persistent, and hardworking (Hough 1992; Mount, Barrick, and Stewart 1998). Put simply, conscientious people tend to perform their professional tasks more thoroughly than less conscientious people. In fact, conscientiousness has been shown to be related to strong performance in virtually all jobs (Barrick, Mount, and Judge 2001).

Conscientiousness also influences how people learn about the world. Scholarship shows that conscientious individuals tend to look for more information – and do so more carefully – than others. Heinström (2003) finds that conscientious people tend to seek out more information – and more complex information – to support their positions than less conscientious people. Heinström examined how graduate students sought out information to work

---

[12] For a similar definition, see Roberts et al. (2004).

on their research. The study investigated how students evaluated information, how they selected the documents they used for their research, and the
effects of time pressure on their information gathering. The results showed
that conscientious people sought out thought-provoking documents instead of
documents that simply confirmed previous ideas. The conscientious students
appeared to engage with the material more extensively and push themselves
to consider more complex material. On the other hand, students with lower
levels of conscientiousness tended to choose their information sources based
on how easily they could obtain those sources. Similarly, Gul et al. (2004,
359) find "[h]igh level conscientious scholars being very competent, disciplined and achievement striking are found to make extra efforts in database
searching to get required information." In a study on how people search the
Internet, Schmidt and Wolff (2016, 6) find that "[c]onscientious people have
a high level of activity and an exhaustive exploitation of the search space,"
while less conscientious individuals use "a search pattern that aims at finding
results fast but with little reflection" (see also Halder, Roy, and Chakraborty
2010).

In terms of work readiness, conscientious people tend to be more prepared.
Caldwell and Burger (1998) find that conscientiousness is associated with
job candidates preparing more for interviews, both in terms of using social
resources (talking to friends and relatives) and researching the company. The
larger point this research underscores is that the influence of personality does
not start the day a person begins a job or even the day of the interview.
Personality's influence starts *before* the interview takes places.

Conscientious people also seek to manipulate and control their social environment. Conscientious people deploy different tools when they interact with
others. Buss (1992), for example, finds that people who are conscientious are
more likely to use reason – rather than emotion or coercion – to influence
people in the context of marital relationships. In a study that examines how
conscientiousness affects workplace influence, Caldwell and Burger (1997)
find that conscientiousness is positively associated with the "involvement strategy" (e.g., involving others by consulting them or by inspiring them) and
negatively associated with the "exchange of benefits strategy" (e.g., offering
help in return or reminding of past favors).[13] Similarly, Baker and McNulty

---

[13] Though it is important to note that Caldwell and Burger (1997) did find, however, that conscientiousness was not associated with the strategies of ingratiating themselves with others,
   assertiveness, rational persuasion, or using others. The null finding for the rational persuasion
   strategy differs from the findings of Buss (1992), but that may be due to the different contexts:
   marital or personal relations versus professional relations.

(2011) find that conscientious people are more likely to work to improve their personal relationships.

Looking to political elites, scholarship shows that conscientious legislators behave differently than less conscientious legislators. Ramey, Klinger, and Hollibaugh (2017) show that highly conscientious members of Congress spend less of their campaign war chest in order to save for future campaigns, and to become committee chairs. They also propose more bills. Among the bills they do propose, they have a relatively lower proportion of ceremonial bills than other members. Conscientious majority-party legislators enjoy higher rates of legislative effectiveness. And, the more conscientious a legislator, the lower his or her rate of absenteeism in lame-duck sessions – especially when the legislator is a lame duck (see also Ramey, Klinger, and Hollibaugh 2019).[14] In general, Ramey et al. argue that these findings are due to conscientious legislators being concerned with future-oriented activity (in the case of having lower campaign spending), or with the managerial aspects of chairmanships incentivizing leadership to seek out conscientious legislators (in the case of receiving chairmanships). They argue that highly conscientious legislators propose more bills because doing so cultivates their reputations as policy entrepreneurs, which provides long-term benefits.[15]

* * *

What can these studies tell us about justices? A lot, actually. Here, we begin to sketch out the theoretical connections between conscientiousness and judicial behavior. We don't lay out testable hypotheses here. We do that in later chapters. The goal of the following discussion is to establish the theoretical

---

[14] Dietrich et al. (2012) examine the survey responses of ninety-three state legislators from Arizona, Connecticut, and Maine to estimate the Big Five for these individuals. They do not hypothesize – nor, surprisingly, do they find – any systematic relationship between conscientiousness and other survey items regarding a legislator's reported interest in running for higher office as well as their differential enjoyment of meeting with voters/constituents, participating in committee hearings, and working on legislation.

[15] Scholars have shown that conscientiousness correlates with good health. For example, Bogg and Roberts (2004) find that conscientious people live longer. In their meta-analysis of 194 studies, they find that conscientiousness is negatively correlated with risky health behaviors and positively correlated with beneficial health-related behaviors (see also Kern and Friedman 2008). Others have found similar results (Hampson et al. 2007). In fact, Roberts et al. (2007) find that conscientiousness is just as important as socioeconomic status and education in predicting good health. And why should we care about good health in our context? We show in the next chapter that our measure of conscientiousness is strongly correlated with the justices' longevity. Thus, because we know that conscientiousness is a very important construct in a nonjudicial domain (e.g., health), we are able to provide a strong piece of validation for our measure. But more on that later.

foundation for how conscientiousness relates to the aspects of judging that we explore. In other words, we discuss how these studies, taken together, might apply to judicial decision-making on the Court.

Conscientious people *follow the rules*. Based on these findings, we expect conscientiousness to influence many of the justices' tasks. For example, we expect conscientious justices, who are diligent, methodical, and thorough, to care about fulfilling their obligations to things like resolving lower court conflict. One of the Court's major roles in the current legal system is to ensure uniformity among the lower courts. The Court's own rules declare that justices are more likely to grant review to cases in order to clear up conflict. One would think, then, that conscientious justices treat conflict resolution differently than less conscientious justices. They also might be less likely to cast forward-looking votes to achieve policy goals.

Along the same lines, a diligent, methodical, and thorough justice whose personality tends toward following rules should expect the same from attorneys. So when it comes to legal persuasion, conscientious justices might be more persuadable via certain kinds of arguments. Court norms counsel against attorneys making impassioned emotional arguments to the justices. As norms and rules followers, conscientious justices are likely to oppose attorneys who make careless arguments. And so we expect that conscientious justices are more likely to be persuaded by methodical, logical, and legally strong arguments.

Conscientious justices also should be more likely to follow precedent. Judging is often viewed as making decisions within constraints. These constraints tend to take the form of rules or precedents. Because conscientious justices are rule abiding, we anticipate conscientious justices will want to interpret and treat past precedent positively. The rule abiding tendency is important, we argue, because justices have a strong interest in maintaining the legitimacy of the Court as an institution. Failure to follow precedent can be seen by the public and other legal elites as a violation of a legal norm. Along the same lines, we expect that conscientious justices will be more likely to recuse themselves from cases than their less conscientious colleagues. The Judicial Code of Conduct and federal law outlines a number of rules that guide justices as to when they must recuse themselves and avoid conflicts of interest. We suspect that justices who are rule followers will be quicker to recuse than their less conscientious colleagues.

Not only are conscientious people rules followers; they also care more about their *work product* than less conscientious people. They are more *deliberate* and *seek out more information* than others. These findings would seem to translate to a number of judicial actions as well. At the agenda stage, for example, conscientious justices should be likely to cast clear rather than tentative votes. As deliberate people, they are likely to eschew vague actions and, instead, cast clear votes. Additionally, because conscientious people are more deliberate, we suspect conscientious justices might require more time to write opinions. They may similarly write longer opinions that incorporate more information. Moreover, assuming the opinion assignor cares about a quality product (a reasonable assumption), it seems likely the assignor would favor highly conscientious justices. They can be trusted to craft solid opinions.

Because conscientious people also tend to be *responsible* and *concerned with the future*, we believe conscientious justices will be likely to consider external dynamics that could influence the Court's legitimacy. We will look, specifically, at the Court's deference to the Solicitor General's office and whether it follows public opinion. Thinking, first, of the justices' decisions to follow the SG's recommendations, we can see a strong separation of powers interest in deferring to the position of the executive. We can also see justices valuing the quality of legal arguments coming from the SG's office. The same logic suggests that conscientious justices might pay attention to public opinion. After all, a Court that deviates from the public's will can soon find itself under attack. And that, we believe, is something a future-oriented conscientious justice will seek to avoid.

There are, of course, other reasons to expect conscientious justices to behave differently than less conscientious justices, but we think we've made the point. The scholarship strongly suggests that conscientiousness influences individual behavior. And we believe those same principles apply to judicial behavior. Our remaining chapters seek to show just how.

2.4 CONCLUSION

There is a popular television show called *Fixer Upper*. It stars a married couple in Texas who work with clients to purchase rundown homes and renovate them. Some are large and some are small. The common denominator among the shows, though, is the couple's desire to take what exists and improve upon it.

Like home renovation, social science is about improving knowledge that currently exists. The goal (at least ours) is not to demolish an existing edifice but, rather, to build upon and improve it. We seek to improve existing theories and understanding of judicial behavior by incorporating personality.

The central thesis of this book is that conscientiousness influences justices. We test these claims throughout the remainder of the book. But before we can begin, we first need a suitable measure of conscientiousness (and, to be complete, the other four personality traits). We now turn to that task.

3

Measuring Justices' Conscientiousness

It would be difficult to overstate the importance of measurement. Imagine your doctor telling you that a disease has left you with anywhere between one to sixty years to live. Not a very precise or helpful measure. People today seek accurate measures for important life activities. And we're not unique in that capacity. Our ancestors had to devise measurements to pursue trade and agriculture. The Old Testament discusses an ancient measurement called cubits (equivalent to about eighteen inches), even going so far as to describe the number of cubits needed to build the Ark of the Covenant.[1] Richard the Lionheart adopted the Assize of Measures in 1196 because he understood the importance of standardizing measures across England. Recent measurement debates focus on how people can measure difficult concepts like pain, love, aesthetics, and the like. Actuaries make good money seeking to measure and manage risk. Scholars have even traded blows over measurements that examine whether Americans have become more politically tolerant (compare, e.g., Nunn et al. 1978 versus Sullivan et al. 1979). In short, measurement is critical.

To determine how conscientiousness influences justices' behavior, we must first *measure* it. But measuring the personality traits of Supreme Court justices is no easy task. There are numerous challenges. The first is our lack of access to the justices. In a world without constraints, we would simply administer a battery of personality tests on justices. Regrettably, we do not live in such a world. The second challenge turns on human longevity. Even if today's justices were courteous enough to complete some personality tests for us, we still would be unable to examine deceased justices.

Luckily, scholars have devised sophisticated methods to measure personality from a distance. The method we employ uses people's words to measure

---

[1] That is, 2.5 cubits in length and 1.5 cubits in both height and width. Eat your heart out, Indiana Jones.

their personalities. Studies have shown that a writer's (or speaker's) words can actually reveal his or her personality. As Pennebaker et al. (2015, 1) note, "The ways people use words in their daily lives can provide rich information about their beliefs, fears, thinking patterns, social relationships, and personalities." We agree. And so we follow the path set out by Winter (2003), who broke ground in measuring the personality components of political actors by analyzing the words they use. In a series of studies, Winter examined the words various political actors used and, from them, measured aspects of their personalities. He employed this method to determine the personalities of presidents, other world leaders, and even individuals in the business world. Others have undertaken similar analyses (see, e.g., Keller and Foster 2012).

In this chapter, we discuss how we measure justices' personalities. The first half of the chapter examines our measurement approach. We walk through the three steps we take to create our measures. Step one involves identifying and collecting the texts we use. Step two discusses cutting-edge methods for translating those texts into measures of traits. Step three involves a novel standardization process we developed to account for the fact that we investigate text from a variety of document types (e.g., speeches, writings, opinions). After these three steps, we undertake an exhaustive analysis to establish our measure's criterion validity. All of that takes place in the first half of the chapter. The second half of the chapter examines Hall's (2018) recent alternative approach to measuring justices' personalities. We explain the limitations of Hall's personality measurements and discuss why we, respectfully, believe our measures are superior.

3.1 STEP ONE: IDENTIFYING AND COLLECTING TEXTS

To estimate justices' personality traits, we analyze the text of their preconfirmation speeches and writings. We are on well-trodden ground when using text to measure personality. For example, Ramey, Klinger, and Hollibaugh (2017, 2019) examine thousands of congressional floor speeches to estimate personality traits for members of Congress. They show that personality predicts a number of noteworthy behaviors: conscientious members are less likely to be absent than their less conscientious, hooky-playing counterparts – even more so when the member is a lame duck (Ramey, Klinger, and Hollibaugh 2017, 175–184). Recently, Hall (2018) applied a similar approach to the study of US Supreme Court justices (discussed in more detail later). Work in the non-legal and non-political world finds similar results. Liu et al. (2016) show that Twitter-derived personality traits (drawn from tweet texts) can be used to predict the purchasing behaviors of individuals across more than one hundred distinct product types. De Choudhury, Counts, and Horvitz (2013) use social media gathered from Twitter to build a predictive model of postpartum depression in new mothers. In short, using text to measure personality is an appropriate method.

Fortunately for us, most Supreme Court justices have lengthy paper trails that precede their elevation to the High Court. Before they ascended to the Supreme Court, most justices engaged in extensive political and legal service (Epstein, Knight, and Martin 2003). Many of them delivered speeches and wrote articles. We use these texts to estimate their preferences. To gather justices' preconfirmation speeches and writings, we start with the corpus of preconfirmation documents collected by Owens and Wedeking (2012) in their analysis of ideological drift on the Supreme Court. Their data consist of three inputs: (1) published articles or other writings penned by a justice prior to his or her confirmation; (2) preconfirmation separate opinions authored by a justice while serving as a circuit court judge, state supreme court justice, or other lower court judge; and (3) speeches delivered by a justice prior to his or her confirmation.

To collect the justices' published articles, Owens and Wedeking (2012) searched HeinOnline and Google Scholar for every article written by a justice prior to the date of his or her confirmation. To obtain each justice's preconfirmation opinions (where relevant), they searched LexisNexis for separate opinions written by the justice when he or she was a circuit court judge, state supreme court justice, or other lower court judge. As for gathering speeches, this was considerably more challenging. Owens and Wedeking turned to archival data in presidential libraries and the justices' private papers at the Library of Congress (and elsewhere), taking digital images of each page in each speech, which they subsequently converted to text files that could be machine processed.

Our text inputs consist of approximately 1,400 documents containing a total of more than 4 million words across 38 unique justices. Hugo Black (appointed in 1937) is the earliest justice in our data. Elena Kagan (appointed in 2010) is the most current justice in our data.[2] The data contain 635 court opinions (1.2 million words), 476 speeches (1.3 million words), and 288

---

[2] We note that our decision to exclude the two most recent appointees to the Court (as of mid-2019), Justices Gorsuch and Kavanaugh, is due not to a lack of available data for estimating their personalities, but rather a lack of data to assess how personality influences their behavior as justices. That is, as both have only recently joined the Court, we would have scant observations in terms of the dependent variables we use throughout the many chapters that follow.

publications (1.8 million words). At the justice level, the median level of input data is 36.5 documents and 88,873 words. The 5th and 95th percentile values for word count are 16,112 (Harlan II) and 296,564 (Frankfurter), respectively.

To put some of these numbers in perspective, consider that the US Constitution, with amendments, contains just under 7,600 words. Roald Dahl's *Charlie and the Chocolate Factory* contains roughly 31,000 words. The Unibomber's manifesto, *Industrial Society and Its Future,* has approximately 35,000 words (of crazy). Jules Verne's *20,000 Leagues Under the Sea* registers at about 138,000 words (or about 7 words per league traveled).[3] As for lengthier tomes, the 7 books in J. K. Rowling's *Harry Potter* series consist of 1.08 million words.[4]

We observe reasonably complete input data across justices and document types. Of the thirty-eight justices in our data, we have at least two distinct types of input sources (e.g., speeches and opinions) for all but three: Souter, White, and Whittaker. We have only lower court separate legal opinions for those three.[5] Nearly one-third (twelve out of thirty-eight) of our justices generated all three document types. Furthermore, we achieve good balance in terms of the comparative frequency of document types. That is, one type does not disproportionately dominate the mixture. A total of twenty-two justices have opinions in their preconfirmation portfolio, thirty have speeches, and thirty-one have publications. To be sure, the situational context in which a particular article is written – or a speech is delivered – might differentially activate various aspects of the writer or speaker's personality (Aliotta 1988, 270). We deal with this concern in step 3. But the bottom line here is that we have a healthy mix of speeches, lower court opinions, and writings for our justices – textual information that allows us to estimate their personality traits.

Before moving to the next step, it's worth pointing out the texts we do *not* use. We do not employ texts created while a justice served on the Supreme Court. This means that their written opinions and comments during oral argument are out. At first blush, this might seem like leaving a lot of data on the table. It also precludes us from assessing whether judicial personality is dynamic as opposed to static. As a principled matter, however, it is right to ignore these texts. Our goal is to explain the behavior of Supreme Court

---

3   http://commonplacebook.com/art/books/word-count-for-famous-novels/.
4   https://electricliterature.com/infographic-word-counts-of-famous-books/.
5   We use the term *legal opinion* somewhat loosely here, as Justice Byron White never served as judge prior to his appointment to the High Court. He did, however, work as a law clerk for Chief Justice Fred Vinson. Our input data for White thus come from certiorari memoranda written by White during his time as a law clerk.

justices. Using a measure that itself comes from the behavior of Supreme Court justices is inherently circular. It's no different than using judicial votes to explain judicial votes, which is inappropriate (Martin and Quinn 2002, 2005). And so, much like Segal and Cover's (1989) decision three decades ago to craft an exogenous indicator of ideology, we seek an indicator of personality that is independent of the behavior we explain.[6] What is more, as we demonstrate in detail in the following discussion, approaches that use justices' Supreme Court opinions to estimate their personality traits are exceedingly sensitive to the types of opinions included in the estimation.[7]

We also do not use justices' testimony during their confirmation hearings. These proceedings constrain what nominees can and do say. Using text to estimate personality depends upon the author's ability to speak freely. Supreme Court nominees have a strong incentive to censor what they say. Conference hearings do not, therefore, reflect a nominee's normal "voice." What is even more concerning for our particular quantity of interest – conscientiousness – is that the context provides incentives for the nominees to create a false impression of who they are and who they might be as a justice. It is quite plausible that most nominees will strive to create the impression that they will be conscientious justices because most everyone's stereotype of a "good judge" is a conscientious one.

To be sure, relying on speeches, writings, and lower court opinions is not without its potential drawbacks. Lower court opinions are likely distinctive from speeches, which are dissimilar from law review articles and other writings. To treat them all as equivalent would be misguided. We take up this point in much greater detail below (see step three), but for now it is sufficient to say that we avoid this erroneous action.

In a slightly different vein, one might wonder whether preconfirmation documents actually provide an unguarded view of a justice's personality. After all, a speech or article might target the president or senators in an effort to get nominated (Graetz and Greenhouse 2016). Black and Owens (2016) show, for example, that during a Supreme Court vacancy, federal circuit judges on the

---

[6] As they sagely observed, "One cannot demonstrate that attitudes affect votes when attitudes are operationalized from those same votes" (1989, 558).

[7] One possible extension to our efforts here is to examine the relationship between preconfirmation speeches or off-the-bench writings (i.e., our data) with what a justice says or writes once she is on the High Court. Using these data as "true" indicators of personality is likely problematic since justices use these opportunities to pursue their goals (Baum 2006). Thus, we have some doubts about whether such data could be used to produce a dynamic estimate of a justice's personality. That being said, it would still be a worthwhile endeavor to examine and model variation in this post-confirmation content as a function of other theoretically informed quantities.

president's shortlist alter their behavior (see also Epstein, Landes, and Posner 2013). It's possible that some of the justices' prenomination texts are not unbiased windows into justices' personalities. Ultimately, we are not especially troubled by the possibility of such forward-looking behavior. People signaling their potential for elevation focus on their *policy* alignment with key policy makers.[8] Although we have no doubt that the career trajectory and document trail of individuals who go on to become Supreme Court justices are in no way representative of the population, and may in fact contain some strategic language, we see little reason to believe that this systematically leads them to alter how they present their *personality* across all of these documents.

3.2 STEP TWO: TRANSLATING TEXTS INTO TRAITS USING IBM WATSON PERSONALITY INSIGHTS

To translate these texts into measures of personality traits, we use IBM Watson Personality Insights (WPI). (Note: Much of the following discussion comes directly from the IBM Watson Personality Insights documentation [2017].) Interacting with WPI is fairly straightforward. We use a Java program to access the service and provide a directory containing whatever text files for which we wish WPI to generate personality scores. The Java program uploads our files to WPI, a cloud-based service, where the IBM program analyzes them. The results come back in individual JSON files that we subsequently aggregate and postprocess using a basic R script.

When WPI analyzes our text files, it performs two initial tasks. First, it divides each text file into individual tokens. For example, the tokenized representation of the first few words in the previous sentence would yield: [First] [it] [divides] [each] [text]. Tokenization also encodes each word into a unique symbol. The token "[consider]," for instance, might be represented as "token0108." Second, tokens in hand, WPI next converts these values into vector representations. (This is also referred to as word-embedding in the natural language processing literature.) The goal of this process is to reduce the dimensionality of raw text, which is useful for the same reasons as more commonly used tools like principal-component or factor analysis; the analyst can take complicated data and simplify them in a way that makes them easier to analyze, while preserving their key substantive features. Rather than

---

[8] For example, Warren Burger, in railing about the difficulty "to convict even those who are plainly guilty" (Graetz and Greenhouse 2016, 237), signaled to President Nixon that he would be no Earl Warren.

treating each word as uniquely distinctive, it is possible to group an individual word, along with other words that have similar meanings. For example, one cluster of similarity might aggregate the words "ocean" and "sea" together. Broadening the category a bit would allow for words like lake, river, stream, or tributary. To determine which words are similar to others, WPI uses an approach called the Global Vectors for Word Representation (GloVe) (Pennington, Socher, and Manning 2014). Researchers trained GloVe on tens of billions of tokens extracted from things like Wikipedia (1.6 billion tokens) and massive crawls across the web (42 billion tokens). The resulting classification scheme determines how (dis)similar one word is to another and, importantly, outperforms other earlier approaches on a variety of diagnostic tasks.

These two initial steps tee up our data for the main measurement task of translating tokens (i.e., text) into trait estimates. WPI combines cutting-edge machine learning techniques with recent advances in natural language processing. To learn how text can reveal traits, IBM gathered data from thousands of Twitter users' feeds. It then had those very same Twitter users complete traditional personality surveys. With these two sets of data, IBM researchers used machine learning to train classification models to uncover the relationship between an individual's personality survey responses and the words those same people used in their tweets. WPI uses those known relationships to generate personality trait estimates when researchers have access only to text.

Before we move to step three, we should point out that although the WPI approach is conceptually similar to earlier efforts in this area, head-to-head comparisons show that WPI is significantly better. As such, it represents the (current) cutting edge in the field of translating text to traits. It significantly outperforms Personality Recognizer, which is the program that both Hall (2018) and others (Ramey, Klinger, and Hollibaugh 2017) employ to measure personality. Personality Recognizer was created by Mairesse et al. (2007) and was one of the first efforts at "automatic recognition of personality traits" (2007, 457). Personality Recognizer examined how undergraduate students' word use in open-ended written essays correlated with their responses to personality surveys. This is substantively equivalent to what WPI does. Where the two approaches part ways, however, is in the way they treat input text.

Personality Recognizer uses predetermined word categories from the Linguistic Inquiry and Word Count (LIWC) program. For example, it establishes ex ante the existence of a "family" category of words, which includes distinctive words like mom, wife, or cousin. So far as Personality Recognizer is concerned, mom, wife, and cousin can be used interchangeably. Personality

Recognizer takes as its inputs the percentage of words used in a document that fall into more than eighty categories and uses those predefined categories to attempt to predict personality traits.[9]

WPI, by contrast, uses a more recent open-vocabulary approach developed by Schwartz et al. (2013). This approach eschews arbitrary ex ante categorization and instead lets the data decide what words, phrases, and topics best predict personality traits. Using the previous example, it seems unlikely that a writer would be comfortable substituting "wife" for "mom" or "cousin" as used in most personal contexts (e.g., "my wife and I took a much-needed romantic vacation to the Caribbean"). WPI captures those nuanced but significant substantive differences; Personality Recognizer does not.

Similarly, the LIWC dictionary, which serves as the key input for Personality Recognizer, relies almost exclusively upon fewer than 5,000 single word entries (i.e., unigrams). WPI, by contrast, looks at one, two, and three-word phrases (i.e., unigrams, bigrams, and trigrams, respectively). It also uses advances in latent topic modeling to identify what general topics of discussion correlate with an individual's personality traits. These enhancements more effectively capture the specific context in which a speaker uses an individual word or phrase. Greater context means greater fidelity to how a writer intended to use a word, which, in turn, provides a clearer window into that individual's personality (i.e., less measurement error).

From our perspective, Personality Recognizer was more impressive as a proof-of-concept demonstration as opposed to a mature tool that could (or rather should) be used to estimate traits. That is, Personality Recognizer's performance was not particularly strong. For example, one way to evaluate a text-to-trait algorithm is by comparing the trait estimates it produces against a baseline that one would obtain by simply predicting the sample average for a specific trait value.[10] This is analogous to always guessing the mode in the context of a dichotomous outcome like yes or no. The error rate for Personality Recognizer, then, is relative to that baseline such that a value of 100 "implies a performance equivalent to that baseline" while values below 100 indicate "that the model performs better than the constant mean baseline"

---

9   Mairesse et al. (2007) report that the trait of conscientiousness, for example, is positively correlated with the aforementioned family category of words. Conscientiousness is negatively correlated with LIWC's "body" category of words, which includes cheek, hands, spit, and more than 170 other words.

10 Another approach is to divide the real (i.e., survey) trait values into two categories – above or below the median value – and see how often the estimated traits (from text) are able correctly predict the dichotomous outcome. Personality Recognizer achieves an average accuracy rate of 57.1 percent. Given that one could achieve a prediction rate of 50 percent by just flipping a coin, Personality Recognizer's performance for even this basic task is not strong.

(Mairesse et al. 2007, 480). The Personality Recognizer results range from 94.2 for openness (i.e., better than the baseline) to 100.7 for extraversion (i.e., slightly worse than the baseline). Values for the other three traits are agreeableness (100.3), conscientiousness (99.3), and neuroticism (98.4).

These values are, however, just point estimates, which is to say they have some uncertainty around them. In terms of providing a *statistically signif-icant* improvement over always guessing the sample average, Personality Recognizer does so for only *one* of the five traits (openness). This suggests, sub-stantively, that the underlying model does not add much useful information in terms of being able to predict an individual's personality accurately. Thus, from our perspective, Personality Recognizer – the first preliminary attempt to automate personality measurement – has large limitations and should not be considered a viable way to estimate personality traits from text.

WPI is a continually updated method with fewer assumptions, and thus performs much better than Personality Recognizer – a program that its devel-oper orphaned more than ten years ago.[11] In this regard, Schwartz et al. (2013) provide the gold-standard comparison: how well do text-derived trait estimates correlate with those that come directly from surveys?[12] Across all five traits, WPI's open-vocabulary approach significantly outperforms the LIWC-based approach of Personality Recognizer. WPI's text-trait correla-tions average 0.35 across the five traits compared to a correlation of 0.26 for the LIWC/Personality Recognizer approach. This is an average relative performance boost of at least 35 percent.[13] Perhaps more tellingly, Schwartz

---

[11] "[U]nfortunately I currently do not have the time to support or maintain this software." Personality Recognizer v1.03 software page (release date June 24, 2008). http://farm2.user .srcf.net/research/ personality/recognizer (last accessed November 3, 2018). So significant are the subsequent developments in the underlying software required to run Personality Recog-nizer (e.g., Java) that it took an experienced (with more than ten years' experience) software developer approximately eight hours of dedicated effort to modify Personality Recognizer so that it would run on one our contemporary computers.

[12] The original Mairesse et al. article does not report any correlations for the trait predictions and the actual trait scores for the specific Personality Recognizer model used by Hall and Ramey et al., but it is possible to use what they do report for other models and arrive at the conclusion that they are probably very weak. Mairesse et al. experiment with five approaches. The strongest performance they obtain for predicting the specific trait estimates comes from a M5 model tree with linear models, which has sub-100 values in the previously discussed prediction task for all five traits and two that are statistically significant improvements: 96.4 for neuroticism and 93.3 for openness. The bivariate correlation between the predicted estimates and actual values for these two results were 0.24 and 0.33, respectively. Given this relationship, we can estimate that the trait-survey correlations for the Hall and Ramey et al. approach aver-ages 0.18, with a range between 0.12 (extraversion) and 0.30 (openness). Conscientiousness, our trait of interest, has a correlation of just 0.16.

[13] We note this LIWC value is considerably higher than what Mairesse et al. achieve for Personality Recognizer. We attribute this difference to advances in the machine learning

et al. also find that combining the LIWC to the WPI approach yields *zero* additional explanatory power over an approach that relies solely on open vocabulary (Schwartz et al. 2013, 13).[14] In short, the approach we utilize represents the current state of the art in translating text into trait estimates.

3.3 STEP THREE: STANDARDIZING THE MEASURE ACROSS DOCUMENT TYPES

As we stated previously, we use justices' preconfirmation speeches, publications, and lower court opinions to estimate their personalities. While this is a fairly exhaustive set of sources, it is also a nonstandardized set. The different document types might systematically diverge in important ways. Perhaps there are patterns that arise in some of those texts due not to personality but, rather, to social context or to the specific purpose for which a justice created a document. In the parlance of social science, there could be some unmeasured confounding variable that influences our eventual measurement values. Further compounding this concern is variation in the mixture of documents across different justices, with some justices writing or speaking more than others, which could be related to their personality differences. For example, an introverted justice might have been less likely to deliver a speech than an extrovert. In short, there will be some inherent personality hardwired into some texts that is not driven wholly by the personality of the writer or speaker.[15] Accordingly, we must find ways to purge our measures of these confounding effects.

To do so, we must first back up a bit. In a perfect world, each text created by a justice prior to her confirmation would be motivated by nothing except her personality. It would be thoughtful, revelatory, and untainted by the specific context for which it was created. These texts would provide an error-free view into each justice's personality. Alas, such is not possible. But, we do propose an alternative that leverages what we see as the *complement* to complete measurement accuracy: total randomness. Stated a bit differently, suppose that instead

incorporated by Schwartz et al. Note that such gains are *not* incorporated in Personality Recognizer, which means that the advantage of WPI over it is even larger.

[14] Other research shows that WPI's open vocabulary approach is also able to more efficiently (i.e., with less input text required) produce accurate trait estimates as compared to the LIWC-based one utilized by Personality Recognizer (Arnoux et al. 2017). This is not a significant concern for our data, where we have, at minimum, thousands of words of text, but we note it for future applications that might take place in more data-sparse environments.

[15] Truth be told, this factor could also contaminate even the ideal personality survey. The Hawthorne effect, nonresponse bias, the social desirability effect, or other dynamics could influence respondents.

of providing completely truthful responses to a multiple-choice personality survey, some people answered purely at random. These random results would give us a baseline sense of what the *absence of meaningful personality* looked like as an empirical matter. Teachers and professors who use multiple choice exams do this all the time when they examine whether the proportion of students who correctly answered a question is significantly greater than 0.25 when a question has four possible answer options. Or, to change fields entirely, the randomness baseline can also be thought of as a placebo drug. In clinical medical trials, the power of a proposed drug is found in the extent to which it provides relief above and beyond the baseline of randomness from the placebo. The same logic applies here.[16] What we seek to do, then, is generate an empirical portrait of what documents would look like in the *absence* of systematic personality traits.

How do we create documents with the *absence* of systematic personality traits? Consider the 476 speeches included in our preconfirmation corpus. We started by merging all 476 speeches into one single mega-speech. Next, we split this outstretched oration into 64,581 individual sentences using the R package quanteda (Benoit 2018). We then created a new document comprised of a random sample (with replacement) from this big pool of sentences. That is, we made a new "speech" that consisted of randomly selected sentences from the pool of all sentences spoken in actual speeches by individuals who would later go on to become justices. We then repeated this procedure 499 more times to generate a total of 500 fake, randomized speeches. Now, a careful reader might observe that we did not say how many sentences we randomly sampled from this mega-document. The 5th and 95th percentile values for document length in our data are 14 and 308 sentences, respectively. As such, before we randomly pulled sentences out of the mega-document, we first randomly selected a number between 14 and 308. In short, then, to create random speeches, we:

1. Aggregated every sentence in all speeches into one document;
2. Selected a random number between 14 and 308;
3. Randomly sampled that many sentences from the mega-document;
4. Created a new document that contained those randomly selected sentences; and
5. Executed steps 2 to 4 a total of 500 times.

[16] We should note that this random approach accomplishes another goal as well. It keeps our language rooted in the legal world. The types of documents generated by individuals who go on to become Supreme Court justices might contain a distinct vocabulary. If we use random documents generated from the same underlying legal content as a baseline, we can control for any unique vocabulary that could be generating our results.

We followed the same procedure for the lower court opinions (70,062 sentences) and the preconfirmation publications (96,306 sentences) in our data. All told, we generated 1,500 documents that contained 4.5 million words of random content.[17] They are "placebo personality" documents against which we will compare our personality estimates. They are also, at times, amusing in terms of their content. Two sentences from one random speech read: "Nineteen additions have so far been made to the park system of the State and a comprehensive program launched for building riding and hiking trails for public use. We impoverish ourselves, intellectually and spiritually."[18]

We used WPI to generate document-level trait scores for each of the 1,500 randomly generated documents. We then calculate the document-type mean and standard deviation for each of the Big Five traits. This is to say that we go from having a total of 1,500 sets of trait scores (i.e., one per document) to one set of means and standard deviations for each of the three document types. Substantively, this provides us with a baseline estimate of how much personality is present when the documents were "written" randomly by "someone" *with absolutely no personality*. We then use these values to standardize the raw scores for our original corpus of pre-confirmation texts. That is, we take the raw WPI trait score we discussed in step two, subtract the average (mean) random text trait score for that document type, and divide by the standard deviation of the random text trait score for that document type. The resulting standardized scores, then, identify personality above and beyond documents on a similar topic generated in the absence of meaningful personality. Since it is a standardization process, these scores should be interpreted like z-scores.

An example illustrates the value – and necessity! – of standardizing our raw WPI scores. One speech in our corpus comes from Hugo Black. It has a raw WPI conscientiousness score of 0.6720. An article by Lewis Powell has a raw WPI conscientiousness score of 0.6718. Rounded to the tenths, hundredths, or even thousandths place, these two (non-standardized) documents would be identical in terms of their conscientiousness. Yet, such equivalence belies the fact that speeches, as a document type, contain higher baseline levels of conscientiousness than do articles.[19] Once we account for

---

[17] The median document length was 3,122 words. The 5th and 95th percentile values are 543 words and 5,628 words, respectively.

[18] The first sentence comes from a radio address given by then governor of California Earl Warren. The second originates in a campaign speech given by Frank Murphy, who would also serve as governor (of Michigan).

[19] Not only is the average in the random documents higher, but the standard deviation is smaller, too. The means and standard deviations for the randomly generated files are 0.698/0.0073 (speeches) and 0.687/0.0081 (publications).

this underlying difference, and after we standardize the measure, the corrected document scores are −3.57 for Powell's speech and −1.86 for Black's article. Powell's speech moves from the 30th percentile of conscientiousness to the 15th percentile. Black's article moves considerably less, going from the 30th to the 31st percentile.

The standardization process fixes similarly poignant differences within a single justice as well. Consider three pre-confirmation documents associated with Justice Scalia. One is an article Scalia wrote in 1980. The second is a 1972 speech he delivered on the Fairness Doctrine. The third is a dissenting opinion he penned on the DC Circuit. In terms of their conscientiousness, the documents' raw WPI scores are a very similar 0.6692, 0.6694, and 0.6685, respectively. But, as we said previously, publications, speeches, and opinions are horses of distinctively different colors in terms of their ability to activate words, phrases, and topics associated with conscientiousness. Once we standardized the three documents, the resulting z-scores are −2.20 for the article, −3.92 for the speech, and −1.58 for the opinion. Clearly, it is important to standardize these texts.

After converting the raw document trait scores to standardized trait scores, our final step was simply to determine the median of these values for each justice. Figure 2 plots the conscientious trait score for all thirty-eight justices in our data. Consider Justice William Douglas, whom we estimate to have a conscientiousness score of approximately −3.7. This indicates that a typical (i.e., median) preconfirmation document for Douglas evinced significantly lower conscientiousness as compared to a baseline of randomly generated texts. At the other end of the spectrum of conscientiousness, we see Chief Justice Earl Warren, whose conscientiousness score is 1.16. Overall, the mean across the 38 justices in our data is −0.69, with a standard deviation of 1.13. The 5th and 95th percentiles are −3.27 and 0.90, respectively.

Naturally, there's quite a bit more we could say about how certain justices fare with respect to their conscientiousness scores. We imagine that if you haven't already, you'll probably spend a few moments pouring over this figure to determine how our ordering of the justices comports with your prior expectations. Is Thurgood Marshall *really* the second most conscientious justice? I see David Souter hanging out there toward the bottom. That seems about right/horribly flawed to me. Having presented these results a number of times to various audiences, we completely understand where you're coming from. You're concerned about validity. It turns out that we have quite a bit to say about validity in the coming pages.

But, before we get to that discussion, we offer Figure 3, which presents estimates for the remaining four traits: agreeableness, neuroticism, openness, and

Conscientiousness

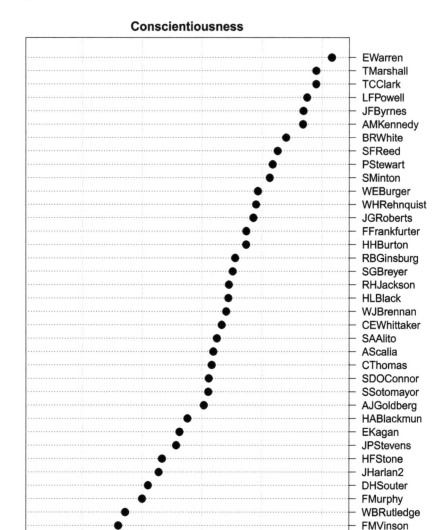

FIGURE 2: *Supreme Court Justice Conscientiousness Trait Estimates.* These values come from IBM Watson's Personality Insight service, which we subsequently standardized with regard to placebo personality documents (see accompanying text for details). The x-axis corresponds to the standardized trait values.

extraversion. The interpretation for these additional panels remains the same as before, although in the interest of space considerations, we use the justices' initials in lieu of their names. We observe considerable variation in the range of the scores across all five of the traits, with the difference between each trait minimum and trait maximum being, on average 5.67 units of measurement.

We also see that individual justices move around in terms of their relative ranking across the various traits. For example, Earl Warren (EW), whom we estimate to be the most conscientious of the justices in our data, ends up being at the very bottom in terms of openness. William Douglas (WOD), the least conscientious justice, is near the middle in terms of openness. Fred Vinson (FMV), by our accounting, scores quite low in terms of both conscientiousness and openness.

Other than asking for your patience with us a couple of paragraphs ago, we've been otherwise silent on whether these scores "seem right." By this, we mean their face validity. Some researchers deploy face validity to show that a new measurement procedure is a "good" one. Indeed, we've done so ourselves in some of our previous joint work on a different topic (e.g., Black, Owens, Wedeking, and Wohlfarth 2016*b*, 51–53). As we suggested previously, although we have no doubt some readers will carefully study the foregoing figures to see how their favorite (or not-so-favorite) justice fares on our measures, we are, on balance, dubious of the *scientific* value of such activity.

For starters, justices are public figures, and in recent decades, they have started to "go public" with increased regularity through their travel (Black, Owens and Armaly 2016), public speeches (Krewson 2018), and television appearances (Davis 2011). This is to say nothing of the inevitable biographies (and autobiographies) that are written both after and, increasingly, during their time on the bench. When a justice dies, volumes of law reviews detail their legacy, with former law clerks, judicial colleagues, and scholars opining on (and usually celebrating) them. All of this is simply to say that we suspect, with sufficient dedication, one could cull these various materials to find support for just about *any* characterization of *any* justice. Such an endeavor, however, is "like walking into a crowded cocktail party and looking over the heads of the guests to pick out your friends" (Breyer 1992, 101).

Take, for example, Justice Clarence Thomas. According to our measures, he scores somewhat below average on the trait of extraversion, which is associated, generally speaking, with a person's tendency to seek stimulation in the company of others. One could point to Thomas' well-documented silence during oral argument as "facial evidence" consistent with this result. But Thomas also spends his summers traveling around the United States in his

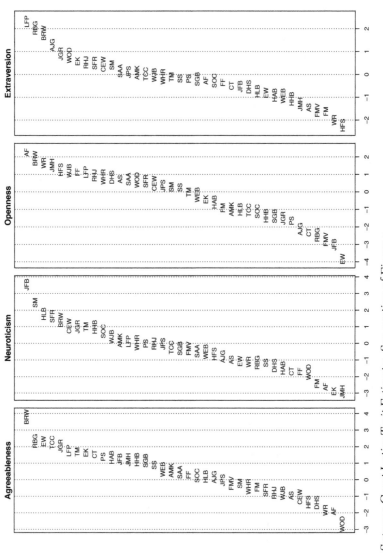

FIGURE 3: *Supreme Court Justice Trait Estimates. See caption of Figure 2.*

RV, speaking with "regular" people, and camping in the parking lots of Wal-mart, which does not seem especially antisocial. A 2016 *Washington Post* article on the social lives of Supreme Court justices similarly suggests: "People have a gross misunderstanding [of Thomas] because he doesn't ask questions during oral arguments. In the Supreme Court building, he is the most beloved justice. He is unbelievably gregarious, knows every staffer's name" (Roberts 2016). With the proper framing, we suspect a talented writer could tout one set of these anecdotes while simultaneously giving short shrift to the other. That doesn't strike us as a good way to go about assessing face validity.

To be clear, one could attempt to get a bit more systematic. For instance, one could look at justices identified by the measures as being at the top and bottom of a specific trait and see how that aligns with available information. At first blush, this seems to be better than cherry-picking individual justices, but we're still unconvinced that it's a good idea. First, even though such efforts would be yeoman's work (if one does ten comparisons per trait, it would be fifty overall), they would be incomplete and are almost guaranteed to be misleading. By letting the top and bottom values drive the validation inquiry, one would ignore the possibility that the approach failed to identify a justice as being very high/low in a trait when she actually was.

In that vein, let's return to the example of Justice Thomas. Suppose that the above description of Thomas is true – he really is "unbelievably gregarious." If Thomas emerges in the top five for extraversion, then that gets labeled as a clear win for the measure (as it should). In contrast, if he ends up in the bottom five, then that's an unambiguous loss. But, what if he ends up somewhere in the murky middle? Quantitatively, this is the most likely outcome (i.e., $1 - \frac{10}{38} \approx 0.74$). But it is one that would be missed by this approach. Objectively, it also seems as though it should be viewed is a significant loss; the measure failed to classify him correctly as being high in extraversion. And yet, by letting the superlative values *as measured* drive the validation, the researcher assumes no such errors occur. We see this as a critical limitation.

The logical retort to this critique is to expand the scope of the validation efforts to include *all* the justices for whom one has estimated personality traits. Go gather a bunch of qualitative data and then see how the measure stacks up. This would effectively address the concern about false negative classifications. It still has serious limitations, however. In particular, both this and the more limited approach described previously still rely upon what information the person doing the inquiry is able to find, how they decide to interpret it, and the way they go about reporting it in the analysis.

So that we are crystal clear, we are not suggesting any sort of conscious scholarly shenanigans on the part of anyone. But it seems woefully naive to think that decades of research from psychology – the very field that provides the foundation for our inquiry in this book – on things like confirmation bias (Nickerson 1998) and motivated reasoning (Kunda 1990) are somehow inapplicable when it comes to the behavior of even the most careful and talented scholars. If, as we firmly believe, judges are people, too, then it seems obvious that, well, so are we. To prove the point, research shows that coders for the US Supreme Court Database tend to gravitate toward issue codes that allow them to classify otherwise similar cases as being liberal during the Warren Court years but as conservative during the Rehnquist Court era (Harvey and Woodruff 2013). Importantly, this is not thought to be a conscious effort on the part of the coder. Instead, it occurs "unwittingly, without intending to treat the evidence in a biased way or even being aware of doing so" (Nickerson 1998, 175; quoted in Harvey and Woodruff 2013, 423). So, face validity requires quite a lot of work, but with very little guaranteed to be gained due to these subjectivity concerns.

3.4 MEASUREMENT VALIDITY

Still, it is essential that we show our measurement validity spans beyond the "just trust us" or "let's just see how things work out in the models" approach. To that end, we examine criterion validity, which is unmistakably an *objective* approach to assessing measure validity. The underlying logic of criterion validity is straightforward. If our personality measurements actually tap into personality, then we should see the measures correlate with other outcomes scholars know tap into personality. In what follows, we review the correlations between our measure of justice conscientiousness and a variety of outcomes that existing research has found to be correlated with conscientiousness. Lest there be any confusion, the results show that our measure provides a valid empirical indicator of conscientiousness. (We review the measurement validity of the remaining four traits in the appendix.)

As we stated in Chapter 2, studies show that highly conscientious people enjoy longer lives than less conscientious people. This should not come as much of a surprise. Conscientious people are self-disciplined (don't eat that extra slice of pizza!), responsible (don't procrastinate!), dutiful (wear your seatbelt!), and goal directed (go the extra mile, literally!). If that's not a recipe for getting to spend more years on this earth, we don't know what is. Indeed, Friedman et al. (1993) demonstrate that conscientiousness in childhood predicts survival to both middle and old age. Kern and Friedman (2008) likewise provide a review of nearly two dozen separate, independent samples, and find a positive and statistically significant relationship between longevity and conscientiousness, with an average correlation of 0.11 [0.05, 0.17]. Roberts et al. (2007) report that the substantive effect of conscientiousness on longevity is just as large as an individual's socioeconomic status.

Our analyses show that increasingly conscientious justices live longer than their less conscientious colleagues. The left panel of Figure 4 presents a scatterplot of a justice's conscientiousness (x-axis) and how old he or she was at time of death (y-axis). (Note that for this and several of the following plots, the number of observations will fluctuate. For some comparisons, it makes sense to examine only justices who have already died or retired versus the full slate of previous and current justices.) As the figure makes clear, the data reveal a positive, statistically significant, and substantively strong relationship between longevity and justice conscientiousness. This finding provides strong criterion validity.

Studies also reveal a strong correlation between conscientiousness and the number of children people beget. Roberts and Bogg (2004) conducted a longitudinal study of women at ages twenty-one, forty-three, and fifty-two. They found that a twenty-one-year-old woman's increased social responsibility, a facet of conscientiousness, predicted the number of children she would go on to have by the age of forty-three. A later study replicated these findings in a large sample of women from the Netherlands; once again, conscientiousness positively correlated with the number of children women had (Dijkstra and Barelds 2009).[20]

Our analyses show that increasingly conscientious justices have more children. The right panel in Figure 4 shows the relationship between justice conscientiousness (the x-axis) and the number of children a justice had (the y-axis). Our analysis includes all thirty-eight justices in our sample. We feel comfortable including all of them here because it is highly unlikely that even the youngest justice in our sample (Kagan at 58) will bear children in the future.[21] (Recall that we do not have conscientiousness scores for the

---

[20] Being the conscientious researchers that we (mostly) are, we should point out that we also found two studies less supportive of this relationship. Judge, Martocchio, and Thorensen (1997) find no relationship between the number of dependent children and conscientiousness. Their underlying sample was a strange one though: nonacademic employees at a large Midwestern university (i.e., staff and administrators). Another study found an overall negative relationship between conscientiousness and the number of children (Jokela et al. 2011). When the authors of this study disaggregated the relationship by gender, however, the effect was null for men and negative for women.

[21] Of course, a number of famous people have had children late in life. Mick Jagger had a child when he was seventy-three, for instance, and Steve Martin had his first child at age sixty-seven. Both of these outliers share something in common, however: a female partner who is

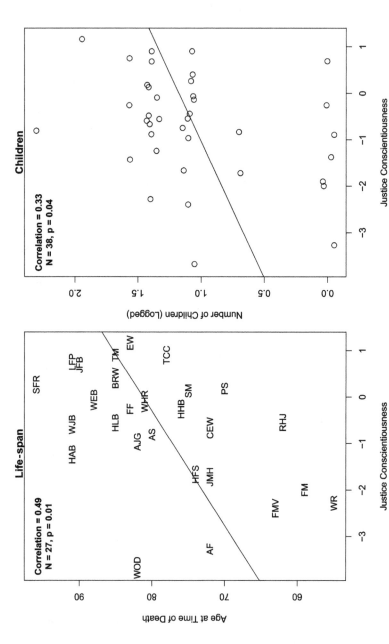

FIGURE 4: *Relationship between justice conscientiousness and longevity (left panel) and number of offspring (right panel). If we examine the raw number of children, then the correlation and p-value drop to values of 0.30 and 0.07, respectively. This is due to the clear outlier point of Justice Scalia, who had nine children (2.5 on the logged scale). Excluding Scalia yields correlations of 0.36 (logged children, p = 0.03) and 0.39 (raw count, p = 0.02).*

two newest – as of mid-2019 – members of the Court: Justices Gorsuch or Kavanaugh, aged fifty-one and fifty-three, respectively.) Another thing worth mentioning is that we present not the raw count of children; rather, we use (one plus) the natural logarithm of that value. We do so in an attempt to neutralize a clear outlier in the data, Justice Scalia, who had a total of nine children. As of 2018, only around 8 percent of the nearly 83 million households in the United States had three or more children. One would need to go back to the 1850s to see even (very small) single-digit percentages of households with so many children. As Figure 4 shows, we find, yet again, a positive and statistically significant correlation between a justice's conscientiousness and his or her proclivity for procreation – yet another representation of criterion validity.

Keeping things at home, we next examine conscientiousness as it relates to marriage and love. A number of studies document a systematic relationship between an individual's conscientiousness and love. For instance, Solomon and Jackson (2014) find a positive and statistically significant correlation between relationship duration and an individual's conscientiousness. Thus we analyze marriage length. We focus on the twenty-six deceased justices who were married at some point during their lives (this excludes Justice Frank Murphy). We focus on the deceased because living justices can theoretically still divorce. The left panel of Figure 5 shows that there is a positive and statistically significant correlation between increased justice conscientiousness and years of marriage.

The literature also considers how conscientiousness correlates with whether someone is lucky (or unlucky) in love. Surveys show that increased conscientiousness is positively associated with marital satisfaction (e.g., Heller, Watson, and Ilies 2004) and negatively correlated with divorce (Roberts and Bogg 2004). We created a dichotomous variable called *Unlucky in Love*, which takes on a value of 1 if a justice either never married (e.g., Kagan) or married but subsequently divorced (e.g., Justices Sotomayor and Douglas). The right panel of Figure 5 illustrates the results for our unlucky in love measure. Because this outcome only takes on two values – yes or no – we assess statistical significance by way of a difference-in-means test. The box plots in the panel show the distribution of our conscientiousness measure on the y-axis. This comparison is expanded to include all thirty-eight justices in the data as opposed to only the twenty-six that have since died. We do so because only two of the twenty-seven justices who are no longer living are

significantly younger than them. Jagger's girlfriend was thirty years old (younger than Jagger's oldest child, who was born in 1970). Martin's wife was twenty-six years younger than him.

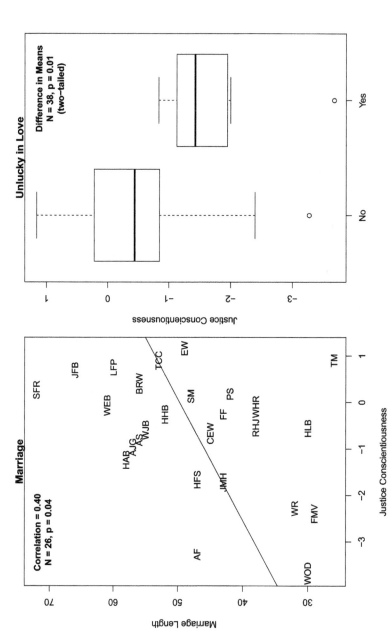

FIGURE 5: *Relationship between justice conscientiousness and marriage duration (left panel) and whether a justice was "unlucky in love" (right panel).* The data for the left panel include the twenty-six justices who are no longer alive but were, at some point in their lives, married. Unlucky in love is coded as "yes" if a justice never married or married and divorced; "no" otherwise. This panel includes all justices in our data. Restricting the analysis to the same comparison group as the left panel actually strengthens the magnitude of the difference (i.e., it jumps from 1.28 to 2.36; $p = 0.01$) but makes the figure look ugly because there are only two such justices in the data.

coded as being unlucky in love (Justices Murphy and Douglas). But, to be clear, both approaches show a statistically significant difference in terms of conscientiousness for justices who are lucky in love and those who are not. This is another example of criterion validity.

We now consider the relationship between conscientiousness and workplace performance. We examine two similar concepts: work productivity and job satisfaction. Existing studies reveal a significant correlation between an individual's conscientiousness and both performance on a specific task as well as the more general quality of job performance (Hurtz and Donovan 2000). Dudley et al. (2006, 45) corroborate this link between conscientiousness and positive work, while also showing that conscientiousness is negatively correlated with counterproductive work behaviors such as "not adhering to policies and procedures, theft, and disciplinary problems." In terms of job satisfaction, a longitudinal analysis of women's participation in the workforce found, for example, that women who scored high in conscientiousness at the age of twenty-one were more likely to be strong professionally more than twenty years later – and to have more positive attitudes about the importance of their work (George, Helson and, John 2011). Related work by Judge et al. (1999) recovered a positive and statistically significant correlation between job satisfaction and an individual's level of conscientiousness.[22]

Figure 6 provides two empirical perspectives on the relationship between a justice's conscientiousness and his or her job performance and job satisfaction. Both panels show conscientiousness on the x-axis and the outcome of interest on the y-axis. The left panel shows each justice's Segal-Cover (1989) qualifications score. To create these qualification scores, Segal and Cover read through and content analyzed newspaper editorials of every nominee to the High Court in recent years across six national newspapers. These editorials often discussed a nominee's perceived qualification for the position. Low values reflect a lack of qualifications whereas larger values indicate justices perceived to be more qualified. As the plot and its annotation make clear, there is no statistically significant relationship between our conscientiousness measure and a justice's preconfirmation qualification score. This null effect is robust to looking at any number of possible cutting lines for determining whether someone is very (un)qualified to be on the Court.[23] To be clear, this

---

[22] We acknowledge at least one mixed finding. Roberts and Bogg (2004) show that a woman's social responsibility – a facet of conscientiousness – as measured at the age of twenty-one was negatively correlated with workforce participation at age forty-three and uncorrelated with workforce participation at the age of fifty-two.

[23] Although the measure can theoretically range between 0 and 1, with a median value of roughly 0.89, it is quite skewed. Indeed, the 25th percentile value is 0.77, which means that even a

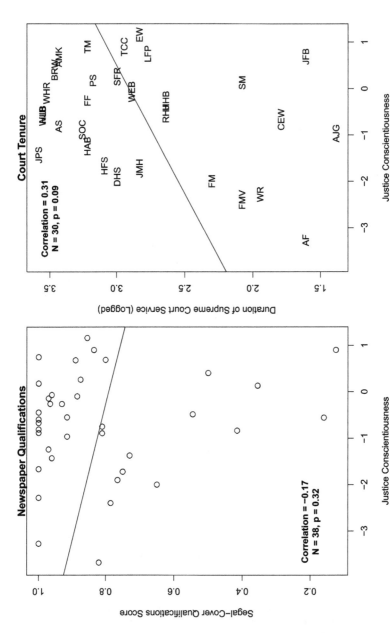

FIGURE 6: *Relationship between justice conscientiousness and Segal-Cover qualifications score (left panel) and tenure of service on the Supreme Court (logged, right panel).* The right panel includes only justices no longer on the Court and excludes Justice William O'Douglas. Douglas is a "double outlier" who served for thirty-six years (longest in history) and has the lowest conscientiousness score in our data (−3.67). If we include him in the calculations, then the correlation drops to 0.17 and the associated p-value is 0.35.

is less than phenomenal news for our measure. We report it, however, because to the extent it is believed to tap into an individual's work quality or performance, it is one of the most logical places one might look when thinking about conscientiousness. And we, too, strive to be conscientious.

That being said, we note that concepts such as performance or quality are difficult to measure. One problem is logistical. Although lower court judges are routinely reviewed by higher courts, Supreme Court justices, seated at the top of the judicial hierarchy, undergo no such review. Other preconfirmation assessments – such as those given out by the American Bar Association – have been shown to be contaminated by ideological bias (Smelcer, Steigerwalt, and Vining 2013). At the other end of the extreme, although many have engaged in cumulative assessments of which justices were the "greatest" (Schwartz 1995) or "most persuasive" (Kosma 1998), these listings do not provide a strong theoretical linkage to a specific aspect of the Big Five, but rather are likely driven by some combination of strengths across multiple traits. And even the newspaper-assessed qualification measure isn't without its warts. Indeed, the measure has not, so far as we know, been subjected to critical validity analyses.[24] We find it peculiar that Justice Gorsuch, a Harvard Law graduate, clerk to Justice Kennedy, and eleven-year circuit court alum scores at the same qualification level as Justice Burton, who never served as a judge before being appointed.

When it comes to correlations between conscientiousness and justices' job satisfaction and productivity, however, we obtain stronger and more logical results. The right panel of Figure 6 plots the duration of service (measured in logged years) for the thirty justices who are no longer on the Court. We treat duration here as job satisfaction, because justices could always retire and make large amounts of money in private practice or by hitting the speaker circuit. Again, we remove justices who are currently on the Court, since we would otherwise artificially censor their careers. We

nominee who is moderately qualified is, compared to his peers who would become justices, comparatively unqualified. Comparing those who had values of one versus those that did not does not yield a significant difference in conscientiousness (p = 0.81, two-tailed test). Alternatively, if we remove the observations with the six lowest qualification scores and examine only justices with a qualification score of .6 or higher, the correlation becomes 0.17 (p = 0.36, two-tailed test). The correlation is now signed in the expected direction, but still not statistically significant.

[24] That is, the first published use of it occurs in Cameron, Cover, and Segal (1990). In describing their measure, the authors write, "We note here that the data are reliable and appear to be valid" (1990, 529). A footnote appears at the end of that sentence, which reads, "We have discussed details of the content analysis elsewhere," referencing an unpublished conference paper of the same title. A more recent application of the measure by Epstein et al. (2005) is similarly silent on anything beyond the face validity of the measure.

also omitted Justice Douglas, who ends up being a "double outlier" in our data. That is, in addition to having served on the Court for nearly three thousand years (OK, really almost thirty-seven years), he also has the lowest conscientiousness score of any justice in our data.[25] Regardless, with Douglas omitted, we recover a positive correlation between tenure on the Court and conscientiousness.

Finally, we examine conscientiousness and ideology. A long line of research demonstrates that increased conscientiousness correlates with increased conservatism (e.g., Carney et al. 2008). Gerber et al. (2010) provide evidence that conscientiousness is correlated with an individual's self-reported ideology (e.g., calling yourself conservative), as well as with revealed preferences in terms of support for (or opposition to) both economic and social policy. To assess whether this relationship holds for justices, we turn to Figure 7, which places justices' conscientiousness along the x-axis and their ideology on the y-axis. We measure ideology from two different sources. In the left panel, we use the values calculated by Segal and Cover's (1989) newspaper editorial approach. In addition to canvasing editorials for statements about a nominee's qualifications, Segal and Cover also searched editorials for comments about the nominees' perceived ideologies. In terms of validation, Segal and Cover do show a very strong and statistically significant relationship (correlation = 0.80) between their editorial measure of ideology and the subsequent votes justices cast in civil liberties cases. Note that Segal and Cover report their measure in terms of a nominee's liberalism, such that a value of 1.0 is a "perfect" liberal and a value of 0.0 is a "perfect" conservative. Thus, we expect to see a negative relationship between conscientiousness and the Segal-Cover measure. This is precisely what we observe in the left panel of Figure 7. The strength of the relationship might not be jaw-dropping, but it is in the expected direction and flirts with general levels of statistical significance (i.e., it would be a mistake to accept the null hypothesis of no relationship given the data we observe).

Turning to the right panel of Figure 7, we plot conscientiousness against a justice's actual voting behavior – as measured by Martin and Quinn (2002) – during their first terms on the Court. Martin-Quinn scores are scaled such that negative values correspond to liberal preferences and positive values are associated with conservative ones. Thus, and in contrast to the left panel,

---

[25] There is also, arguably, a good substantive justification for his omission. By this we mean that his lengthy tenure belies a key fact about Douglas. As recounted by Murphy's (2003) wonderful biography of him, Douglas eagerly sought to leave the Court for possible elected office throughout his career. We know of no other justice who served in the modern era who has tried to run (away) from the Marble Palace.

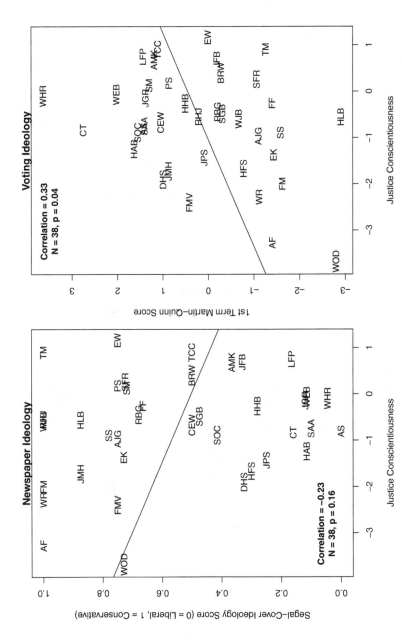

FIGURE 7: *Relationship between justice conscientiousness and their Segal-Cover pre-confirmation newspaper editorial ideology estimate (left panel) and their first term Martin-Quinn ideal point (right panel).*

we expect to see a positive relationship between conscientiousness and the justices' first term Martin-Quinn scores. We do. The correlation is actually about 43 percent stronger when we use actual behavior (i.e., Martin-Quinn) as opposed to predictions before someone became a justice (i.e., Segal-Cover). We take these to be results that, once again, validate our conscientiousness measure.

This exhaustive battery of analyses validates our measurement approach. The same, however, cannot be said for the SCIPE measures employed in Hall (2018). As we noted in Chapter 2, Hall (2018) examines personality and the Court. Figure 8 reproduces the correlations we just presented (dark gray bars) alongside the analogous correlations using Hall's SCIPE measures (light gray bars). We report statistical significance by annotating the ends of the correlation bars, with *, **, and *** corresponding to significance levels of 0.20, 0.10, and 0.05, respectively. We use "n.s." to abbreviate not statistically significant (i.e., p > 0.20).

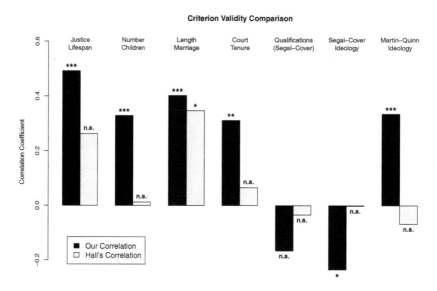

FIGURE 8: *Comparison of criterion validity correlations.* The dark bars reproduce the bivariate correlations presented earlier in this chapter from Figures 4-7. The lighter bars are the analogous correlation between the outcome variable of interest and the Hall/Hall et al. measure of conscientiousness. *, **, and *** correspond to levels of statistical significance, at the 0.20, 0.10, and 0.05 levels, respectively. n.s. means not statistically significant (i.e., p > 0.20).

The results are clear. Whereas we obtain significant correlations between our measure of conscientiousness and the outcome criterion of interest for all but one analysis, Hall's measures merely come close to significant correlations in only one instance (length of marriage).[26] Additionally, recall that one comparison we presented earlier was not of the correlational variety but rather a difference in means test for whether conscientiousness varied significantly if a justice was unlucky in love. Using our measure, we found that unlucky in love justices evinced significantly lower conscientiousness than their lucky in love counterparts (p = 0.01). Using the Hall et al. measure, however, we fail to find any such difference (N = 34, p = 0.36 [two-tailed test]). Put simply, our measures have strong criterion validity; the SCIPE measures have none.[27]

* * *

So far, we have explained the texts we used to measure personality. We discussed IBM's Watson Personality Insights. We then analyzed the importance of standardizing our measurements. And then we validated them, showing that, even though we cannot directly measure justices' conscientiousness, our measures correlate strongly with things we know, themselves, correlate with conscientiousness.

In the remainder of this chapter, we shift our focus to providing a critical assessment of Hall and his SCIPE approach. We do so in acknowledgment that his efforts preceded ours and, as a result, represent the status quo. And if we seek to change the status quo, we must discuss its limitations. This airing of differences is especially important because we believe personality scholarship will soon join the mainstream of empirical legal scholarship. It would be ill-advised to deploy measures that are unfit for the task at hand. Instead, scholars should employ our measures.

---

[26] Hall (2018) provides two assessments of the validity of his resulting personality measures. He looks at both the year-by-year Martin-Quinn scores and the proportion of liberal votes cast by the justices in his data. In terms of the Martin-Quinn result, he finds that conscientiousness is negatively related with liberalism. Why, then, do we report an insignificant correlation that is in the wrong direction? It is a question of the unit of analysis. Hall uses multiple observations for each justice (e.g., Chief Justice Roberts in 2012, 2013, and so on). We only use a single observation: Each justice's score after his or her first term. This is methodologically appropriate since the explanatory variable is static. That is, Roberts's score does not change from year-to-year. Adding more terms just makes it easier to find statistical significance because the size of the standard errors decreases.

[27] Given the magnitude of these differences, it likely comes as little surprise that the correlations between our trait estimates and Hall's are not especially strong. They are as follows: conscientiousness = −0.09, agreeableness = 0.09, neuroticism = −0.14, openness = 0.06, and extraversion = 0.37.

3.5 THE MULTIPLE HAZARDS OF USING CONCURRING OPINIONS TO ESTIMATE PERSONALITY

Like us, Hall (2018) investigates how personality influences the behavior of Supreme Court justices. But the analysis employs measures of justices' personalities that are inappropriate and lack reliability. He estimates justices' preferences by analyzing their concurring opinions written while on the Court. Hall argues that "formal written opinions are the only comprehensive, consistent, and routinized source of the justices' language" (2018, 37). But the winnowing goes even narrower than that. Only concurring opinions are sufficient, he claims, to represent justices' personalities. Unlike other opinions, concurrences "minimize appropriated and stylized language" (Hall 2018, 39). A related benefit of using concurrences, he claims, is that a concurring opinion writer, unlike the author of a majority or dissenting opinion, "has little incentive to accommodate the views of other justices" (2018, 39).

In what follows, we describe and document why relying upon justices' concurring opinions to estimate their personalities is improper. First, we show that concurring opinion content is endogenous to the Court's majority opinions and, as a result, does not accurately reflect the concurring justice's personality. Second, the SCIPE measures lump all concurring opinions together as a singular type, which ignores their nonrandom heterogeneity. Consequently, the SCIPE measures are flawed.

3.5.1 *Concurring Opinions Are Not Sincere Reflections of Their Writers' Personalities*

Concurring opinions are not sincere reflections of their writers' personalities. They tend to reflect majority opinions. As one of the leading studies of concurring opinions observes, "concurrences are the perfect vehicle in which the justices can communicate their understanding *of the majority opinion*" (Corley 2010, 96, emphasis added). Another authority observes that "by writing separately, a concurring author always offers an internal commentary on the court's judgment" (Ray 1990, 783). Rather than provide an open-ended opportunity for expression, the content of concurring opinions is fundamentally constrained.[28]

---

[28] This stands in contrast to previous usage of Personality Recognizer. To wit, the underlying models it uses to bridge text to traits were developed using thousands of essays written by students told to write whatever they want for twenty minutes (Mairesse et al. 2007, 463). When applying these models to estimate personality traits for members of the US Congress, Ramey, Klinger, and Hollibaugh (2019) turn to a very close verbal approximation of that task: what

The analyses suggest as much. We gathered the 2719 concurring opinions (in cases with a signed majority opinion) written by 35 different justices during the Court's 1946–2016 terms. We also gathered the 2088 corresponding majority opinions for these cases (the lower number of majority opinions reflects the fact that some cases have multiple concurrences). We then estimated personality trait scores for each concurring and majority opinion using Personality Recognizer, employing the same settings as used by Hall (2018).

We undertake four comparisons. First, we examine the correlations between the Big Five traits of a concurring opinion with the same Big Five traits of the *majority opinion in that same case*. If concurrences provide a chance for a justice to shuck "off the normal restraints of writing for a panel" – as Hall suggests they do (2018, 38) – the correlation should be minimal. Conversely, if concurring opinions reflect the content of majority opinions, the correlation between them and their majority opinions will be sizable. Second, we paired each of the 2719 concurring opinions in our data set to a *randomly selected majority opinion* (i.e., a majority opinion in a different case). We undertake this comparison to determine whether there simply is overlap among the words used generally in legal opinions. Third, we paired each concurring opinion with a *randomly selected majority opinion in the same issue area* (via the Supreme Court Database's "issueArea" variable). This acknowledges the possibility that language overlap may be driven by issue-specific content that arises in opinions. Fourth, we paired each concurring opinion with a randomly selected *concurring opinion written by the same justice*. For example, Justice Thomas wrote a concurring opinion in *Weaver v. Massachusetts* (2017). We randomly paired this concurrence with one of Thomas's other 154 concurring opinions. If concurring opinions reflect a justice's personality, the data should reveal a significant correlation among concurrences written by the same justice.

Figure 9 presents the results of these comparisons. The y-axis shows each of the Big Five personality traits while the x-axis shows the correlation for each of our four pairings. Consider the comparison between the personality content of a justice's concurring opinion and that of the majority opinion in the same case (reflected by the black square markers). These correlations range from 0.31 (openness) to 0.43 (neuroticism), with a median value of 0.37. Although they fall well short of being perfectly correlated, these values nevertheless show some systematic connection between the

members said during floor speeches that are governed by scant content rules. Concurring opinions are much more limited in what justices can say.

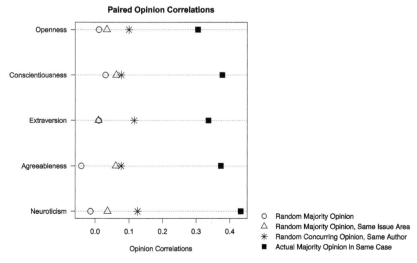

FIGURE 9: *Correlation between personality trait estimates for a justice's concurring opinion and four other comparison opinions* (N = 2719).

revealed personality content of concurring opinions. And they are unquestionably greater than one would observe if concurring opinions were primarily reflections of justices' personalities and were independent of the majority opinion.

To help provide some additional interpretative context, consider the relationship between concurring opinion personality content and the two types of randomly selected majority opinions (the circles and triangles). For both of these comparisons, we find little to no correlation across all five of the traits. This suggests that the majority-concurrence connection is not driven by either some general or issue-specific legal language used throughout opinions.

Perhaps most important is the comparison between a justice's concurrence in a case and his or her concurrence in other cases. If justices' personalities drove their concurring opinions, their own concurring opinions should be highly correlated to one another. But they are not. The correlations range from a low of 0.08 (conscientiousness and agreeableness) to a high of just 0.13 (neuroticism). There is startlingly little consistency across concurring opinions written by the same justice.

Simply put, concurring opinions do not reveal justices' personalities. The data show a moderate correlation where there should be very little correlation (concur versus majority opinion) and next-to-no correlation where there should be a sizable correlation (concur versus concur). Taken together, the results provide strong evidence against using concurring opinions to estimate justices' personalities and, thus, challenge the SCIPE measures of justices' personalities.

3.5.2 *Concurrences Are Not All the Same*

The SCIPE measures are flawed for a second reason: they ignore the fundamental heterogeneity among concurring opinion types. "Not all concurrences are created equal" (Kirman 1995, 2088). Various justices write various concurring opinions for various reasons. And while variety may be the spice of life, it undermines the reliability of the SCIPE measures.

Regular and Special Concurrences Are Distinct. The SCIPE measures rely on the content of justices' concurring opinions – all their concurring opinions. This includes "regular concurrences" as well as "special concurrences." A regular concurring opinion is one in which a justice agrees with both the final disposition of the case (reverse or affirm) and with the reasoning the majority used to reach that disposition. The justice writes separately to hash out some point separate from the majority opinion or (less commonly) to challenge the dissent. By contrast, a special concurrence is one in which a justice agrees with the final disposition but not the reasoning used to reach that disposition. The justice writes separately to explain the rationale the majority should have used. These two kinds of concurrences are, of course, wildly different. Indeed, some jurists even question whether special concurrences should even be considered concurrences. As Justice Scalia (1994, 33) once stated: "Some such opinions, when they happen to reach the same disposition as the majority ... are technically concurrences rather than dissents. To my mind, there is little difference between the two ... to get the reasons wrong is to get it all wrong, and that is worth a dissent, even if the dissent is called a concurrence."

We examine whether regular concurrences reveal the same personality traits as special concurrences. We return to the 2,719 concurring opinions we evaluated in our previous analysis. We classified each concurring opinion as either regular or special based on the language used at the start of each opinion. We coded a concurrence as "special" if the justice concurred "in the judgment." We coded it as "regular" if it did not include this phrase. For example, "Mr. Justice Fortas, with whom the Chief Justice joins, concurring" is a regular concurrence written by Fortas. Conversely, "Justice Thomas, concurring in judgment" is a special concurrence written by Thomas. Mixed concurrences, when a justice, for example, "concurring in part and concurring in the judgment" were coded as special concurrences since the phrase "in judgment" appears in them.

As a preliminary matter, the data reveal ample variation in the relative frequency with which a justice specially concurs. Figure 10 provides a descriptive comparison of the data. The x-axis shows the proportion of special – as opposed to regular – concurrences written by each justice in our data (y-axis). Among justices with at least ten total concurrences (counts are reported in parentheses next to each justices' name), Justice Douglas used special concurrences with the lowest relative frequency – just 10 percent of his total concurring opinions. The highest relative frequency goes to Justice Scalia, for whom special concurrences constitute fully 65 percent of his concurring opinions. This is somewhat ironic, given his quotation provided previously about believing such opinions are not distinct from dissents.

The large difference between Douglas and Scalia is, of course, statistically significant. We find additional systematic differences among the less dramatic pairings, as well. We conducted a difference-in-proportion tests for each of the 561 unique justice pairings. All told, fully 36 percent of these comparison indicate statistically significant difference ($p \leq 0.10$, two-tailed test). This is well above – more than triple – the expected rate we would expect to see by chance alone under the null hypothesis that no differences existed (i.e., 10 percent).

That justices vary significantly in their relative use of special concurrences is a necessary, but not sufficient, condition for our conclusion that the content of these opinions is heterogeneous. That is, it must also be the case that the types of words used are dissimilar enough as to produce discrepant trait estimates when one uses one set of inputs as opposed to another. To examine this possibility, we estimated two separate sets of personality scores for each justice. One set employed only the justice's regular concurrences. The other set employed only her special concurrences. As before, we used Personality Recognizer, with settings identical to those of Hall (2018).

As Figure 11 shows, far from being similar, the personality scores derived from regular and special concurrences are ships that pass in the night. Each panel title identifies the personality trait under analysis as well as the correlation (r) and Cronbach's alpha (a) for the regular concurrence and special concurrence trait estimates. The x-axis reports scores from using only regular concurrences. The y-axis reports scores from using only special concurrences. We identify justices in each plot by their initials. If regular and special concurrences provide the same information about a justice's personality, the scores estimated from these two separate data sources will be highly correlated. They are not.

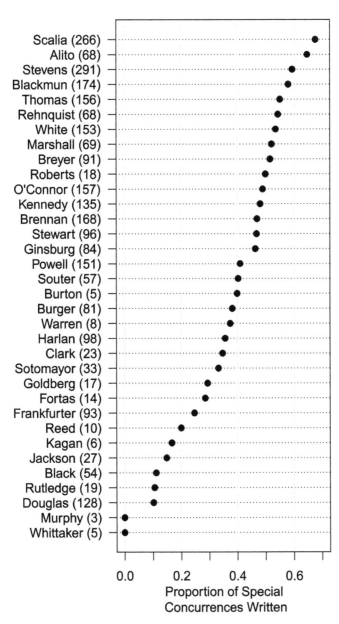

FIGURE 10: *Relative proportion of a justice's written concurrences that were special (as opposed to regular).* The number in parentheses identifies the total number of concurrences written by a justice in our data. Of the 561 unique justice pairings, we observe significantly different proportions for 36 percent of them (i.e., 204; p ≤ 0.10).

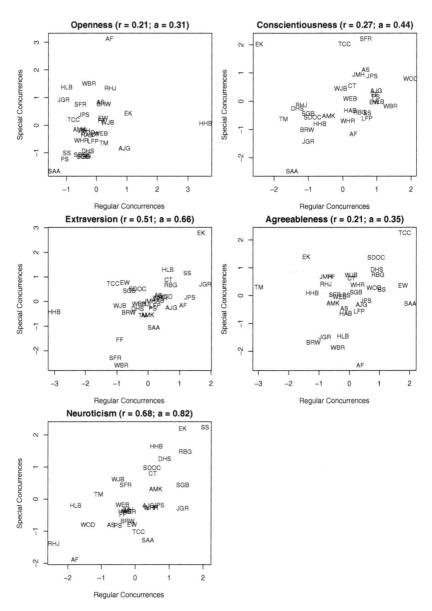

FIGURE 11: *Comparison of justice trait estimates depending on concurrence type (regular versus special).*

For a majority of the traits, regular and special concurrences provide wholly different personality estimates. The correlations of trait estimates from regular and special concurring opinions for the traits of openness, conscientious-ness, and agreeableness are at levels where "little if any" relationship exists (Asuero, Sayago, and Gonzalez 2006, 47). The Cronbach's alpha also show the two types of concurring opinions generate dissimilar personality estimates. As one source counsels: "where measurements on individuals are of interest ...a reliability of 0.90 is the minimum [Cronbach's alpha] that should be tolerated, and a reliability of 0.95 should be considered the desirable stan-dard" (Corp. 2017, 15). Here, the three alpha values are not even close to 0.90. The two remaining traits – extraversion and neuroticism – offer "mod-erate" evidence with respect to the correlation. Both, however, still fall short of the 0.90 minimum alpha threshold (albeit to varying degrees). In short, the SCIPE approach assumes text homogeneity when significant textual vari-ation exists. This heterogeneity injects measurement error into the SCIPE measures.

Solo Concurrences Are Different than Joined Concurrences. There is also reason to question whether concurrences provide justices the opportunity to express their own views without need to accommodate colleagues. Hall claims, "Concurrences are especially well-suited for these analyses because the author of a concurring opinion has little incentive to accommodate the views of other justices" (2018, 38). We disagree. A concurring opinion, after all, can overtake the initial draft of the majority opinion. A draft majority opinion becomes the Court's opinion if, and only if, at least four other justices join it. Until that point, any other opinion drafts are viable alternatives. As Justice Scalia notes, "Not often, but much more than rarely, an effective dissent or concurrence ...changes the outcome of the case, winning over one or more of the Justices who formed the original majority" (1994, 41–42). Because it is always possible to overtake the majority opinion, justices have incentives – at least at times – to grow their coalition. And that likely means accommodating other justices' concerns.

To examine whether concurrences reflect justices' sincere personality traits or whether they are diluted by the need to accommodate, we return to our 2,719 concurring opinions. With assistance from the `firstAgreement` and `secondAgreement` variables in the justice-centered version of the Supreme Court Database, we classified concurring opinions as either solo or joined by another justice.[29] Again, we begin with a descriptive snapshot of the data. Figure 12 illustrates. As it makes clear, justices varied quite a bit in

---

[29] http://scdb.wustl.edu/.

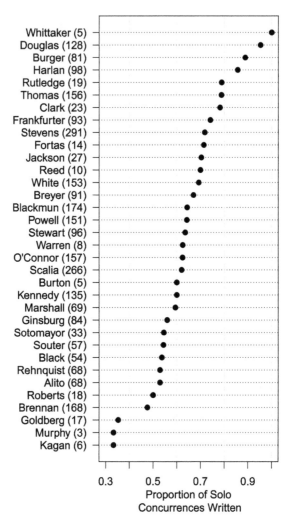

FIGURE 12: *Relative proportion of a justice's written concurrences that solo (i.e., not joined by another justice).* The number in parentheses identifies the total number of concurrences written by a justice in our data. Of the 561 unique justice pairings, we observe significantly different proportions for 29 percent of them (i.e., 161; p ≤ 0.10).

how often they wrote solo or joined concurring opinions. Among justices with at least ten opinions, the solo percentage goes as low as 35 percent for Justice Goldberg and as high as 95 percent for Justice Douglas. And, just like before, we see substantial evidence of systematic difference among the possible justice comparisons. Twenty-nine percent of the unique justice pairings are statistically significant.

We turn next to evaluating whether the personality content of these opinions differs as much as the relative frequency in which justices author solo versus joined concurrences. To remain consistent with Hall et al., we again use Personality Recognizer to generate two sets of trait scores using each justice's solo and joined concurrences as the inputs. The results appear in Figure 13. If solo and joined concurring opinions revealed the same personalities, we would see a strong correlation between their resulting personality scores. We do not.

The median correlation between the two sets of trait estimates is 0.37 with an observed range of 0.17 (agreeableness) to 0.81 (neuroticism). Correlations for the three traits of openness, conscientiousness, and extraversion would be classified as "low" (Asuero, Sayago, and Gonzalez 2006, 47). Agreeableness would be "little to none." Only neuroticism would be assessed as "high." Results for Cronbach's alpha are similar, with only neuroticism's value nearing the 0.90 minimum-recommended threshold. Substantively, this implies that – contrary to the assumption of the SCIPE measures – the amount and nature of personality embedded in concurring opinions varies dramatically depending on whether a justice writes alone or writes an opinion on to which her colleagues sign.[30] And, since not all justices write alone with an equal relative frequency, this demonstrates another source of systematic measurement error in the SCIPE measures.

3.6 CONCLUSION

In this (admittedly lengthy) chapter, we laid out a dozen figures and numerous analyses to make our point. But what we've done here is critical for the rest of the book. It would be difficult to overstate the importance of measurement in the context of this book. It is always important, but here it is vital. Our goal is to show that justices' conscientiousness exerts an independent and important effect on top of all the things we already know motivate them. If we are going to move the field in the direction we want it to go, we had better get this right.

---

[30] We acknowledge that these results cannot tell whether other justices *cause* joined opinions to reveal different personality from solo opinions or whether these other justices are simply more likely to *sign on* to opinions with different personality. This distinction, however, is irrelevant. Regardless of the underlying cause, these data establish that the two types of opinions reveal very different personalities and cannot, therefore, be combined without some corrective steps.

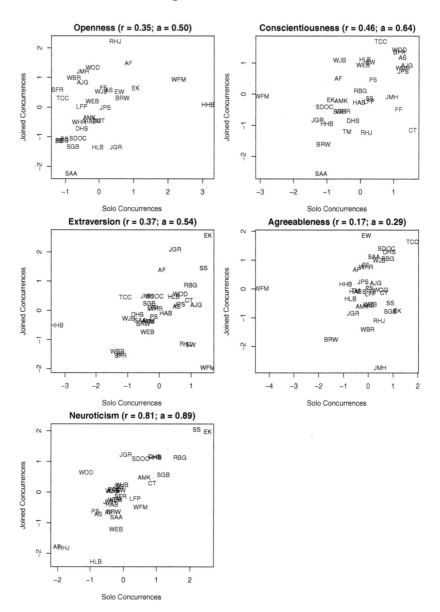

FIGURE 13: *Comparison of justice trait estimates depending on concurrence type (solo versus joined).*

To recap, we explained the texts we use to measure personality: precon- firmation speeches, writings, and lower court opinions. We discussed IBM's Watson Personality Insights and how we employed it to measure traits. We then analyzed the importance of standardizing our measurements, recogniz- ing that only by doing so would we generate trait measures the discipline will use. We validated those measures, showing that, even though we can- not directly measures justices' conscientiousness, our measures are correlated strongly with things we know are, themselves, strongly correlated with consci- entiousness. What is more, we discovered that the sole other measure used in the discipline is bereft of any criterion validity.

Moving on, we directly addressed that existing work. In applying careful scrutiny to Hall's approach, we have thrown more than a few numbers at you in the preceding pages, so let's pause for a moment to summarize the rea- sons we reject his approach. First, we have a fundamental disagreement over what input texts to use. This stems both from the endogenous nature of the measures and the circularity of the underlying reasoning Hall employs. Sec- ond, we showed that a key assumption of his approach – that concurrences are equivalent – is demonstrably untrue. These statistical results strongly suggest that using concurring opinions to measure justices' personalities is erroneous.

We also showed that even if Hall's inputs were appropriate, there are strong reasons to eschew the methodological approach he utilized. Though it was a fascinating proof-of-concept exercise, Personality Recognizer has since been surpassed by superior approaches that translate text into traits. The combi- nation of these broad points is that our measures have tremendous objective validity whereas Hall's SCIPE scores have virtually none at all.

Taken together, the findings of this chapter offer strong support for our trait measures. The question, now, is whether conscientiousness influences justices' behavior. It is to that task that we now turn.

3.7 APPENDIX

3.7.1 *Measurement Validity of Agreeableness, Neuroticism, Openness, and Extraversion*

In this section, we review the measurement validity for the other four traits. We examine how each trait correlates with the same covariates that we exam- ined for conscientiousness earlier in this chapter. This is to say that we did not go out and do additional canvassing to look for specific criterion validity measures associated with the particular trait of neuroticism, for example. We made this decision based on the fact that this book is ultimately one about conscientiousness. We have no doubt that the other four traits are interesting and worthy of their own, lengthier treatment. But we happily leave such low-hanging fruit for future researchers. Instead, we hope to merely seed their interest in taking up this cause by showing that it is not *only* our conscientiousness measure that has validity. Indeed, as we demonstrate herein, correlations between our other four traits and the various outcome measures fall within the range of correlations observed in the broader literature on personality.

It should be noted at the outset that this is a challenging enterprise for various reasons. On the one hand, we generated trait estimates of a highly idiosyncratic sample – Supreme Court justices. These individuals are extremely well educated, lawyers, political elites, wealthy individuals, and mostly white males, who tend to prefer privacy in their profession. This is relevant because one of the enduring questions in psychology is whether psychological phenomena vary across cultures and different populations and samples. This includes traits. The implication is, in practice, that comparisons are not always straightforward, as traits may have different effects in different samples or populations.

At the same time, we have the simultaneous challenge of having only thirty-eight observations. Fewer observations means weaker statistical power (or that outliers carry more weight). This is important because when we compare the results of our correlations to the studies (mostly) from psychology that have hundreds or thousands of observations, it is not as simple as checking to see if both correlations report a significant correlation with a low p-value. In other words, finding significant results when the number of observations are large is less challenging. For studies with small sample sizes such as ours, one must occasionally also gauge the size of the p-value in relation to the magnitude of the coefficient when comparing the results.

To complicate matters further, not every study publishes the correlations of their variables, or their correlations with all five traits. Some may simply describe the results. In the validation that follows, we tried to use studies that published the correlations and we tried to find any meta-analyses that summarized numerous studies. We also offer Hall's (2018) correlations for comparison.

With those provisos out of the way, we begin with Table 1, which examines the relationship between the four remaining traits and the justices longevity (age at their death). We offer two studies for comparison that report results for all five traits. For conscientiousness (results not shown), both studies

TABLE 1: *Trait Correlations with Justice Lifespan (Age at Time of Death)*

Study	Agreeableness	Neuroticism	Openness	Extraversion
Our Study (n = 27)	.35 (p = .07)	−.37 (p = .06)	−.05 (p = .80)	.44 (p = .02)
Hall (2018) (n = 23)	.33 (p = .13)	.47 (p = .02)	−.32 (p = .13)	.235 (p = .28)
Chapman et al. (2011)	weak	inconsistent	modest positive	inconsistent
McCann (2005) (n = 32)	−.07 (n.s.)	.17 (n.s.)	.26 (n.s.)	−.28 (n.s.)

Note: The top row represents the pairwise correlations between our four trait estimates and the justices age at their time of death; p-values in parentheses for two-tailed test. Chapman et al. (2011) qualitatively summarize numerous studies. "sig." or "n.s." = "significant" or "not significant" at the thresholds reported in the study.

report a strong and significant relationship with longevity, consistent with our evidence provided previously. For agreeableness, we observe a positive and significant (p = 0.07) correlation with longevity. In their qualitative review and summary of numerous studies of personality and longevity, Chapman, Roberts, and Duberstein (2011) found some weak evidence that agreeableness aided longevity, which is consistent with our findings. In contrast, McCann (2005), who examines thirty-two presidents, finds a nonsignificant relationship between agreeableness and longevity. For neuroticism, we find a significant, negative correlation with longevity. This is within the normal range of findings as cited by Chapman, Roberts, and Duberstein (2011), who found both positive and negative correlations in the literature. In contrast, McCann (2005) reports a null finding.

We find a null relationship between openness and longevity. This is different from Chapman, Roberts, and Duberstein (2011), who summarize the review of studies as having a modest positive relationship. However, we find consistent results with McCann (2005), who also reports a null correlation coefficient for openness and longevity. For extraversion, we find a strong and positive correlation with longevity. This is within the range of findings from Chapman et al. (2011), who found both positive and negative correlations, while McCann (2005) reported a nonsignificant correlation.

Table 2 examines the relationship between the four traits and the justices' number of children (logged). It offers three studies for comparison. For agreeableness, we find consistency with the modest and positive correlation found in the Judge, Martocchio, and Thorensen (1997) study. The

TABLE 2: *Trait Correlations with the Justices, Number of Children (Logged)*

Study	Agreeableness	Neuroticism	Openness	Extraversion
Our Study (n = 38)	.07	−.33	−.11	.04
	(p = .66)	(p = .04)	(p = .52)	(p = .79)
Hall (2018) (n = 34)	.14	−.25	−.07	−.16
	(p = .44)	(p = .15)	(p = .69)	(p = .36)
Dijkstra and Barelds (2009) (n = 2,618)	.10 (sig.)	−.02 (n.s.)	−.03 (n.s.)	.05 (sig.)
Judge et al. (1997) (n = 73)	.12	−.19	−.23	.02
Jokela et al. (2011) (n = 15,729)	.07 (sig.)	−.05 (sig.)	−.19 (sig.)	.12 (sig.)

Note: The top row represents the pairwise correlations between our four trait estimates and the justices number of children (logged); p-values in parentheses for two-tailed test. The Judge et al. (1997) study does not report significance levels, only the correlation coefficient. Jokela et al. (2011) estimates are from a regression that controlled for gender and age. "sig." or "n.s." = "significant" or "not significant" at the thresholds reported in the study.

magnitude is approximately the same for the other two studies, though they have substantially larger sample sizes. For neuroticism, we find a strong negative correlation with the logged number of children. The Judge, Martocchio, and Thorensen (1997) study also reports a correlation of the same magnitude, and the Jokela et al. (2011) study also reports a significant, negative correlation. There is inconsistency with the Dijkstra and Barelds (2009) correlation. For openness, we find a null relationship with a negative sign. We find consistency with the Dijkstra and Barelds (2009) and Judge et al. (1997) studies. The Jokela et al. (2011) study reports a negative coefficient, the same as ours, though slightly higher in magnitude and significant.

Table 3 examines the relationship between the remaining four personality traits and marriage length. Our study found a positive correlation between agreeableness and marriage duration, and it would be statistically significant with a one-tailed test. This coefficient is consistent with the findings of Solomon and Jackson (2014), which was one study that we could find that published their correlation between relationship duration and personality traits.[31] We find that neuroticism is negatively signed and has a coefficient of similar magnitude to Solomon and Jackson (2014). The correlation for openness shares a consistent negative sign, though it is not significant like Solomon and

---

[31] Most studies in this area tend to look at relationship satisfaction, a similar construct that we examine next.

TABLE 3: *Trait Correlations with the Justices, Marriage Length*

Study	Agreeableness	Neuroticism	Openness	Extraversion
Our study (n = 26)	.29 (p = .15)	−.23 (p = .25)	−.07 (p = .74)	.25 (p = .21)
Hall (2018) (n = 22)	.29 (p = .19)	.50 (p = .02)	−.07 (p = .75)	.03 (p = .91)
Solomon and Jackson (2014) (n = 8,206)	.10 (sig)	−.16 (sig.)	−.16 (sig.)	−.05 (sig.)

Note: The top row represents the pairwise correlations between our four trait estimates and the length of the justices marriage; p-values in parentheses for two-tailed test. "sig." or "n.s." = "significant" or "not significant" at the thresholds reported in the study.

TABLE 4: *Mean Trait Level, by Relationship Satisfaction (Unlucky in Love)*

Study	Agreeableness	Neuroticism	Openness	Extraversion
Our Study (n = 38)	unlucky −.058 lucky .527 (p = .32)	unlucky 1.596 lucky −.005 (p = .01)	unlucky −.214 lucky −.261 (p = .94)	unlucky .182 lucky .143 (p = .93)
Hall (2018) (n = 34)	unlucky −.046 lucky .012 (p = .89)	unlucky .709 lucky −.184 (p = .03)	unlucky .168 lucky −.044 (p = .63)	unlucky .416 lucky −.108 (p = .22)
Heller, Watson, and Ilies (2004)	.24 (sig.)	−.26 (sig.)	.08 (sig.)	.14 (sig.)
Malouff et al. (2010)	.15 (sig.)	−.22 (sig.)	.03 (n.s.)	.06 (sig.)

Note: The top two rows represents the group means for the two groups ("unlucky in love" or "lucky in love"). The third row is the p-value for a two-tailed test. Remaining entries are average correlations found in the meta-analyses. Heller, Watson, and Ilies (2004) provide a meta-analysis of approximately seventy studies. Malouff et al. (2010) provide a meta-analysis of approximately nineteen samples. "sig." or "n.s." = "significant" or "not significant" at the thresholds reported in the study.

Jackson's report. Our coefficient for extraversion is positive but null, while Solomon and Jackson's correlation is negative and significant. This suggests that most of the evidence in Table 3 supports the validation of the estimates. Let's move to the evidence for relationship satisfaction.

Table 4 shows the results for our unlucky in love variable, our proxy for relationship satisfaction. Recall, this variable is coded "1" for justices who are either divorced or never married (e.g., the justice was not lucky in love);

justices who married and stayed married are coded "0" (e.g., assumed to be lucky in love). Cell entries report the results from a difference of means t-test, with the different group means and a p-value for a two-tailed test. Recall, our "lucky in love" group was significantly more conscientiousness than the unlucky in love group. We find the same pattern for agreeableness, with the "lucky" group, which is our proxy for those that are more satisfied with their relationship. This is consistent with both of the studies who did very large meta-analyses. The advantage of the meta-analyses is that they survey all of the studies they can find and then calculate an average correlation. Both of the studies found a strong, positive average correlation between agreeableness and being satisfied with their relationship (e.g., more agreeable people were more satisfied in their relationships). For neuroticism, we found a strong and statistically significant difference. Those justices who were more neurotic tended to be more unlucky in love, while those that were less neurotic were lucky in love. This is highly consistent with one of the main findings in the relationship satisfaction literature – that higher neuroticism correlates with lower relationship satisfaction.

For openness, we did not find much of a difference in our two groups of justices, and this is consistent with one of the meta-analyses, Malouff et al. (2010), which also found no difference. The other study, Heller, Watson, and Ilies (2004), found a very mild average correlation. We also did not find a difference of group means for extraversion, and this differed from the two studies who both found a strong positive correlation. While this may seem alarming at first, it is important to know that Malouff et al. (2010), when examining the effect sizes, found significant heterogeneity for openness, extraversion, and agreeableness. This suggests that it is certainly possible that our measures for openness and extraversion are within the boundaries of other studies in the literature.

Table 5 shows the correlations between the traits and our proxy for professional job performance, the justices, qualifications as rated based on newspaper statements at the time of their confirmation. Putting aside the issues with the qualifications measure that we identified earlier, we find that our correlations for agreeableness and neuroticism are largely inconsistent. Specifically, our measure of agreeableness is significant and negatively signed, and only the two coefficients for the Judge et al. (1999) study are negatively signed, though they fail to reach statistical significance.[32] In contrast, we find some support for our measures of openness and extraversion. Specifically,

---

[32] This may be an example where this sample is unique in that one is professionally rewarded in the law profession for being argumentative and disagreeable, as opposed to agreeable.

TABLE 5: *Trait Correlations with Job Performance (Qualifications)*

Study	Agreeableness	Neuroticism	Openness	Extraversion
Our Study (n = 38)	−.28 (p = .09)	.16 (p = .33)	.17 (p = .30)	−.01 (p = .96)
Hall (2018) (n = 34)	−.13 (p = .46)	−.01 (p = .97)	.18 (p = .32)	.09 (p = .60)
Hurtz and Donovan (2000)	.13 (n.s.)	−.14 (sig)	.07 (n.s.)	.10 (n.s.)
Judge et al. (1999) (n = 194)				
occupational status	−.04 (n.s.)	−.27 (sig.)	.26 (sig.)	.09 (n.s.)
extrinsic career success	−.11 (n.s.)	−.34 (sig)	.14 (sig.)	.19 (sig.)

Note: The top row represents the pairwise correlations between our four trait estimates and the covariate of interest; p-values in parentheses for two-tailed test. Coefficients from Solomon and Jackson (2014) are from a regression that controls for gender, income, education, children, and aspects of relationship status. Coefficients for Hurtz and Donovan (2000) are true-score correlations for a meta-analysis that examined approximately twenty-six studies, and reported the correlation for emotional stability, which we reversed for neuroticism. Coefficients for Judge et al. (1999) are from two variables that measured performance: "occupational status" and "extrinsic career success." "sig." or "n.s." = "significant" or "not significant" at the thresholds reported in the study.

TABLE 6: *Trait Correlations with Job Satisfaction (Court Tenure; Logged)*

Study	Agreeableness	Neuroticism	Openness	Extraversion
Our Study (n = 30)	.27 (p = .15)	−.02 (p = .93)	.20 (p = .28)	.01 (p = .98)
Hall (2018) (n = 26)	.19 (p = .35)	.25 (p = .22)	−.57 (p = .01)	−.06 (p = .77)
Judge et al. (1999) (n = 194)	−.26 (sig.)	−.26 (sig.)	−.09 (n.s.)	.12 (n.s.)
Solomon and Jackson (2014) (n = 3,777)	.06 (sig.)	−.06 (sig.)	−.02 (n.s.)	.06 (sig.)
Heller et al. (2004)	.13 (sig.)	−.24 (sig.)	.01 (n.s.)	.19 (sig.)

Note: The top row represents the pairwise correlations between our four trait estimates and the covariate of interest; p-values in parentheses for two-tailed test. Coefficients for Judge et al. (1999) are from their measure of job satisfaction. Coefficients from Solomon and Jackson (2014) are from a regression that controls for gender, income, education, children, and aspects of relationship status. Coefficients for Heller et al. (2004) are average correlations from a meta-analysis that examined approximately seventy studies. "sig." or "n.s." = "significant" or "not significant" at the thresholds reported in the study.

TABLE 7: *Trait Correlations with Ideology*

Study	Agreeableness	Neuroticism	Openness	Extraversion
Our Study (n = 38)	.24 (p = .15)	−.12 (p = .48)	−.10 (p = .53)	.01 (p = .96)
Hall (2018) (n = 34)	.29 (p = .09)	.08 (p = .64)	−.15 (p = .39)	.05 (p = .76)
Carney et al. (2008)	4 null, 2 positive (sig.)	3 null, 2 negative (sig.), 1 positive (sig.)	6 negative (sig.)	5 null, 1 positive (sig.)
Gerber et al. (2010)	1 null, 1 positive (sig.), 1 negative (sig.)	3 negative (sig.)	3 negative (sig.)	3 positive (sig.)
Gosling et al. (2003)	3 null	3 negative (sig.)	3 negative (sig.)	3 null

Note: The top row represents the pairwise correlations between our four trait estimates and ideology. Ideology is the first term Martin-Quinn score for each justice, with higher values representing more conservativeness. The second row contains p-values in parentheses for two-tailed test. Carney et al. (2008) report on six studies with different personality measures; NEO-PI-R, Big Five Inventory (BFI), Ten Item Personality Inventory (TIPI), and coefficients come from multiple regressions. Gerber et al. (2010) report from three different measures of ideology (self-reported, economic policy issues, and social policy issues) and results are taken from regression equations that control for a host of demographic variables; Gerber et al. report a reverse direction of ideology and also report stability, which we reverse for neuroticism. Gosling et al. (2003) reports correlations from three different measures of personality – the BFI, Five Item Personality Inventory (FIPI), and TIPI; and report emotional stability that we reverse for neuroticism. "sig." or "n.s." = "significant" or "not significant" at the thresholds reported in the study.

both measures are of relatively low magnitude and not significant, and the large meta-analysis study of Hurtz and Donovan (2000) found similar non-significant correlations across twenty-six studies.[33] We also see some support from the Judge et al. (1999) measures for openness, which both have a similar positive sign. In addition, the occupational status measure has a null finding for extraversion, which is the same as our correlation.

Table 6 examines the trait correlations with our proxy for job satisfaction, court tenure, as measured by the logged number of years on the Court (excluding justices still on the Court and William O. Douglas, for reasons we listed previously). We find support for our measure of agreeableness based on its sizable coefficient relative the size of the standard error, and this is consistent with the two larger studies from the literature. For neuroticism, we find a largely null correlation for our measure, and this differs from all three of the studies in the table. Perhaps this profession (Supreme Court justice) is an exception in the career field where one can be highly neurotic and still serve a long time in the profession. Our measure of openness enjoys consistent support in that it is not significant and none of the three studies are. Extraversion also enjoys some limited support, with a null finding that is the same as the Judge et al. (1999) finding, though it differs from the two large studies.

Table 7 contains the trait correlations with our behavioral measure of ideology, the Martin-Quinn score from each justice's first term. Our correlation for agreeableness is positive and close to conventional levels of statistical significance. It is consistent with the null findings of the three studies. The neuroticism correlation is negatively signed but not significant. It is consistent with the three null findings of the Carney et al. (2008) study, but not the Gerber et al. (2010) or Gosling, Rentfrow, and Swann Jr. (2003) studies, though they do share the negative sign. The openness correlation is negatively signed, which is consistent with the findings from all three studies, but our correlation is not significant while the others are. Finally, we find an almost nonexistent correlation for extraversion that is not statistically significant and that is consistent with two out of three studies.

---

[33] Hurtz and Donovan (2000) report the 90 percent credible interval for the lower bound, and for the nonsignificant variables, it includes zero.

4

Conscientiousness and Supreme Court Agenda Setting

Melvin Hicks worked for five years as a correctional officer and supervisor at Saint Mary's halfway house in Saint Louis, Missouri. After Saint Mary's disciplined Hicks for a number of infractions, it fired him. Hicks contested his termination, alleging that Saint Mary's fired him for racially motivated reasons, in violation of Title VII of the 1964 Civil Rights Act. As evidence, he claimed that over a twelve-month period, Saint Mary's received numerous complaints about white officers but fired only one. Conversely, it fired twelve black officers during the same time. In defense, Saint Mary's challenged Hicks's assertions, but its responses, as one court held, were contrived after the fact to make Saint Mary's appear blameless.

After the District Court ruled against Hicks, the Eighth Circuit reversed. It held that because Saint Mary's reasons for firing Hicks were contrived, Title VII compelled the Court to rule in favor of Hicks. That is, in race discrimination cases, when a court finds an employer's reasons for termination to be pretextual, the employee automatically wins the case without investigating the facts and law further. But the Eighth Circuit's interpretation of Title VII conflicted with the First and Seventh Circuits' rulings in similar cases. So, Saint Mary's filed a petition for a writ of certiorari (cert) that asked the Supreme Court to review the case. The Court granted the petition and, in a 5–4 decision, reversed the Eighth Circuit. The High Court declared that a contrived justification for termination under Title VII did not automatically trigger a win for the employee; rather, that fact simply helped to establish the bad intent of the employer.[1]

Hicks was an important case in labor law. It attracted considerable attention when the Court released it, receiving front-page coverage in three of the four major national newspapers (Collins and Cooper 2012). In the intervening quarter century, it continues to provoke both judicial and scholarly interest.

---

[1] *See Saint Mary's Honor Center v. Hicks*, 509 U.S. 502 (1993).

It has been cited in more than 25,000 judicial decisions and 1,100 law review articles.[2] But *Hicks* also demands attention because of three agenda-related features.

First, the Court decided to hear the case because it involved legal conflict among the lower federal courts. As we noted previously, the Eighth Circuit's decision conflicted with decisions of the First and Seventh Circuits. When lower courts conflict like this, the Supreme Court is expected to step in and clear up that conflict (Black and Owens 2009a). Indeed, the Court's own Rules state as much: "A petition for a writ of certiorari will be granted only for compelling reasons [such as when] a United States court of appeals has entered a decision in conflict with the decision of another United States court of appeals on the same important matter."[3] This feature did not escape the attention of the law clerk responsible for providing a summary and assessment of the contentions involved in the case. Thanks to the Digital Archive of the Papers of Harry A. Blackmun, we can journey back to January 1993 and read the actual memorandum distributed to the Court's "cert pool."[4] Figure 14 does exactly that and shows the initial overview the law clerk provided, which recommended the Court grant review. As the memo writer stated: "the [lower court] ruling raises a circuit split on the proper interpretation of the Court's opinion regarding the burdens of production in a private Title VII action ... An issue of importance, and a circuit split lead me to recommend a grant (weak)."[5]

Second, the vote to grant review involved an unusual vote called a "Join-3." As the Court's docket sheet in Figure 15 shows (again courtesy of the Blackmun Archives), when the justices met in their private conference on January 11, 1993 to decide whether to grant review to the case, only Chief Justice Rehnquist, Justice White, and Justice Scalia cast votes to hear the case. Ordinarily,

---

[2] *Shepard's* report retrieved via Lexis Advance on October 15, 2018.

[3] See Supreme Court Rule 10(a).

[4] To quote the late Justice Scalia, reviewing cert petitions is among the "most onerous" tasks the justices face (C-SPAN 2009). To address this concern, the justices created the "cert pool" in the early 1970s. The cert pool is a labor-sharing agreement whereby only a single law clerk, out of a "pool" of those from a number of chambers, is responsible for providing an in-depth review and analysis of the materials in each certiorari petition. As of February 2017, all of the justices except Justices Alito and Gorsuch contribute to the cert pool. Pool memos contain a basic summary of the case, the facts and proceedings at the lower court level, the parties' arguments and amicus brief arguments, and the clerk's discussion and recommendation of the worthiness for review. Once complete, the pool memos are then copied and distributed to each participating justice's chamber, where they are typically reviewed by a justice's clerks before being read by the justice herself (Lane and Black 2017, 6).

[5] See http://epstein.wustl.edu/research/blackmunDockets/1992/Paid/docket-92-602.pdf.

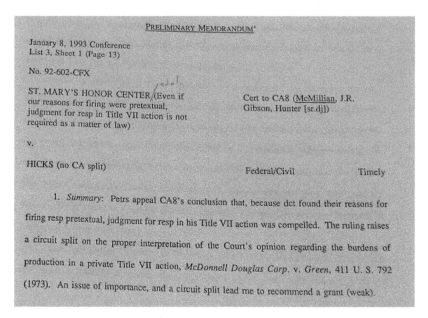

FIGURE 14: *Cert pool memo in Saint Mary's Honor Center v. Hicks (92–602)*. The pool memo writer noted the presence of conflict among the lower courts.

earning only three such "grant" votes means the Court will deny the petition. For the Court to hear a case, at least four justices must agree to hear it.[6] Justice Souter, however, introduced a wild card. He cast what is called a "Join-3" vote. Pursuant to informal Supreme Court norms, three grant votes plus a Join-3 vote will trigger review. And so Melvin Hicks's case made it to the Court.

Third, the vote to grant review clearly involved strategic, forward-looking behavior by some justices. When justices decide whether to grant or deny review to a petition, they often make their determinations based on whether they expect the Court to make better policy than the status quo. If so, they may grant. If not, they may deny. Surely, some of the justices (Rehnquist, Scalia) voted to grant because they wanted to move policy in a conservative direction, away from the status quo. (A conservative vote in the case made it easier for businesses to defend against claims of racial bias.) Others, like Blackmun, surely wanted the opposite. Indeed, Figure 16 shows that Blackmun's clerk

---

[6] Congress requires the Court to hear and decide only a handful of cases in the modern era. See, e.g., 28 U.S.C. §§1251, 1253. For all others, the Court hears them only when four or more justices vote to hear them (Leiman 1957).

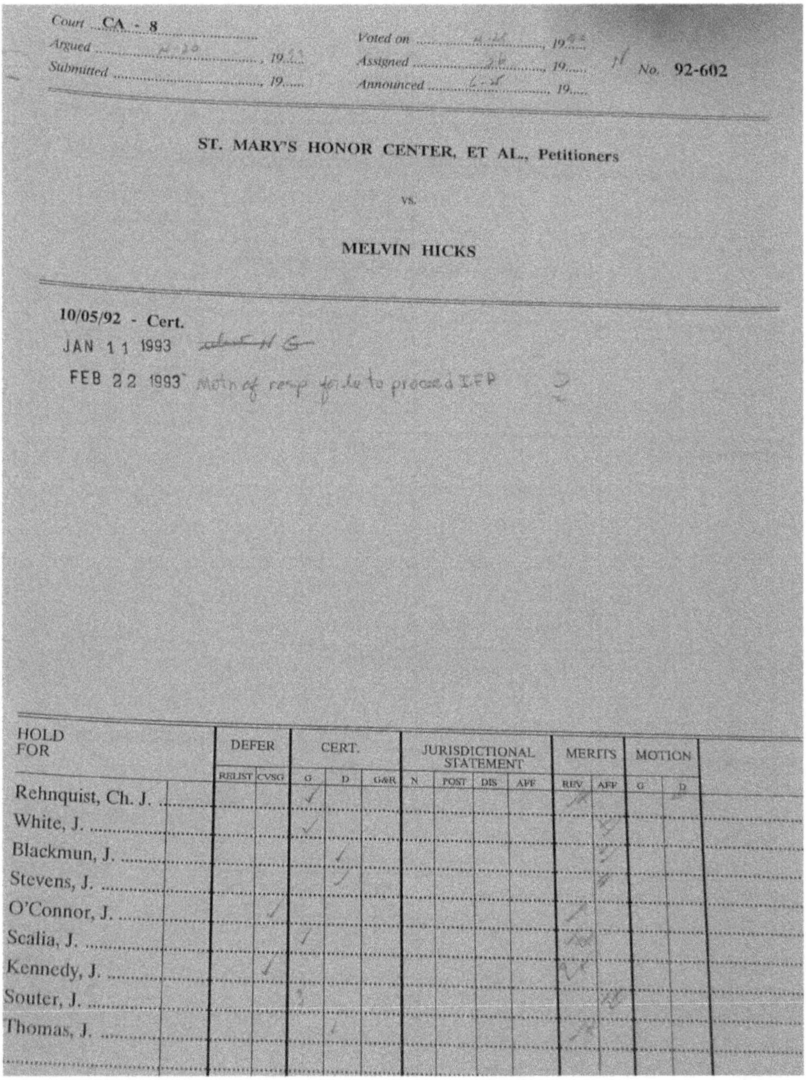
Court CA - 8
Argued ..., 19...
Submitted ..., 19...
Voted on ..., 19...
Assigned ..., 19...
Announced ..., 19...
No. 92-602

ST. MARY'S HONOR CENTER, ET AL., Petitioners

vs.

MELVIN HICKS

10/05/92 - Cert.
JAN 11 1993
FEB 22 1993

HOLD FOR	DEFER		CERT.			JURISDICTIONAL STATEMENT				MERITS		MOTION	
	RELIST	CVSG	G	D	G&R	N	POST	DIS	AFF	REV	AFF	G	D
Rehnquist, Ch. J.			✓							✓			
White, J.			✓								✓		
Blackmun, J.				✓							✓		
Stevens, J.				✓							✓		
O'Connor, J.		✓								✓			
Scalia, J.			✓							✓			
Kennedy, J.		✓								✓			
Souter, J.			✓								✓		
Thomas, J.				✓						✓			

FIGURE 15: *Justice Blackmun's docket sheet in Saint Mary's Honor Center* v. *Hicks* (92–602). The Court granted review after the case received three grant votes plus a Join-3 vote.

suggested he vote to deny review for precisely this reason, stating, "It seems to me that no good could come from a grant at this time."

But what about the justices' personalities? How did the justices' conscientiousness influence their behavior? Our results reveal that legal conflict – even

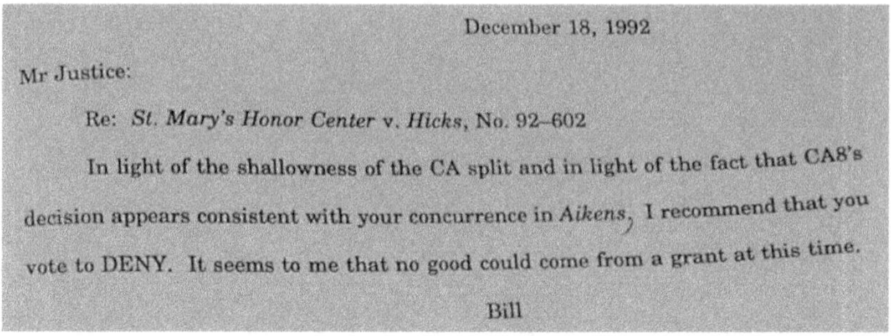

December 18, 1992

Mr Justice:

    Re: *St. Mary's Honor Center* v. *Hicks*, No. 92–602

    In light of the shallowness of the CA split and in light of the fact that CA8's decision appears consistent with your concurrence in *Aikens*, I recommend that you vote to DENY. It seems to me that no good could come from a grant at this time.

Bill

FIGURE 16: *Justice Blackmun's clerk notes in Saint Mary's Honor Center* v. *Hicks* (92–602).

weak legal conflict – influences conscientious justices more than less conscientious justices. Conscientious justices were more likely to grant review in *Hicks* because of the weak circuit split. At the same time, our data reveal that conscientious justices are less likely to cast Join-3 votes. Perhaps it is no surprise, then, that Justice Souter voted to cast a Join-3 vote in the case. He is among the least conscientious justices in our sample. Finally, the data show that conscientious justices are less likely to cast forward-looking policy-based agenda votes. This may explain why Justice White voted to grant review in *Hicks*, despite the fact that he later voted (in the minority) to affirm the lower court. White is among the more conscientious justices in the sample.

In this chapter, we focus on how conscientiousness influences justices' behavior at the agenda-setting stage. And our results reveal a strong effect.

4.1 THE AGENDA-SETTING PROCESS

Before the Court decides a case, the justices must determine whether they want to hear it in the first place. That decision occurs at the agenda-setting stage. The Court's agenda-setting process begins when a litigant files a petition for a writ of certiorari, asking the Supreme Court to review (and reverse) a lower court decision. The petitioner's attorneys craft a brief in support of the petition. The respondent's attorneys typically file a brief in opposition to review. (In some instances, like when a case is clearly nationally important, the respondent's attorneys will simply concede that the Court should review the case.) After the parties file such materials, the Supreme Court Clerk's office circulates them to each of the nine justices' chambers.[7]

---

7   In a small handful of cases, litigants file "appeals" rather than petitions for a writ of certiorari. By law, the Court is required to hear these cases. But there are not many. "Today, the Court

At this point, the justices' law clerks get involved. Their actions, and their workload, are a function of whether their justice is in the "cert pool." As we mentioned earlier, the purpose of the cert pool is to divide up into manageable numbers the thousands of cert petitions the Court receives, thus allowing the law clerks enough time to draft adequate memoranda regarding each case (Ward and Weiden 2006). As its name suggests, the cert pool is simply the pooling together of the justices' law clerks to make recommendations to the justices in the pool regarding whether the Court should or should not hear and decide a case.

Each cert pool memo provides significant information to the Court, including information about the parties, the procedural history of the case, the identity of the lower court judges, and other information. As the cert pool memo in *Saint Mary's* v. *Hicks* (Figure 14) showed, pool memos begin by identifying the parties, often including a quippy statement summarizing the parties' main points. The memo identifies the lower court that heard the challenged decision as well as the judges – and opinion authors – who presided in the lower court decision. Each pool memo briefly summarizes the dispute, then turns to the lower court decisions and procedural history of the case. The memo then carefully lays out the arguments made by each party and the outside amici groups, if any, who filed briefs in support of or opposition to Supreme Court review. It concludes with the clerk's recommendation (and rationale therefor) to the pool. That memo is then sent out to each pool justice's chambers. The clerks will often "mark up" the pool memo for their own justices, adding information and recommendations their justices may want. (See, e.g., Figure 16.) The justices and their clerks review this information before the Court's conference.

Two features distinguish the behavior of clerks who are in the cert pool from those who are not. The first difference is simply workload. Today, the cert pool consists of all the law clerks from seven of the nine justices' chambers. Only Justices Alito and Gorsuch refuse to participate in the cert pool.[8] Since each justice employs four law clerks, this means there are twenty-eight (seven times four) clerks in the pool. Each clerk in the pool, then, reviews and summarizes only about 3.5 percent of all the Court's cert petitions that term. Clerks whose justices are *not* in the cert pool must review every cert petition that comes to the Court and make a recommendation to their justices. This

---

is legally obligated to hear only those few cases (typically involving the Voting Rights Act) appealed from special three-judge district courts" (Epstein and Walker 2010, 12).

[8] During the terms of our analysis (1986–1993), Justices Brennan, Marshall, and Stevens did not participate in the cert pool.

means that clerks whose justices are not in the pool review and summarize 25 percent of all filed petitions. The second difference involves the fullness of the cert memo. Whereas clerks in the cert pool write for a broad and ideologically diverse group of justices, clerks whose justices are not in the pool write personalized and sometimes very short memos on each case, with an emphasis on, or prolonged attention to, cases the clerk knows the justice keeps an eye out for, salient cases, and legally important cases.

Prior to each conference in which the Court will discuss cert petitions, the Chief Justice circulates a list with the names of all petitions he thinks the Court should discuss at the conference. This list is called the "Discuss List." Associate justices can add petitions to the Discuss List but no one can remove a petition put on by another justice (Black and Boyd 2013).[9] Once finalized, the Chief sends out the Discuss List to the full Court. It provides the names of all petitions the Court will discuss at the next conference. Petitions that appear on the Discuss List receive at least some discussion by the justices and a recorded vote. Petitions that do not appear on the Discuss List are summarily denied cert by the Court without a formal vote. The justice who placed the petition on the Discuss List – generally the Chief – begins the conference discussion, stating why he or she thinks the Court should (or should not) grant review. That justice then casts his or her vote. In order of seniority, the remaining justices provide their views and votes.

The justices can exercise a number of voting options at the agenda stage. They can, of course, vote to grant or deny review to the case. But there are other options as well. They can vote to *call for the views of the Solicitor General*.[10] They can also *hold* a case. A hold keeps the case at the Court without a formal determination. Generally, the Court will hold a petition when it is similar to a case the justices are in the process of deciding or will decide shortly. Once they decide that case, they can then GVR (grant, vacate, and remand) the held petition and order the lower court to rehear it in light of the recently decided case. They can also *summarily affirm* or *summarily reverse* the lower court decision. They can *relist* a case for another conference if a justice needs more time to decide how to vote.[11] And, they can cast a Join-3 vote. As we noted above, a Join-3 vote is like a conditional grant vote: If at

---

9   A justice can remove a petition from the list that s/he placed on it, but other justices are then free to put it back on.

10 Upon the votes of four justices, the Court will publish an order reading: "The Solicitor General is invited to file a brief in this case expressing the views of the United States." Even though it is formally an invitation, the CVSG is, in practice, an order to the SG's office to submit a brief to the Court (Black and Owens 2012*a*).

11 The Roberts Court seems to have undertaken the practice of relisting cases multiple times before voting to grant or deny review.

least three other justices vote to grant review to the case, a justice's Join-3 vote becomes the equivalent of a grant vote. If fewer than three other justices vote to grant review, the Join-3 is treated as a denial.

With so much discretion to hear cases, one critical question to ask is: what factors make a justice more or less likely to vote to grant review? One place to look for answers to this question is to the justices' own comments. But these comments are somewhat unhelpful. Like magicians trying to obscure their craft, justices often suggest their agenda-setting behavior is largely subjective. After sixteen years of service on the Court, Justice Brennan labeled the agenda setting decision "inherently subjective" (Brennan 1973, 481). Chief Justice Rehnquist called it "rather subjective ... made up in part of intuition and in part of legal judgment" (Rehnquist 2001, 234). In Perry's exhaustive interviews with justices and their clerks about agenda setting, one respondent stated that the "certworthiness" of a case "is ultimately subjective" (Perry 1991, 253). While the decision might seem to some to be subjective, there are nevertheless systematic predictors of grant votes.

Academic research has identified a number of factors that strongly predict whether justices vote to grant review to cases (see, e.g., Tanenhaus, Schick, and Rosen 1963; Ulmer, Hintz, and Kirklosky 1972; Brenner 1979; Songer 1979; Caldeira and Wright 1988; Caldeira, Wright, and Zorn 1999; Black and Owens 2009a). A justice is more likely to vote to hear:

- Cases that are part of an interpretive split among the lower courts (Legal Conflict);
- Cases that will advance the justice's policy preferences (Policy Considerations);
- Cases where a lower court struck down a statute (Judicial Review); and
- Cases that are nationally important (Case Importance).

Legal Conflict. One of the Supreme Court's primary obligations is to resolve conflict among lower court judges over how to interpret federal laws. As Chief Justice Rehnquist once stated, "One factor that influences every member of the Court is whether the case sought to be reviewed has been decided differently from a very similar case coming from another lower court" (Rehnquist 2001, 234). The Court's own rules highlight the fact that justices use the agenda-setting process to clear up legal conflicts among the lower courts. Supreme Court Rule 10 states:

A petition for a writ of certiorari will be granted only for compelling reasons. The following, although neither controlling nor fully measuring the Court's discretion, indicate the character of the reasons the Court considers: (a) a United States court of appeals has entered a decision *in conflict* with the decision of another United States court of appeals on the same important matter; has decided an important federal question *in a way that conflicts* with a decision by a state court of last resort; or has so far departed from the accepted and usual course of judicial proceedings, or sanctioned such a departure by a lower court, as to call for an exercise of this Court's supervisory power; (b) a state court of last resort has decided an important federal question *in a way that conflicts* with the decision of another state court of last resort or of a United States court of appeals; (c) a state court or a United States court of appeals has decided an important question of federal law that has not been, but should be, settled by this Court, or has decided an important federal question *in a way that conflicts* with relevant decisions of this Court. (Emphasis added.)

The Court's cert pool memos also focus extensively on the presence or absence of conflict among the circuits, further signaling the importance of legal conflict to the justices. For example, the cert pool memo writer in *O'Melveny & Myers* v. *FDIC* (93–289) wrote, "This case seems to be a clear GRANT. Both parties acknowledge a [court of appeals] conflict." Likewise, in *Digital Equipment Corp.* v. *Desktop Direct Inc.* (93–405), the pool memo writer declared, "There is a clear split on this issue; [the Tenth Circuit] expressly disagreed with the published views of the [Second Circuit, Fifth Circuit, and Eleventh Circuit] ... GRANT." Conversely, in *Gambino* v. *United States* (90–1689), the pool memo writer noted, "Although there are hints that a split [among the lower courts] might develop, there is no split as yet on this precise issue. DENY." These were not isolated memos, either. Nearly every cert pool memo contains at least some reference to the presence or absence of legal conflict.

Empirical scholarship supports the claim that the Court is more likely to review cases where lower courts conflict over the proper interpretation of federal law. For example, Caldeira and Wright (1988) find that the presence of lower court conflict increases the probability the Court will grant review to cases – from a probability of 0.01 in cases without conflict to 0.33 in cases with conflict. Other studies unearth similar results. Ulmer (1984) finds that conflict, along with other contextual factors, leads to a dramatic increase in the probability of review. Caldeira and Wright (1990) show that the presence of conflict predicts a case's placement on the Discuss List as well as its eventual review. Black and Owens (2009a) find that the Court's duty to resolve conflict is so strong that the presence of conflict can motivate justices to vote to grant review even in cases when they expect their favored policy to lose on the merits.

Policy Considerations. Scholarship also shows that policy considerations influence how justices set their agenda. Decades of legal realism research shows that justices seek to craft national legal policy and want to etch their policy preferences into law (Segal and Spaeth 2002). Conservatives want to make conservative legal policy, while liberals want to make liberal policy – or so the argument goes. If they hold those goals, it makes sense to believe, then, that they grant review to cases by calculating whether those cases serve as good vehicles to satisfy their goals. The results largely concur.

Archival evidence from the Court's internal documents suggests that justices and their clerks make policy calculations when setting the agenda. For example, in the markup to one pool memo, a Blackmun clerk told the Justice, "I am reluctant to recommend granting here because I am uncertain about what the Court as presently constituted would do with this question."[12] The cert pool memos are plastered with such comments. In one case, the clerk wrote, "given the current mood of the Court, I am not eager to see the petition granted."[13] In another, the clerk counseled Justice Blackmun to deny review "because nothing good can come from this case."[14]

A host of empirical scholarship highlights just how important policy considerations are to justices at the agenda-setting stage. Songer (1979) finds that justice use policy cues to decide which cases to review. Palmer (1982) finds that justices are both reverse-minded and strategic when they set the Court's agenda. Others have argued that affirm-minded justices strategically anticipate the Court's likely merits ruling and vote with that outcome in mind (Benesh, Brenner, and Spaeth 2002; Boucher and Segal 1995; Brenner 1979). Caldeira, Wright, and Zorn (1999) find that the more ideologically proximate a justice is to the majority, the more likely she is to grant review. Black and Owens (2009a) find that justices are more likely to vote to grant review when they are closer to the expected outcome on the merits than they are to the status quo. Conversely, they are more likely to vote to deny review when they are closer to the status quo than to the expected outcome on the merits. In other words, justices are forward-looking, strategic actors at the agenda-setting stage.[15]

Judicial Review. Justices admit that they are more likely to vote to grant review to a case where the lower court struck down a federal law. One justice stated, "[I]f a single district judge rules that a federal statute is unconstitutional, I think we owe it to Congress to review the case and see if, in fact, the

---

[12] *Franklin v. Gwinett County Public Schools* (90–918).
[13] *Freeman v. Pitts* (89–1290).
[14] *National Advertising Company v. Raleigh* (91–1555).
[15] Still, despite the fact that justices appear to be forward-looking policy actors, the analyses show that they still largely care about resolving legal conflict among the circuits (Black and Owens 2009a).

statute they've passed is unconstitutional" (Perry 1991, 269) Legal practitioners echo the sentiments of the justices, as well. As Stern et al. (2002, 244) state, "Where the decision below holds a federal statute unconstitutional or where a federal statute is given an unwarranted construction in order to save its constitutionality, certiorari is usually granted because of the obvious importance of the case." The empirical scholarship agrees. When a lower federal court strikes down a law as unconstitutional, legal norms strongly push the Supreme Court to grant review to the case. Black and Owens (2009a) find that judicial invalidation of a law by a lower court significantly increases the likelihood of review, even by those justices who desire to deny review to the case on policy grounds (see also Owens 2010a).

Case Importance. Justices are more likely to vote to hear important cases. For example, as the cert pool memo writer noted in *Eli Lilly* v. *Medtronic, Inc.* (89–243): "patent issues decided by [the Court of Appeals for the Federal Circuit] qualify for cert because of their importance." Circumstantial evidence also supports the belief that justices are more likely to hear important cases: the Obamacare cases, *Bush* v. *Gore* (2000), and President Trump's travel bans were all important cases the Court heard. Empirical studies support the claim that importance leads justices to grant review. Caldeira and Wright (1988) show that the presence of amicus curiae briefs filed at the agenda-setting stage leads to a higher probability the Court will review the case. By bearing the costs to participate in the proceeding, organized interests show that the case has important distributional consequences. The same principle obtains when the Solicitor General elects to weigh in (Caldeira, Wright, and Zorn 1999).

Clearly, there is strong empirical and circumstantial evidence to support the importance of these four factors in the agenda-setting process. But personality, we believe, also matters. In our view, a justice's conscientiousness will influence his or her behavior.

Only one study of which we are aware examines how conscientiousness (or other personality traits) influences justices' agenda votes. Hall (2018, 55) hypothesizes that "more-conscientious justices are less likely to cast a grant vote because pursuing policy objectives violates their judicial duty." His results purport to show this. But there are two major problems with this claim (in addition to the measurement concerns we addressed in Chapter 3). First, the hypothesis assumes that granting review somehow automatically triggers the pursuit of policy objectives in violation of the judicial duty. It does nothing of the sort. It simply puts the case on the Court's docket (assuming three others also vote to grant) for the Court to decide. What happens next is within the control of the justices. Second, the logical implication of this statement is that conscientious justices – those who are strongly motivated by duty and obligation – would not grant review to *any* cases. Clearly, that cannot be. The idea that the justices who are most responsible, most dutiful, and most rule abiding would simply decline to hear any cases flies in face of everything we know about conscientiousness. And so we seek to determine whether conscientiousness influences agenda setting.

4.2 A THEORY OF CONSCIENTIOUSNESS AND AGENDA SETTING

As we discussed in Chapter 2, conscientiousness is "a spectrum of constructs that describe individual differences in the propensity to be self-controlled, responsible to others, hardworking, orderly, and rule abiding" (Roberts et al. 2014, 1315). John and Srivastava (1999, 121) argue that conscientiousness "describes *socially prescribed impulse control* that facilitates task- and goal-directed behavior, such as thinking before acting, delaying gratification, following norms and rules, and planning, organizing, and prioritizing tasks" (emphasis in original; see also Roberts et al. 2004). People who are less conscientious tend to be careless (McCrae and John 1992) and display disinhibition, with an orientation toward immediate gratification and impulsive behavior (Krueger and Markon 2014). Highly conscientious people tend to be deliberate, self-disciplined, well-organized, competent, dutiful, orderly, responsible, goal directed, and thorough.

These qualities surely matter when justices set the Court's agenda. Hardworking and deliberate justices who follow the rules and know what is expected of them are likely to pay careful attention to legal conflict in the lower courts. We further suspect that they will be clear and decisive with their votes. And, we expect them to be less likely to allow policy considerations to influence their agenda votes. We elaborate on each of these expectations in turn.

4.2.1 *Conscientiousness and Legal Conflict*

If there is one action the legal community expects the Supreme Court to take, it is to clear up legal conflict in the circuit courts. We already mentioned Rule 10 as well as the empirical findings surrounding the role of legal conflict. The effect of legal conflict, though, should be especially influential to conscientious justices. After all, conscientious workers "are predisposed to be organized, exacting, disciplined, diligent, dependable, methodical, and purposeful ... [they] thoroughly and correctly perform work tasks [and] take initiative in solving problems" (Witt et al. 2002, 164). One of the justices' main tasks is to ensure uniformity in the law. It is a task that the Court – and only the Court – can accomplish. And, it is precisely the kind of concern that should motivate a conscientious justice.

Of course, not all legal conflict is the same. Here, we distinguish between strong and weak conflict. Strong conflict exists when there is a square conflict between or among lower courts, and the conflict does not appear to be clearing itself up. In other words, if the same legal question has come up in multiple circuits and those circuits have reached opposing answers, there is strong legal conflict involving that issue. In such a case, we would expect all justices to be sensitive to the conflict and vote to resolve it – even if it meant sacrificing their policy goals (e.g., Black and Owens 2009a, 2012c). Everyone expects the Court to resolve such legal conflict. There is little escape from such cases. If justices are to comply with settled expectations about their role, and protect the Court's integrity, they must hear these cases whether they want to or not.

Weak conflict, on the other hand, is another matter. Here, although there is tension among lower court decisions, the nature of the conflict is qualitatively different from strong conflict. The need to address it is not as pressing – at least for some justices. At the most basic level, the two circuit court decisions purportedly at loggerheads might not address an identical legal question. This means a conflict might be characterized as "shallow" or indirect. Or, it could be that the circuit courts appear to be working out the conflict on their own, by virtue of one answer to a legal question gaining favor over another and moving the circuits toward uniformity.

Figure 17 offers an example of how the cert pool memos distinguish weak as opposed to strong conflict. The case, *Mertens v. Hewitt Associates* (1993), involved whether retirees could sue the providers of a health care plan for acting in bad faith. After discussing the circuits that appeared to be in conflict,

2

distinguishable from this one. Because the only true conflict is
with CA7, and because the current validity of CA7's reasoning is
in doubt in light of a subsequent decision of this Court, I would
deny the petition, but it's a close one.

FIGURE 17: *Portions of the pool memo from Mertens v. Hewitt Associates (91–1671).*

the pool memo writer summed things up this way: "Because the only true conflict is with CA7 [Court of Appeals for the Seventh Circuit], and because the current validity of CA7's reasoning is in doubt in light of a subsequent decision of this Court, I would deny the petition, but it's a close one." The Court ultimately decided to grant review in the case, but did so by a vote of 5–4.

Some justices seem particularly disposed to clear up any and all legal conflict – even weak legal conflict. Consider Justice White, who possessed an "unswerving view that the Court ought not let circuit splits linger, that it should say what the federal law is sooner rather than later" (Ginsburg 2003, 1285). Studies show that White alone was responsible for the Court granting a substantial number of cases (Owens and Simon 2012; Cordray and Cordray 2008). What is more, White often dissented from the denial of cert because he thought the Court had an obligation to grant review to petitions that presented even weak amounts of conflict among the circuits. Stern et al. (2002) show that White dissented from the denial of cert sixty-seven times during the 1989 term and more than ninety times in 1991, largely based on his view that the lower courts impermissibly conflicted over the proper interpretation of federal law and the Court had an obligation to hear those cases. He believed the Court should hear and decide cases where legal conflict existed, and not just the cases with strong legal conflict.

We believe conscientious justices will treat petitions with weak legal conflict more seriously than do justices with less conscientiousness. Conscientious people take their professional obligations seriously. Conscientious justices, then, should take their *judicial* obligations seriously. One of the key obligations of the High Court is to resolve legal conflict among the lower courts. In cases where the conflict is strong, all justices will be inclined toward granting review. But it is in cases with weak legal conflict that the conscientious justice's heightened level of duty and discipline come through. We therefore expect that *increasingly conscientious justices are more likely than less conscientious justices to vote to grant review to cases that present weak legal conflict.*

4.2.2 *Conscientiousness and Join-3 Votes*

At the same time, we believe that conscientious justices will be less likely to cast Join-3 votes than their colleagues. Recall that conscientious people tend to be *deliberate*. They are goal directed and thorough. And, as we discussed in Chapter 3 when we validated our measures, conscientiousness correlates with better job performance and workers who set higher goals. Conscientious people also seek to take charge of their environments. They are not people who behave tentatively.

Recall what the Join-3 vote is. It is a tentative vote to grant. It counts as a grant vote if and only if three or more other justices vote to grant. If fewer than three other justices vote to grant, the Join-3 is treated as a deny vote. (So, even if two justices vote to grant and two vote to Join-3, the Court will deny the petition.) The Join-3 vote is highly conditional, highly tentative, and highly apprehensive.

Even the justices themselves have remarked about the tentative nature of Join-3 votes. Stated one justice: "[T]he way [a Join-3 vote] is generally used is that it is a timid vote to grant. At times maybe there is doubt about something" (Perry 1991, 167). Similarly, when asked what a Join-3 vote meant to him, Chief Justice Rehnquist replied that Join-3 votes are more tentative than grants. They allow justices to switch their votes later in the voting process with greater ease: "[M]y sense has always been that [a Join-3] is a more tentative vote than a 'grant,' and that if there are three to join, the person who casts the vote may nonetheless reconsider it" (O'Brien 1997, 788). Similar language appears in the pool memo markups. For example, even though a Justice Blackmun clerk recommended granting review in her memo to the cert pool in *Argentine Republic* v. *Amerada Hess Shipping Corp.* (87–1372), she added a hand-written note for Blackmun's eyes only, stating: "My hesitancy [about the petition] inspires me to recommend to you a [Join-3]." Highly conditional. Highly tentative. Highly apprehensive. These are not descriptions of people who are highly conscientious. As such, we expect that *increasingly conscientious justices are less likely to cast Join-3 votes.*

4.2.3 *Conscientiousness and Strategic Policy Votes*

Finally, recall from Chapter 2 that conscientiousness touches on impulse control, with increasingly conscientious people better able to control their impulses than less conscientious people. They delay gratification and follow norms and rules. This impulse control for the sake of broader considerations translates well to the justices' agenda-setting behavior.

The literature (as discussed previously) shows that although justices pay close attention to legal factors when setting the Court's agenda, their policy considerations often motivate them. The archival images from *Hicks* show firsthand evidence of that. When it comes to setting the agenda, justices regularly consider policy goals. They grant review to cases in which they believe they can "win" by improving legal policy and deny review to cases they expect to lose. But conscientious justices, we believe, will be less likely than other justices to act on these policy motivations.

When it comes to "deciding to decide," the Court has a number of critical institutional roles to play. Just as we expect a conscientious justice to be more attuned to the presence of legal conflict, we expect a conscientious justice to reconcile what he or she ostensibly wants to do on policy grounds versus what he or she needs to do from an institutional perspective. The conscientious justice will rein in those policy behaviors and instead, do what they think is best for the Court as an institution, or for the law. In short, the conscientious justice will be better able to contain his or her policy behavior at the agenda stage.

As such, we expect that *increasingly conscientious justices are less likely to cast policy-based agenda votes than less conscientious justices.*

4.3   DATA, MEASUREMENT, AND ANALYSIS

To test our hypotheses, we randomly sampled 360 paid, non–death penalty petitions appealed from the federal court of appeals that made the Court's Discuss List during the 1986–1993 terms.[16] From these 360 petitions, we recovered a total of 3,024 individual justice votes. We obtained data on the justices' votes from the digital images of Justice Harry A. Blackmun's docket sheets, which we retrieved from Epstein, Segal, and Spaeth (2007).

Using these data, we present three statistical analyses to test our theory that conscientiousness influences justices' agenda-setting behavior. The first analysis examines whether conscientious justices are more likely than less conscientious justices to vote to grant certiorari in cases with weak legal conflict. The second analysis considers whether conscientious justices are less likely to cast Join-3 votes. Our third analysis considers whether conscientious justices are less likely than their colleagues to cast policy-based strategic votes.

4.3.1   *Conscientiousness and Lower Court Legal Conflict*

Dependent Variable. The dependent variable, *Grant*, measures whether each justice cast a vote to grant or deny review to each cert petition in the sample.

---

[16] We sample petitions from the Court's discuss list because these are petitions that have a nonzero probability of being granted, since at least one justice deemed it worthy of some discussion. We examine only petitions from federal courts of appeals because current data allows ideologically estimably comparisons only between Supreme Court justices and lower federal court judges. We exclude capital petitions because they were treated differently than their non-capital counterparts during the time period of our study. The Court automatically added capital cases to the discuss list. Once there, Justices Brennan and Marshall always voted to grant the petition, vacate the death penalty, and remand the case (Woodward and Armstrong 1979; Lazarus 2005).

We assign the dependent variable a value of 1 if the justice voted to grant review, and a value of 0 if the justice voted to deny review. Following Spaeth (2001), we code votes to "note probable jurisdiction" (in appeals) as votes to grant. Similarly, we code "dismiss" votes and votes to "dismiss for want of jurisdiction" (also in appeals) as votes to deny. This coding scheme produces our sample of 3024 justice votes. This value falls 198 votes short of the theoretical maximum for a nine-member body voting on 358 petitions (i.e., 360 × 9 = 3240), because in some cases fewer than nine justices sat on the Court (i.e., vacancy or non-participation), or because Justice Blackmun's docket sheets, which have been shown to be reliable and valid indicators of agenda-setting votes (Black and Owens 2009*b*), contained missing entries.

Other missing values were votes to call for the views of the Solicitor General (CVSG), votes to hold over the petition to a later date, or some other action that is not directly mappable onto our grant/deny framework. Rather than arbitrarily code these votes, we simply counted them as missing data. For similar reasons, we opted to exclude from our analysis petitions where the outcome was to grant, vacate, and remand. As for votes to Join-3, our second model will address their specific determinants, but for the time being we follow standard practice in the agenda-setting literature (Black and Owens 2009*a*; Black and Boyd 2012*a,b*) and code these conditional votes as being votes to grant review. (We obtain substantively similar results if we instead treat these observations as missing values.)

Conscientiousness. As our primary independent variable, we focus on each justice's conscientiousness, which we describe in great detail and validate in chapter three. Larger values correspond to more conscientiousness. We also control for justices' scores on the four other personality trait dimensions – *Openness*, *Extraversion*, *Agreeableness*, and *Neuroticism*.

Legal Conflict. We create four dummy variables to measure the presence and extent of lower court conflict within the case. We derive these measures from reading the cert pool memo in each case. It should be noted that this approach is similar to the one utilized by Caldeira and Wright (1988), who used law students to assess the presence of actual conflict in cert petitions. Our approach, however, has two added advantages. First, the cert pool memos are the actual materials used by the justices in the cert pool.[17] Second, our approach avoids the risk of confirmation bias. Caldeira and Wright had law students assess conflict *after* the Court had decided to grant (or deny) review to a petition.

---

[17] Black and Owens (2009*a*) conducted an intercoder reliability study for these variables. All measures were reliable by commonly used metrics.

Strong Conflict. Following the approach taken by Black and Owens (2009a), *Strong Conflict* represents instances when the pool memo writer acknowledges a clear and deep split among the lower courts. An example comes from *Digital Equipment Corp. v. Desktop Direct Inc.* (93–405). There, the pool memo writer declared, "There is a clear split on this issue; [the Tenth Circuit] expressly disagreed with the published views of the [Second Circuit, Fifth Circuit, and Eleventh Circuit] ... GRANT." If the cert pool memo writer acknowledges strong conflict, we code *Strong Conflict* as 1; 0 otherwise. Thirty-one percent of the petitions in our sample have this level of conflict.

Weak Conflict is present when the law clerk, while assessing the presence of alleged conflict, suggests that immediate review may not be necessary. Sometimes, this means that the split is shallow and involves only two circuits. Other times, it means the conflict appears to be clearing itself up. For example, in *Gardner v. Sea-Land Services, Inc.* (2012), the pool memo author noted that although the lower court's decision conflicted with an existing decision "in principle," the would-be conflicting decision "did not address the question explicitly." He went on to note that "[t]his certainly has not developed into an irreconcilable conflict demanding this Court's intervention."[18] If the cert pool memo writer acknowledges that some conflict exists, but somehow minimizes its importance, we code *Weak Conflict* as 1; 0 otherwise. Twenty-five percent of petitions in our sample have this level of conflict.

Alleged Conflict occurs if the petitioner in the case alleges a conflict among lower courts but the pool memo writer denies the existence of this conflict. For example, in *New York v. Eastway Corporation* (87–359), the petitioner alleged that the lower court's decision conflicted with existing decisions of two other circuits. The pool memo author, after summarizing the competing claims of the respondent, agreed that the respondent correctly characterized the lack of conflict: "For the reasons articulated by resp[ondents], this case does not warrant further review by this Court. There is no conflict with the decision of any other [circuit courts] or of this Court. [The Second Circuit]'s decision is consistent with the approach taken by other [circuits] and the principles enunciated by this Court."[19] In such situations, we record *Alleged*

---

[18] See page 4 of the cert pool memo in *Gardiner v. Sea-Land Services, Inc.* (86–329). Accessible online through the Digital Archive of the Papers of Harry A. Blackmun (last accessed October 17, 2018).

[19] See page 5 of the cert pool memo in *New York v. Eastway Corporation* (87–359). Accessible online through the Digital Archive of the Papers of Harry A. Blackmun (last accessed October 17, 2018).

Conflict as 1; 0 otherwise. Twenty-five percent of petitions in our sample have this level of conflict.

No Conflict. This category, which we designate as the baseline category in our subsequent statistical models, represents instances where the petitioner did not allege any legal conflict among the lower courts. This occurs, for instance, when a petitioner is simply alleging that a lower court somehow erred in the substance of its decision-making. Less commonly, it occurs when a case presents a legal question that is the first of its kind and, therefore, has not had an opportunity to trigger conflict across the circuits. If the pool memo writer did not discuss the presence of conflict or otherwise note the allegation of conflict among the lower courts, we give this variable a value of 1; 0 otherwise. Nineteen percent of petitions in our sample have this level of conflict.

With these four binary variables in hand, we then proceed to interact them with our *Conscientiousness* measure. In the tables that follow, recall that *No Conflict* is the omitted baseline category, whose effect is picked up by the model's intercept term. Similarly, the interaction between *No Conflict* and *Conscientiousness* is accounted for simply through the *Conscientiousness* measure. As noted previously, we expect the presence of weak conflict will induce conscientious justices to vote to grant certiorari more than it induces less conscientious justices to grant.

We also control for multiple factors that previous research has shown to influence the policy and legal motivations behind Supreme Court agenda setting (see, e.g., Black and Owens 2009a). Unless otherwise indicated, the source of information we use to code these variables is the cert pool memos written for each petition.

US Supports Grant. This variable reflects cases in which the Solicitor General (SG) recommends that the Court grant review to a petition, acting as either the petitioner or amicus curiae in favor of review. Given the notable influence of the US government and SG on the Court's decision-making (e.g., Black and Owens 2012b; Wohlfarth 2009), we account for cases in which the SG has taken a favorable position on a petition. We code the variable as 1 when the SG supports the grant of review, 0 otherwise.

US Opposes Grant. This variable reflects instances when the SG recommends that the Court deny review to a petition, acting as either the respondent or amicus curiae opposed to review. We code the variable as 1 when the SG opposes review; 0 otherwise.

Intermediate Court Reverses. We account for instances where the US Court of Appeals reversed the decision of the lower court (usually a trial court). Justices might be more inclined to review such cases, given the disagreement between the trial and appellate courts. *Intermediate Court Reverses* receives a value of 1 when the Court of Appeals reversed the court below it; 0 otherwise.

Intermediate Court Dissent. The presence of a dissent in the lower court often sends a strong signal to justices about the importance of a case. Circuit court judges tend not to dissent. Their refusal is partly a function of time constraints (they hear so many cases per year that they cannot dissent often) and partly a function of norms against dissenting. Whatever the reason, it is clear that a dissent signals something important. And so circuit court decisions accompanied with a dissent signal a greater need for Supreme Court review. Thus, we control for cases with dissent in the appellate court, coding *Intermediate Court Dissent* as 1 when the pool memo writer notes a dissent in the lower court; 0 when the memo writer does not mention dissent.

Intermediate Court Judicial Review. We also account for cases where the appellate court exercised judicial review by striking a federal statute. Justices might perceive a greater need to review such cases (Black and Owens 2009a). We code *Intermediate Court Judicial Review* as 1 if the pool memo writer noted the lower court's exercise of judicial review of a federal statute; 0 otherwise.

Intermediate Court Unpublished. Judges on federal appellate courts may use a brief, unpublished opinion to dispose of easy or mundane cases that lack precedential value. The High Court is unlikely to review such decisions because they tend to be of little legal or policy value. We code *Intermediate Court Unpublished* as 1 when the pool memo writer noted that the Court of Appeals' opinion was unpublished; 0 otherwise.

Amicus Briefs. A major indicator of legal importance is the number of amicus curiae briefs filed in support of, or opposition to, a petition (Caldeira and Wright 1988). Greater involvement by interest groups should reflect a petition that is more salient and thus a better candidate for review by the Supreme Court. We code *Amicus Briefs* as the total number of amicus briefs filed at the agenda-setting stage, as recorded in the cert pool memos.

US Law Week Article. Another indicator of legal importance – and thus perhaps a sign that a petition is more certworthy – occurs when the legal periodical *US Law Week* publishes a summary of the Court of Appeals decision that a party appealed to the Supreme Court. We code this variable as 1 if the periodical included coverage about the appellate court's decision; 0 otherwise. As this information is exogenous to the cert pool memo, we used LexisNexis to gather data for it.

Merits Outcome Closer. We include a variable to control for a justice's potential desire to review a case for strategic, policy-based reasons. We assign

Merits Outcome Closer a value of 1 if the voting justice's policy preference is ideologically closer to the expected merits outcome (if the Court were to decide the case) than to the status quo; 0 otherwise. To code this variable, we rely on the Judicial Common Space (JCS) (Epstein, Martin, Segal, and Westerland 2007), which offers the ideal points of Supreme Court justices on the same ideological scale as federal circuit court judges. We identify the expected merits outcome using the ideal point of the Court's median justice. To identify the status quo, we use the JCS scores of the circuit court judges who reviewed the case. Given a unanimous three-judge panel decision, we identify the status quo as the JCS score of the median panel judge. When the lower court decision involved a dissent or special concurrence within a three-judge panel, we code the status quo as the midpoint between the two judges in the majority. If the lower court decision was rendered en banc, we identify the status quo as the median judge in the en banc majority. And, when district court judges sat by designation on the circuit panel, we follow Giles, Hettinger, and Peppers (2001) and code the district court judge's ideal point consistent with the norm of senatorial courtesy.

Given the dichotomous dependent variable, we employ logistic regression models. We estimate robust standard errors but note that all subsequent results remain statistically significant if we estimate classical standard errors. We begin with two models: (1) a baseline traits-only model that specifies the interaction terms between *Conscientiousness* and each of the three legal conflict variables, along with the four other personality traits; and (2) a full model specification that includes all control predictors.[20] Table 8 reports the regression results. Both models support our theoretical expectations. The impact of legal conflict varies significantly based on *Conscientiousness*, and in a way that is most evident among petitions with weak legal conflict – that is, weak legal conflict effects conscientious justices more than it effects less conscientious justices.

Consider Figure 18, which shows the average marginal effects (with 90 percent confidence intervals) of each legal conflict category (compared to the baseline of no conflict) across the range of *Conscientiousness* using the results from Model 2 in Table 8. Figure 18(a) (i.e., the top left panel) shows, as expected, that the impact of *Strong Conflict* is always statistically significant and positive, and its magnitude increases ever so slightly across the range of *Conscientiousness*. That is, when confronted by a petition that conveys a

---

[20] The interactive effects between conscientiousness and legal conflict are substantively consistent when specifying a baseline model that does not include the other personality trait variables (nor the other control predictors).

TABLE 8: *The Conditional Impact of Justice Conscientiousness and Lower Court Conflict on Supreme Court Agenda Setting*

	(1)	(2)
Conscientiousness	−0.45*	−0.50*
	(0.14)	(0.15)
Strong Conflict	1.77*	1.86*
	(0.15)	(0.17)
Weak Conflict	0.76*	0.85*
	(0.16)	(0.18)
Alleged Conflict	0.04	0.05
	(0.17)	(0.18)
Conscientiousness × Strong Conflict	0.27*	0.28*
	(0.15)	(0.17)
Conscientiousness × Weak Conflict	0.39*	0.38*
	(0.16)	(0.17)
Conscientiousness × Alleged Conflict	0.23	0.23
	(0.17)	(0.19)
Openness	0.11*	0.13*
	(0.04)	(0.05)
Extraversion	0.07	0.01
	(0.09)	(0.09)
Agreeableness	0.24*	0.28*
	(0.04)	(0.05)
Neuroticism	−0.09	−0.11
	(0.07)	(0.08)
US Supports Grant		0.91*
		(0.13)
US Opposes Grant		−0.21*
		(0.11)
Intermediate Court Reverses		0.39*
		(0.09)
Intermediate Court Dissent		0.30*
		(0.10)
Intermediate Court Judicial Review		1.65*
		(0.23)
Intermediate Court Unpublished		−0.38
		(0.23)

(continued)

TABLE 8: (*continued*)

	(1)	(2)
Amicus Briefs		0.21*
		(0.05)
US Law Week Article		0.22*
		(0.10)
Merits Outcome Closer		0.46*
		(0.10)
Constant	−1.92*	−2.89*
	(0.14)	(0.19)
N	3024	3024
χ^2	353.32*	490.68*

Note: Table entries are coefficients from a logistic regression model with robust standard errors in parentheses; * denotes $p < 0.05$ (one-tailed). The dependent variable indicates whether each justice cast a vote to grant certiorari, among a random sample of 360 paid, non–death penalty petitions (1986–1993 terms) that were appealed from a federal court of appeals and made the Court's discuss list.

strong degree of lower court conflict (compared to one with no conflict), all justices are generally much more likely to seek to grant certiorari. Increasingly conscientious justices are only somewhat more likely to do so than less conscientious justices.

At the other end of the spectrum, consider the top-right panel – that is, Figure 18(b). It shows the impact of alleging a nonexistent conflict on the likelihood that a justice votes to grant review. The shaded gray confidence interval contains zero across the entire range of justice conscientiousness. This is to say that, substantively speaking, no justice, regardless of his or her conscientiousness, appears any more (or less) likely to grant review when conflict is alleged but not present in any form. Alleged conflict alone moves no one.

Figure 18(c) is the most important figure. It highlights how justices treat petitions with weak legal conflict. Recall that these are cases where some circuits have conflicted with each other over how to interpret law, but the conflict is either very new or has not yet percolated across the circuits. These are cases where the law is muddled in the lower courts but not completely unclear – like twilight as opposed to the dark night. As the figure makes clear, weak conflict fails to move less conscientious justices. It does, however, move conscientious justices. Less conscientious justices do not distinguish between weak conflict and no conflict. As a justice's conscientiousness increases,

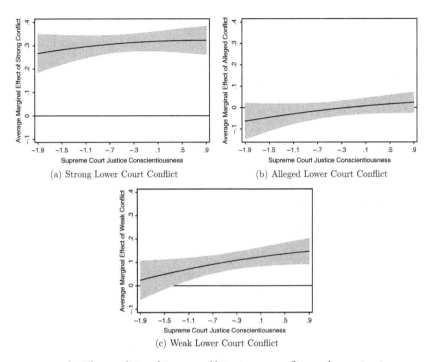

FIGURE 18: *The conditional impact of lower court conflict and conscientiousness on Supreme Court justices' votes to grant certiorari.* Panel (a) displays the average marginal effect of *Strong Conflict* (with 90 percent confidence intervals) across the range of *Conscientiousness* using results from Model 2 in Table 8. Panel (b) displays the average marginal effect of *Alleged Conflict*, and Panel (c) displays the results for *Weak Conflict*.

though, the justice becomes significantly more likely to grant review. Indeed, when *Conscientiousness* is at its sample maximum, a justice is 0.15 more likely to vote to grant review in a petition with weak conflict (0.26) as compared to one where no conflict (0.11) exists, which is well over twice the likelihood of review. This provides considerable support for the role of conscientiousness in addressing conflict at the agenda stage.

Among the control predictors, justices scoring higher on *Openness* and *Agreeableness* are significantly more likely to vote to grant certiorari. Next, the results confirm the importance of the SG's agenda-setting recommendations, as justices are substantially more likely to vote to review a case when the US government supports the petition and are less likely to do so when the US opposes the petition. The results also suggest that justices are more likely to vote to grant review when the court of appeals reversed the trial court, when there was dissent in the appeals court's decision, and when the appeals court exercised judicial review. Justices are more likely to vote to grant review in cases with more amicus briefs and when *U.S. Law Week* published a summary of the Court of Appeals decision. Lastly, the results confirm that justices are much more likely to seek review of a case when the expected merits outcome is closer to the justice's ideal policy preference than to the status quo.

4.3.2 *Conscientiousness and Join-3 Votes*

We turn, next, to examine how conscientiousness influences justices' propensities to cast Join-3 votes.

Dependent Variable. The dependent variable, *Join-3*, indicates whether the justice cast a Join-3 vote. We reviewed each justice's agenda-setting vote recorded on each docket sheet in our sample of cases. We give *Join-3* a value of 1 if the docket sheet indicates that the justice cast a Join-3 vote; 0 otherwise. We expect that justices' *Conscientiousness* scores negatively predict Join-3 voting behavior.

We include the same set of variables we included in our previous models. Once again, our primary covariate of interest is *Conscientiousness*. We also include *US Supports Grant, US Opposes Grant, Intermediate Reverses Trial, Dissent in Intermediate, Intermediate Judicial Review, Intermediate Unpublished, Amicus Briefs, US Law Week Article, Merits Outcome Closer, Strong Conflict, Weak Conflict, Alleged Conflict,* and *No Conflict*. We also control for the other four personality traits.

Due to the dichotomous dependent variable, we report the results from a logistic regression model with robust standard errors. Again, all subsequent results remain statistically significant if we estimate classical standard errors. Table 9 shows that, as expected, increasingly conscientious justices are significantly less likely to cast Join-3 votes than justices who score lower on *Conscientiousness*. And this effect is evident in both the baseline traits-only model and one that includes the full complement of controls.[21]

Figure 19 displays the magnitude of *Conscientiousness* on the probability of casting a Join-3 vote. It reports the predicted probability a Supreme Court justice casts a Join-3 vote across the range of *Conscientiousness* (with 90 percent confidence intervals) using results from Model 2 in Table 9. A justice that displays the least conscientiousness in the data exhibits an expected 0.059

---

[21] All subsequent empirical results are consistent when specifying a bivariate model that includes only conscientiousness (and no control predictors).

TABLE 9: *The Impact of Supreme Court Justice Conscientiousness on Join-3 Agenda-Setting Votes*

	(1)	(2)
Conscientiousness	−0.32*	−0.32*
	(0.17)	(0.17)
Openness	−0.02	−0.02
	(0.08)	(0.08)
Extraversion	−0.40*	−0.43*
	(0.22)	(0.22)
Agreeableness	0.30*	0.31*
	(0.12)	(0.12)
Neuroticism	−0.01	−0.01
	(0.19)	(0.19)
Strong Conflict		0.14
		(0.28)
Weak Conflict		−0.12
		(0.29)
Alleged Conflict		−0.16
		(0.30)
US Supports Grant		0.03
		(0.28)
US Opposes Grant		−0.14
		(0.23)
Intermediate Court Reverses		0.30
		(0.20)
Intermediate Court Dissent		0.18
		(0.22)
Intermediate Court Judicial Review		−0.18
		(0.47)
Intermediate Court Unpublished		−1.24*
		(0.72)
Amicus Briefs		0.12*
		(0.06)
US Law Week Article		0.00
		(0.21)
Merits Outcome Closer		0.23
		(0.20)
Constant	−3.63*	−3.93*
	(0.20)	(0.34)
N	3024	3024
χ^2	15.60*	35.45*

Note: Table entries are coefficients from a logistic regression model with robust standard errors in parentheses; *p < .05 (one-tailed). The dependent variable indicates whether each justice cast a Join-3 vote, among a random sample of 360 paid, non–death penalty petitions (1986–1993 terms) that were appealed from a federal court of appeals and made the Court's discuss list.

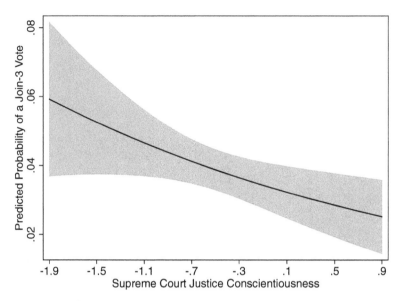

FIGURE 19: *The impact of conscientiousness on Supreme Court justices' Join-3 votes.* Estimates represent the predicted probability (with 90% confidence intervals) that a Supreme Court justice casts a Join-3 vote across the range of *Conscientiousness* using results from Model 2 in Table 9.

[0.033, 0.086] probability of casting a Join-3 vote. By contrast, a justice that displays the most conscientiousness in the data exhibits an expected 0.025 [0.012, 0.038] probability of casting a Join-3 vote. This shift from the minimum to maximum conscientiousness score yields an expected decrease of approximately 0.034 in the probability that a justice casts a Join-3 vote – a 58 percent change. Even a less extreme difference in *Conscientiousness* exhibits a substantial change. A one standard deviation increase (0.832) above the mean conscientiousness score leads to an expected 0.009 decrease in the probability of a Join-3 vote – a 24 percent change. In short, *Conscientiousness* is not only statistically significant in explaining Join-3 votes; it is substantively meaningful. And once again, we retrieve these results even after accounting for a number of other legal and policy considerations that influence agenda-setting behavior.

Turning to the control predictors, the results suggest that more extraverted justices are less likely to cast Join-3 votes. Justices scoring higher on the agreeableness trait are significantly more likely to Join-3. The results also indicate that justices are less likely to cast Join-3 votes when considering appeals to unpublished lower court decisions. The presence of more amicus briefs leads justices to be more likely to cast Join-3 votes.

4.3.3 *Conscientiousness and Strategic Policy-Based Voting*

In our third analysis, we review how conscientiousness effects a justice's pursuit of policy. This analysis requires us to revisit one of our previous variables: *Merits Outcome Closer*. Recall from above that we sought to predict whether the expected outcome on the merits would be better for the justice – on policy grounds – than the status quo. We argued that policy-motivated justices would be more likely to vote to grant review to a case when they expected to benefit from the Court's decision. In this section, we examine the conditions under which they actually vote in that manner.

Dependent Variables. We employ two dependent variables: one accounts for whether the justice cast a forward-looking policy-based grant vote; the other accounts for whether the justice cast a forward-looking policy-based deny vote. To make these determinations, we turn to the *Merits Outcome Closer* variable described previously. Recall that this variable is coded as 1 if a justice is spatially closer to the likely merits outcome as opposed to the legal status quo. It asks, in other words, am I better off ideologically by hearing this case or rejecting it? To code the strategic grant variable, we look at the 1886 instances where a justice is theoretically closer (ideologically) to the likely merits outcome of the case than he or she is to the legal status quo. We then code whether the justice did, in fact, vote to grant review in that case. *Policy Grant*, then, takes on a value of 1 if a justice voted to grant review when doing so would be the strategically sound policy move. (Justices did so in 647 of these chances, or about 34 percent of the time.) If the justice voted to deny review, we code *Policy Grant* as 0. To code the strategic deny variable, we look at the 1,138 instances where a justice is theoretically closer to the status quo than to the likely decision on the merits. If the justice voted to deny review here, we code *Policy Deny* as 1. If the justice voted to grant review, we code the variable as 0. *Policy Deny* is coded as 1 about 25% of the time (i.e., 281 out of 1,138).

Our primary covariate of interest remains *Conscientiousness*. We control for *Strong Conflict, Weak Conflict, Alleged Conflict, No Conflict, US Supports Grant, US Opposes Grant, Intermediate Reverses Trial, Dissent in Intermediate, Intermediate Judicial Review, Intermediate Unpublished, Amicus Briefs*, and *US Law Week Article*. We also control for the four other personality traits. We do not include *Merits Outcome Closer* as a control predictor in this analysis because it represents part of the dependent variables.

Following Black and Owens (2009a), we also include several additional control predictors that are relevant when predicting a justice's proclivity to cast a policy-based strategic vote.

Freshman Justice. It is possible that freshman justices may be less likely to pursue their policy goals at the expense of nonpolicy, or legal, motivations. We assign a value of 1 to *Freshman Justice* if the voting justice served fewer than two full terms when the Court issued a final decision on the petition; 0 otherwise.

Merits Outcome Uncertainty. It may sometimes be more (less) difficult for a justice to form expectations about the anticipated outcome on the merits, which might affect his or her willingness to cast a policy-based strategic vote. We create a variable that reflects the probability the median justice is actually the median on the Court (and thus accurately reflects the location of the expected merits outcome), using the probability value that Martin and Quinn (2002) assign to the estimated median justice. Larger values amount to greater certainty about the location and identity of the median.

Outcome-Status Quo Difference. We account for the possibility that issuing a policy-based strategic agenda-setting vote may become more difficult for a justice as the distance between the expected merits outcome and the status quo decreases. We capture this potential effect such that *Outcome-Status Quo Difference* represents the absolute value of the distance between the expected merits outcome (i.e., JCS score of the Supreme Court's median justice) and the status quo.

Procedural Complexity. Lastly, it may become more difficult for justices to look forward strategically and anticipate the merits outcome when reviewing a more complex petition. We measure *Procedural Complexity* as the proportion of the pool memo's pages that a clerk devoted to discussing the petition's procedural history in the lower courts.

Table 10 reports the logistic regression results (with robust standard errors) predicting when justices cast policy-based strategic votes to grant certiorari (Models 1–2) and then policy-based strategic votes to deny certiorari (Models 3–4).[22] Models 1 and 3 report the baseline results.[23] Models 2 and 4 report full specifications. In Models 1 and 2, we uncover evidence that increasingly

---

[22] All results are similar if we estimate the models using classical standard errors.

[23] Note, though, that the effect of conscientiousness changes direction when predicting strategic grants while specifying a bivariate model that includes only conscientiousness and does not account for other factors known to affect such agenda-setting votes.

TABLE 10: *The Impact of Supreme Court Justice Conscientiousness on Politically Strategic Agenda-Setting Votes*

	Strategic Grants		Strategic Denials	
	(1)	(2)	(3)	(4)
Conscientiousness	−0.21*	−0.27*	0.03	−0.11
	(0.08)	(0.09)	(0.13)	(0.16)
Openness	0.08	0.12*	−0.12	−0.03
	(0.05)	(0.06)	(0.10)	(0.12)
Extraversion	0.02	−0.01	−0.18	−0.35*
	(0.10)	(0.12)	(0.16)	(0.20)
Agreeableness	0.24*	0.32*	−0.11	−0.05
	(0.05)	(0.06)	(0.08)	(0.10)
Neuroticism	−0.07	−0.11	−0.12	−0.28
	(0.08)	(0.10)	(0.15)	(0.19)
Strong Conflict		1.84*		−1.74*
		(0.19)		(0.24)
Weak Conflict		0.77*		−0.63*
		(0.19)		(0.26)
Alleged Conflict		−0.21		−0.28
		(0.21)		(0.27)
US Supports Grant		0.82*		−0.97*
		(0.16)		(0.21)
US Opposes Grant		−0.38*		−0.09
		(0.15)		(0.18)
Intermediate Court Reverses		0.49*		−0.21
		(0.12)		(0.16)
Intermediate Court Dissent		0.30*		−0.39*
		(0.14)		(0.17)
Intermediate Court Judicial Review		1.67*		−1.76*
		(0.30)		(0.34)
Intermediate Court Unpublished		−0.93*		−0.33
		(0.32)		(0.36)
Amicus Briefs		0.27*		−0.11
		(0.06)		(0.07)
US Law Week Article		0.23*		−0.19
		(0.12)		(0.17)
Freshman Justice		−0.24		0.67*
		(0.17)		(0.37)

(continued)

TABLE 10: (*continued*)

	Strategic Grants		Strategic Denials	
	(1)	(2)	(3)	(4)
Merits Outcome Uncertainty		−0.25		−0.01
		(0.24)		(0.33)
Outcome-Status Quo Difference		1.20*		−0.14
		(0.34)		(0.45)
Procedural Complexity		−0.64		0.39
		(0.45)		(0.61)
Constant	−0.95*	−2.22*	1.16*	2.32*
	(0.08)	(0.36)	(0.13)	(0.48)
N	1886	1886	1138	1138
χ^2	68.53*	374.37*	6.90	152.57*

Note: Table entries are logistic regression coefficients with robust standard errors in parentheses; *$p < 0.05$ (one-tailed). The dependent variable indicates whether each individual Supreme Court justice casts a strategic, policy-based agenda-setting vote, among a random sample of 360 paid, non–death penalty petitions (1986–1993 terms) that were appealed from a federal court of appeals and made the Court's discuss list.

conscientious justices, as expected, are significantly less likely than nonconscientious justices to cast policy-based grant votes. That is, they are less likely to put cases on the Court's docket strategically for policy reasons.

Figure 20 displays the magnitude of this effect. It reports the predicted probability a justice casts a policy-based grant vote across the range of *Conscientiousness* (with 90% confidence intervals) using results from Model 2 in Table 10. A justice with the minimum conscientiousness score exhibits an expected 0.41 [0.36, 0.46] probability of casting a policy-based strategic vote to grant cert. A justice at the maximum end of the conscientiousness scale, by contrast, is likely to cast a strategic grant vote with an estimated 0.29 [0.25, 0.33] probability. This shift from the minimum to maximum conscientiousness score yields an expected decrease of 0.12 in the probability a justice strategically votes to grant review – representing a roughly 30 percent decrease. Looking at a less severe change, a one standard deviation increase above the mean conscientiousness score leads to an expected 0.04 decrease in the probability of a strategic grant vote – more than a 10 percent decrease from the mean probability. In short, there is compelling evidence that conscientiousness plays an important role in Supreme Court agenda setting that is independent of established factors that shape justices' votes.

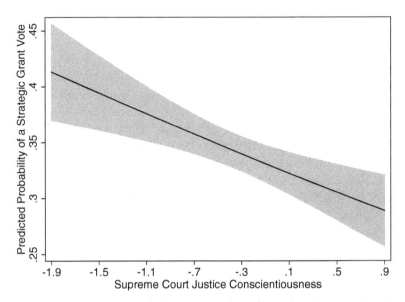

FIGURE 20: *The impact of conscientiousness on Supreme Court justices' policy-based strategic agenda-setting votes.* Estimates represent the predicted probability (with 90 percent confidence intervals) that a Supreme Court justice casts a strategic, policy-based agenda-setting vote across the range of *Conscientiousness* using results from Model 2 in Table 10.

Although we do not uncover a similar effect of justice conscientiousness on strategic denials (i.e., Models 3 and 4), one should expect conscientiousness to exhibit its greatest mitigating effect on the decision to review a case to move policy closer to one's preferred policy outcome (i.e., a strategic grant). We might expect conscientiousness to pump the breaks on granting rather than moving with more certainty to deny.

When viewing the control predictors, the results suggest that more open and agreeable justices are significantly more likely to cast strategic grant votes. Alternatively, more extraverted justices are less likely to cast strategic denials. The results also show that the presence of legal conflict has the expected effects on justices' certiorari votes. That is, justices are more likely to cast policy-based strategic grants and less likely to cast strategic deny votes in the presence of either strong or weak lower court conflict. And, the magnitude of strong conflict's effect is considerably greater than that of weak conflict. In other words, the presence of legal conflict can help justices justify voting to grant review. Next, justices are more likely to cast strategic grants and less likely to exhibit strategic denials when the SG supports the petition. Similarly, when the SG opposes the petition, justices are significantly less likely to issue strategic grant votes.

When the lower appellate court reversed the trial court's decision, justices are more likely to cast strategic grants. Similarly, justices are more likely to cast strategic grants and less likely to issue strategic denials when there was dissent among the judges in the lower court panel, or when the Court of Appeals exercised judicial review. Strategic grants are more common in cases with greater amicus participation, when *US Law Week* published a summary of the circuit court's decision, and when the distance between the expected merits outcome and the status quo increases. Lastly, the results suggest that justices are less likely to cast strategic votes to grant review when the lower court's decision was unpublished and more likely to exhibit strategic denials if the voting justice was in his or her first two terms on the Court.

4.4 CONCLUSION

We're going to get a bit more colloquial here. Imagine yourself building a LEGO set. Picture yourself on the living room floor or dining room table putting them together. Perhaps you're assembling the ultimate collector series of the Millennium Falcon. Or maybe it's something from the Harry Potter movies (Hogwarts Express train?). Or, in a less branded way, maybe it's a modular building like the 1950s diner. Whatever the case, you'll have multiple LEGO bags to open. Each bag is numbered sequentially. You begin with bag number 1 and then move to bag number 2, and so on. After you've put everything together, you can (hopefully) sit back and enjoy your creation (and then wait for your children to break it).

This chapter was bag number 1. Together, we constructed portions of the foundation for our eventual product. We can start to see how things are shaping up. Conscientiousness influences judicial behavior at this stage of the Court's decision-making process.

We inquired whether conscientiousness influences justices' agenda-setting behaviors. We examined the link between conscientiousness and legal conflict, the link between conscientiousness and Join-3 voting, and the link between conscientiousness and forward-looking policy votes. We accounted for the features scholars believe influence these behaviors. And even after doing so, we discovered a profound effect of conscientiousness. Conscientious justices are more attuned to the influence of weak legal conflict than other justices. They are less likely to cast tentative votes than other justices. And they are less likely to cast policy-based grant votes than their less conscientious colleagues.

These results establish a strong beginning for our argument that conscientiousness influences justices' behavior. But we have more work to do – more bags to open before we are done assembling our full argument. And so we move on now, to our next chapter, which discusses the role of conscientiousness and legal persuasion.

5

Conscientiousness and Legal Persuasion

Ships that pass in the night, and speak each other in passing,
Only a signal shown and a distant voice in the darkness;
So on the ocean of life we pass and speak one another,
Only a look and a voice, then darkness again and a silence.

–Henry Wadsworth Longfellow (1874)

In *Bailey* v. *U.S.* (2013), the Supreme Court had to decide whether police officers with a warrant to search a home could seize and search a person who had
left that home minutes before they arrived or, whether they were, as Longfellow wrote, merely "ships that passed in the night."[1] The anticipated vote
breakdown in the case was more uncertain than usual, but one thing seemed
clear: Justice Scalia had a high probability of being one of the swing justices.
Court watchers commented on the important role Justice Scalia would play.
His vote was up for grabs in Fourth Amendment cases. He might even control the case's outcome. Perhaps not surprisingly, Bailey focused his brief,
and his oral arguments, on winning Scalia's vote. Argument after argument
targeted Scalia. Indeed, because Bailey's brief relied on so many of Scalia's
previous opinions – and employed language he often used – one commen-
tator remarked that the brief read like "a love letter to Justice Scalia" (Epps
2012).

The arguments paid off. Not only did Bailey capture Scalia's vote – and
the votes of five other justices; he was able to get Scalia to write a helpful
concurring opinion that "rode shotgun." (A concurring opinion that rides
shotgun is one that agrees fully with the majority and attacks the dissent.)
Scalia ripped the dissent's position as a "promiscuous" interpretation of existing law. "The dissent [which consisted of Justices Breyer, Thomas, and Alito]
...would harvest from [past law] what it likes (permission to seize without

---

[1] *See Bailey* v. *U.S.*, 586 U.S. 186 (2013).

probable cause) and leave behind what it finds uncongenial." In short, Bailey persuaded Scalia, and then some.

How was Bailey able to persuade these six justices? Surprisingly, the general topic of legal persuasion is understudied from an empirical perspective. Court scholars know little about how persuasion works at the Court. Thankfully, however, we can draw from thousands of years of discussion on the topic of persuasion more broadly. The study of persuasion is an ancient one that dates back at least to Aristotle. Aristotle argued that persuasion is a function of credibility, logic, and emotion.

So that there is no confusion about our results, we summarize them here. Credibility and logic influence all justices, but they influence highly conscientious justices the most. Conscientious justices are less likely to rule in favor of the party with emotionally tainted briefs than their less conscientious colleagues. They also are more likely to be persuaded by legally strong oral arguments than less conscientious justices. These findings present yet further evidence that justices' personalities matter.

5.1 PERSUASION: THE ROLES OF CREDIBILITY, EMOTION, AND LOGIC

Persuasion is an ancient topic. We know, historically, that the Greeks and Romans took the concept seriously and dedicated substantial time and reflection to its study. For example, as a young man, Demosthenes exercised with a pebble in his mouth in order to overcome a speech impediment and to make the elocution of his words more authoritative and persuasive (Pearson 1975). Cicero spent considerable effort to understand speech and persuasion. He examined the *inventio*, or substance of the speech, and *dispositio*, or disposition or order of the speech (Ochs 1989). Plato's *Gorgias* compares Callicles' various speeches, designed to appeal to "fickle" audiences, with the approach of Socrates (Kapust 2011, 92). And Aristotle, of course, examined how speakers could persuade their audiences. As he saw it, persuasion was, in part, a function of the speaker's credibility (or *ethos*), appeals to logic (*logos*), and appeals to emotion (*pathos*) (Kennedy 2007).

Aristotle believed that a speaker had to be perceived as credible by listeners to persuade them. He claimed that an argument could be made "in such a way as to make the speaker worthy of credence" (Kennedy 2007, 38). The credibility of the speaker needed to be established "from the speech, not from a previous opinion that the speaker is a certain kind of person" (Kennedy 2007, 39). In other words, *ethos* is the "projection of the character of the speaker as trustworthy" (Kennedy 2007, 15). One could conceive of *ethos* as the adaptation of speech to the character of the audience. One should know one's audience to be credible.

Aristotle also recognized that logic (i.e., logos) would persuade (most) listeners. Logic was critical to make a persuasive point. Logic could win an argument even when the speaker lacked other virtues. As he put it, "[p]ersuasion occurs through the arguments when we *show* the truth or the apparent truth from whatever is persuasive, in each case" (Kennedy 2007, 69, emphasis added). *Logos* is about showing your audience, step by step, the logical conclusions of your argument and winning them over accordingly.

We make the (we hope) uncontroversial statement that credibility and logic matter when seeking to persuade Supreme Court justices (Scalia and Garner 2008). The attorney making an argument must be seen as credible by the justices. And while we cannot say, exactly, what makes a lawyer more credible, we do know that some things can make them look *less* credible – like using highly emotional language in their briefs (Black, Hall, Owens, and Ringsmuth 2016).[2] And so we examine how credibility and emotion interact when justices read party briefs. Additionally, we know that justices value crisp and coherent legal arguments, and that such oral arguments can influence justices (Johnson, Wahlbeck, and Spriggs 2006). A strong oral argument can even win over ideologically skeptical justices. We examine whether strong oral arguments influence conscientious justices more than less conscientious justices.

5.2 A THEORY OF CONSCIENTIOUSNESS AND BRIEF WRITING

We follow Black, Hall, Owens, and Ringsmuth (2016) and argue that justices are less likely to side with parties who draft briefs that use emotionally charged language. Briefs that employ emotional language – and the attorneys who write them – are seen by justices as less *credible* than those employing non-emotional legal arguments. And we believe this effect is felt most acutely by conscientious justices. But before we examine source credibility and brief writing more specifically, we take a moment to discuss briefs more generally.

It is beyond controversy to state that the brief is the most important communicative tool available to lawyers today. Nearly all of the attorneys' arguments hinge on their briefs. According to one important work, the brief is "the

---

[2] For a particularly galling example of a lack of credibility at oral argument, see O'Brien (2009, 30–35).

central feature of modern appellate practice" (Martineau et al. 2005, 770). Similarly, Judge Frank M. Coffin once stated:

"I know of no other field of human endeavor where a limited number of pages of written and structured argument can be so decisive as in appellate decision-making. The heavy artillery of appellate practice *is* the brief" (Coffin 1994, 107, emphasis in original).

Attorneys must file briefs at all stages of the Court's decision-making process. When a party wishes the Supreme Court to review a lower court decision, they file a petition for a writ of certiorari along with a brief in support thereof. If the respondent wishes to persuade the Court to deny review to the case, its attorneys submit briefs in opposition to certiorari. According to the Supreme Court's Rules, once the Court grants review to a case, the petitioner's attorney has forty-five days to file forty copies of their main brief. The respondents then have thirty days after that to submit forty copies of their own brief. The petitioner then has the opportunity to submit a reply brief. These briefs lay out the parties' legal arguments.

Before justices attend oral arguments in a case or hold a merits conference to discuss it, they carefully read these briefs. As Chief Justice Rehnquist once wrote:

When I start to prepare for a case that will be orally argued, I begin by reading the opinion of the lower court . . . I then read the petitioner's brief, and then the respondent's brief. Meanwhile, I have asked one of my clerks to do the same thing, with a view to our then discussing the case. (Rehnquist 2001, 240)

Other judges have indicated that they rely extensively on the parties' briefs, with one judge saying, "the brief is the companion of the judge from before oral argument until after the rehearing is denied" (Martineau et al. 2005, 800). If there was any doubt that justices read the briefs, it could be dispelled by the finding that they often borrow large portions of text from them (Corley 2008; Black and Owens 2012*b*).

Because of the Court's norm against issue creation (Epstein, Segal, and Johnson 1996), the issues presented to the Court in the parties' briefs define the set of issues it will address in its ruling. The arguments attorneys present in their briefs can set the boundaries of the issues the Court will address. A poorly crafted brief can fail to address (or barely address) issues that might be important to the Court's determination. Along the same lines, the information contained in the briefs can help justices learn about the policy consequences of their decisions, the law involved in the case, and the preferences of actors with whom they must interact. The briefs may even help justices locate where their policy preferences are in a case.

Briefs are also important because they allow parties to frame the issues how they want – to present their arguments coherently and without interruption. Briefs allow parties to frame their arguments strategically. And brief writers usually understand their framing powers. For example, Wedeking (2010) shows that brief writers employ certain frames depending on context and lower court opinions. He also finds that strategic framing can lead to a heightened probability of success: "how litigants frame a case does affect the likelihood of receiving a favorable ideological decision even after accounting for other potential explanations" (Wedeking 2010, 627; see also Teply 1990; Sokol 1967). As Justice Scalia once stated, "Many advocates fail to appreciate that the outcome of a case rests on what the court understands to be the issue the case presents" – in other words, framing (Scalia and Garner 2008, 83).

Yet, despite the importance of briefs, scholars know little about whether the information contained in them can translate into litigant influence. Only a handful of studies briefly investigate this empirically and systematically. Corley (2008) uses plagiarism software to determine whether Supreme Court opinions rely on the language found in party briefs. (They do.) Epstein and Kobylka (1992) analyze the arguments parties and amici made in abortion and death penalty cases to determine whether their arguments led to success. (They did.) Wedeking (2010) examines whether attorneys use frames strategically to influence the dimension on which the High Court evaluates cases. (They do.)

While highly useful, none of these studies directly examine credibility and emotion. We believe that using highly emotional language in briefs can reduce an attorney's credibility and harm his or her case. Evidence supports this claim. Black, Hall, Owens, and Ringsmuth (2016) find that justices are significantly less likely to side with parties whose briefs contain extensive amounts of emotional language. As they put it:

> When the petitioner uses little emotional language in its brief (approximately the 10th percentile in our sample), a justice has a .61 [.58, .63] probability of voting for her. When, however, the petitioner uses significantly more emotional language – about the 90th percentile in our sample – that probability decreases to around .56 [.53, .58], a relative decrease of about 8%. (Black, Hall, Owens, and Ringsmuth 2016, 389–390)

The reason, as they saw it, was that increased emotional language "decreases an attorney's perceived credibility, a key component of persuasion" (397).

Some of the justices have made remarks that corroborate these results. Justice Scalia once stated:

> Appealing to judges' emotions is misguided because it fundamentally mistakes their motivation. Good judges pride themselves on the rationality of their rulings and the suppression of their personal proclivities, including most especially their emotions ... don't make an overt, passionate attempt to play upon the judicial heartstring. It can have a nasty backlash. (Scalia and Garner 2008, 32)

Other judges agree. One judge once remarked:

> When a lawyer resorts to a jury argument [i.e., emotional] on appeal, you can just see the judges sit back and give a big sigh of relief. We understand that you have to say all these things to keep your client happy, but we also understand that you know, and we know, and you know we know, that your case doesn't amount to a hill of beans, so we can go back there in the conference room and flush it with an unpublished disposition. (Scalia and Garner 2008, 32)

Taken together, these studies and comments suggest that attorneys who make emotional arguments to the Court will be perceived as less credible and will, therefore, be less likely to win their cases. Still, however, we do not expect the negative effects of emotion on credibility to be constant across all justices. Instead, we expect them to attach more profoundly to conscientious justices.

As we described in Chapter 2, conscientious people tend to be deliberate, self-disciplined, dutiful, and responsible. Conscientiousness is associated with the pursuit of excellence and a diligent effort to accomplish tasks in the most proper way. One important dimension of conscientiousness is a desire to maintain professionalism and proper decorum. As Roberts et al. (2014, 1315) claim, conscientiousness is "a spectrum of constructs that describe individual differences in the propensity to be self-controlled, responsible to others, hardworking, orderly, and rule abiding." Similarly, Buss (1992) finds that conscientious people are more likely to use reason – rather than emotion – to influence people in the context of marital relationships. Psychology research also indicates that people lacking in conscientiousness often exhibit careless behavior (McCrae and John 1992) and disinhibition (Krueger and Markon 2014).

Extending the principles of this research to decision making on the Supreme Court, conscientious justices should place a premium on the professionalism of briefs submitted by litigants. Since conscientious justices themselves value dutifulness and disciplined work, they should expect that attorneys appearing before them will exhibit those same qualities. That is, they should expect professionalism and sound legal argumentation. A legal presentation laced with emotion is likely to offend a conscientious justice's professional sensibilities and his or her respect for proper norms of behavior.

As Justice Scalia (among others) remarked, the use of emotion in briefs is "misguided" and may "have a nasty backlash" (Scalia and Garner 2008, 32). When litigants present such emotional language, their briefs should be less compelling and credible to the conscientious justice. This is not to say that other justices do not value professionalism or that they respond positively to emotional language. Indeed, Black, Hall, Owens, and Ringsmuth (2016) show how such an emotional presentation, on average, can inhibit a litigant's fortunes on the merits. Instead, we argue that the most conscientious justices on the Court levy the greatest penalty for emotional language, as they are the most likely to find it off-putting and unpersuasive.

In short, the credibility of arguments in legal briefs is central to their ability to persuade and affect how justices view a case. The use of emotional language should undermine a brief's credibility, especially among conscientious justices. Therefore, we expect that *a justice will be more likely to vote for a party whose brief uses less emotional language, and this effect will be more pronounced as a justice becomes more conscientious.*

5.3 A THEORY OF CONSCIENTIOUSNESS AND ORAL ARGUMENTS

The Honorable, the Chief Justice and Associate Justices of the Supreme Court of the United States. Oyez! Oyez! Oyez! All persons having business before the Honorable, the Supreme Court of the United States, are admonished to draw near and give their attention, for the Court is now sitting. God save the United States and this Honorable Court!

Those words from the Court Marshal begin each oral argument session of the High Court. The Chief Justice then bangs his gavel and calls to order the first case of the day. The petitioner's attorney approaches the Court's lectern. After raising or lowering the lectern to an appropriate height, the attorney begins, stating, "Mr. Chief Justice, and may it please the Court."

The attorneys each receive thirty minutes of oral argument time to make their case to the justices.[3] It is not uninterrupted time, however. In fact,

---

3   The Court occasionally allows an interested nonparty (an *amicus curiae,* or "friend of the Court") to share time with one of the parties. The Court may (and sometimes does) waive the

nothing could be further from the truth. During oral argument, justices regularly interrupt the attorneys with questions, comments, and hypothetical scenarios related to the case, a practice that makes it difficult for attorneys to make coherent and persuasive arguments.

Oral argument today serves at least three purposes. First, justices use oral argument to collect information about each other. Justice Kennedy once declared that, at oral argument, "the court is having a conversation with itself through the intermediary of the attorney" (qtd. in O'Brien 2005). As Greenhouse explains, "Court protocol does not permit justices to address one another directly from the bench, so, as often happens when justices want to do so anyway, the debate between the two [is] conducted through questions that each pose[s]" (Greenhouse 1989). Black, Johnson, and Wedeking (2012, 15) find that Justice Powell recorded notes of his colleagues' questions at oral argument "to listen to those with whom he may join a coalition."

Second, oral argument enhances the Court's legitimacy in the eyes of the public and the attorneys who appear before the justices. This is the case because the only time the public actually observes the Court conducting its work is when justices are on the bench, either at oral argument or when they announce opinions from the bench. What the public witnesses during oral argument – chiefly, legal symbols – tends to enhance the Court's legitimacy. As Gibson and Caldeira (2009) explain, the public generally holds a "positivity bias" toward the Court, rooted in perceptions of judicial symbols and impartiality that motivate the vast majority of citizens to confer legitimacy on the Court's decisions – even those with which they might initially disagree (see also Gibson, Caldeira, and Baird 1998; Ura 2014). These symbols include the black judicial robes, the high back chairs elevated on a pedestal on which the justices sit, and the "marble palace" itself. They lead citizens to think of the Supreme Court as different than other institutions (Gibson and Caldeira 2011).

Third, and most important for our purposes here, oral argument allows attorneys to make or refine their cases. Despite the fact that justices interrupt the attorneys regularly, those attorneys still can use oral argument to make their case. And many do. Indeed, some of what they tell justices at oral argument are new topics not addressed in their briefs. For example, Johnson (2004) finds that oral argument allows justices to obtain unique information about

thirty minutes per side rule in highly salient or important cases. For example, oral argument in *Bush* v. *Gore* lasted an hour and a half. The Affordable Care Act cases lasted six and a half hours over three days.

policy and about the preferences of external actors. More specifically, justices often use oral argument to find out how the political branches could respond to certain Court rulings. As Johnson shows, 80 percent of the issues raised in justices' questions appear for the first time at oral argument; that is, the particular issue did not appear in the attorneys' briefs. And 33 percent of the issues raised uniquely at oral argument make it into the Court's final opinions (Johnson 2004).

Johnson, Wahlbeck, and Spriggs (2006) find that attorneys who provide a stronger oral argument are more likely to win their cases. Justices, of course, are more likely to side with the attorney making an argument consistent with the justices' preferences. But a strong legal argument mitigates the negative effects of ideological distance. That is, even justices disposed to dislike an argument are more likely to side with it if it comes on the heels of a strong oral argument performance.

Our question, derived from these findings, is whether conscientious justices are more susceptible to strong legal arguments than less conscientious justices.

The relationship between conscientiousness and job performance is especially relevant to the persuasive impact of an attorney's performance during oral argument. As Witt et al. (2002, 164) argue, "Workers high in conscientiousness are predisposed to be organized, exacting, disciplined, diligent, dependable, methodical, and purposeful ... [and] they are more likely than low-conscientiousness workers to thoroughly and correctly perform work tasks." What is more, increased conscientiousness correlates with better job performance among a wide variety of workplace settings (Barrick and Mount 1991; Barrick, Mount, and Judge 2001). This is the case because high-conscientiousness people, generally, are the most dependable, orderly, self-disciplined, and hardworking individuals.

In the context of oral argument on the US Supreme Court, one might expect a conscientious justice to be especially receptive to a skilled presentation – or, critical of an inept performance – during oral argument. Experienced, skillful attorneys experience greater success on the merits (McGuire 1993, 1995), and this result can be at least partly attributed to performance during oral argument (Johnson, Wahlbeck, and Spriggs 2006). But these effects likely vary across justices, and for reasons that include personality. We expect that although justices on average may be persuaded by a compelling oral argument, the most conscientious justices on the Court should be the most discerning. Their propensity for organized, thorough, and meticulous work should inform their expectations of others' work. And, in the crucible of a Supreme Court oral argument, these same personal qualities that resonate with a conscientious justice should also be those that make for a skilled oral presentation. Put simply, conscientious justices should demand – and reward – a thorough, skilled presentation from attorneys appearing before the Court. Thus, we hypothesize that *increasingly conscientious justices are more receptive to strong oral arguments than less conscientious justices.*

5.4 DATA AND MEASURES

We approach these questions by undertaking two separate analyses. The first focuses on brief writing and the second on performance during oral argument.

5.4.1 *Persuasion and Briefs*

To test our hypothesis, we replicate the work of Black, Hall, Owens, and Ringsmuth (2016). But unlike them, we include measures of justices' conscientiousness. We analyze how each justice voted in 1,677 orally argued cases decided during the Court's 1984–2007 terms.[4] Our unit of analysis is the justice vote in each case.

Dependent Variable. The dependent variable, *Vote for Petitioner*, measures whether each justice voted for the petitioner (=1) or the respondent (=0). Black, Hall, Owens, and Ringsmuth (2016) find that justices are more likely to vote for the party whose brief employs less emotional language. We argue that this effect will be magnified among the most conscientious justices.

Conscientiousness. As our primary independent variable, we focus on each justice's conscientiousness (described in Chapter 3). Larger values correspond to greater conscientiousness. We also control for justices' scores on the four other personality trait dimensions – *Openness*, *Extraversion*, *Agreeableness*, and *Neuroticism*.

Emotional Language in Briefs. To examine the emotional language of briefs, Black, Hall, Owens, and Ringsmuth (2016) employed the software program "Linguistic Inquiry and Word Count" (LIWC; Pennebaker and King 1999). LIWC uses a number of dictionary-based word lists, read and created by human coders, to classify the content of text. LIWC analyzes "attentional focus, emotionality, social relationships, thinking styles" and other things associated with language and language use (Tausczik and Pennebaker 2010, 24).

---

4 Black, Hall, Owens, and Ringsmuth (2016) examine only cases with a single initial merits brief submitted by each party. They also examine only the parties' initial merits briefs. This approach yields 85 percent of all the cases decided during those terms.

To put it in more concrete terms, LIWC scans through text, looking for words or word stems; after scanning the text, LIWC counts the number and percent of words from various categories.

Petitioner Brief Emotion and *Respondent Brief Emotion.* Black, Hall, Owens, and Ringsmuth (2016) focused on LIWC's "affective language" category. These are words like "discourage," "considerate," "charming," and "sad." They downloaded all the parties' briefs and examined them using LIWC. They retrieved the percent of emotional words in the argument section of each party's brief. *Petitioner Brief Emotion* and *Respondent Brief Emotion* measure the percent of affective language words contained in the petitioner's and respondent's brief on the merits, respectively.

Brief Emotion × *Conscientiousness.* Because we are interested in the interactive effect between brief emotions and conscientiousness, we create two interaction terms – *Petitioner Brief Emotion* × *Conscientiousness* and *Respondent Brief Emotion* × *Conscientiousness.*

Dissent Noted in Lower Court. To control for the quality of the case – and the fact that justices might vote for the side with the better quality case, regardless of emotional briefs – Black, Hall, Owens, and Ringsmuth (2016) created *Dissent Noted in Lower Court*, which takes on a value of 1 if the Supreme Court opinion noted the presence of a dissenting opinion in the lower court; 0 otherwise. The logic here is that because the cost of dissent is fairly high in the circuit courts (because of a high workload and concomitant collegiality concerns), the presence of a dissent likely signals that the petitioner has a strong case.

Petitioner Legal Authority and *Respondent Legal Authority.* In another attempt to control for case quality, Black, Hall, Owens, and Ringsmuth (2016) included variables called *Petitioner Legal Authority* and *Respondent Legal Authority.* This variable broadly examines the legal authority in the litigants' briefs. The more legal authority a side has, the stronger, on average, its case should be. Looking at the Tables of Authorities in each party's briefs, they identified the total number of unique authorities listed in the Table of Authorities for all briefs in that side (including any amicus briefs). They then computed the natural logarithm of these totals. *Petitioner Legal Authority* and *Respondent Legal Authority* measure these values for each side.

SG Petitioner and *SG Respondent.* Black, Hall, Owens, and Ringsmuth (2016) included variables to measure whether the United States, represented by the Solicitor General, was the petitioner or respondent in the case. Since the SG wins so much more often than other parties, they wanted to make sure any effects they discovered from briefs were not a function of the high quality representation delivered by the SG. If the SG was the petitioner (or respondent), the variable takes on a value 1; 0 otherwise.[5]

SG Amicus for Petitioner and *SG Amicus for Respondent*. For similar reasons, the authors controlled for instances in which the SG filed an amicus brief for the parties. If the SG filed an amicus brief for the petitioner (or respondent), the variable takes on a value 1; 0 otherwise.

Petitioner Status and *Respondent Status* reflect the resources of each party in a case. Scholarship suggests that parties' resource advantages might influence the Court's decisions (Black and Boyd 2012a; Black et al. 2011). Black, Hall, Owens, and Ringsmuth (2016) follow the coding scheme of Collins (2004, 2007) and use the Supreme Court Database party codes to determine which status category each party fell into: poor individuals, minorities, individuals, unions or interest groups, small businesses, businesses, corporations, local governments, state governments, and the US government. The weakest category (poor individuals) is coded 1, whereas the strong category (the U.S. government) is coded 10.

Petitioner Experience and *Respondent Experience*. These variables account for the total number of oral arguments each attorney engaged in prior to the case under consideration (McGuire 1995). To account for the non-linear nature of oral argument experience, Black, Hall, Owens, and Ringsmuth (2016) calculated the natural logarithm of (one plus) each attorney's past oral argument experience.

Questions for Petitioner and *Questions for Respondent* reflect the number of questions asked of each party during oral arguments. These variables seek to control for the fact that the attorney who receives more oral argument questions tends to lose (e.g., Johnson et al. 2009; Black et al. 2011).

Petitioner Amicus Support and *Respondent Amicus Support* measure the number of amicus briefs for each side in each case. These variables are included because evidence suggests that amicus briefs can help a party win (Collins 2008).

Brief Readability. Black, Hall, Owens, and Ringsmuth (2016) control for the readability of the briefs, as readability is linked to clarity and persuasion. To code for readability, they measure the Coleman-Liau Index for each merits brief. The Coleman-Liau Index examines the length of words and sentence length. Texts with longer words and sentences will have higher values, which indicate *less* readability.

---

5   The results are consistent with those reported below when dropping the SG party predictors and, instead, relying solely on the petitioner and respondent status variables to capture differences across litigant type.

Lower Court Decision Liberal × *Justice Ideology*. Black, Hall, Owens, and Ringsmuth (2016) control for the ideological congruence between the justice and the party's position. To measure *Justice Ideology*, they identified the justice's Segal-Cover score, which is the perceived liberalism of a justice at the time of his or her nomination (Segal and Cover 1989). The variable ranges from 0 (most conservative) to 1 (most liberal). They then code *Lower Court Decision Liberal* as 1 if the Supreme Court Database codes the lower court decision as liberal and 0 if conservative. They then multiply these two variables to create the interactive term.

5.4.2 *Persuasion and Oral Argument*

We seek to replicate the findings of Johnson, Wahlbeck, and Spriggs (2006) while examining the effects of conscientiousness. We discuss how they coded their variables as follows.

Dependent Variable. The dependent variable, *Justice Reverse*, examines whether each justice voted to reverse the lower court's decision. We code votes to reverse as 1 and votes to affirm as 0.

Conscientiousness. As our primary independent variable, we focus on each justice's conscientiousness (described in Chapter 3). Larger values correspond to more conscientiousness. We also control for justices' scores on the four other personality trait dimensions – *Openness, Extraversion, Agreeableness,* and *Neuroticism*.

Oral Argument Grade. Johnson, Wahlbeck, and Spriggs (2006) combed through Justice Blackmun's personal papers and discovered that he graded each attorney who appeared before him at oral argument. They were able to use those grades as proxies for the strength of the argument presented to the Court. They then took the grades of the attorneys, arguing each case, and subtracted the appellee's grade from the appellant's grade. Larger values of the variable reflect that the appellant presented a stronger oral argument than the appellee.

Conscientiousness × *Oral Argument Grade.* Because we are interested in the interactive effect of conscientiousness and strength of oral argument, we create an interaction term – *Conscientiousness* × *Oral Argument Grade.*

Ideological Compatibility with Appellant. Johnson, Wahlbeck, and Spriggs (2006) next created a variable that examined the ideological distance between each justice and the attorney making his or her case. To do so, they started by gathering Martin-Quinn scores for each justice (Martin and Quinn 2002). They then determined the ideological outcome sought by the petitioner and the respondent. If the lower court decision was liberal, they assumed the petitioner sought a conservative outcome while the respondent sought a liberal outcome. If an attorney argued for the liberal side, they coded the variable as the negative value of the justice's Martin-Quinn score. If the attorney argued for the conservative position, they coded the variable as the justice's Martin-Quinn score. This means that larger values reflect that a justice is ideologically closer to the attorney's position.

Ideological Compatibility × *Oral Argument Grade.* Johnson, Wahlbeck, and Spriggs (2006) then interact these two variables to examine how the strength of the attorney's oral argument interact with ideological compatibility.

Case Complexity. To measure the complexity of a case, Johnson, Wahlbeck, and Spriggs (2006) used a factor analysis that included the number of legal provisions in a case and the number of issues involved in the case.

Oral Argument Grade × *Case Complexity.* Johnson, Wahlbeck, and Spriggs (2006) then interacted case complexity with the attorney's oral argument grade to determine whether justices consider stronger oral arguments in more complex cases.

U.S. Appellant or *Appellee.* These variables code whether the United States was either the appellant or the appellee in the case, but were not represented by the Solicitor General or Assistant Solicitor General. If the US was the appellant, *US Appellant* is coded as 1; 0 otherwise. If the US was the appellee, we code *US Appellee* as 1; 0 otherwise.

SG Appellant or *Appellee.* These variables code whether the Solicitor General's office argued the case. If the SG argued as the appellant, *SG Appellant* is coded as 1; 0 otherwise. If the SG argued as the appellee, we code *SG Appellee* is 1; 0 otherwise.

Washington Elite Appellant or *Appellee.* These variables reflect whether the arguing attorney's firm was located in Washington, DC. (It excludes federal government attorneys.) If so, the variables are coded 1; 0 otherwise.

Law Professor Appellant or *Appellee.* These variables examine whether the arguing attorney was a professor at a law school. If so, they are coded as 1; 0 otherwise.

Former Court Clerk Appellant or *Appellee.* These variables represent whether the attorneys who argued were former Supreme Court clerks. Former clerks are coded as 1; nonclerks are coded as 0.

Elite Law School Appellant or *Appellee.* These data come from Lexis/Nexis, Westlaw, or the Martindale Hubbell directory (the issue published during the year the case was argued). Attorneys who attended one of the elite law schools (Harvard, Yale, Columbia, Stanford, Chicago, Berkeley, Michigan, and Northwestern) are coded 1, whereas all other attorneys are coded as 0.

Difference in Litigating Experience. Using McGuire's (1993) definition of experience, we coded the number of times an attorney previously appeared before the US Supreme Court at oral arguments. We gathered these data through searches on Lexis/Nexis for each attorney's name to determine past cases in which they appeared in this capacity. A case was only counted if the attorney in the case was listed as having been the attorney to argue orally (being on a brief does not count for this purpose).

5.5 METHODS AND RESULTS

5.5.1 *Briefs*

We begin with our analysis of briefs. Because our dependent variable is dichotomous, we estimate a logistic regression model. We employ robust standard errors clustered on each justice. Table 11 shows parameter estimates for both a smaller model that includes only our primary variables of interest (i.e., Model 1), as well as a full model that includes the full suite of controls included by Black et al.[6] As our underlying argument is conditional, however, we turn to simulations and graphical representations of our results to understand how conscientiousness affects the impact of briefs.

Figure 21 examines the probability a justice votes for the petitioner (the y-axis) as a function of the emotional content in the brief, for both low- and high-conscientious justices. Consider the panel on the left, which displays the effect of emotional language in the petitioner's briefs on the probability a justice votes for the petitioner. The results from Black, Hall, Owens, and Ringsmuth (2016) suggest that as the emotional language in petitioner's brief increases, the probability a justice votes for the petitioner will decrease. Our expectation, however, is that the conscientious justices drive these results.

The analyses concur. When the petitioner employs next to no emotional language in its brief, conscientious justices have nearly a 0.69 probability of voting for the petitioner. But when the petitioner employs a large amount of emotional language, near the sample maximum of 9 percent, that probability drops substantially, down to nearly 0.35. What once had been a strong case

---

[6]   The empirical results are consistent when specifying a baseline model that includes only the interaction between conscientiousness and brief emotion (and no other personality trait indicators or control predictors).

TABLE 11: *Personality Traits, Litigant Brief Content, and Supreme Court Voting*

	(1)	(2)
Petitioner Brief Emotion	−0.080*	−0.121*
	(0.031)	(0.032)
Justice Conscientiousness	0.065	0.041
	(0.083)	(0.088)
Petitioner Brief Emotion × Justice Conscientiousness	−0.057*	−0.080*
	(0.032)	(0.033)
Respondent Brief Emotion	0.132*	0.157*
	(0.032)	(0.033)
Respondent Brief Emotion × Justice Conscientiousness	0.039	0.070*
	(0.033)	(0.035)
Justice Openness	−0.038*	−0.048*
	(0.016)	(0.018)
Justice Extraversion	0.032	0.045
	(0.027)	(0.030)
Justice Agreeableness	−0.024	−0.021
	(0.020)	(0.022)
Justice Neuroticism	0.009	−0.033
	(0.025)	(0.029)
Dissent Noted in Lower Court		0.119*
		(0.042)
Petitioner Legal Authority		0.209*
		(0.034)
Respondent Legal Authority		−0.121*
		(0.033)
US Petitioner		0.272*
		(0.075)
US Respondent		−0.520*
		(0.073)
US Amicus for Petitioner		0.769*
		(0.055)
US Amicus for Respondent		−0.885*
		(0.063)
Petitioner Status		0.026*
		(0.011)
Respondent Status		−0.002
		(0.010)

(continued)

TABLE 11: (*continued*)

	(1)	(2)
Petitioner Experience		0.053*
		(0.018)
Respondent Experience		−0.009
		(0.020)
Questions for Petitioner		−0.020*
		(0.001)
Questions for Respondent		0.020*
		(0.001)
Petitioner Amicus Support		0.029*
		(0.009)
Respondent Amicus Support		−0.033*
		(0.008)
Petitioner Brief Readability		−0.037*
		(0.013)
Respondent Brief Readability		−0.004
		(0.013)
Lower Court Decision Liberal		0.908*
		(0.064)
Justice Ideology		1.299*
		(0.114)
Lower Liberal × Justice Ideology		−3.242*
		(0.139)
Constant	0.156*	0.371
	(0.080)	(0.370)
N	14,888	14,888
χ^2	33.93*	1815.48*

Note: Table entries are coefficients from a logistic regression model. Model 2 replicates Table 1 of Black, Hall, Owens, and Ringsmuth (2016, 389) with the addition of our justice personality trait measures. *$p < 0.05$ (one-tailed).

for petitioners, and a likely win, has become a likely loss of that vote among conscientious justices.

The inverse applies to respondents. When the respondent employs next to no emotional language in its brief, conscientious justices have nearly a 0.46 of voting for the petitioner. This is telling, since the Court on average votes to

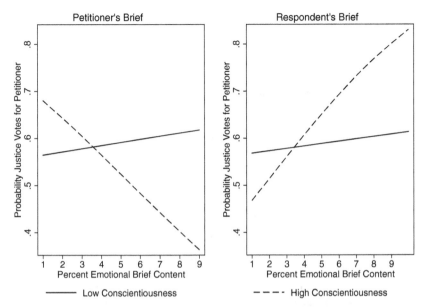

FIGURE 21: *Predicted probability a justice votes for the petitioner, conditional on the emotive content of a brief (x-axis) and a justice's conscientiousness (line type).* The left panel shows the effect of emotional content in the petitioner's brief and the right panel shows the respondent's brief. All other variables are held at their median values. We used the `margins` command in Stata 15.1 to generate these estimates. See Table 11 for a table with parameter estimates for the underlying model.

reverse about 60 percent of the time. When the respondent employs a large amount of emotional language, the probability of voting for the petitioner skyrockets to roughly 0.85. Respondents have a tough time before the reverse-minded Court, but increasing the amount of emotional language they use in their briefs is the death knell – at least in terms of acquiring the votes of conscientious justices.

As we anticipated, low conscientious justices are not influenced by emotional language in briefs. Figure 22 provides further information on this. It shows the marginal effect of a one unit increase in emotional brief content on justices. That is, for each justice-conscientiousness value, we increase the emotional language value one unit and determine the effects that has on the probability the justice votes for the petitioner. The different symbols and shaded confidence intervals distinguish between emotional content in the petitioner's brief (solid line) versus the respondent's brief (dashed line). As we can see, among low conscientious justices, increasing the amount of

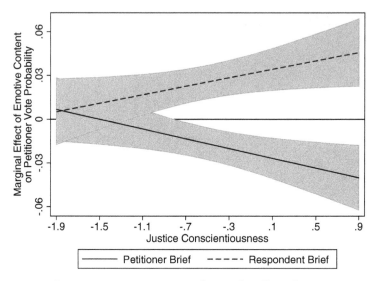

FIGURE 22: *Justice conscientiousness conditions the effect of emotive content in both the petitioner's and the respondent's briefs.* The x-axis shows the range of our conscientiousness variable. The y-axis shows the marginal effect of a one-unit increase in brief emotive content on the probability a justice votes for the petitioner. All other variables are held at their median values. We used the margins command in Stata 15.1 to generate these estimates. See Table 11 for a table with parameter estimates for the underlying model.

emotional language in the briefs does little. Here, the marginal effects for both petitioner and respondent are small and the confidences intervals for the effect easily contain zero – which is to say, no significant effect exists. Substantively, this means that when either litigant's brief contains additional emotional content, a nonconscientious justice is no more or less likely to give that litigant his or her vote.

As we begin to look at increasingly conscientious justices, things change dramatically. A couple of things happen as justices become more conscientious. First, the marginal effects separate depending on whether we examine the impact of the petitioner's brief or the respondent's brief. In particular, the addition of more emotive content in the petitioner's brief results in a decrease in the likelihood that a justice will vote for the petitioner (i.e., the solid line is in the negative zone). This is the result that Black, Hall, Owens, and Ringsmuth (2016) obtain in their original study. Also, there is the complementary effect for the presence of more emotional writing in the respondent's brief; the respondent is less likely to win, which means the petitioner's probability goes up (i.e., the dashed line is in the positive zone). And, if one examines the shaded regions that accompanies each line, one observes that the region no longer includes zero in the confidence area, which means the effect is statistically significant.

Justices are not, of course, uniformly distributed across the range of conscientiousness. The original Black, Hall, Owens, and Ringsmuth (2016) data cover nearly 15,000 justice votes cast across nearly a quarter century of Supreme Court decision-making. In terms of being blind to a petitioner's emotional appeals, fully 35 percent of the observations in the data are associated with a justice who falls in the null region identified above. As for respondents who appeal to emotional content, 19 percent of our observations are in that null region. Thus, although many justices continue to penalize litigants who appeal to emotional content, it is not a constant on the Court, but rather, an aspect that is conditioned by a justice's conscientiousness.

Taken together, these findings show that emotional content does indeed establish a lack of credibility among attorneys, an effect that reduces their likelihood of success, but only among highly conscientious justices.

As for the other personality traits included in our model, we find no relationship between a justice's propensity to reverse the lower court decision and her agreeableness, neuroticism, or extraversion. The coefficient on our openness variable is negative and statistically significant, suggesting that justices scoring higher on the openness trait are less likely to reverse a lower court. The other controls perform as expected.

5.5.2 *Oral Argument*

We turn now to oral argument strength discussion. We argued that attorneys who made stronger legal arguments would be more likely to win justices' votes, and that that effect would be heightened among conscientious justices. Because our dependent variable is dichotomous (whether the justice votes for the petitioner), we employ a logistic regression model with standard errors clustered on the case.

As Table 12 shows, the results confirm our expectations.[7] Figure 23 examines the predicted probability a justice votes for the petitioner (y-axis) as the petitioner's attorney increasingly outperforms the respondents' attorney. (Recall that the variable is coded as petitioner grade – respondent grade.

---

7 The empirical results are consistent when specifying a baseline model that includes only the interaction between conscientiousness and oral argument grade.

When the respondent made a stronger argument, the value on the covariate is negative; when the petitioner made a stronger argument, the value on the covariate is positive.) For a highly conscientious justice, the probability of voting for the petitioner when the respondent made a manifestly better argument is 0.30. This is striking because, again, the Court reverses in roughly 60% of its cases. As the petitioner's argument improves, and becomes manifestly better than the respondent's, the probability a justice votes for the petitioner skyrockets to nearly 0.80. Among low conscientious justices, however, nearly the opposite is evident.

TABLE 12: *Personality Traits, Oral Argument Performance, and Supreme Court Voting*

	(1)	(2)
Ideological Compatibility	0.294[*]	0.309[*]
	(0.036)	(0.038)
Case Complexity	0.066	0.078
	(0.061)	(0.072)
Oral Argument Grade	0.274[*]	0.209[*]
	(0.045)	(0.047)
Conscientiousness	0.037	0.036
	(0.067)	(0.066)
Openness	0.030	0.032
	(0.036)	(0.036)
Extraversion	−0.040	−0.037
	(0.025)	(0.027)
Agreeableness	0.100[*]	0.095[*]
	(0.034)	(0.034)
Neuroticism	0.172[*]	0.162[*]
	(0.057)	(0.058)
Conscientiousness × Oral Argument Grade	0.082	0.083
	(0.054)	(0.059)
Ideological Compatibility × Oral Argument Grade		0.018
		(0.013)
Case Complexity × Oral Argument Grade		−0.079
		(0.099)
US Petitioner		0.463[*]
		(0.100)
US Respondent		−0.797[*]
		(0.098)
		(*continued*)

TABLE 12: (*continued*)

	(1)	(2)
SG Petitioner		0.334*
		(0.104)
SG Respondent		−0.204
		(0.134)
Washington Elite Petitioner		0.398*
		(0.103)
Washington Elite Respondent		0.073
		(0.141)
Law Professor Petitioner		−0.749*
		(0.171)
Law Professor Respondent		−1.565*
		(0.200)
Former Law Clerk Petitioner		−0.234*
		(0.096)
Former Law Clerk Respondent		−0.165
		(0.197)
Elite Law School Petitioner		0.023
		(0.112)
Elite Law School Respondent		−0.128
		(0.082)
Difference in Litigating Experience		−0.127*
		(0.014)
Constant	0.191*	0.247*
	(0.067)	(0.068)
Observations	3331	3331
Pseudo-R^2	0.098	0.124

Note: Table entries are coefficients from logit regression models with clustered standard errors (on the case) in parentheses. This table replicates Table 3 of Johnson, Wahlbeck, and Spriggs (2006, 109) with the addition of our justice personality trait measures. *$p < 0.05$ (one-tailed).

Figure 24 speaks to a slightly different question: How does a justice's conscientiousness condition the impact of an attorney's oral argument performance? The x-axis shows a justice's conscientiousness. The plot portrays the effect of a one-unit increase in the petitioner's oral argument performance on the probability that a justice votes for the petitioner. (When the shaded gray area cross the dashed horizontal line, the data suggest that a better performance

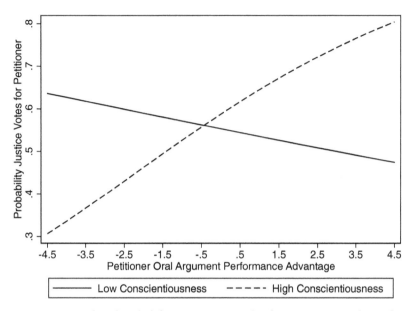

FIGURE 23: *Predicted probability a justice votes for the petitioner, conditional on the petitioner's oral argument performance advantage (x-axis) and the voting justice's conscientiousness (different line type).* All other variables are held at their median values. We used the `margins` command in Stata 15.1 to generate these estimates. See Table 12 (column 2) for a table with parameter estimates for the underlying model.

does not translate into a higher likelihood of winning.) The effect of having the better argument does not appear to correlate with the voting behavior of justices low in conscientiousness. This is true, all told, for fully 405 of the 3,331 observations in the Johnson et al. data (about 12 percent). What can easily be seen is that for justices low in conscientiousness, it does not matter whether the petitioner or respondent makes the stronger oral argument. When, however, we examine justices who are more conscientious, we find a statistically significant and substantively strong positive effect for argument quality. These conscientious justices are significantly more likely to vote for the petitioner when he or she makes the stronger argument.

Turning our attention, ever so briefly, to the other four traits, we find that more agreeable and neurotic justices are more likely to reverse the lower court decision. Extraversion and openness, by contrast, appear to be uncorrelated with reversal. The remaining controls perform as expected.

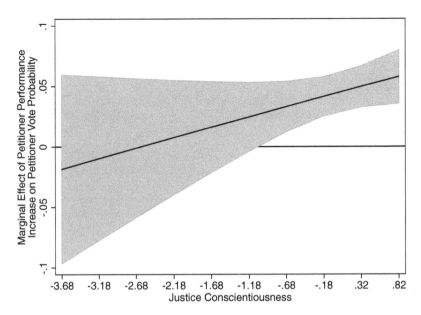

FIGURE 24: *Marginal effect of a one-unit increase in petitioner oral argument performance advantage on the likelihood a justice votes for the petitioner, conditional on the voting justice's conscientiousness.* Shaded region identifies the 95 percent confidence interval. All other variables are held at their median values. We used the margins command in Stata 15.1 to generate these estimates. See Table 12 (column 2) for a table with parameter estimates for the underlying model.

5.6 CONCLUSION

In this chapter, we considered whether conscientiousness influences the persuasive impact of briefs and oral argument on justices' merits decisions. The results uncover substantial effects for conscientiousness among justices on the Court. Conscientious justices are more likely than other justices to penalize a litigant for using emotional language in a written brief. What is more, they are also more likely to reward attorneys who perform skillfully and effectively at oral argument. Taken together, these two results support the general idea that legal persuasion is partly tied to justices' conscientiousness, and they contribute to literatures on the impact of briefs and oral argument on the Court.

These results also enable us to take one additional step toward supporting our larger claim about the importance of conscientiousness on the Supreme Court. Importantly, they speak to the role of personality during the process through which the Court adjudicates disputes. And they highlight how taking account of personality is essential to understand how briefs and oral argument can shape final outcomes on the merits. To this point, we have shown that a justice's conscientiousness exhibits a meaningful impact on his or her agenda-setting votes and the impact of litigant briefs and oral argument. Next, we move to another empirical application of our larger argument – the impact of a justice's conscientiousness on his or her support for the US Solicitor General.

6

Conscientiousness and the US Solicitor General

Local 144 Nursing Home Pension Fund v. *Demisay* (1993) is not a Supreme Court decision most people have heard of.[1] And with good reason. It's a statutory interpretation case that involved pension funds, the Labor Management Relations Act, and the Employee Retirement Income Security Act of 1974. An employer switched pension plans for its union employees. The question in the case was whether the old pension plan could be required to transfer previous employee savings to the new pension plan. It's not the kind of case that receives attention. Indeed, reading the Court's opinion tests a person's ability to stay awake in the face of sleepy obstacles.

But underneath that collection of yawns was an interesting exchange on the Court. Despite the fact that the pool memo writer discovered little conflict among the circuits – something the justices look for when granting review to cases – and therefore recommended the Court deny review, the Court voted to call for the views of the Solicitor General (CVSG). The justices wanted to know the SG's thoughts before they decided whether to hear the case. The Solicitor General recommended the Court grant review, noting that there was a growing conflict among the circuits and that the case was important. The Court then granted review.

Interestingly, some justices changed their votes after receiving the SG's brief. As Figure 25 shows, Justices White and Kennedy both voted to deny review in the Court's December 9th conference. Yet, after receiving the SG's brief, they changed their votes to grant and Join-3, respectively. On the other hand, Justice Stevens voted to deny review at both conferences. Justice Blackmun, too, refused to follow the SG's recommendation (after having voted to CVSG). Blackmun's clerk told the justice: "There's no real split ... This is just another anti-labor stance of the SG."

---

[1] See *Local 144 Nursing Home Pension Fund* v. *Demisay*, 508 U.S. 581 (1993).

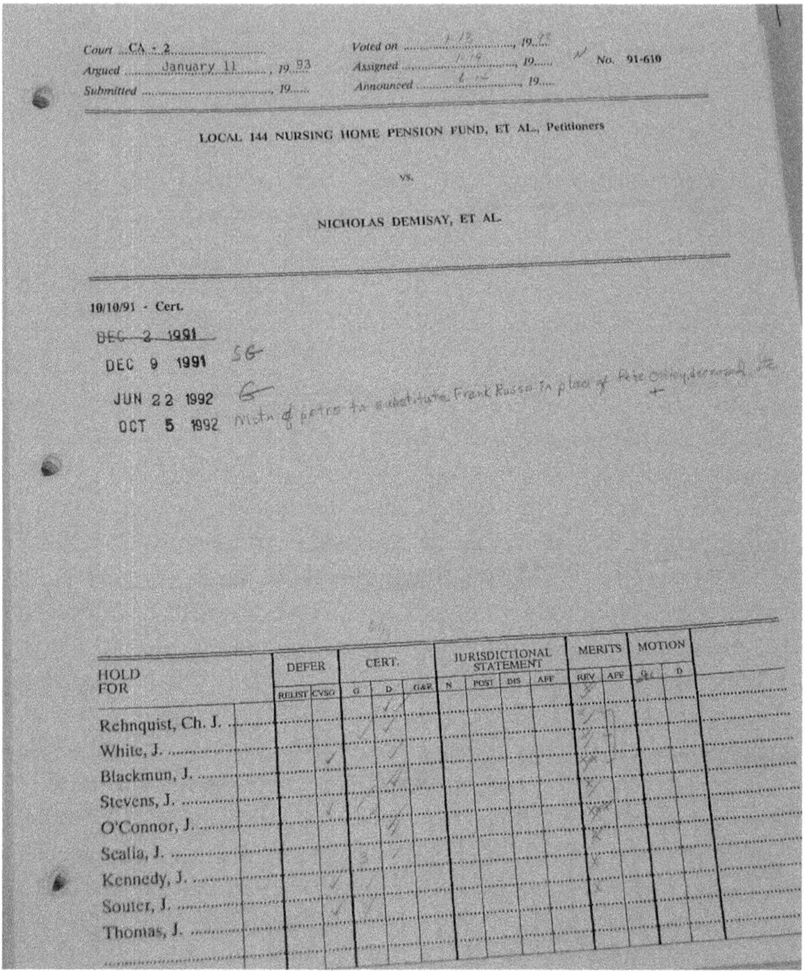

Court CA - 2 Voted on ..., 19.. No. 91-610
Argued January 11, 19 93 Assigned ..., 19...
Submitted ..., 19... Announced ..., 19...

LOCAL 144 NURSING HOME PENSION FUND, ET AL., Petitioners

vs.

NICHOLAS DEMISAY, ET AL.

10/10/91 - Cert.
~~DEC 2 1991~~
DEC 9 1991 SG
JUN 22 1992 G
OCT 5 1992 Motn of petrs to substitute Frank Russo in place of ...

HOLD FOR	DEFER RELIST	DEFER CVSG	CERT. G	CERT. D	CERT. G&R	JURISDICTIONAL STATEMENT N	POST	DIS	AFF	MERITS REV	MERITS AFF	MOTION G	MOTION D
Rehnquist, Ch. J.													
White, J.													
Blackmun, J.													
Stevens, J.													
O'Connor, J.													
Scalia, J.													
Kennedy, J.													
Souter, J.													
Thomas, J.													

FIGURE 25: *Docket sheet in Local 144 Nursing Home Pension Fund v. Demisay (91–610).*

Is it coincidence that Kennedy and White – who are among the most conscientious justices in our sample – switched positions in line with the SG? Conversely, is it coincidence that Justices Stevens and Blackmun – two of the less conscientious justices in our sample – refused the SG's suggestion? We think not.

In this chapter, we examine whether conscientiousness leads justices to support the US Solicitor General (and attorneys from that office). Personality scholarship shows that conscientious people are more dutiful and deliberate.

We therefore expect conscientious justices to rely more extensively on attorneys who are, themselves, more dutiful and deliberate. The results concur. Justices who are more conscientious are more likely to support the SG's position both at the merits stage and at the agenda stage. These results show yet again that conscientiousness strongly influences judicial decision-making.

6.1 THE ROLE OF THE SOLICITOR GENERAL

The Office of the Solicitor General (OSG) serves two important roles today (Black and Owens 2011*b*). First, it coordinates the United States's appellate strategy. The SG determines which cases the government will appeal to the Supreme Court. That is, the government appeals cases to the Supreme Court only when the Solicitor General agrees to do so.[2] Along the same lines, the SG determines whether the government will file an amicus curiae brief in the Supreme Court. An amicus curiae brief is a brief filed by a person or entity, not a party to the dispute, but who has an interest in its outcome (Owens and Epstein 2005). If the government is not involved in a case, the SG can inform the Court of its views.[3] When the government files an amicus brief with the Court, it is able to present its views on a case – and the broader policy consequences of a decision in the Court – despite the fact that it is not a named party in the suit. For the government to engage the Court in either capacity, the SG must first give his or her consent.

By controlling which cases the government will take to the Court (and thereby wield negative agenda control), the SG can set policy. The SG pursues cases with legal issues he or she wants the Court to expand or contract. He or she can try to push the Court to develop law in certain areas and try to prevent it from developing law in others. And the SG can favor some agencies over others. Consider the following statement by former Solicitor General Rex Lee, who said: "If we've got the [FCC] on one side of an issue and the Commerce Department on the other, and I decide that the government's over-all [*sic*] interest is better served by the F.C.C. …that means we'll take the F.C.C.'s position to the Supreme Court and the Commerce Department won't go there at all" (*quoted in* Jenkins 1983, 737). By controlling and coordinating the government's access to the Court, the SG can allow only the "right" cases to proceed to review.

---

[2] Occasionally, the SG will allow independent agencies to argue their own cases and/or pursue appeals without the SG's express permission (Chamberlain 1987).
[3] See Supreme Court Rule 37.

The OSG's second role is to provide the United States with quality legal representation in the Supreme Court. When the SG is involved with a case at the Court, the entire office works together to support the government's position. OSG staff attorneys consult with attorneys from the agencies and divisions of the Department of Justice who were originally involved in the case (Salokar 1992, 63). After discussing the case with them, the OSG staff attorneys conduct legal research and craft the brief. They then work with the Deputy Solicitor General who specializes in the issue involved in the case. The Deputy edits the brief and then sends it to the Solicitor General (Chamberlain 1987, 382). The SG then reads, reviews, and revises the brief before submitting it to the Court (Cooper 1990). If the Court grants review to the case, the OSG attorneys present capable oral arguments to justices (Johnson, Spriggs, and Wahlbeck 2007). Everything that comes out of the OSG has been vetted by three layers of lawyers, with all lawyers bringing their own expertise to bear on the legal dispute.

Perhaps not surprisingly, the Court often sides with the OSG. Consider the OSG's success at the agenda stage. The Supreme Court is more likely to grant review to OSG petitions – and petitions the office supports – than any other petition (Black and Owens 2009a; Caldeira and Wright 1988; Provine 1980). The Court votes to review between 75 percent to 90 percent of the SG's cert petitions, a standard that no other regular party or law firm comes close to matching (Perry 1991). Indeed, Caplan (1987) points out that while the Court grants review to roughly 80 percent of SG cert petitions, it grants review to a mere 3 percent of those filed by other lawyers (see also Jenkins 1983; Scigliano 1971).

The OSG is also highly successful at the merits stage (Epstein, Segal, Spaeth, and Walker 2007). Black and Owens (2011b) find that the OSG can influence justices to vote in ways other lawyers cannot.[4] When comparing an OSG lawyer to a lawyer who never worked in the OSG (but who otherwise is nearly identical to the OSG lawyer and who argues a nearly identical case), the authors find that the OSG lawyer enjoys a significantly higher probability of winning. Additionally, when comparing an OSG lawyer to an otherwise identical lawyer who formerly worked in the OSG, the (current) OSG lawyer still enjoys a higher probability of winning. Combined, these findings show that not only is the SG's office successful before the Court; it is uniquely influential.

---

4 Such heightened success is also evident among state solicitors general (Owens and Wohlfarth 2014).

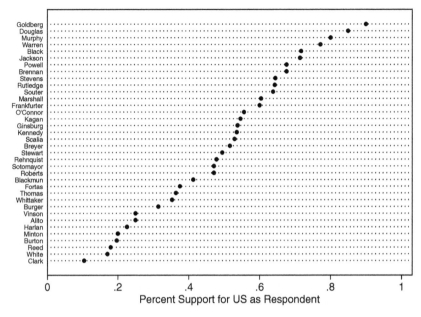

FIGURE 26: *Percent of cases in which justices voted for the United States as respondent, 1946–2016 terms (among cases where the United States was the respondent).*

Still, we know that *some justices* are more likely to side with the OSG than others. Figure 26 provides a simple display that highlights this fact. It shows the percent of times each justice voted for the United States as respondent, among all the cases in which the "United States" or an agency for the federal government appeared as respondent in the Supreme Court Database. It is clear that some justices have voted more for the SG as respondent than others.

Archival records also suggest that some justices are more or less likely to support the OSG. Consider the following memos written by Justice Blackmun's clerks to the Justice.[5] In *National Advertising Co.* v. *City of Raleigh* (91–1555), one clerk told Blackmun, "As we know from *Lucas*, the SG's view will be very slanted." In *Securities Industry Association* v. *Board of Governors of the Federal Reserve* (87–1513), Blackmun's clerk wrote, "The SG's brief was poor and, I suspect, ideologically slanted." And, in *Florence County School District* v. *Carter* (91–1523), Blackmun's clerk told him, "I also don't trust the SG on this."

5 See http://epstein.wustl.edu/blackmun.php.

These examples suggest that ideological differences caused some justices to vote with the OSG more than others. But surely other factors lead justices to side with the OSG more or less. We ask: Are justices with different personalities more likely to support the OSG than others? Are conscientious justices more likely to vote with the OSG than less conscientious justices?

6.2 A THEORY OF CONSCIENTIOUSNESS AND SUPPORT FOR THE OSG

As we discussed in Chapter 2, conscientiousness reflects a person's tendency to act in an organized or thoughtful way. In a general sense, it captures whether a person is dutiful, deliberate, driven, persistent, self-assured, and hardworking. Roberts et al. (2014, 1315) define conscientiousness as "a spectrum of constructs that describe individual differences in the propensity to be self-controlled, responsible to others, hardworking, orderly, and rule abiding."

Conscientious people have certain tendencies that would appear to make conscientious justices more likely to be receptive to the OSG and its arguments. For starters, when seeking to answer questions, conscientious individuals tend to look for more information – and to rely on more objective information – than less conscientious individuals. For example, Heinström (2003) examined how graduate students conducted research. Among other things, the study investigated how students evaluated information, how they selected the documents they used for their research, and the effect of time pressure on their information gathering. The results showed that conscientious people sought out thought-provoking and objective documents rather than documents confirming previous ideas. Conversely, less conscientious students tended to choose their information sources based on how easy the information was to access.[6] Conscientious individuals rely on greater amounts of information and more objective information than less conscientious individuals.

Because conscientious individuals are dependable, efficient, and hardworking, it seems reasonable to believe that they are inclined to use objectively reliable information. A person who is dependable, after all, would not use unreliable information to solve problems. Dutiful workers tend to use the best information they can get. Persistent people do not accept middling materials. These kinds of people rely on objective and credible information.

---

[6] Along similar lines, Gul et al. (2004, 359) finds, "High level conscientious scholars being very competent, disciplined and achievement striking are found to make extra efforts in database searching to get required information."

Supreme Court justices should be no different. Indeed, Chapter 5 tells us that justices are more likely to side with the party whose brief is more legally reliable, and whose attorney makes a more legally reliable argument. All this points to the conscientious justice being more likely to rely on objective information.

If it is reliable and objective material that conscientious justices want, they need look no further than to the information they receive from the OSG. There is perhaps no more objective Supreme Court litigant than the Office of the Solicitor General. Despite occasionally pressing an argument too far or acting ideologically, attorneys in the OSG are highly professional and, on average, present the Court with impartial information. They generally do not make legal arguments or otherwise take action that would impair the integrity of the Court (Caplan 1987). Both Black and Owens (2011b) and Wohlfarth (2009) argue that OSG success has been tied to the office's objective and professional behavior. Some scholars even call the Solicitor General a "Tenth Justice" (Caplan 1987) to underscore the general notion that the OSG is an objective purveyor of legal information (Salokar 1992; Scigliano 1971). One former Supreme Court clerk, in fact, told us that the SG is expected to "play as an honest broker of the facts" when communicating with the Court. Perry's (1991) seminal text is filled with comments from justices and clerks who assert that the OSG, overall, can be trusted.

The OSG is able to offer this credible and professional information, in part, because it hires and relies on professionals within the Office (Black and Owens 2013). While the SG changes over presidential administrations, the bulk of OSG attorneys remain professional staff attorneys dedicated to the rule of law and good lawyering. Employing professionals over various presidential administrations signals to the Court that the OSG's information can largely be trusted and is not tainted by partisan motivations. Moreover, given that the OSG must appear before the Court regularly, lawyers within that office know they must be honest. They tend to disregard short-term gains for longer-term benefits that reflect on the institutions within which they act.

We also believe conscientious justices will be more likely to follow the SG's position for a second reason – one that turns on the Court's external support. Justices care a great deal about the Supreme Court as an institution. Justices are sensitive to outside criticism that may challenge the Court's legitimacy. A good way to mitigate those criticisms is to rely on and defer to an important external actor like the SG. Importantly, research shows that key elements of conscientiousness facilitate justices' abilities to do that. Specifically, key components of conscientiousness are responsibility, conventionality, and formalness. Formalness is a tendency to follow rules of decorum. Responsibility is a "tendency ... to follow rules that make social groups work more smoothly" (Roberts et al. 2014, 1317). And conventionality "is the inclination to support and follow the norms of society in order to maintain good social environments ... [and] uphold ... traditions" (Mike et al. 2015, 659).[7] These three aspects, combined, suggest that in order to make the institution run smoothly and preserve the legitimacy of the institution, highly conscientious justices should be more receptive to the arguments of important external actors like the OSG.

Taken together, increasingly conscientious individuals tend to acquire more information to solve problems than less conscientious individuals. The information they obtain is more reliable and objective. Highly conscientious justices should therefore be more likely to seek out and rely on credible information. The Office of the Solicitor General tends to provide the Court with the most reliable and objective legal information. Everything adds up for conscientious justices to pay more attention to the OSG than less conscientious justices. We hypothesize, therefore, that *increasingly conscientious justices are more likely to side with the position advocated by the OSG than less conscientious justices.*

To analyze our theoretical claims, we perform two empirical analyses. The first considers how conscientiousness influences justices' support for the OSG's positions at the merits stage. The second examines how conscientiousness influences justices' support for the OSG's positions at the agenda stage.

6.3 DATA AND MEASURES: SUPPORT FOR THE OSG AT THE MERITS STAGE

We first analyze how justices' conscientiousness influences their treatment of the OSG at the merits stage. We construct a data set of individual justice votes in all orally argued Supreme Court decisions, from the 1953 to 2013 terms, in which the Solicitor General participated as voluntary amicus curiae or as a party to a case.[8] To identify those cases where the SG filed a voluntary amicus

---

7   Roberts, Jackson, Burger, and Trautwein (2009) note that most inventories of conscientiousness fail to incorporate conventionality because it is often mistakenly identified as an aspect of low openness. However, they found that conventionality is more strongly related to conscientiousness than openness. In fact, McCrae and Costa (1987) examined eighty adjective trait measures and found that the "traditional-untraditional" adjective loaded highly on the conscientiousness trait in addition to the openness trait.

8   We use the justice-centered Supreme Court Database organized by case citation, which is available at http://scdb.wustl.edu. We exclude those decisions that the Database identifies as a nonorally argued per curiam or a decree (i.e., "decisionType" = 2 or 4).

brief, we rely on data from Wohlfarth (2009) and update it through the 2013 term.[9] To identify those cases where the SG represented the government as party, we use the Supreme Court Database to identify all cases where the US government (or a federal agency) was the petitioner or respondent.[10] The unit of analysis is the justice vote among all orally argued cases where the SG or US government was a participant.

Dependent Variable. Our dependent variable, *Vote with SG*, represents whether a justice cast a merits vote to support the position advocated by the OSG. Since we look at cases where the OSG acts as amicus participant and cases where the OSG represents the United States as party, we require two coding methods. To code *Vote with SG* when the OSG was an amicus participant, we read the OSG's brief to determine whether it recommended reversal or affirmance.[11] To code *Vote with SG* when the government was a party to the case, we looked to see whether the United States was the petitioner or respondent. Next, we identified whether the Court's decision supported the petitioner or respondent and, then, whether each justice was in the majority or dissenting coalition.[12] We code *Vote with SG* as 1 when the justice's vote supported the OSG's position; 0 otherwise.

Conscientiousness. Our main covariate is each justice's score for the *Conscientiousness* measure that we discussed in Chapter 3. We also include as control predictors the justices' scores on the four other personality trait dimensions – *Openness, Extraversion, Agreeableness*, and *Neuroticism*.

---

9   We drop the SG's amicus briefs that were invited by the Court (i.e., CVSG) because they effectively represent Court orders instructing the SG to offer the government's views. Justices should be naturally inclined to support the SG's positions. To identify the invited amici, we look to the "Interest of the United States" section of each brief. By custom, the SG will state explicitly that the Office's amicus participation was invited by the Court. Nevertheless, all subsequent results are substantively consistent when including the invited amici in the analyses.

10 We include all cases where the Supreme Court Database identified the US government, Department of Justice, or a federal agency as a party, and we use the Database's "petitioner" and "respondent" variables to identify the litigants. See the replication data set for the full list of litigant identification codes used in the analysis. The subsequent results are consistent if you limit the party cases to only those where the Supreme Court Database identifies the petitioner or respondent as the "United States" (i.e., where the "petitioner" or "respondent" variables equal 27).

11 Occasionally, the SG files an amicus brief that reflects a neutral position, that does not explicitly take a side, or that advocates both a partial reversal and affirmance of the lower court decision. We drop these amicus briefs (87, or 7.6 percent, of the voluntary amici from 1953 to 2013) due to the inability to definitively determine the SG's position in the case.

12 We use the "partyWinning" and "majority" variables in the Supreme Court Database to identify when the petitioner received a favorable disposition and the justices in each coalition, respectively.

Justice Ideology. We recognize that various justices are ideologically predisposed to vote in liberal or conservative directions, which might also correlate at times with the identity of the SG and his or her position. We therefore employ a measure of ideology to account for their likely votes in cases. We use the Segal and Cover (1989) scores as estimates of justices' policy preferences. We do so because they were generated using content analyses of newspaper editorials about justices *before* they got to the Supreme Court, and thus are exogenous to their actual votes. In other words, Segal and Cover estimate justices' preferences without using votes to explain votes. Although these scores are most closely connected to justices' preferences regarding civil liberties and civil rights issues, they represent the most appropriate exogenous measures of preferences currently available. The scores range from 0 to 1, with larger (smaller) values signifying more liberal (conservative) attitudes.

Liberal SG Position. We create a single dummy variable to capture the ideological direction of each position taken by the Solicitor General. To do so, we refer to the ideological direction of the lower court's decision and the litigant supported (represented) by the SG (United States).[13] For instance, a liberal position reflects one where the SG supported (or the United States was) the petitioner (respondent) and the lower court issued a conservative (liberal) decision. Conversely, we code the position as conservative when the SG supported the petitioner (respondent) in the wake of a liberal (conservative) lower court decision. We assign a value of 1 to liberal positions and a value of 0 to conservative positions.

Ideology × Liberal SG Position. We include an interactive term to account for each justice's ideological predisposition interacted with the SG's position. We expect that increasingly liberal (conservative) justices will be more (less) likely to support liberal SG positions and less (more) likely to support conservative SG positions.

Justice-President Ideological Distance. We also account for the likelihood that justices may support the SG due to an affinity for the sitting president. To capture this effect, we create a predictor reflecting the degree of ideological congruence between the justice and sitting president. We use the Judicial Common Space (JCS; Epstein, Martin, Segal, and Westerland 2007) to identify the ideal points for the justice and president. (The JCS scores were generated with a common scale, and thus they provide suitable indicators

---

[13] We use the Supreme Court Database's "lcDispositionDirection" variable to identify the ideological direction of the lower court's decision. We code this variable as missing if the database indicates that the ideological direction cannot be specified clearly.

for this predictor.[14]) Next, we compute the absolute value of the difference between them. Smaller values thus reflect justices who are ideologically closer to the president. Justices who are ideologically similar to the sitting president should be more inclined to support the SG.[15]

Public Mood. We also control for the likelihood that public opinion shapes justices' votes (e.g., Black, Owens, Wedeking, and Wohlfarth 2016b; Enns and Wohlfarth 2013; Casillas, Enns, and Wohlfarth 2011; Epstein and Martin 2011; McGuire and Stimson 2004) using the indicator created by Stimson (1991).[16] Stimson's public mood measure is a longitudinal indicator of the public's general preference for more or less government over time. It is an aggregate, dynamic reflection of the general tenor of public opinion (and preference over desired public policy) on the standard liberal-conservative dimension (Stimson 1991). Scholars who examine public opinion in the courts use this measure frequently (e.g., Black, Owens, Wedeking, and Wohlfarth 2016b; Enns and Wohlfarth 2013; Casillas, Enns, and Wohlfarth 2011; Epstein and Martin 2011; Giles, Blackstone, and Vining 2008; McGuire and Stimson 2004).[17] Larger values of *Public Mood* reflect a more liberal public while smaller values reflect a more conservative public.

Public Mood × Liberal SG. We interact *Liberal SG Position* with *Public Mood*. We expect that as public opinion becomes more liberal (conservative), justices will be more (less) likely to support liberal SG positions and less (more) likely to support conservative SG positions.

---

[14] The JCS scores are available at http://epstein.wustl.edu/research/JCS .html.

[15] One might also control for the degree to which solicitors general use the office to push a political agenda, as greater politicization should lead justices to discount the SG's recommendations (Wohlfarth 2009). We opt not to include Wohlfarth's (2009) indicator of politicization – measured as a running proportion of voluntary, merits-stage amicus briefs that the SG files in the ideological direction most favored by his or her appointing president – in the present analysis because it would limit the sample to the start of Archibald Cox's tenure in the office (i.e., the 1961 term). The infrequency with which solicitors general filed voluntary amicus briefs in the 1950's makes it difficult to construct a reliable measure. Nevertheless, all subsequent results are substantively consistent if we include the politicization indicator in the analysis (of post-1960 cases). And, in such an alternative analysis, the SG politicization predictor exhibits a statistically significant, negative effect on the likelihood that justices support the SG's amicus positions, thereby offering evidence consistent with Wohlfarth's (2009) finding that greater politicization inhibits the SG's success on the merits.

[16] We use updated estimates of public mood (May 2, 2016 data release) retrieved from http:// stimson.web.unc.edu/data/.

[17] Consistent with most prior studies, we match the public mood score each calendar year to the Supreme Court term – that is, public mood in 2000 predicts Court decisions in the 2000 term, thereby creating a nine-month lag. This ensures that changes in public opinion temporally precede the Court's decisions.

SG Amicus Reversal and *US Petitioner*. Next, we account for the Supreme Court's well-known proclivity to reverse lower court judgments. We include two dummy variables to capture this effect. *SG Amicus Reversal* takes on a value of 1 when the SG files an amicus brief that supports the petitioner; o otherwise. *US Petitioner* takes on a value of 1 when the United States was the petitioner; o otherwise.[18]

Issue Area. Lastly, we account for differences in behavior across issue areas by including fixed effects for the primary issue of each case.[19] We include a dummy variable for each broad issue area among those identified by the Supreme Court Database.[20]

6.4 METHODS AND RESULTS: SUPPORT FOR THE OSG AT THE MERITS STAGE

We estimate logistic regression models with robust standard errors.[21] We estimate six total models in Table 13, three of which are baseline traits-only models without control predictors for the three different scenarios (Models 1, 3, and 5).[22] The three remaining models are fully specified models among: only SG amicus curiae briefs (Model 2); only the United States as a party (Model 4); and SG amici and US party cases combined (Model 6).

Table 13 shows that increasingly conscientious justices are indeed more likely to vote for the Solicitor General's position. Figure 27(a) displays the magnitude of this effect (from Model 2), expressed as the predicted probability a justice will support the SG across the observed range of *Conscientiousness*.[23] Justices with the minimum level of *Conscientiousness* exhibit a 0.59 [0.54, 0.64] predicted probability of supporting the SG's amicus position. Justices with the maximum level of *Conscientiousness* exhibit a 0.70 [0.68, 0.73] predicted probability of supporting the SG's amicus position – a total expected increase of 0.11, or nearly 20 percent. A shift of one standard deviation (0.89)

---

[18] Again, we exclude those SG amicus briefs that do not clearly support a particular position in the case, which includes briefs that do not take a clear side or those that support both partial reversal and affirmance of the lower court decision.

[19] We use the "issueArea" variable in the Database to identify the primary issue area within each case.

[20] One might also control for differences across presidential administrations. All subsequent results are substantively consistent when we include fixed effects for each president.

[21] All subsequent results remain statistically significant if we employ classical standard errors.

[22] All subsequent empirical results are consistent when specifying a bivariate model that includes only conscientiousness (and no control predictors).

[23] We compute predicted probabilities using the observed values of the control predictors (see Hanmer and Kalkan 2013).

TABLE 13: *The Impact of Supreme Court Justice Conscientiousness on Support for the US Solicitor General on the Merits*

	Amicus Cases (1)	(2)	Party Cases (3)	(4)	Amicus & Party (5)	(6)
Conscientiousness	0.11*	0.11*	0.11*	0.10*	0.12*	0.11*
	(0.04)	(0.04)	(0.02)	(0.02)	(0.02)	(0.02)
Openness	−0.02	−0.02	0.12*	0.11*	0.08*	0.07*
	(0.02)	(0.02)	(0.01)	(0.01)	(0.01)	(0.01)
Extraversion	0.04	0.07*	−0.09*	−0.08*	−0.06*	−0.04*
	(0.03)	(0.03)	(0.02)	(0.02)	(0.02)	(0.02)
Agreeableness	−0.03	−0.02	0.13*	0.13*	0.10*	0.09*
	(0.02)	(0.03)	(0.01)	(0.02)	(0.01)	(0.01)
Neuroticism	0.04	−0.00	0.01	−0.01	0.02	−0.00
	(0.03)	(0.03)	(0.02)	(0.02)	(0.01)	(0.02)
Justice-President Distance		−0.73*		−0.29*		−0.44*
		(0.07)		(0.05)		(0.04)
Liberal SG/US Position		−2.90*		−3.44*		−3.29*
		(0.70)		(0.46)		(0.38)
Justice Ideology		−1.83*		−1.41*		−1.52*
		(0.11)		(0.06)		(0.05)
Ideology × Liberal Position		3.17*		2.39*		2.54*
		(0.16)		(0.10)		(0.08)
Public Mood		0.00		−0.02*		−0.01*
		(0.01)		(0.00)		(0.00)
Mood × Liberal Position		0.03*		0.04*		0.04*
		(0.01)		(0.01)		(0.01)
SG Amicus Reversal		0.66*				0.76*
		(0.05)				(0.04)
US Petitioner				0.61*		0.58*
				(0.03)		(0.03)
Constant	0.74*	1.06*	0.40*	2.09*	0.50*	1.90*
	(0.04)	(0.50)	(0.02)	(0.29)	(0.02)	(0.25)
Issue Area Controls	No	Yes	No	Yes	No	Yes
N	9223	9170	20,588	20,182	29,718	29,174
χ^2	14.31*	906.49*	355.98*	1895.99*	294.81*	2727.51*

Note: Table entries are logistic regression coefficients with robust standard errors in parentheses; *p < .05 (one-tailed). The dependent variable represents whether each individual justice cast a vote to support the SG/United States on the merits, among orally argued cases where the SG participated as voluntary amicus curiae and/or the United States (or a federal agency) was a party, 1953–2013. Models 2, 4, and 6 include, but do not display, fixed effects controls for the issue area of each case.

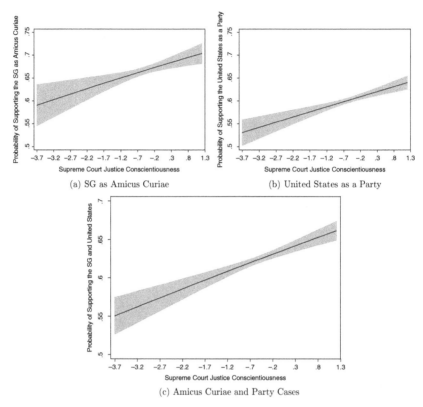

(a) SG as Amicus Curiae   (b) United States as a Party

(c) Amicus Curiae and Party Cases

FIGURE 27: *The impact of conscientiousness on justices' support for the solicitor general and United States on the merits.* Panel (a) displays the predicted probability that a Supreme Court justice supports the SG's position as amicus curiae (with 90 percent confidence intervals) across the range of *Conscientiousness* using results from Model 2 in Table 13. Panel (b) displays the predicted probability that a justice supports the United States' position as a party using results from Model 4. Panel (c) reports the predicted probability when combining amicus curiae and party cases using results from Model 6.

above the mean level of justice *Conscientiousness* yields an expected increase of 0.02 in the probability the justice will support the SG's amicus position. It is noteworthy that we retrieve these results even after controlling for the prevailing explanations for justices' voting behavior in general and support for the SG in particular.

To be sure, the data confirm the primacy of ideological considerations on justices' support for the SG as amicus curiae. For instance, a shift from the minimum to maximum level of *Justice-President Ideological Distance* exhibits an expected decrease of 0.18 in the predicted probability of supporting the SG. Still, the impact of *Conscientiousness* remains profound. Its magnitude begins to approach that of ideological congruence between the justice and president.

Next, consider how *Conscientiousness* shapes justices' support for the OSG when the US participates as a party. The results in Models 3 and 4 in Table 13 display effects that are comparable to the analysis of the SG's amicus participation. Once again, increasingly conscientious justices are significantly more likely to vote in favor of the OSG's position. Figure 27(b) shows that the magnitude of this effect is comparable to that of the amicus cases. A justice with the minimum level of *Conscientiousness* exhibits a 0.53 [0.50, 0.56] predicted probability of supporting the OSG while a justice at the maximum end has a probability of 0.64 [0.62, 0.66] – a predicted difference of 0.11, or more than 20 percent. A shift of one standard deviation above the mean *Conscientiousness* score again yields an expected increase of 0.02 in the probability of supporting the OSG as a party.

The impact of *Conscientiousness* is even more impressive in this context when evaluated relative to the *Justice-President Ideological Distance* control predictor. A minimum-to-maximum increase in *Justice-President Ideological Distance* exhibits an expected decrease of only 0.08 in the probability of supporting the United States as a party. Thus, the total potential impact of *Conscientiousness* among the party cases actually *exceeds* the predicted effect of justice-president ideological congruence by nearly 40 percent. Conscientiousness is strong medicine.

Lastly, the regression results from Models 5 and 6 in Table 13 show that the impact of *Conscientiousness* is substantively consistent when combining the amicus and party cases. Figure 27(c) displays the predicted probability a justice will support the OSG across the observed range of *Conscientiousness* (using results from Model 6). A justice at the minimum level of *Conscientiousness* exhibits a predicted probability of 0.55 [0.52, 0.58] of supporting the SG's position, yet the model predicts that a justice at the maximum level of *Conscientiousness* will support the OSG with a probability of 0.66 [0.65, 0.68] – a total expected increase of 0.11, or approximately 20 percent once again. This total impact among the combined amicus and party cases is roughly equivalent to the magnitude of *Justice-President Ideological Distance*'s negative impact (i.e., a 0.12 min-to-max decrease). In short, the data suggest that conscientious justices are most likely to support the OSG, both as amicus curiae and a party.

Among the control predictors, there is some evidence that increasingly extraverted justices are more likely to support the SG as amicus curiae, although the effect is only statistically significant in the fully specified model (Model 2). No other personality trait exhibits an impact on support for the SG as amicus curiae. Among the party cases, the data suggest that justices with greater openness and agreeableness are more likely to support the US government on the merits, yet greater extraversion seemingly predicts less support. On the whole, conscientiousness is the single most consistent personality predictor of support for the SG on the merits.

The impact of *Justice Ideology* exhibits the effects one would expect. Among those cases where the SG takes a conservative position, more liberal (conservative) justices are significantly less (more) likely to support the SG.[24] Similarly, the state of public opinion exhibits a similar positive effect when the SG advocates a liberal policy, and a negative impact among conservative positions. In other words, as prevailing public mood becomes more liberal (conservative), justices are more (less) likely to support liberal SG positions and less (more) likely to support conservative SG positions.[25] Lastly, the *SG Amicus Reversal* and *US Petitioner* predictors exhibit their expected positive effects – that is, justices are significantly more likely to support the SG as amicus curiae when he or she advocates for a reversal of the lower court decision, and they are more likely to rule in favor of the United States on the merits when the government is the petitioner.

6.5 DATA AND MEASURES: SUPPORT FOR THE OSG AT THE AGENDA-SETTING STAGE

We next analyze how justices' conscientiousness influences their treatment of the OSG at the agenda-setting stage. Here, we use data from Black and Owens (2011*a*), who examined the conditions under which justices voted to follow the OSG's agenda recommendations after the Court called for the views of the Solicitor General's office. We examine all cases originating in the US Courts of Appeals where the SG filed an agenda-stage amicus curiae brief

---

[24] A full examination of the interactive effects in Models 2, 4, and 6 shows that the average marginal effect of *Justice Ideology* is positive and statistically significant when the SG supports a liberal position ($p < 0.001$) and negative and significant among conservative positions ($p < 0.001$).

[25] The average marginal effect of *Public Mood* is positive and statistically significant when the SG supports a liberal position ($p < 0.001$) and negative and significant among conservative positions ($p < 0.001$). The one exception is that when analyzing only the amicus cases (i.e., Model 2), the impact of public mood is not statistically distinguishable from zero among those cases where the SG files a conservative amicus brief.

from 1970 to 1993 (N = 277).[26] Black and Owens (2011*a*) examined the docket sheets and cert pool memos of Justice Harry A. Blackmun (collected from the Library of Congress [for the 1970–1985 terms] and from Epstein, Segal, and Spaeth (2007) [for the 1986–1993 terms]). They used the docket sheet in each case to record the justices' votes and the cert pool memos to code the SG's recommendation.[27] Our unit of analysis, like theirs, is the justice vote.

Dependent Variable. Our dependent variable, *Vote with SG*, represents whether a justice cast a vote to support the position advocated by the OSG at the agenda stage. *Vote with SG* receives a value of 1 if the justice voted consistent with the SG's position; 0 otherwise. For example, if the OSG recommended the Court grant review and the justice so voted, we code *Vote with SG* as 1. On the other hand, if the OSG recommended the Court grant review and the justice voted to deny review, we code *Vote With SG* as 0.

Conscientiousness. Once again, our primary independent variable is *Conscientiousness*. We also control for the four other personality traits of the Big Five.

Policy Agreement. We account for whether the justice's policy preferences align with the OSG's recommendation. We use Black and Owens's (2011*a*) indicator of when the SG's recommendation is consistent with the justice's policy preferences. As Figure 28 shows, this predictor accounts for (1) the ideological distance between the justice's ideal point (using the JCS scores) and the status quo policy position (indicated by the preferences of those judges who sat on the circuit court that heard the case), and compares it to (2) the ideological distance between the justice's ideal point and the location of the expected merits outcome if the Court were to review the case (a proxy measure using the composition of the majority coalitions in the Supreme Court's recent previous cases in the same general issue area). If a justice is ideologically closer to the expected merits outcome than to the status quo, we expect that justice will vote to grant review. If the justice is closer to the status quo, we expect him or her to vote to deny review.[28]

As Table 14 shows, we assign a value of 1 to justices who were expected to grant (deny) review and the SG recommended a grant (deny); otherwise the variable takes on a value of 0.

---

[26] This includes cases in which the Court invited the SG to participate (i.e., CVSG), in addition to the few cases where the SG submitted a brief voluntarily.

[27] We drop cases where the SG did not make a clear policy recommendation on certiorari. Thus, the analysis includes recommendations to grant or deny review, note probable jurisdiction, or to affirm or dismiss the appeal. Black and Owens (2011*a*) note that these recommendations represent 91 percent of all SG recommendations from 1970 to 1993.

[28] See Black and Owens (2011*a*) for the full coding details.

TABLE 14: *Policy Agreement Coding*

Expected Justice Policy Vote	OSG Recommends	Policy Agree Value
Grant	Grant	1
Deny	Deny	1
Grant	Deny	0
Deny	Grant	0

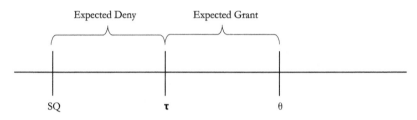

FIGURE 28: *Forward-looking policy calculations at agenda stage.* Justices closer to the status quo (SQ) should be more likely to deny review. Justices closer to the expected outcome on the merits (θ) should be more likely to grant review. Cutpoint τ represents the indifference point between the status quo and expected outcomes on the merits.

Policy Confusion. We next account for the uncertainty involved when a justice becomes indifferent about the status quo versus the expected outcome on the merits – that is, the closer the justice gets to τ. The forward-looking policy calculation we describe in Figure 28 assumes (implausibly) that all justices can discern whether they prefer the status quo or the expected outcome on the merits. Sometimes, though, it is unclear which is better. Sometimes, they are indifferent between the two. To account for this, we compute the absolute value of the ideological distance between the justice's ideal point and the cutpoint between the expected merits outcome and the status quo (i.e., τ). The smaller the value, the more likely a justice is to indifference between the expected outcome and the legal status quo.

Legal Consistency. We next control for whether the SG's agenda recommendation accords with the legal aspects of a petition. We examined the cert pool memos written by the pool clerks for each case and analyzed their discussions of the cases, focusing on the legal factors they used to justify their recommendations to grant or deny review. If the pool memo identified one or more legal reasons that would support review (e.g., strong circuit conflict, or the lower court exercised judicial review) *and* the SG recommended granting the petition, we code *Legal Consistency* as 1. For the same reasons, if the memo identified one or more legal grounds on which to deny the petition (e.g., no circuit conflict, or an unpublished lower court decision) and the SG recommended denial, we code *Legal Consistency* as 1.[29] Alternatively, if the pool memo identified one or more legal reasons that would support review but the SG recommended denial, *Legal Consistency* equals −1. And if the memo identified one or more legal grounds on which to deny the petition but the SG recommended a grant, *Legal Consistency* equals −1. Finally, we identified, and categorized as legally neutral, those petitions that possessed no legal reasons to grant or deny review, as well as the small number of petitions (11 out of 277) where there are legal reasons both to grant *and* deny the petition. For example, a case may have genuine conflict but justiciability concerns.[30] We code *Legal Consistency* as 0 when petitions are legally neutral.

Political Salience. Our next control predictor captures the political salience of each case at the agenda stage. Salient cases, because of the policy stakes at issue, may lead justices to deviate from the SG's recommendation. We measure this dynamic by counting the total number of amicus curiae briefs filed at the agenda stage. This variable ranges from zero to eight, with a mode of zero amici.

Initial Agreement. We next account for instances where a justice cast an agenda-setting vote consistent with the SG's eventual recommendation, but did so prior to the Court issuing its CVSG order. Back up a bit. Recall that for the Court to CVSG, at least four justices must so vote. There are numerous instances where some justices vote to grant or deny while others vote to CVSG. And those justices who vote to grant or deny have revealed a preference in the case. For example, consider Figure 29, which is the Court's docket sheet in *Mertens v. Hewitt Associates* (91–1671). As can be seen, the Court voted to CVSG on June 8, 1992, after Justices White, Blackmun, Stevens, and O'Connor so voted. The remaining justices, however, revealed a preference right away. Chief Justice Rehnquist would have voted to deny review, as

---

[29] A possible alternative measure for law might combine the reasons to grant (or deny) certiorari into a scale of legal support. That is, if there were three reasons to grant a petition, the law might be considered clearer (and thus more compelling) than a petition with only one legal reason to grant. Unfortunately, our sample contains no petitions with multiple legal reasons to grant. Further, out of the 2,151 observations, only 129 have two legal reasons to deny and only 17 have three reasons to deny. In short, while scaling the legal variable might help us determine whether legal influence is stronger when "stacked," we do not have adequate data to sufficiently test that proposition.

[30] We note that separating them out into a fourth category (i.e., "Legally Ambiguous") does not appreciably alter the results we report herein.

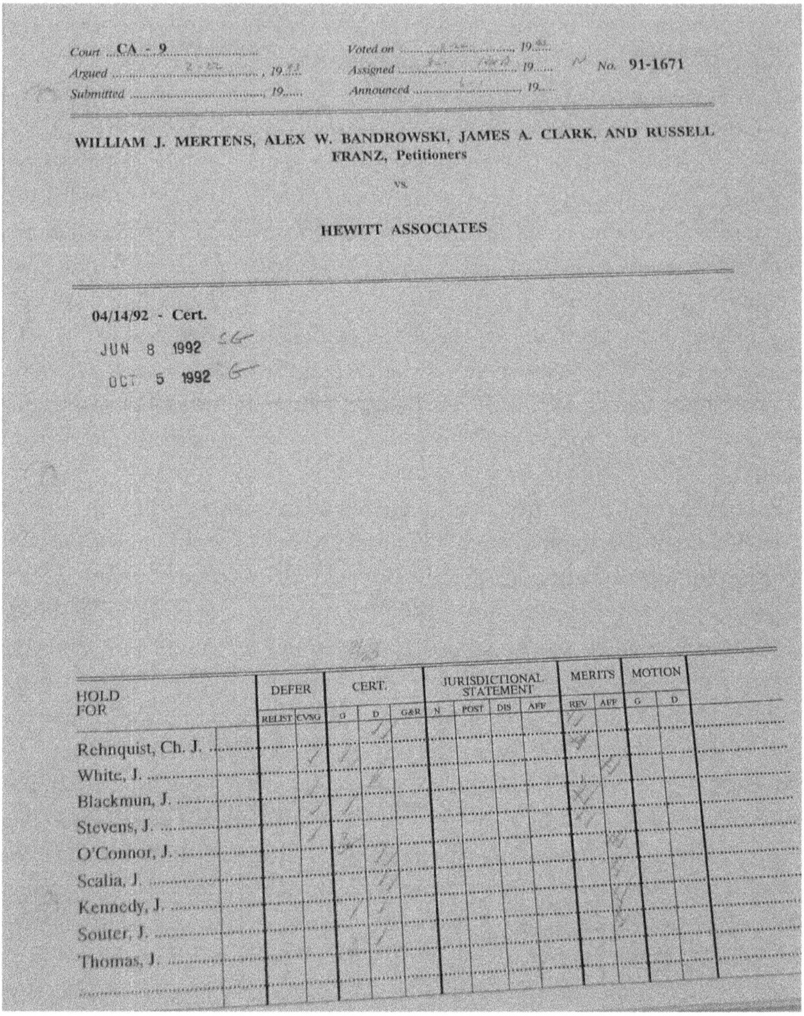

Court **CA - 9**   Voted on ...., 19....   No. **91-1671**
Argued ...., 19....   Assigned ...., 19....
Submitted ...., 19....   Announced ...., 19....

WILLIAM J. MERTENS, ALEX W. BANDROWSKI, JAMES A. CLARK, AND RUSSELL FRANZ, Petitioners

vs.

HEWITT ASSOCIATES

04/14/92 - Cert.

JUN 8 1992

OCT 5 1992

	DEFER		CERT.			JURISDICTIONAL STATEMENT			MERITS		MOTION	
HOLD FOR	RELIST	CVSG	G	D	G&R	N	POST	DIS	AFF	REV	AFF	G	D
Rehnquist, Ch. J.													
White, J.													
Blackmun, J.													
Stevens, J.													
O'Connor, J.													
Scalia, J.													
Kennedy, J.													
Souter, J.													
Thomas, J.													

FIGURE 29: *Court's docket sheet in Mertens v. Hewitt Associates (91–1671).*

would Justices Scalia, Kennedy, Souter, and Thomas. We assign a value of 1 to instances where the justice originally voted to support the position ultimately recommended by the SG; 0 otherwise.

Voluntary SG Recommendation. We also control for whether the SG's submission was voluntary or whether the Court invited the SG to participate. Given that voluntary agenda-setting briefs are relatively uncommon, the voluntary brief may signal to the Court the importance of the case for the government and induce justices to be more likely to agree with the SG. We assign a value of 1 to voluntarily filed OSG briefs and 0 for those filed at the invitation of the Court.

Separation of Powers Predictors. Consistent with Black and Owens (2011a), we account for multiple separation of powers predictors that may affect the Court's decision to issue a CVSG order and side with the SG (see also Owens 2010b; Johnson 2003). First, we control for the presence of a *Presidential Honeymoon*, which takes on a value of 1 if the president was in the first year of his first term when the justice cast the agenda-setting vote; 0 otherwise. Next, we code *Presidential Election Year* as 1 if the agenda-setting vote occurred during a presidential election year. Lastly, we include predictors for *Presidential House Strength* and *Presidential Senate Strength*, which we code as the percentage of seats held by the legislators of the president's party in the House and Senate, respectively.[31]

Pro-SG Amicus Briefs. Justices might also be more likely to support the SG's recommendation when there is greater external support for that position. Thus, we count the total number of agenda-stage amicus briefs that agreed with the SG's certiorari recommendation.

6.6   METHODS AND RESULTS: SUPPORT FOR THE OSG AT THE AGENDA-SETTING STAGE

Using these data, we estimate a logistic regression model (with robust standard errors) to examine the conditions under which justices vote consistent with the SG's agenda-setting recommendation.[32] Table 15 reports the empirical results of two models – a baseline traits-only model and a second model that includes the full complement of control predictors. As the results show, a justice's conscientiousness significantly predicts his or her support for the SG's agenda-setting recommendation in the fully specified model, though not in the traits-only model.[33] Thus, the data offer some, if uneven, evidence that increasingly conscientious justices are more likely support the SG's position when casting agenda-setting votes.[34]

---

[31]   Additionally, one might also further control for differences across presidential administrations. All subsequent results are substantively consistent if also including fixed effects controls for each president.

[32]   All results are substantively consistent if we estimate the models using classical standard errors.

[33]   The conscientious predictor does not exhibit a statistically significant effect in a bivariate model (without control predictors).

[34]   Specifically, one must account for *Initial Agreement* and *Policy Confusion* in order to uncover statistically significant evidence for *Conscientiousness*. The results are robust, however, to the inclusion/exclusion of the other control predictors.

TABLE 15: *The Impact of Supreme Court Justice Personality Traits on Agenda-Setting Support for the Solicitor General*

	(1)	(2)
Conscientiousness	0.04	0.18*
	(0.09)	(0.09)
Openness	−0.23*	−0.31*
	(0.06)	(0.07)
Extraversion	0.02	0.05
	(0.08)	(0.09)
Agreeableness	−0.03	−0.08
	(0.05)	(0.05)
Neuroticism	0.02	0.05
	(0.08)	(0.09)
Policy Agreement		0.53*
		(0.11)
Legal Consistency		0.51*
		(0.08)
Political Salience		−0.21*
		(0.09)
Initial Agreement		2.52*
		(0.19)
Voluntary SG Recommendation		0.70*
		(0.22)
Presidential Honeymoon		0.07
		(0.17)
Presidential Election Year		0.02
		(0.12)
Presidential House Strength		−2.25
		(1.98)
Presidential Senate Strength		3.10
		(3.16)
Policy Confusion		−0.89*
		(0.23)
Pro-SG Amicus Briefs		0.08
		(0.11)
Constant	1.16*	0.40
	(0.08)	(0.73)
N	2151	2151
χ^2	20.36*	280.85*

Note: Table entries are coefficients from a logit regression model with robust standard errors in parentheses; *$p < 0.05$ (one-tailed). The dependent variable represents whether a justice cast a vote consistent with the SG's agenda-setting recommendation, among all cases originating in the US Courts of Appeals where the SG filed an agenda-stage amicus curiae brief, 1970–1993.

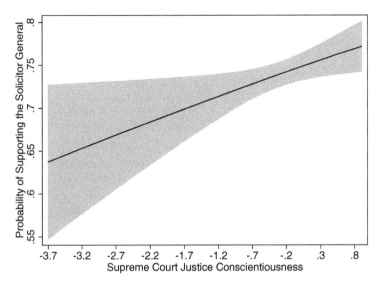

FIGURE 30: *The impact of conscientiousness on justices' agenda-setting support for the solicitor general.* Estimates represent the predicted probability (with 90 percent confidence intervals) that a Supreme Court justice casts a liberal vote across the range of *Conscientiousness* using results from Model 2 in Table 15.

Figure 30 displays the magnitude of the predicted effect of *Conscientiousness* using results from Model 2 in Table 15. It reports the predicted probability a justice will support the OSG's recommendation across the range of *Conscientiousness*. A justice who scores the lowest on *Conscientiousness* in the sample is likely to support the SG's position with a probability of 0.64 [0.53, 0.74]. This probability increases to 0.77 [0.74, 0.81] among justices at the maximum level of *Conscientiousness*. Thus, the range of variation in justices' conscientiousness exhibits an expected increase of up to 0.13 in the probability of supporting the SG's agenda position – a 20 percent change. In addition, we retrieve these results even while controlling for factors known to shape justices' agenda-setting behavior in general, and support for the SG in particular.

Among the control predictors, justices who score higher on the openness trait are less likely to support the SG at the agenda stage. Greater policy agreement and legal consistency both induce justices to follow the SG's recommendations. Similarly, as expected, justices that supported the SG's eventual position prior to a CVSG invitation are more likely to support the SG's recommendation subsequently. Justices are more likely to support the SG when he or she submits an agenda recommendation voluntarily.

Alternatively, cases with greater political salience lead to less support for the SG, as does greater policy confusion.

6.7 CONCLUSION

In this chapter, we examined how conscientiousness influences the behavior of Supreme Court justices when interacting with the SG. The results show that justices who are more conscientious are considerably more likely to support the Solicitor General than less conscientious justices. Conscientious people are more likely to seek out and rely on credible information than less conscientious people. Conscientious people are more responsible, conventional, and formal. As such, we argued that justices would operate the same way. We argued that because conscientious justices seek out and rely on credible and objective information, they would be more likely to vote in the manner recommended by the SG. Lawyers in the OSG are the most objective and reliable lawyers who appear before the Court. The findings illuminate our understanding of the Court's relationship to the OSG.

But what do these findings suggest about the law more generally? The connection between personality and the OSG is crucial. If the OSG loses its credibility as being objective and providing high quality information, the conscientiousness of the justices may be of little consequence. Most immediately, it means the OSG may expect to lose more often (or at least not win at the same rates as before). While this may or may not be a normatively "bad" thing, it does change the landscape for how the executive branch approaches the law and legal change.

We leave those debates for another time. For now, however, the results indicate, once again, that conscientiousness plays a major role among justices – a role that heretofore has gone unnoticed.

7

Conscientiousness and Majority Opinion Assignments

On May 13, 1978, Warren McCleskey picked up Ben Wright, Bernard Dupree, and David Burney. They looked like four friends going out to have fun on a spring day. But on that spring day, their fun was vile and vicious. They decided to rob the Dixie Furniture Store in Atlanta, Georgia. McCleskey carried a .38 caliber revolver. His friends armed themselves with different weapons for the dirty deed. When they arrived at the furniture store, McCleskey innocently entered the front of the store; the other three entered the rear of the store. Then, all hell broke loose.

Wielding his pistol, McCleskey controlled the front of the store – at least for the moment. Wright, Dupree, and Burney tied up people in the store. The four then ordered the manager to give them his watch and six dollars. At that point, police officer Frank Schlatt answered a silent alarm. As he walked through the front door, bullets tore through his skin and bones. One split his skull and killed him. Days later, police captured McCleskey in another armed robbery. He confessed to the Dixie Furniture Store robbery. And though he denied shooting officer Schlatt, the evidence suggested otherwise. So a jury imposed the death penalty.

McCleskey challenged the imposition of the death penalty. He argued that he received the death sentence because he was black and killed a white person. Citing studies by David Baldus, he presented data which suggested that the death penalty was assessed in 22 percent of cases involving black defendants and white victims, 8 percent of cases involving white defendants and white victims, 1 percent of cases involving black defendants and black victims, and 3 percent of cases involving white defendants and black victims. The data, he claimed, showed a general pattern of racial bias, which violated his rights to equal protection and due process.

The Supreme Court, in an opinion by Justice Powell, disagreed.[1] McCleskey provided no evidence the state discriminated against *him*

---

[1] *See McCleskey v. Kemp*, 481 U.S. 279 (1987).

personally. The data might have shown overall patterns, but the Court's duty, said Powell, was to review discrete cases and rulings. Overall patterns are for legislatures to examine. Courts decide individual cases. And so McCleskey's arguments failed. Powell's opinion was critical to death penalty litigation.

Why did Chief Justice Rehnquist assign this important case to Powell? Surely, Powell's conservative voting record in criminal cases helped. But Rehnquist could have assigned to the similarly conservative Scalia, or O'Connor, or even to himself. Something else seems to have mattered.

Are Chiefs more likely to assign opinions in important cases to their conscientious colleagues than to their less conscientious colleagues? We believe so. Despite numerous analyses of Chief Justices (Danelski and Ward 2016; Ruger 2006; Cross and Lindquist 2006; Danelski 1960) and opinion assignments generally (Wahlbeck 2006; Wahlbeck and Maltzman 2005; Maltzman and Wahlbeck 2004; Maltzman, Spriggs, and Wahlbeck 2000; Maltzman and Wahlbeck 1996; Rohde 1972), we do not know the answer to this question. We know that opinion assignors consider the expertise of the opinion writer, the efficiency of the opinion writer, and, of course, the ideology of the opinion writer. But scholarship has largely ignored whether assignors consider the conscientiousness (or any other personality trait) of justices when assigning cases.

In this chapter, we investigate whether opinion assignors are more likely to assign opinions to conscientious justices. At least among the most legally important cases on the docket, they do. The Chief Justice is as much as 70 percent more likely to assign the opinion in a legally salient case to a more conscientious colleague.

7.1 THE OPINION ASSIGNMENT PROCESS

Discussing opinion assignments is a bit like stepping into a moving river. A number of things have occurred before the Chief (or the senior associate justice in the majority) assigns opinion authorship. We've already discussed how the Court sets its agenda, and we've analyzed litigant briefs and oral arguments. The opinion assignment comes after the Court's conference shortly following oral argument.

The Court typically holds Wednesday and Friday conferences to discuss the cases justices heard that week. During Wednesday afternoon conferences, justices discuss the cases they heard on Monday. During the Friday conferences, justices discuss the cases they heard on Tuesday and Wednesday. (The

Court does not usually hear oral arguments on Thursdays or Fridays.) The Chief begins these conferences by discussing each case, what it is about, the relevant law, and then explains how he or she votes. In order of seniority, the remaining justices then explain their views and cast their votes in order of seniority. Former Chief Justice Rehnquist described the conference process well:

> As soon as we come off the bench Wednesday afternoon around three o'clock, we go into private "conference" in a room adjoining the chambers of the Chief Justice. At our Wednesday afternoon meeting, we deliberate and vote on the four cases which we heard argued the preceding Monday. The Chief Justice begins the discussion of each case with a summary of the facts, his analysis of the law, and an announcement of his proposed vote (i.e., whether to affirm, reverse, modify, etc.). The discussion then passes to the senior Associate Justice, presently Mr. Justice Brennan, who does likewise. It then goes on down the line to the junior Associate Justice. When the discussion of one case is concluded, the discussion of the next one is immediately taken up, until all the argued cases on the agenda for that particular Conference have been disposed of. (Rehnquist 1977, 559–560, n.1)

Typically, after all the justices have spoken, a majority coalition will have formed in support of a legal position (affirm, reverse). Shortly thereafter, the senior justice in the majority coalition selects a justice from that coalition to write the opinion for the Court. The Chief Justice is always the most senior justice regardless of the number of years he has served. So if he is in the majority, he assigns the opinion. If the Chief is in the minority coalition, the Senior Associate Justice in the majority selects the opinion author. The opinion assigner can either self-assign or assign to another majority coalition justice. Usually, the Chief will wait until the end of the sitting, and then determine who was in the majority in all the cases for that sitting and what other opinions those justices must write. (The Court holds two-week sittings in which it hears oral argument. After the two weeks are up, the Court waits for two more weeks until beginning its next sitting.) After balancing all those factors, the Chief (or Senior Associate in the majority) will assign the majority opinion. Again, Chief Justice Rehnquist states:

> At the beginning of the week following the two-week sessions of oral argument, the Chief Justice circulates to the other members of the Court an Assignment List, in which he assigns for the writing of a Court opinion all of the cases in which he voted with the Conference majority. Where the Chief Justice was in the minority, the senior Associate Justice voting with the majority assigns the case. (Rehnquist 1977, 559–560, n.1)

Consider *Saint Mary's Honor Center* v. *Hicks* (1993), a case we discussed in our chapter on agenda setting.[2] The case involved whether employees who challenged their terminations on grounds of racial discrimination must prove that employers fired them because of race, or whether an employer's failure to rebut a prima facie case of discrimination was enough to trigger employer liability. At the Court's post-oral argument conference, Chief Justice Rehnquist began the discussion. He led off by explaining the case and stating his view that the lower court committed legal error when it ruled Hicks did not have to carry the burden of persuasion throughout the trial. As Figure 31 shows, Rehnquist then voted to reverse. Justices White, Blackmun, and Stevens followed, with the three of them all siding with Hicks. The vote was now 1-3 in favor of affirming. Justices O'Connor, Scalia, and Kennedy then voted to reverse, making the tally 4-3 in favor of reversing. Justice Souter voted to affirm, making the vote 4-4, and leaving Justice Thomas, the most junior justice, the pivotal vote. Thomas voted to reverse, making the final vote 5-4 to reverse. Soon, the Chief would assign the majority opinion to one of the members of the majority. In this case, he assigned it to Justice Scalia.

For a more complete understanding of what the process in fact looks like, Figure 32 shows an example of one of the Court's assignment sheets. It reflects how the Court divided up its majority opinions after the first sitting in November, 1993. Each of the justices received one majority opinion assignment except for Justices O'Connor and Scalia, who each received two. Chief Justice Rehnquist assigned all the opinions except for *Ratzlaf* v. *United States* (1994),[3] which Justice Stevens assigned, and *Tennessee* v. *Middlebrooks* (1993)[4] and *J.E.B.* v. *T.B.* (1994),[5] which Justice Blackmun assigned.

7.2 FACTORS LEADING TO OPINION ASSIGNMENT

When it comes to explaining the factors that lead the Chief (or the senior Associate Justice) to assign opinions to some justices rather than others, scholarship has lined up behind two major theories. The first is that Chiefs assign opinions based on ideological congruence with prospective writers. The second is that Chiefs consider various institutional dynamics when assigning opinions. We examine both theories.

---

[2] See *Saint Mary's Honor Center* v. *Hicks*, 509 U.S. 502 (1993).
[3] *Ratzlaf* v. *United States*, 510 U.S. 135 (1994).
[4] *Tennessee* v. *Middlebrooks*, 510 U.S. 124 (1993).
[5] *J.E.B.* v. *T.B.*, 511 U.S. 127 (1994).

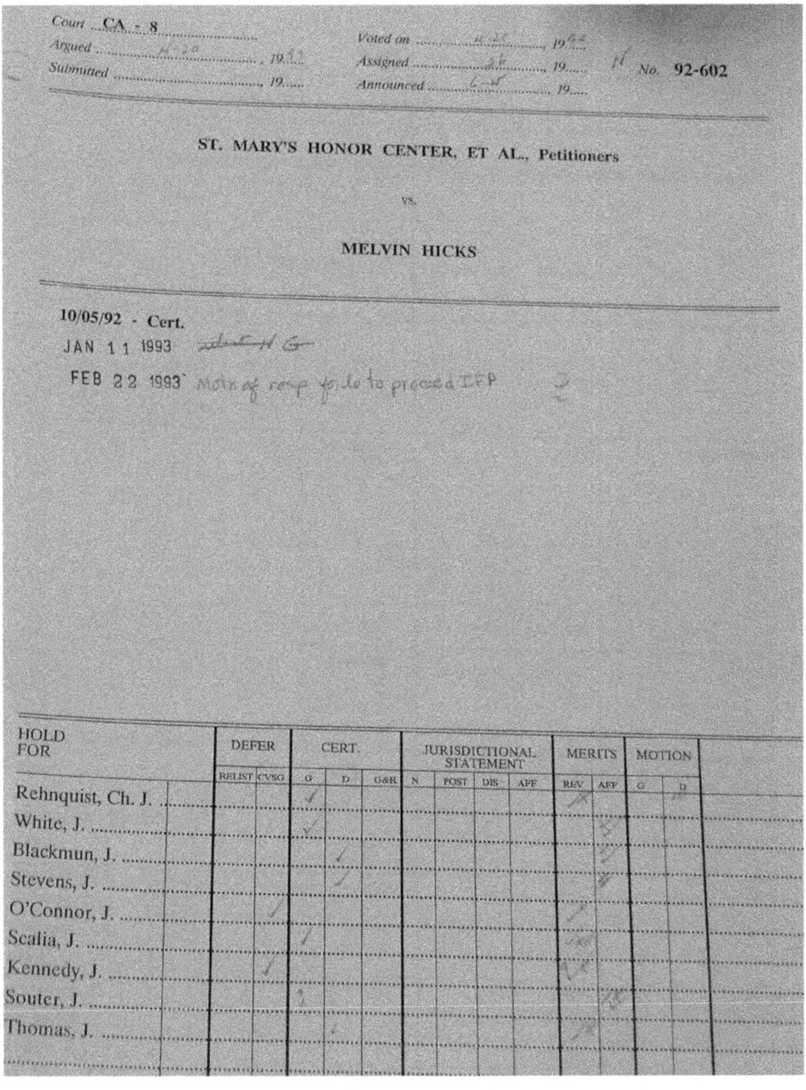

Court CA - 8
Argued .... 19..
Submitted .... 19..
Voted on .... 19..
Assigned .... 19..
Announced .... 19..
No. 92-602

ST. MARY'S HONOR CENTER, ET AL., Petitioners

vs.

MELVIN HICKS

10/05/92 - Cert.
JAN 11 1993
FEB 22 1993 Motn of resp for lv to proceed IFP

HOLD FOR		DEFER		CERT.			JURISDICTIONAL STATEMENT				MERITS		MOTION	
		RELIST	CVSG	G	D	G&R	N	POST	DIS	AFF	REV	AFF	G	D
Rehnquist, Ch. J.				✓							✓			
White, J.				✓								✓		
Blackmun, J.					✓							✓		
Stevens, J.					✓							✓		
O'Connor, J.			✓								✓			
Scalia, J.				✓							✓			
Kennedy, J.			✓								✓			
Souter, J.				✓								✓		
Thomas, J.				✓							✓			

FIGURE 31: *Justice Blackmun's docket sheet in Saint Mary's Honor Center* v. *Hicks (1993).*

7.2.1 *Ideological Considerations*

For years, scholars have argued that justices assign majority opinions for ideological considerations. That is, when the Chief is in the majority coalition, he will assign opinions to ideological allies. And when the Chief is not in

CONFIDENTIAL

ASSIGNMENTS FOR OCTOBER TERM, 1993
November 15, 1993

Justice GINSBURG..(92-1196 - Ratzlaf v. United States (JPS)

Justice THOMAS....(92-1223 - U.S. Dept. of Defense v. FLRA ²/₃₂

Justice SOUTER....(92-1292 - Campbell v. Acuff-Rose Music ³/₇

Justice KENNEDY...(92-74 - Oregon Dept. of Rev. v. Act Industries ¹/₂ᴶ

Justice SCALIA....(92-6921 - Liteky v. U.S. ³/₇
                  (91-1950 - American Dredging Co. v. Miller ¹/₃₂

Justice O'CONNOR..(92-6281 - Hagen v. Utah ²/₂₂
                  (92-7549 - Schiro v. Farley ⁴/₈

Justice STEVENS...(92-989 - Tennessee v. Middlebrooks (HAB)
                                          DIG ¹²/⁹/⁹³

Justice BLACKMUN..(92-1239 - J.E.B. v. T.B. (HAB) ⁴/⁷

C.J. REHNQUIST....(92-1482 - Weiss v. U.S. ⁴/₈

PER CURIAMS.......(92-1510 - Cavanaugh v. Roller (DIG) ¹¹/₂₀

FIGURE 32: *Opinion assignments from the Supreme Court's first sitting in November 1993.* Taken from record of Justice Harry Blackmun and found at http://epstein.wustl.edu/blackmun.php?p=2.

majority coalitions, the Senior Associate Justice will assign opinions to his or her ideological allies (see, e.g., Davis 1990).

There is some evidence to support this policy-driven theory. Using a simple difference in means test, Maltzman, Spriggs, and Wahlbeck (2000, 48) find that Chief Justice Burger was, all else being equal, more likely to assign opinions to his ideological allies. The authors also discovered that Burger was more likely to assign opinions to ideological allies when a case was politically salient (see also Wahlbeck 2006). In an analysis of Chief Justices Warren, Burger, and Rehnquist, Maltzman and Wahlbeck (2004) found that all three Chiefs relied on ideology when assigning opinions. As they put it, "If a justice is relatively close to a chief ... the probability of being assigned the opinion-writing task is 19.8 percent greater than the odds that an ideologically-distant justice will receive the assignment" (558).

The vast majority of studies, however, suggest that Chiefs are more nuanced when it comes to ideological assignments. Instead of simply assigning to allies, Chiefs assign to justices whose ideologies will most effectively keep majority coalitions together. For example, Maltzman, Spriggs, and Wahlbeck (2000) find that Chief Justice Burger was less likely to assign opinions to ideological allies in minimum winning coalitions. Rather, he assigned opinions in these coalitions to justices who could keep the coalition cup from tipping over and spilling majority justices this way and that. Wahlbeck and Maltzman (2005, 436) find that Chief Justice Rehnquist behaved the same way: he was less likely to assign an opinion to an ideological ally in minimum winning coalitions, preferring, instead, to assign to more moderate members (see also Wahlbeck 2006). Maltzman and Wahlbeck (2004, 559) agree, finding that "the effect of ideology is only significant when the chief is freed from the constraint of trying to hold a decision coalition together." Policy matters, and when unconstrained, Chiefs will assign accordingly. But when constrained by context, Chiefs pursue their policy goals more carefully.

7.2.2 *Institutional Considerations*

A second theory argues that institutional considerations motivate opinion assignors – even more so than ideological considerations. The literature shows that Chiefs assign opinions to ensure the smooth functioning of the Court: they assign opinions equitably, they assign opinions to issue experts, and they sometimes favor efficient justices who can work quickly.

In recent decades, Chiefs and senior Associate Justices have assigned opinions equitably. When sitting down to determine who will write which opinions, Chiefs ensure that all justices receive a similar number of assignments in order to achieve equity. Often, this means working with the Senior Associate Justice to find out the justices to whom they have assigned opinions. The Chief then works around those assignments. Chief Justice Warren once reported that "if it [opinion assignment] wasn't done with regard to fairness, it could well lead to great disruption on the Court" (quoted in Slotnick 1979a, 319). The data suggest that Chief Justice Rehnquist assigned opinions so as to achieve equity in each sitting (Wahlbeck 2006). Maltzman and Wahlbeck (1996) find that Rehnquist was "less likely to assign an additional case to a justice who was being assigned a majority opinion by a senior associate justice" in order to retain an equitable distribution. According to their data, a justice with no other opinion assignments had a 10.7 percent chance of being assigned a case, while a justice who already received an opinion from another assignor had a 6 percent chance of being assigned the case, even after controlling for things like ideological congruence with the assignor.

Other recent Chiefs also assigned opinions equitably. In their study of Chief Justices Warren, Burger, and Rehnquist, Maltzman and Wahlbeck (2004) find that "if a justice is assigned two opinions by associate justices, the chances of a chief justice giving him or her an additional assignment are 9.3 percent lower" than when the justice has no pending assignments. Slotnick reports that Chiefs from Taft to Burger cared a lot about "absolute" equity in opinion assignments, though not as much in important cases (Slotnick 1979a,b). That is, Chiefs cared about the raw numbers of assigned opinions as opposed to the percent of time a justice was in the majority and received an opinion (see also Benesh, Sheehan, and Spaeth 1999).[6]

Contemporary data reveal that Chief Justice Roberts is just as equitable. Figure 33 shows the Court's opinion assignments for the 2017 Term. It is obvious from this Figure that Roberts seeks equity when he assigns opinions. Each justice authored either six or seven opinions during the Court's term. No justice received more than two opinions per sitting. Each justice received at least one opinion in nearly every sitting. Indeed, so strong is the norm of equitable assignments that Court watchers can often predict who will write a majority opinion by examining who has already written during a sitting. For example, near the end of the Court's 2017 term, most Court watchers confidently predicted Chief Justice Roberts would write the majority opinion in *Gill v. Whitford* (2018) because he was the only justice who, at that time, had yet to release an opinion from the October sitting, when the Court heard *Gill*. They were right.

Chiefs also appear more likely to assign opinions to justices who are experts on the legal issues involved in cases. Some cases are more complicated than

---

[6] Earlier Chief Justices, however, were not so enamored of opinion equity. As Wood et al. (2000) report, earlier Chiefs were "less egalitarian" than recent Chiefs, perhaps because the Court's workload was so much greater (Owens and Simon 2012), thereby necessitating a greater need for efficiency.

	Oct.	Nov.	Dec.	Jan.	Feb.	March	April	Total
Argued	9	6	10	9	9	8	12	**63**
Roberts	1		1	1	1	1	1	6
Kennedy	1		1	1	1	1	1	6
Thomas	1	1	1	1	1	1	1	7
Ginsburg	1	1	1	1		1	1	6
Breyer	1	1	1	1	1		2	7
Alito	1	1	1	1	1	1	1	7
Sotomayor	1	1	1	1	1		2	7
Kagan	1	1	1	1		1	1	6
Gorsuch	1		2	1	1	1	1	7
Per Cur.					2	1	1	4
Remaining	0	0	0	0	0	0	0	**0**
	Oct.	Nov.	Dec.	Jan.	Feb.	March	April	Total

FIGURE 33: *Opinion assignments from the Supreme Court's 2017 Term as shown by SCOTUSblog. See* http://www.scotusblog.com/statistics/.

others, and in those cases it is useful to have an expert take on the challenge of writing the opinion. Justices overall tend to be generalists when they arrive at the Court. But some justices come to the Court having specialized in certain areas of the law. And these justices tend to get tapped for such cases more than their non-expert colleagues. One study discovered that "[i]n cases where a justice is considered an expert ... the likelihood that he or she will be assigned the opinion is 7.8% greater than for a non-expert in that area" (Maltzman and Wahlbeck 2004, 558). So, for example, Justice Scalia often received the Court's telecommunications opinions because he once was general counsel in the Office of Telecommunications Policy (OTP) in the Nixon White House.

Some studies also show that assignors are more likely to reward "efficient" justices (i.e., those who complete their writing assignments quickly). That is, they are more likely to assign opinions to justices who require less time to write them. Maltzman and Wahlbeck (2004) find that efficient justices are 28.5 percent more likely to receive an opinion assignment than inefficient justices. Perhaps not surprisingly, efficient justices benefit from the end of term crunch. Assignors are more likely to lean on them at the end of the term when the Court must complete its work quickly. Wahlbeck (2006) finds that Chief Justice Rehnquist was more likely to assign opinions to efficient justices – but only as the end of the term neared. As the end of the term approached, efficient justices were 1.4 times more likely to receive an opinion assignment than inefficient justices (Maltzman and Wahlbeck 1996). Looking further back in time, Brenner and Palmer (1988) find that for Chief Justice Vinson, efficiency mattered dramatically. More efficient justices received more opinions from him than inefficient justices, even when those efficient justices were ideologically distant from him. And looking even further back than that, Wood et al. (2000) examine all opinion assignments made by Chief Justices from 1888 to 1940. Their results suggest that Chief Justices historically assigned more cases to efficient justices.

Alas, the Court's smaller docket, combined with a strong norm of equity, has in recent years decreased the importance of efficiency in the opinion assignment decision. Still, we wonder whether, even with the norm of equity, justices who are more conscientious receive more opinions, or more important opinions. How relevant, in other words, is a justice's conscientiousness to the Chief when he assigns opinions?

Two studies come close to answering this question. The first was conducted by Brenner in 1985. Brenner sought to examine whether justices whom historians and experts rated as "great" or "more competent" were more likely to receive opinion assignments than justices rated as failures. Brenner wondered whether justices' reputations for competence in writing opinions (as reflected in polls about the justices) correlated with their actual numbers of written opinions. The study revealed little, with one largely artificial result. When Brenner compared "failure" justices (as one group) against "the greats," "the near greats," and those rated as "average" (lumped together as one group), he discovered that failures received fewer opinion assignments than non-failures. Justices rated as "great," however, were no more likely to receive opinion assignments than others.[7]

The second study is Hall's recent analysis on personality and the Court (Hall 2018). Hall finds no correlation between conscientiousness and receiving an opinion assignment from the Chief.[8] But this analysis is limited in

---

[7] Of course, these results stemmed from subjective evaluations of greatness. Moreover, Brenner had to infer whether the majority opinion writer was indeed the justice to whom the opinion had been assigned. He was unable to use archival records that showed the justice to whom the Chief (or SAJ) assigned the case. Inferring the identity of that justice, as we explain below, can lead to erroneous conclusions.

[8] Hall seeks to explain this null result by claiming that Chiefs may not actually want to assign opinions to hardworking and dutiful justices because they may take more time to write the

important ways. First, as we discussed in Chapter 3, the SCIPE measures Hall uses to estimate justices' preferences are highly suspect. Second, Hall does not accurately identify actual opinion assignments. Rather than employing actual archival data that shows which justices, in fact, received the opinion assignment, he looks to the Supreme Court Database. The Database, however, *imputes* the majority opinion assigner from the final vote breakdown in the case. That is, it assumes the final author of the opinion was the justice who received the original assignment. This is wrong. In fact, the authors of the Database suggest that scholars should be wary of using their approach. As they put it, "According to several scholarly studies, considerable voting shifts occur between the final conference vote (where the assignment is made) and the vote that appears in the Reports. As a result, *in approximately 16 percent of the cases*, a person other than the one identified by the database actually assigned the opinion."[9] Put simply, without certainty over who really received the original opinion assignments, one can hardly claim that their results "[rival or exceed] that of several legal, institutional, and ideological influences on assignments" (Hall 2018, 74).

7.3 A THEORY OF CONSCIENTIOUSNESS AND OPINION ASSIGNMENT

We believe Chiefs (and senior Associate Justices) favor conscientious justices in important cases for one overarching reason. Important cases present the chance to make "good law" or legal policy. While norms of equity seemingly dominate assignment of the "average" or regular cases, there are incentives to put the important opinions in the hands of a more conscientious justice. The assignor wants a good opinion that is a solid piece of craftsmanship.

Recall what conscientiousness represents. Conscientiousness is a person's tendency to act in an organized or thoughtful way. It captures whether a person is dutiful, deliberate, driven, persistent, self-assured, and hardworking. Conscientious people are self-controlled and responsible to others. They

---

opinion and could slow down the Court (77). This concern seems trivial to us. Certainly, the Chief will be the one to get blamed for a slow Court, but so long as the opinions come down by the end of the term, it's hard to believe there would be much blowback. And even if there was, it would be a small price to pay in exchange for a better opinion. Hall also suggests Chiefs might not want to assign to conscientious justices because they might be "less likely to pressure other justices to abandon their own views for political expediency" (77). But this cuts against his own findings in chapter 6 that conscientious justices circulate *more* suggestions and fewer join statements.

9 http://scdb.wustl.edu/documentation.php?var=majOpinAssigner (emphasis added).

abide by rules. They are good at organizing and prioritizing tasks. These certainly seem to us like characteristics an opinion assignor would value when searching to assign an important case.

Indeed, there is circumstantial evidence to support our theory. Chief Justice Burger assigned Harry Blackmun the Court's opinion in *Roe* v. *Wade* (1973). Scholars have shown that Burger may have manipulated the process to do so (Graetz and Greenhouse 2016; Maltzman, Spriggs, and Wahlbeck 2000; Woodward and Armstrong 1979). For his part, Blackmun privately believed Burger had to assign him the opinion. After all, Blackmun had extensive expertise and experience in the area. Blackmun had been Mayo Clinic's legal counsel for nearly ten years and knew much about the doctor-patient relationship (Greenhouse 2005). And that was, for Blackmun, a major part of the case. What is more, many of the other justices had "public perception" problems in the case and might not have been able to write an opinion that would earn public support. For example, Brennan was Catholic and would not want backlash from Catholics. An opinion by Marshall, Blackmun believed, might "racialize" the issue of abortion. And Douglas . . . Well, Douglas had his own problems. Blackmun believed to his core that Burger could not have assigned the opinion to Douglas because Douglas wrote poorly reasoned opinions. Douglas's opinions, Blackmun believed, had "deteriorated" and "become increasingly superficial" (Woodward and Armstrong 1979, 206). Burger could not assign Douglas the opinion, in other words, because he would have written a *careless and perfunctory* opinion. The Chief would want a more conscientious writer for such an important case.

All things being equal, we expect the Chief will be more likely to assign opinions to increasingly conscientious justices. But given the norm of equity so strongly prevalent today, the Chief does not have the luxury of always favoring such justices. The Court's history contains conscientious justices as well as those who are less demanding. The Chief must assign to them all. And so the Chief's favoritism likely comes through in selecting *which kind* of opinions to assign to which justices. In our view, the Chief will favor conscientious justices in the most important cases. That is, we expect that *the Chief will be more likely to assign opinions in legally and politically salient cases to increasingly conscientious justices.*

7.4 DATA AND MEASURES

Our data and measures come primarily from Maltzman and Wahlbeck (2004). But to their study, we add our conscientiousness measures. We discuss the data and measures in this section, but note that we necessarily draw on

Maltzman and Wahlbeck (2004, 554–556) for much of the discussion. To determine how justices assign opinions on the High Court, Maltzman and Wahlbeck examined the initial assignment sheets and docket sheets from the personal papers of Chief Justice Earl Warren, and Justices William Brennan and Thurgood Marshall. These assignment sheets describe how Chief Justices Warren, Burger, and Rehnquist assigned opinions from 1953 to 1990. Maltzman and Wahlbeck restricted the analysis to the 3,494 cases where the assignment sheets indicated the Chief assigned the opinion. Doing so generates 23,970 observations in which the unit of analysis is the individual (conference majority) justice within each case.

Dependent Variable. The dependent variable, *Assigned*, indicates whether a justice, who had voted with the majority at conference, received the opinion assignment from the Chief Justice. We assign a value of 1 if the justice under analysis received the opinion assignment; 0 otherwise.

Conscientiousness. Our main covariate of interest is *Conscientiousness*. We also control for justices' four other personality traits – *Openness, Extraversion, Agreeableness*, and *Neuroticism*.

Legal Salience. To measure the legal salience of a case, Maltzman and Wahlbeck (2004) created a binary indicator that measured whether the Court struck down a law as unconstitutional or whether the Court formally altered precedent.[10] We code a legally salient case as 1; 0 otherwise.

Conscientiousness × Legal Salience. A conscientious justice may be more likely to receive the assignment in legally salient cases. To examine the conditional effect of conscientiousness and legal salience, we interact the two variables.

Political Salience. To measure the political salience of a case, Maltzman and Wahlbeck (2004) identified the number of amicus curiae briefs filed in every case. They then calculated term-specific z-scores for amicus participation. That is, they computed the difference between the number of case-specific amicus filings and the average number of amici per case during that term, and then divided that difference by the term-specific standard deviation in amicus filings. Larger values reflect cases with greater than average amici participation.

Conscientiousness × Political Salience. A conscientious justice may be more likely to receive the opinion assignment in politically salient cases. To examine the conditional effect of conscientiousness and political salience, we interact the two variables.

---

[10] This indicator includes cases that struck down federal, state, or local laws as unconstitutional.

Winning Margin. To code *Winning Margin*, Maltzman and Wahlbeck (2004) first identified the size of the majority conference coalition. They then subtracted the number of votes needed to form a winning coalition from the number of justices voting with the assignor. Thus, minimum winning coalitions (5-4) equal 0, while a nine-person unanimous coalition would take on a value of 4.

Conscientiousness × Winning Margin. We also examine whether conscientious justices are more likely to receive an opinion assignment in close cases, in order to maintain a winning coalition. (We perform this interaction because we are replicating the models in Maltzman and Wahlbeck 2004.)

End of Term. We measure the number of days remaining in the Court's term. This, of course, accounts for the time remaining for the prospective assignee to complete the opinion. Maltzman and Wahlbeck (2004) identified the number of days between the date an opinion was assigned and July 1, which they argue is the traditional end of the Court's term. Larger values reflect opinions assigned earlier in the term. Smaller values reflect opinions assigned at the end of the term.

Conscientiousness × End of Term. To determine whether the Chief is more likely to assign an opinion to a conscientious justice as the end of terms nears, we create an interactive variable. (Again, we perform this interaction because we are replicating the models in Maltzman and Wahlbeck 2004.)

Ideology. We control for the ideological compatibility between the Chief Justice and each individual justice who might receive the opinion assignment. To determine each justice's ideological compatibility for each case, Maltzman and Wahlbeck (2004) calculated an issue-specific compatibility score between the Chief and the justices in the majority conference coalition. They first identified each case's primary substantive issue area, among the Supreme Court Database's twelve issue area values. They then measured the percent of cases in which each justice voted in the liberal direction in that issue area among all previous cases (during that justice's time on the bench). For each justice, this created a percent liberal score per issue area. They then determined the absolute value of the difference between each justice's value-specific liberalism score and the assignor's liberalism score. Larger values reflect more ideological distance between the justice and the Chief.

Chief Justice. Maltzman and Wahlbeck (2004) created a binary indicator to determine whether the Chief was the justice under consideration. If so, the variable takes on the value of 1; 0 otherwise.

Equity. As we discussed previously, Chiefs in recent years have tended to assign opinions in an equitable fashion. To account for this dynamic,

Maltzman and Wahlbeck (2004) measured the number of associate justice assignments each justice received between each set of assignments made by the Chief. The more assignments a justice received from someone other than the Chief, the smaller the likelihood that the Chief would assign an opinion to that justice.

Expertise. Justices who are experts on an issue are more likely to receive opinions dealing with that issue. To determine whether a justice was a policy expert, Maltzman and Wahlbeck (2004) calculated what they called an "issue-specific opinion ratio" for each justice. As they put it, the opinion ratio "is the number of cases in which a justice wrote a dissent or concurrence divided by the number of like cases that previously had reached the Court since that justice's appointment" (556). Once they determined this ratio, Maltzman and Wahlbeck (2004) created a standardized z-score per justice. They did so by comparing the justice's ratio to the mean for all justices who sat that term. For instance, if a justice's score was one standard deviation above the average justice that term, *Expertise* equals 1. If the score was one standard deviation below the mean, the justice's *Expertise* measure equals −1.

Efficiency. The final control predictor represents each justice's past efficiency when authoring opinions. Maltzman and Wahlbeck (2004) examined the mean number of days each justice took to write the first draft of their majority opinions during each natural Court.

7.5   METHODS AND RESULTS

Because our dependent variable is dichotomous, we estimate logistic regression models. We estimate robust standard errors clustered on the case citation, given that the errors should be correlated across justices within each case.[11] We report the results of five separate analyses – an unconditional specification and four separate analyses where *Conscientiousness* is interacted with *Legal Salience, Political Salience, Winning Margin,* and *End of Term,* respectively. For each analysis, we first report a baseline regression and then a second model that includes the full complement of control predictors.[12]

Table 16 presents the regression results. First, consider the unconditional effects in Models 1 and 2. The statistically insignificant coefficients suggest that increasingly conscientious justices are no more, or less, likely to receive the opinion assignment than less conscientious justices. Given the norm of

[11]   The subsequent results are substantively consistent if alternatively estimating robust (unclustered) or classical standard errors.
[12]   All empirical results are substantively consistent when specifying a baseline model that does not include the other personality trait indicators (nor other control predictors).

TABLE 16: *The Conditional Impact of the Conscientiousness Trait on Majority Opinion Assignments on the US Supreme Court*

	Unconditional		Legal Salience		Political Salience		Winning Margin		End of Term	
	(1)	(2)	(3)	(4)	(5)	(6)	(7)	(8)	(9)	(10)
Conscientiousness	−0.03 (0.03)	−0.02 (0.03)	−0.05 (0.03)	−0.04 (0.03)	−0.03 (0.03)	−0.02 (0.03)	−0.04 (0.03)	−0.02 (0.03)	−0.03 (0.03)	−0.02 (0.03)
Openness	−0.03* (0.02)	−0.01 (0.02)	−0.03* (0.02)	−0.01 (0.02)	−0.03* (0.02)	−0.01 (0.02)	−0.03 (0.02)	−0.01 (0.02)	−0.03* (0.02)	−0.01 (0.02)
Extraversion	0.06* (0.03)	0.01 (0.03)	0.06* (0.03)	0.02 (0.03)	0.06* (0.03)	0.01 (0.03)	0.06* (0.03)	0.01 (0.03)	0.06* (0.03)	0.01 (0.03)
Agreeableness	−0.02 (0.02)	−0.001 (0.02)	−0.02 (0.02)	−0.002 (0.02)	−0.02 (0.02)	−0.001 (0.02)	−0.02 (0.02)	−0.002 (0.02)	−0.02 (0.02)	−0.001 (0.02)
Neuroticism	−0.04* (0.02)	−0.03 (0.02)	−0.04* (0.02)	−0.03 (0.02)	−0.04* (0.02)	−0.03 (0.02)	−0.05* (0.02)	−0.03 (0.02)	−0.04* (0.02)	−0.03 (0.02)
Legal Salience			0.02 (0.02)	0.036 (0.023)						
Conscientious × Leg Sal			0.16* (0.06)	0.16* (0.06)						
Political Salience					0.012* (0.007)	0.01 (0.01)				
Conscientious × Pol Sal					0.02 (0.02)	0.02 (0.02)				
Winning Margin							−0.17* (0.005)	−0.17* (0.005)		
Conscientious × Margin							0.018 (0.012)	0.019 (0.012)		

	1	2	3	4	5	6	7	8	9	10
End of Term									0.0002 (0.0001)	0.0002* (0.0001)
Conscientious × Term									0.0003 (0.0003)	0.0003 (0.0002)
Ideology (Distance)		−0.005* (0.001)		−0.005* (0.001)		−0.005* (0.001)		−0.004* (0.001)		−0.005* (0.001)
Chief Justice		−0.06 (0.07)		−0.06 (0.07)		−0.06 (0.07)		−0.09 (0.07)		−0.06 (0.07)
Equity		−0.06* (0.02)		−0.05* (0.02)		−0.06* (0.02)		−0.05* (0.02)		−0.06* (0.02)
Expertise		0.04 (0.02)		0.04* (0.02)		0.04* (0.02)		0.04* (0.02)		0.04* (0.02)
Efficiency		−0.004* (0.001)		−0.004* (0.001)		−0.004* (0.001)		−0.004* (0.001)		−0.004* (0.001)
Constant	−1.76* (0.02)	−1.50* (0.06)	−1.76* (0.02)	−1.50* (0.06)	−1.76* (0.02)	−1.50* (0.06)	−1.75* (0.02)	−1.50* (0.06)	−1.76* (0.02)	−1.50* (0.06)
N	23,970	23,970	23,970	23,970	23,970	23,970	23,970	23,970	23,970	23,970
χ^2	13.33*	56.60*	24.38*	68.68*	16.62*	59.43*	83018.2*	41532.9*	15.59	59.40

Note: Table entries are logistic regression coefficients with robust standard errors (clustered on the case citation) in parentheses; *$p < .05$ (one-tailed). The dependent variable represents whether a justice in the majority conference coalition received the initial assignment to author the majority opinion, 1953–1990.

equitable assignments, this result is not surprising. The strong norm of assignment equity dictates that conscientiousness likely plays only a conditional role. And that is indeed what the results show.

Models 3 and 4 report the results while interacting *Conscientiousness* with *Legal Salience*. Chief Justices are more likely to assign opinions to conscientious justices in legally salient cases. The Chief needs to balance out opinion assignments fairly evenly. But as he contemplates how to assign the major and the minor opinions, he takes into consideration the conscientiousness of the available justices.

Given the difficulty of interpreting interactive terms from coefficients in a regression table, we visually present predicted probabilities and average marginal effects. Figure 34(a) shows the predicted probability a justice will receive the majority opinion assignment across the range of *Conscientiousness*. The solid line in the figure represents non–legally salient cases, while the dashed line reports legally salient cases. Consider the non–legally salient case. A justice who scores the lowest on conscientiousness has a 0.16 [0.13, 0.19] probability of receiving the assignment. That probability decreases to 0.14 [0.13, 0.15] when the case becomes highly legally salient.

Figure 34(b) displays the average marginal effect (with 90 percent confidence intervals) of *Legal Salience* across the observed range of *Conscientiousness* using results from Model 4 in Table 16. The figure shows that a justice at the low end of *Conscientiousness* – below −0.377, or roughly 44 percent of the sample observations – is significantly *less* likely to receive the assignment in a legally salient case compared to one that is not legally salient. By contrast, justices scoring above 0.03 (or, 40 percent of the observations) on *Conscientiousness* are significantly *more* likely to receive the assignment in legally important cases. What is more, the impact of *Legal Salience* increases markedly among the most conscientious justices in the sample.

Figure 34(c) shows the average marginal effect of *Conscientiousness* conditional on *Legal Salience*. It indicates that the slope in a non-legally salient case is not statistically distinguishable from zero. Alternatively, in a legally salient case, *Conscientiousness* does exhibit a statistically significant effect on opinion assignments. Specifically, the dashed line in Figure 34(a) shows that the least conscientious justice has a 0.10 [0.06, 0.13] probability of receiving the opinion assignment. But as legal salience increases, so too does the probability of receiving the opinion writing task, such that the most conscientious justice has a 0.17 [0.14, 0.20] probability of receiving the assignment – an increase of 0.07, or 70 percent. And to highlight the magnitude of this effect, we can say that the effect exceeds the total average impact of *Ideology*.

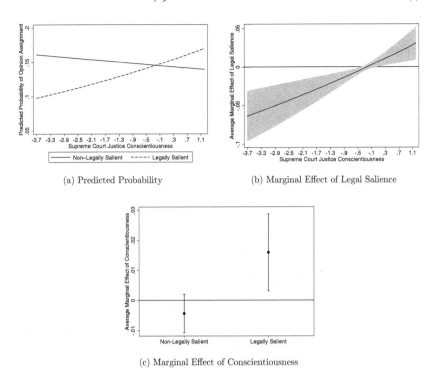

(a) Predicted Probability   (b) Marginal Effect of Legal Salience

(c) Marginal Effect of Conscientiousness

FIGURE 34: *The conditional effect of conscientiousness on majority opinion assignments.* Panel (a) reports the predicted probability that a justice will receive the majority opinion assignment across the range of *Conscientiousness*. The solid line represents non–legally salient cases while the dashed line reports legally salient cases. Panel (b) reports the average marginal effect (with 90 percent confidence intervals) of *Legal Salience*. Panel (c) reports the average marginal effect (with 90 percent confidence intervals) of *Conscientiousness* conditional on *Legal Salience* using results from Model 4 in Table 16.

In short, the Chief Justice tends to assign opinions in legally salient cases to his most conscientious colleagues.

Contrary to our expectations, political salience does not appear to moderate the impact of *Conscientiousness* on opinion assignments; nor do coalition or end of term considerations.

Our controls perform as expected. As the ideological distance increases between the justice and the Chief, the Chief becomes less likely to assign him or her the majority opinion. Specifically, a shift from the minimum to maximum degree of ideological distance diminishes the predicted probability that justice will receive the opinion assignment by 0.043 (or, a roughly 28 percent decrease). We also find strong support for the equity norm. As a justice receives more opinions from a Senior Associate Justice, the Chief becomes less likely to assign him or her the opinion – and this is while accounting for the ideological difference between the Chief and the justice. Lastly, the Chief Justice is significantly more likely to assign opinions to experts and to more efficient justices (i.e., less likely to assign to justices who take longer to write). Looking to the other traits, we find that in the models without controls, justices who are more open and neurotic are less likely to receive an opinion assignment from the Chief, while justices who are more extraverted are more likely to receive the assignment. The effects of these traits disappear, however, when we include the controls in our model.

7.6 CONCLUSION

Chiefs assign opinions for various reasons – some good, some bad. For example, Justice Blackmun once told listeners: "If one's in the doghouse with the Chief, he gets the crud. He gets the tax cases and some of the Indian cases" (Staudt, Epstein, and Wiedenbeck 2006, 1,799, n. 7). Likewise, Justice Powell once told another justice that because Powell had opposed Burger in a case, he was "resigned to writing nothing but Indian affairs cases for the rest of my life" (Schwartz 1990, 4). While there is some evidence to suggest that Chiefs sometimes use opinion assignments to punish justices, the literature suggests that systematically, they value ideological and contextual dynamics. While we certainly do not take issue with these findings, we believe they are incomplete. We believe they omit the important effects of conscientiousness.

We argued that justices receive opinion assignments, in part, because of their conscientiousness. We argued that increasingly conscientious justices would be more likely to receive opinion assignments. At the same time, we argued the Chief's motivations would be limited by the strong norm of equitable assigning. As we saw it, conscientious justices would be more likely to receive opinions than less conscientious justices in the most salient cases. The results support this theory, in part.

Chiefs are more likely to assign opinions to increasingly conscientious justices in legally salient cases. This is precisely what we expected. On the other hand, the results do not support the claim that they are more likely to assign opinions similarly in politically salient cases. Nevertheless, these results provide further evidence that conscientiousness influences judicial behavior.

These findings tell us a number of important things. First, they further solidify our argument that conscientiousness influences justices and case outcomes. This chapter, and the others, show just how important conscientiousness is to the decision-making process and the evolution of law. The finding is, as Pink Floyd might say, another brick in the wall. Second, the results tell us about the opinion writing process. It sounds elementary (and it is), but a justice must be assigned a majority opinion in order to write it (barring switching among the justices after the opinion assignment). The content of the opinion and the quality of it are functions of who wrote the opinion. The decision to assign the opinion, therefore, is incredibly important – and so is knowing how opinion assignments are made.

Think back to our conclusion in Chapter 4. We discussed the process of building LEGOs. Most LEGOs come in packages with numbered bags. Bag number one builds a foundation. Bag number two adds to it. Bag number three might generate the finished product. We've now completed bag number four. The results are stacking up – and they are providing a strong overall theme. Conscientiousness influences judicial behavior.

7.7 APPENDIX

7.7.1 *Interactive Effects*

In the main part of the chapter, we provide the graphical image of the interactive effect of legal salience and conscientiousness. Here, we include figures of all four interactions.

7.7.2 *Winning Margin*

Figure 35(c) reports the average marginal effect (with 90 percent confidence intervals) of *Winning Margin* across the observed range of justice *Conscientiousness* using results from Model 8 in Table 16. The figure seems to indicate that *Winning Margin* has a negative impact on opinion assignment that decreases (i.e., becomes less negative) among more conscientious justices. However, Figure 36(a) indicates that the average marginal effect of *Conscientiousness* is never statistically significant across the entire range of *Winning Margin*. And, similarly, Figure 36(b) shows that the predicted probability of receiving the assignment in a high-margin case (i.e., the dashed line, or 90th percentile) is mostly flat across the range of *Conscientiousness*.

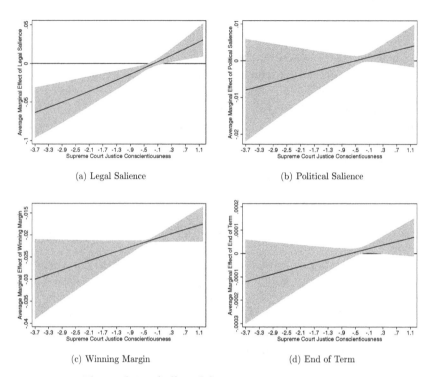

(a) Legal Salience

(b) Political Salience

(c) Winning Margin

(d) End of Term

FIGURE 35: *The conditional effect of the conscientiousness trait on majority opinion assignments.* Estimates represent the average marginal effect (with 90 percent confidence intervals) of *Legal Salience* (panel a), *Political Salience* (panel b), *Winning Margin* (panel c), and *End of Term* (panel d) across the observed range of justice *Conscientiousness* using results from Table 16.

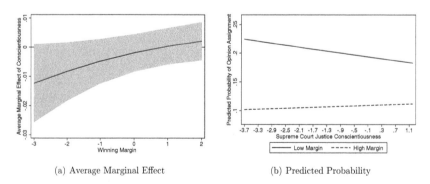

(a) Average Marginal Effect

(b) Predicted Probability

FIGURE 36: *The interactive effect of the conscientiousness trait and winning margin on majority opinion assignments.* Panel (a) reports the average marginal effect (with 90 percent confidence intervals) of *Conscientiousness* across the range of *Winning Margin* using results from Model 8 in Table 16. Panel (b) reports the predicted probability that a justice will receive the majority opinion assignment across the range of *Conscientiousness*. The solid line represents cases with a low winning margin (10th percentile), while the dashed line reports high margin cases (90th percentile).

8

Conscientiousness and Opinion Bargaining

In *Ingraham* v. *Wright* (1977), the Supreme Court faced the question whether corporal punishment at a public school violated the Eighth Amendment's "cruel and unusual punishment" clause.[1] It was a case with significant ramifications in schools across the country. Perhaps not surprisingly, the Court split 5–4. In an opinion written by Justice Lewis Powell, the majority determined that corporal punishment did not violate the Eighth Amendment. Both the common law and the Court's recent decisions, said Powell, dictated such an outcome.

Interestingly, it took Powell 116 days to write the opinion. A full 116 days elapsed between the day he was assigned the opinion and the day he circulated the opinion to his colleagues.[2] Compared to the average amount of time it normally took justices to write, this was lengthy. In fact, it amounted to two standard deviations above the mean number of days justices needed to circulate their first opinions. Clearly, Powell was being careful as he wrote.

Once he circulated his draft, it triggered some consternation. Though the Chief and Justice Blackmun joined the opinion right away, and Justice Stewart asked for a handful of seemingly minor changes, Justice Rehnquist pushed Powell for a number of changes. He expressed particular concern about the portion of Powell's opinion that conceded the paddled students had a "protected liberty interest." He argued, "I would like to see a more explicit and circumscribed approach to the question of why such an interest is held to exist." He went further and told Powell:

---

[1]   See *Ingraham* v. *Wright*, 430 U.S. 651 (1977).
[2]   The archival memos we use here come from the Burger Court Opinion Writing Database (Maltzman, Spriggs, and Wahlbeck 2000).

If you are able to get five votes including your own for your present opinion without me, I will concur in everything except Part IV A of the opinion. Otherwise, I would like to see some changes to part IV A along the lines I have preliminarily suggested herein.

One week later, Rehnquist followed up with an additional memo seeking further changes to the opinion.[3]

Why did Justice Powell take so long to write the first draft of the opinion in *Ingraham*? What led Justice Rehnquist to push for changes? The dominant understanding of opinion writing and bargaining is that ideology and context drive justices' decisions. But these factors surely cannot explain their behavior completely. We believe that the justices' conscientiousness also influences them.

Our theory leads us to believe, first, that conscientious justices will take more time to write the majority opinion in order to craft a careful legal document that satisfies their colleagues and, second, that conscientious justices will be more likely to seek changes from majority opinion writers. The results largely (though with conditions) confirm our expectations.

8.1 BARGAINING OVER SUPREME COURT OPINION CONTENT

Once a justice receives an opinion assignment, he or she has plenty of work to do. Generally, each justice convenes a meeting of his or her law clerks to discuss the majority's position at conference as well as the various and potentially nuanced positions taken by the minority coalition justices. The clerks and the justice formulate a path forward for writing the opinion. The clerk crafts the first draft of the opinion with input from her justice (Peppers 2006; Ward and Weiden 2006). Some justices give their clerks more freedom when writing; others give less. But throughout, the clerk and justice maintain a collaborative dynamic.[4] When the opinion writer is personally satisfied that she

---

3   Lest readers make the mistake of thinking justices do not read academic scholarship, Rehnquist had this to say: "I should add that in footnote 37 on page 20 you cite Professor Monaghan's draft article, 'Of Liberty and Property' to be published in the *Cornell Law Journal*. I do not believe I could join the opinion if that citation is intended as a favorable reference to that article, as a whole. The article is quite critical of *Paul* v. *Davis*, which I wrote, and *Meachum* v. *Fano*, which I joined (and both of which you joined)."

4   Some justices, instead, follow a delegation method, whereby the delegate nearly exclusive authority to the clerk to write the opinion. Others follow a retention approach by which they write most of the opinion themselves, with minimal input from the clerk. The collaborative approach is most common on the Court today (Peppers 2006; Ward and Weiden 2006).

and her clerks have put together an opinion that faithfully reflects her views and those of the majority coalition from the conference, she circulates it to her colleagues.

On the nine-member Court, at least four other justices must join the opinion for it to become precedentially binding, which means that opinion writers must often negotiate and bargain with their colleagues. Sometimes their colleagues simply join the opinion; other times, even the justices who agreed with the writer in principle at conference will seek changes. And if they request changes, the opinion writer has the option to accommodate them or not. Knowing that the author requires a majority of justices to join, the non-writing justices can exercise some leverage.

Upon receiving the majority opinion draft, justices have a number of options available to them. As Maltzman, Spriggs, and Wahlbeck (2000) point out, justices can join the opinion as is, make nonconditional suggestions, threaten the author to make changes or risk losing their vote, tell the author they will wait for the dissent before responding, tell the author they will write a separate opinion, or actually write and circulate a separate opinion. We discuss and provide examples of each.

In most instances, justices respond to the majority opinion writer with a simple *Joinder*. That is, after they receive the majority opinion draft, they tell the author, "Please join me." This is the response opinion authors want more than anything. Quoting Justice Powell's chambers, Maltzman, Spriggs, and Wahlbeck (2000, 63) state that justices "anxiously await responses from other Chambers. The happiest response is simply a note saying, 'Please join me.'" Figure 37 shows an example of a Joinder in *Bowers* v. *Hardwick* (85–140).

Other times, justices make non-conditional *Suggestions* to the opinion writer. These bargaining statements are collegial in nature – simple suggestions to the author to make a change. For example, as Figure 38 shows in *Japan Whaling Association* v. *American Cetacean Society* (85–954), Justice Powell responded to Justice White's opinion thusly:

> Dear Byron. I think your opinion is excellent, and have joined it. I do have one minor suggestion. On p. 11, the sentence ... is not clear as to the scope of the Secretary's discretion ... it would be helpful if you added language ... to make clear that the sentence is illustrative rather than a definition of that discretion. (Wahlbeck, Spriggs, and Maltzman 2009a)

Of course, justices often have more than one suggestion. Usually they have multiple suggestions, but they are nevertheless collegial in nature and designed to improve the opinion.

⌣

Supreme Court of the United States
Washington, D. C. 20543

CHAMBERS OF
JUSTICE WILLIAM H. REHNQUIST

April 23, 1986

Re: NO. 85-140 <u>Bowers</u> v. <u>Harwick</u>

Dear Byron,

Please join me.

Sincerely,

[signature]

Justice White

cc: The Conference

FIGURE 37: *Memo from Justice Rehnquist to Justice White in Bowers v. Hardwick (1986).*

In other instances, justices *Threaten* to withhold their votes conditional on the opinion writer making a change. For example, in *Bowsher* v. *Synar* (85–1377), Chief Justice Burger assigned himself the opinion. But to the chagrin of some of his colleagues, his draft opinion deviated from the conference majority's consensus. As a consequence, nearly all the justices responded with requested changes, but some were more threatening than others. As Figure 39 shows, one such threat came from Justice Stevens, who responded by stating: "Dear Chief . . . I do not agree with [your] rationale and will not be able to join your opinion unless it is substantially revised." In other words, *change the opinion or lose my vote.*

In other instances, justices simply announce their intent to *Wait* and see how other justices respond. Figure 41 shows, in *Bowers*, Justice Marshall responded to Justice White's majority opinion, stating, "Dear Byron: I await the dissent." A wait statement sometimes has the effect of bringing

May 30, 1986

```
85-954 & 85-955   Japan Whaling Assn. v. American
                  Cetacean Society
```

Dear Byron:

I think your opinion is excellent, and have joined it.

I do have one minor suggestion. On p. 11, the sentence beginning "We do not understand...." is not clear as to the scope of the Secretary's discretion. I see no compelling reason to be more specific, but it would be helpful if you added language (e.g., "for example") to make clear that the sentence is illustrative rather than a definition of that discretion.

Sincerely,

Justice White

LFP/vde

FIGURE 38: *Memo from Justice Powell to Justice White in Japan Whaling Association v. American Cetacean Society (1986).*

the majority opinion writer to the bargaining table, as it signals displeasure. But much of the time it simply signals that the justice generally favors the dissenting position.

Yet another option is for a justice to announce that she *Will Write* a separate opinion or in fact to *Circulate* a separate opinion. Figure 41 shows how, in *Bowers* v. *Hardwick*, Justice Blackmun responded to Justice White by stating, "Dear Byron: In due course, I shall try my hand at a dissent in this case."

Though justices often join the opinion without asking for changes, they commonly attempt to bargain with the opinion author for changes (Epstein and Knight 1998). Indeed, Maltzman, Spriggs, and Wahlbeck (2000) tell us

Supreme Court of the United States
Washington, D. C. 20543

CHAMBERS OF
JUSTICE JOHN PAUL STEVENS

June 2, 1986

Re: 85-1377 – <u>Bowsher</u> v. <u>Synar</u>
      85-1378 – <u>United States Senate</u> v. <u>Synar</u>
      85-1379 – <u>O'Neill</u> v. <u>Synar</u>

Dear Chief:

     As I read your opinion, you propose to hold that the functions assigned to the Comptroller General must be assigned to an officer removable by the President of the United States. I do not agree with this rationale and will not be able to join your opinion unless it is substantially revised.

     It was my understanding of the consensus at Conference that the rationale of the decision was that the function performed by the Comptroller General could not be performed by an arm of the Legislature unless Congress itself performed that function by the normal process of legislating described in <u>Chadha</u>. In other words, the central rationale should rest on <u>Chadha</u> rather than <u>Myers</u>. I think your opinion casts substantial doubt on the legal status of independent agencies and that it would be a serious mistake for the Court to adopt this approach.

     If others do not agree, I shall of course be writing separately.

Respectfully,

The Chief Justice

Copies to the Conference

FIGURE 39: *Memo from Justice Stevens to Chief Justice Burger in Bowsher v. Synar (1986).*

that roughly 25 percent of all cases observe a justice either expressly suggesting changes or threatening to withhold his or her vote unless the author changes the opinion. What is more, nearly 44 percent of all responses are some kind of bargaining response (i.e., not a Joinder). In short, bargaining is a common occurrence on the Court.

Scholars understand fairly well the conditions under which justices craft opinions. For example, we know that opinion writers take more time to write

Supreme Court of the United States
Washington, D. C. 20543

CHAMBERS OF
JUSTICE THURGOOD MARSHALL

April 22, 1986

Re: No. 85-140-Bowers v. Hardwick

Dear Byron:

I await the dissent.

Sincerely,

T.M.

T.M.

Justice White

cc: The Conference

FIGURE 40: *Memo from Justice Marshall to Justice White in Bowers v. Hardwick (1986).*

opinions when the majority coalition is ideologically heterogeneous. We also know that writers take more time when they write for a minimum winning coalition, when they write in legally salient cases, and when they have busy workloads. Conversely, they (necessarily) take less time as the end of the term nears (Maltzman, Spriggs, and Wahlbeck 2000).

Omitted from the literature, however, is the effect of conscientiousness on this process (but see Aliotta 1988). Conscientious justices may be more likely to take more time than their less conscientious colleagues. After all, conscientiousness involves "thinking before acting, delaying gratification, following norms and rules, and planning, organizing, and prioritizing tasks" (John and Srivastava 1999, 121). This sounds, to us, like strategic thinking and forecasting what needs to be done to complete a task. For a justice writing an opinion, this must mean engaging in "anticipatory accommodation." Conscientious justices will want to produce a solid piece of judicial craft and their timing is likely to reveal as much. Accordingly, we expect that *an*

𝔖𝔲𝔭𝔯𝔢𝔪𝔢 𝔔𝔬𝔲𝔯𝔱 𝔬𝔣 𝔱𝔥𝔢 𝔘𝔫𝔦𝔱𝔢𝔡 𝔖𝔱𝔞𝔱𝔢𝔰
𝔚𝔞𝔰𝔥𝔦𝔫𝔤𝔱𝔬𝔫, 𝔇. 𝔔. 20543

CHAMBERS OF
JUSTICE HARRY A. BLACKMUN

April 21, 1986

Re: No. 85-140, Bowers v. Hardwick

Dear Byron:

    In due course, I shall try my hand at a dissent in this case.

Sincerely,

FIGURE 41: *Memo from Justice Blackmun to Justice White in* Bowers v. Hardwick *(1986).*

increasingly conscientious justice will take more time to craft an opinion than a less conscientious justice.

Scholarship also tells us a lot about justices' bargaining behavior. We know that justices are more likely to engage with majority opinion writers for ideological reasons. The more distant a justice is from the writer and from the majority coalition, the more likely that justice is to seek changes. We also know that justices in minimum winning coalitions take advantage of their leverage and are more likely to bargain with the opinion author. We know that justices are more likely to seek changes in salient cases, complex cases, and when they are issue experts. Justices who have cooperated with each other in the past are less likely to push for changes in the majority opinion. Justices are also less likely to seek changes as the end of the term nears (Maltzman, Spriggs, and Wahlbeck 2000).

8.2 A THEORY OF CONSCIENTIOUSNESS AND OPINION BARGAINING

We believe conscientiousness influences whether justices bargain with opinion writers. Conscientiousness focuses largely on dependability (Mondak 2010, 53). It captures whether a person is hardworking. Conscientious people tend to be hard workers and perform well at their jobs. They are academically successful. John and Srivastava (1999, 121) remark that conscientiousness involves "following norms and rules, and planning, organizing, and prioritizing tasks." Conscientious people tend to work well on teams because they are more dependable, thorough, persistent, and hardworking (Hough 1992; Mount, Barrick, and Stewart 1998).

These findings demand our attention. Conscientious people are hardworking and successful. They are thorough and seek excellence. Given these findings, we expect conscientious justices to be more likely to engage the opinion writer and ask for changes to the opinion in an effort to improve it. At the same time, existing studies suggest that conscientious employees tend to work well in teams. To be sure, this could mean that they work well on teams because they pick up the slack when others falter. It could also mean, though, that they know their roles – and the roles others play – and respect those roles. If such is the case, we would expect conscientious justices to seek certain *kinds* of changes.

More specifically, we suspect that conscientious justices will be more likely to engage the opinion writer with concrete and specific efforts to change – and to do so from within the majority coalition. What we mean is this: they will be unlikely to issue a wait statement, concur, or dissent. Why? Issuing a wait statement is not what one would expect from a hardworking, no nonsense conscientious person. These people do not wait; they act to control their situations. For similar reasons, we expect conscientious justices to be less likely to dissent. Dissenting, in particular, saps their goals of precedentially binding authority. While we are less certain of concurrences, we do note that concurring opinions muddy the waters for the majority opinion. Orderly individuals are not likely to want that.

On the other hand, we suspect conscientious justices will be more likely to offer suggestions, threats, and will write statements. These options all involve concrete, actionable things. Suggestions and threats reveal precisely what the justice wants. Conscientious people work hard toward their goals. Such justices are more likely to spell out their wishes to the opinion writer. At the same time, we know that conscientious people are willing to put in extra work to achieve their goals. If they are unable to accomplish those goals, we could easily see them informing the opinion author that they will write their own opinions. And even though we expect them, on average, to be less likely to author dissents and possibly concurrences, we suspect they will do so when necessary.

Taken together, we expect that *as a justice becomes more conscientious, she will be more likely to make suggestions, threats, and will write statements, and less likely to make wait statements, to dissent, and to concur.*

Before proceeding to our data, we pause to note that Hall (2018, see Chapter 6) also seeks to examine how personality influences opinion bargaining. But his method of doing so differs from ours. He counts the number of majority opinion drafts and separate opinion drafts justices circulate, as well as the number of suggestions, wait statement, and join statements justices circulate. He claims that increasingly conscientious justices circulate more separate opinion drafts, more suggestions, and fewer join statements than less conscientious justices. He claims to find no evidence that increasingly conscientious justices circulate more majority opinion drafts than less conscientious justices. We have strong concerns over these findings.

We reiterate (see Chapter 3) our methodological concerns about the SCIPE measures used in his analysis. The measurement approach used to calculate those personality estimates relies on an outdated software program that has shown to be a poor estimator of personality. What is more, the SCIPE measures are endogenous (i.e., circular) for this particular analysis. Hall claims to find evidence that conscientious justices write more separate opinions than less conscientious justices. But the scores are derived from the text of the very same concurring opinions Hall examines. This is tremendously problematic.[5] Relatedly, Hall's analysis lumps all concurring and dissenting opinions together as "separate opinions." We know, however, that justices concur and dissent for different reasons. And so the fact that conscientious justices tend to write more *separate* opinions tells us very little. They could write more *concurring* or *dissenting* opinions, and the difference would be meaningful.

Additionally, we have theoretical concerns about the approach. Hall argues that increasingly conscientious justices will circulate more *separate opinion drafts* than less conscientious justices. They do so, he claims, because they put in extra work to make their separate opinions better. Yet (and here's our concern), he also finds that increasingly conscientious justices are no more likely than less conscientious justices to circulate multiple *majority opinion drafts*. This contrast seems odd. It is hard to believe a conscientious justice would sink so much effort into a separate opinion – an opinion that may not be precedential – but *would not invest the same effort into a majority opinion that will be precedential.*

<hr>

[5] Hall also, in chapter 8 of his book, argues that conscientious justices are more likely to concur than less conscientious justices. Again, however, since he measures traits by looking to concurring opinions, he cannot then use those measures to examine concurring behavior.

Hall argues that increasingly conscientious justices circulate fewer join statements than less conscientious justices. After all, join statements are "a much simpler and less effortful response to a draft opinion." Hall does not actually mean joinders when he discusses "join statements," however. Instead, he defines join statements as including joinders (as we discussed previously) but also instances where a justice joins a concurrence or a dissent (among other various joins). Grouping these "joins" together tells us little. Joining a majority opinion is different than joining a dissent or a concurrence. At any rate, lumping them together tells us nothing about the questions we raise here.

8.3 DATA AND MEASURES

To determine whether conscientiousness influences the length of time justices take to circulate their opinions and whether it influences how justices bargain over the content of opinions, we turn to Wahlbeck, Spriggs, and Maltzman (2009*a*), who made photocopies of the 48,524 memoranda and opinion drafts that justices circulated to their colleagues between 1969 and 1986. Using these materials – and following the analytical approach of Maltzman, Spriggs, and Wahlbeck (2000) – we examine (1) the *amount of time* it requires an opinion writer to craft the Court's opinion, and (2) whether conscientiousness influences a justice's decision *to bargain* with the opinion writer.[6]

8.3.1 *Opinion Writing Duration*

In the opinion writing duration analyses, we follow Maltzman, Spriggs, and Wahlbeck (2000) and use the Burger Court Opinion Writing Database to identify each majority opinion writer in cases from 1969 to 1986 and create an observation for each of these justices. The unit of analysis is the majority opinion (or, case).

---

[6] That is, we estimate a model of preemptive accommodation. We do not replicate Maltzman, Spriggs, and Wahlbeck's (2000) analyses of "responsive accommodation," because we have significant reservations over what, exactly, their dependent variable measures. Their dependent variable is coded as 1 if a circulated draft was the final draft; 0 otherwise. As we (and they) are quick to acknowledge, this is merely a surrogate for a more direct measure of responsive accommodation. And it is not a particularly good one. Ideally, what we want are data that examine whether the opinion writer responds to each specific request by another justice. To date, those data are not available. Nevertheless, for the interested reader, we replicate Maltzman, Spriggs, and Wahlbeck's (2000) responsive accommodation models in the appendix. They are substantively similar to the results we present here.

Dependent Variable. We examine how long it takes for the majority opinion writer to circulate the first draft of the opinion. Maltzman, Spriggs, and Wahlbeck (2000) argue that a greater time lag between conference and circulation suggests that the opinion author is expending more effort to write a solid opinion and to accommodate his or her colleagues preemptively. As we are replicating the findings of Maltzman, Spriggs, and Wahlbeck (2000), our dependent variable is the number of days between the case's conference discussion and the date the opinion author circulates the first draft. As Maltzman, Spriggs, and Wahlbeck (2000, 108) explain, this measure carries the "assumption that authors who take the views of other justices into account in crafting the original version of the opinion will take longer than authors who simply express their own policy preferences."

Conscientiousness. Our main covariate of interest is our measure of conscientiousness. Here, it represents the conscientiousness score for the majority opinion writer. We also control for the majority opinion writer's scores on the four other personality traits – *Openness*, *Extraversion*, *Agreeableness*, and *Neuroticism.*

Legal Salience. Justices are likely to take more time to craft an opinion in legally salient cases. Maltzman, Spriggs, and Wahlbeck (2000) use a proxy measure to capture a case's underlying legal importance. They assign a value of 1 to cases that either declared a law unconstitutional or that formally altered precedent; 0 otherwise.[7]

Political Salience. Maltzman, Spriggs, and Wahlbeck (2000) also account for each case's political salience because cases with greater political salience might take more time to write. The authors measure political salience by counting and then standardizing the number of amicus briefs submitted in the case. That is, they generate a case-specific z-score by computing the difference between the number of case-specific amicus filings and the average number of amici per case during that term, divided by the term-specific standard deviation in amicus filings. *Political Salience* reflects the degree to which each case has more (less) amicus participation compared to the norm during that term. Larger (smaller) values represent greater (less) political salience.

Conference Coalition Distance. Justices are likely to require more time to write the Court's opinion when they are ideologically distant from the conference coalition. *Conference Coalition Distance* represents the ideological distance between the majority opinion writer and the average of the other majority coalition members. For each specification of this predictor,

---

7   Specifically, they include cases that declared a federal, state, or local law as unconstitutional, in addition to those that formally altered precedent.

Maltzman, Spriggs, and Wahlbeck (2000) create an issue-specific "compatibility score." To generate this measure, they first approximate each justice's ideology using the percentage of the time he or she supported a liberal policy position in all previous cases (during that justice's time on the bench) in the case's issue area. They then computed the absolute value of the difference between the average of other majority coalition members and the majority opinion author. An ideological distance score of zero reflects perfect compatibility, while larger values indicate justices with increasingly divergent ideological views.

Conference Coalition Heterogeneity. Justices are likely to require more time to write the Court's opinion when the conference coalition is ideologically diverse. *Conference Coalition Heterogeneity* is the standard deviation of the majority coalition members' individual ideological scores (excluding the opinion author). Larger scores represent greater heterogeneity among the majority coalition.

Winning Margin. Maltzman, Spriggs, and Wahlbeck (2000) measure the size of the initial conference coalition. They compute the difference between the number of justices who voted with the majority opinion author at conference and the number of votes necessary to build a winning coalition. Larger values reflect instances where the opinion author has more leeway in pursuit of building a majority coalition.

Cooperation. An additional factor that may affect a justice's time to write opinions is the amount of cooperation he or she received from the other justices in the past. Here, *Cooperation* is the average cooperation score among all the conference's majority coalition members, thereby reflecting the coalition's shared history of cooperation (or not) with the majority opinion author.

Case Complexity. Justices might take more time to write opinions in complex cases. We employ Maltzman, Spriggs, and Wahlbeck's (2000) measure of case complexity, which is a factor-analytic score of the number of issues presented by the case and the number of legal provisions that are relevant to the case. Larger (smaller) values signify increasingly (less) legally complex cases.

End of Term. Justices are likely to take more time to write opinions when there is more time available. *End of Term* accounts for the number of days between the release date of the first majority opinion draft and the end of the term.[8] Larger values of this indicator suggest that justices have more time until the end of the term.

---

[8] Specifically, Maltzman, Spriggs, and Wahlbeck (2000) assume a uniform term end date of July 1.

Workload. The time it takes an opinion writer to put together an opinion might also be a function of the number of competing constraints on his or her time. Justices who are currently working on a greater number of opinions in other cases may have less time to write in the present case. Maltzman, Spriggs, and Wahlbeck (2000) code *Workload* as the number of other majority or separate opinions that the justice is working on at the time of the majority opinion draft's first circulation.

Chief Justice. We also control for differences in timing due to the status of being Chief Justice on the Court and yoked to excessive administrative and institutional obligations. We assign a value of 1 when the justice under analysis was Chief Justice Burger; 0 otherwise.

Freshman Author. Majority opinion authors who are new to the Court may require additional time to write as they get their feet wet and learn the job. We create *Freshman Author*, which take on a value of 1 where the majority opinion author has served fewer than two full years at the time of the opinion draft circulation; 0 otherwise.

Expertise. A justice's subject matter expertise may also influence the length of time required to write, with expert justices requiring less time. Maltzman, Spriggs, and Wahlbeck (2000) create an issue-specific measure of subject-matter expertise that is a standardized indicator of a justice's expertise relative to his or her colleagues. First, the authors count the number of dissents and concurrences written by the justice within the specific issue area of the present case and during his or her time on the Court up to the term preceding the present case. They then divide this count by the total number of cases involving the same issue area decided since the justice's appointment. This procedure creates what they call the issue-specific opinion ratio (OR). Lastly, they standardize this OR measure relative to the average subject-matter expertise among the other sitting justices. That is, the authors compute a z-score, computing the difference between the justice's OR score and mean OR score among the other justices, and then dividing this difference by the standard deviation of all the justices' OR scores. A large (small) score represents a justice with greater (less) subject-matter expertise relative to the other sitting justices.

8.3.2 *Coalitional Bargaining Analysis*

In the bargaining analysis, we identify, for each case from 1969 to 1986, each justice in the conference majority coalition (excluding the opinion author). Our unit of analysis is the individual (majority) justice within each case.

Dependent Variables. We fit two general models in our bargaining analyses. Our first bargaining dependent variable – *Bargain* – is simply a binary variable that indicates whether a justice in the majority coalition sought to bargain with the majority opinion writer. If he or she took any action other than a Joinder, we code the variable as 1; 0 otherwise. The second dependent variable – *Type of Response* – is multinomial and examines the specific type of response the justice provided to the opinion author. Consistent with our previous discussion, the dependent variable can take on one of seven entries. A justice can (a) join the majority opinion draft; (b) state that he or she will wait for another opinion before deciding what to do; (c) make a suggestion to the author; (d) threaten the author; (e) state that he or she will write a separate opinion; (f) circulate a concurrence; (g) or circulate a dissent. We replicate Maltzman, Spriggs, and Wahlbeck (2000) and, thus, use their coding of the dependent variable.

Our covariates of interest include *Conscientiousness, Legal Salience, Political Salience, Winning Margin, Case Complexity, End of Term, Chief Justice, Freshman Author,* and *Expertise.* They take on the same values as in the opinion writing duration analysis. (Again, we also included the other four personality traits as controls.)

We include two additional variables not present in the opinion writing duration analysis. *Author Distance* represents the ideological distance between each justice and the majority opinion author. It is the absolute value of the distance between the justice and the majority opinion writer, using the same issue-specific "compatibility score" approach as noted previously. To measure *Cooperation,* Maltzman, Spriggs, and Wahlbeck (2000) computed the percentage of the time during the previous term the majority opinion author joined a separate opinion written by the justice under analysis. They then regressed this percentage on the ideological compatibility score between these two justices and extracted the residuals as the final cooperation indicator. Larger values of *Cooperation* reflect a greater history of cooperation (that is not driven by ideological compatibility).

8.4 METHODS AND RESULTS

8.4.1 *Opinion Writing Duration*

We begin with the results of our opinion writing duration analyses. Because our dependent variable represents the number of days between each case's conference discussion and the date the opinion author circulated the first draft, we employ a Cox proportional hazard regression model with robust standard errors clustered on the opinion author.[9] This model predicts the "risk" that an opinion author will circulate the first draft opinion over time (i.e., the time since conference), given that the opinion draft has not already been circulated. We follow Maltzman, Spriggs, and Wahlbeck (2000) and estimate time invariant models that assume proportionality of the effects with respect to the time at risk. In the appendix, we include model results when relaxing this assumption.[10]

Table 17 reports the model results. Models 1 and 2 present the baseline and full specifications, respectively, where *Conscientiousness* may have an unconditional effect on the timing of the draft circulation. Models 3 and 4 report regression results where *Conscientiousness* may be conditional on *Legal Salience*. Models 5 and 6 present interactive results for *Political Salience*.

First consider the unconditional model results.[11] The full model specification reports a statistically significant, negative coefficient for *Conscientiousness*.[12] The "hazard rate," or relative risk, of circulating the first opinion draft decreases among more conscientious justices. In plain terms, the data indicate that, once accounting for the various individual and contextual factors that affect the timing of opinion writing, *increasingly conscientious opinion writers take more time to circulate first drafts than less conscientious justices.*

Figure 42(a) displays the dynamic survival rate of the first majority opinion draft, which is equivalent to the probability that the draft will *not* be circulated as a function of the days since opinion assignment.[13] Within that figure,

---

9   The use of ordinary least squares in the present analysis is inappropriate because it is likely to produce biased estimators and invalid hypothesis tests (given that errors should not be normally distributed).

10   We use Schoenfeld residuals to identify those predictors whose effects appear to violate the proportionality assumption and then allow for their effects to vary with respect to time (i.e., the natural log of the time since conference). Importantly, these results continue to indicate that more conscientious opinion writers take more time to circulate the first draft than less conscientious justices, even though the data suggest that the magnitude of this effect decreases with more time at risk.

11   We use the Breslow method for handling ties. The impact of conscientiousness is substantively consistent when employing alternative modeling approaches to deal with ties – that is, the Efron method, exact marginal likelihood, and exact partial likelihood. The results are also robust to estimating the model using a Weibull distribution.

12   Like Model 1 in Table 17, the results of a baseline specification that includes only conscientiousness (and no other personality trait indicators or control predictors) does not exhibit a statistically significant effect. Thus, we uncover a significant marginal effect of conscientiousness only after accounting for other factors known to affect the timing of opinion writing.

13   We generated the predicted survival rate while holding all other predictors at their mean, or modal, values.

TABLE 17: *The Impact of Conscientiousness on Preemptive Accommodation by the Majority Opinion Writer*

	Unconditional		Legal Salience		Political Salience	
	(1)	(2)	(3)	(4)	(5)	(6)
Conscientiousness	−0.13	−0.29*	−0.12	−0.29*	−0.15	−0.29*
	(0.23)	(0.17)	(0.23)	(0.17)	(0.22)	(0.17)
Openness	−0.04	−0.04	−0.04	−0.05	−0.03	−0.04
	(0.12)	(0.10)	(0.12)	(0.10)	(0.12)	(0.10)
Extraversion	0.23	0.33*	0.23	0.33*	0.23	0.32*
	(0.16)	(0.13)	(0.16)	(0.13)	(0.15)	(0.13)
Agreeableness	−0.20*	−0.19*	−0.20*	−0.19*	−0.21*	−0.19*
	(0.09)	(0.06)	(0.09)	(0.06)	(0.09)	(0.06)
Neuroticism	−0.27*	−0.28*	−0.27*	−0.28*	−0.27*	−0.28*
	(0.13)	(0.11)	(0.13)	(0.11)	(0.13)	(0.11)
Legal Salience		−0.13*	−0.14*	−0.15*		−0.13*
		(0.05)	(0.04)	(0.04)		(0.05)
Conscientiousness × Legal Salience			−0.05	−0.12*		
			(0.05)	(0.06)		
Political Salience		−0.02*		−0.02*	−0.03*	−0.02*
		(0.007)		(0.01)	(0.01)	(0.01)
Conscientiousness × Political Salience					0.02*	0.001
					(0.01)	(0.01)
Conference Coalition Distance		0.01*		0.01*		0.01*
		(0.003)		(0.003)		(0.003)
Conference Coalition Heterogeneity		−0.01*		−0.01*		−0.01*
		(0.003)		(0.003)		(0.003)
Winning Margin		0.06*		0.06*		0.06*
		(0.01)		(0.01)		(0.01)
Cooperation		−0.003		−0.01		−0.003
		(1.00)		(1.00)		(1.01)
Case Complexity		−0.05		−0.05		−0.05
		(0.03)		(0.03)		(0.03)
End of Term		−0.005*		−0.005*		−0.005*
		(0.001)		(0.001)		(0.001)
Workload		−0.11*		−0.11*		−0.11*
		(0.01)		(0.01)		(0.01)

(*continued*)

TABLE 17: (*continued*)

	Unconditional		Legal Salience		Political Salience	
	(1)	(2)	(3)	(4)	(5)	(6)
Chief Justice Author		0.01		0.01		0.01
		(0.18)		(0.18)		(0.18)
Freshman Author		−0.28*		−0.29*		−0.28*
		(0.14)		(0.14)		(0.14)
Expertise		−0.01		−0.01		−0.01
		(0.03)		(0.03)		(0.03)
N	2289	2289	2289	2289	2289	2289
χ^2	37.88*	1745.82*	125.79*	7590.05*	112.58*	1766.09*

Note: Table entries are Cox Proportional Hazard regression coefficients with robust standard errors (clustered on the majority opinion author) in parentheses; *p < .05 (one-tailed). The dependent variable represents, for each case, the number of days between the majority opinion assignment and circulation of the first majority opinion draft, 1969–1985.

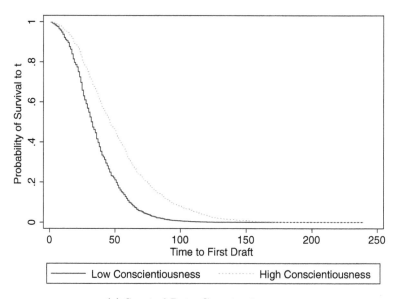

(a) Survival Rate–Conscientiousness

FIGURE 42: *The impact of conscientiousness on the time needed to write and circulate the first draft.* Figure reports the predicted survival rate – the probability that the first majority opinion draft will *not* be circulated – as a function of the days since opinion assignment, using results from Model 2 in Table 17. The darker, solid line represents a justice with low conscientiousness (10th percentile), while the lighter, dashed line represents high conscientiousness (90th percentile).

the darker, solid line represents a justice with less conscientiousness (i.e., the 10th percentile of *Conscientiousness*) while the lighter, dashed line represents an opinion author with more conscientiousness (i.e., the 90th percentile). For the highly conscientious justice, the probability of not circulating the first draft takes noticeably longer to decline. (The average time to first circulation in the sample is approximately forty-eight days.) The model indicates that the hazard ratio associated with a one-unit change in *Conscientiousness* – representing a change of approximately one standard deviation – is 0.75. This means that a majority opinion writer who is one unit more conscientious than another justice in a comparable case is associated with a 25 percent reduction in the risk that he or she will circulate the first opinion draft (given that he or she has not already done so). Thus, these results suggest that the conscientious justice take considerably longer than his or her colleagues to circulate the first opinion draft, which likely indicates a greater effort to craft a solid opinion.

Given the importance of legal and political salience in the opinion assignment models in Chapter 7, we thought it relevant to interact conscientiousness with both salience measures. Although Model 6 suggests that the effect of a justice's conscientiousness does not vary significantly as a function of *Political Salience*, Model 4 indicates that *Legal Salience* does significantly moderate it. The conscientious justice takes even longer to circulate the first opinion draft in cases where the Court alters precedent or strikes down a law (i.e., a legally salient case). In short, the conscientious justice expends greater effort and takes more time when writing, particularly among cases of great legal importance.

8.4.2 *Coalitional Bargaining*

We turn, next, to the results of our bargaining analyses. We estimate two general models. One examines whether justices bargain at all; the other examines the specific type of response justices make.

Any Bargaining Response
Because our first dependent variable is binary (i.e., whether a justice in the conference majority bargains at all with the opinion author), we estimate a logistic regression model. We employ robust standard errors to account for the possibility of correlated errors across observations.[14] Table 18 reports these

---

[14] The results are substantively consistent if we estimate robust standard errors clustered on the individual justice or the opinion author, or if we estimate the model using classical standard errors.

parameter estimates. Models 1 and 2 report the results of a baseline and full specification, respectively, where the impact of *Conscientiousness* is unconditional.[15] Models 3 and 4 test whether the impact of *Conscientiousness* is conditional on *Legal Salience*. Models 5 and 6 test whether the impact of *Conscientiousness* is conditional on *Political Salience*.

Taken together, the results show that a justice's conscientiousness affects his or her proclivity to bargain with the majority opinion writer – but (unexpectedly) in a negative direction. Justices who are more conscientious are less likely to bargain with the majority opinion writer. Figure 43 illustrates predicted probabilities (with 90 percent confidence intervals) that a justice in the majority coalition will bargain with the majority opinion writer across the range of *Conscientiousness* (using results from Model 2 in Table 18). The probability that a justice with the minimum conscientiousness score bargains with the opinion author is 0.274 [0.224, 0.323]. The

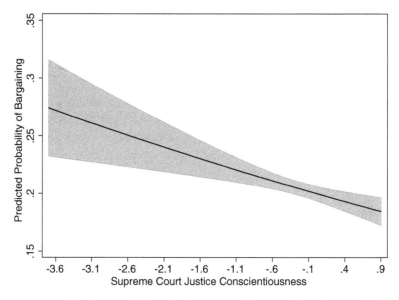

FIGURE 43: *The impact of Conscientiousness on Supreme Court justices' willingness to bargain with the majority opinion writer.* Estimates represent the predicted probability that a justice in the majority conference coalition sought to bargain with the majority opinion writer (with 90 percent confidence intervals) across the range of *Conscientiousness* using results from Model 2 in Table 18.

---

[15] The results are consistent when specifying a baseline model that includes only conscientiousness (and no other personality trait indicators or control predictors).

TABLE 18: *The Impact of Conscientiousness on Supreme Court Justices' Willingness to Bargain with the Majority Opinion Writer*

	Unconditional		Legal Salience		Political Salience	
	(1)	(2)	(3)	(4)	(5)	(6)
Conscientiousness	−0.16* (0.03)	−0.12* (0.04)	−0.16* (0.04)	−0.12* (0.04)	−0.18* (0.04)	−0.13* (0.04)
Openness	−0.04 (0.03)	−0.09* (0.03)	−0.04 (0.03)	−0.09* (0.03)	−0.04* (0.03)	−0.09* (0.03)
Extraversion	0.02 (0.03)	0.01 (0.04)	0.01 (0.03)	0.01 (0.04)	0.02 (0.03)	0.01 (0.04)
Agreeableness	−0.03 (0.02)	0.08* (0.02)	−0.03 (0.02)	0.07* (0.02)	−0.03 (0.02)	0.08* (0.02)
Neuroticism	−0.09* (0.03)	−0.01 (0.04)	−0.08* (0.04)	−0.01 (0.04)	−0.09* (0.04)	−0.01 (0.04)
Legal Salience		0.17* (0.07)	0.33* (0.07)	0.18* (0.07)		0.17* (0.07)
Conscientiousness × Legal Salience			0.04 (0.06)	0.02 (0.06)		
Political Salience		0.04* (0.01)		0.04* (0.01)	0.04* (0.01)	0.04* (0.01)
Conscientiousness × Political Salience					0.02* (0.01)	0.013* (0.008)
Author Distance		0.03* (0.002)		0.03* (0.002)		0.03* (0.002)
Coalition Distance		0.01* (0.002)		0.01* (0.002)		0.01* (0.002)
Winning Margin		−0.02 (0.02)		−0.02 (0.02)		−0.02 (0.02)
Cooperation		−2.27* (0.24)		−2.27* (0.24)		−2.27* (0.24)
Case Complexity		0.08* (0.02)		0.08* (0.02)		0.08* (0.02)
End of Term		0.002* (0.000)		0.002* (0.000)		0.002* (0.000)
Workload		0.005 (0.006)		0.005 (0.006)		0.01 (0.01)
Chief Justice		−0.39* (0.09)		−0.39* (0.09)		−0.39* (0.09)

(continued)

TABLE 18: (*continued*)

	Unconditional		Legal Salience		Political Salience	
	(1)	(2)	(3)	(4)	(5)	(6)
Freshman Author		−0.16*		−0.16*		−0.16*
		(0.09)		(0.09)		(0.09)
Expertise		0.06*		0.06*		0.06*
		(0.02)		(0.02)		(0.02)
Constant	−1.36*	−2.41*	−1.40*	−2.41*	−1.41*	−2.42*
	(0.03)	(0.10)	(0.04)	(0.10)	(0.04)	(0.10)
N	12,648	12,558	12,648	12,558	12,648	12,558
χ^2	42.82*	660.34*	65.29*	661.21*	72.28*	662.91*

Note: Table entries are logistic regression coefficients with robust standard errors in parentheses; *p < .05 (one-tailed). The dependent variable represents whether a justice in the majority conference coalition sought to bargain over the first circulated draft opinion (i.e., any response other than to join the opinion), 1969–1985.

most conscientious justice in the sample is likely to bargain with a probability of 0.184 [0.170, 0.199] – a decrease of 0.09, or 33 percent. Even a more modest shift in *Conscientiousness* exhibits a meaningful effect, as a one standard deviation increase in *Conscientiousness* exhibits an expected 0.02 – or, roughly 10 percent – decrease in the probability the justice will bargain (versus join). What is more, this relationship is statistically significant in both the baseline and full specifications. As an initial test, then, increased *Conscientiousness* appears to predict less bargaining on the Burger Court.

Once again, though, we want to illustrate these effects while interacting conscientiousness with legal and political salience. Figure 44(a) reports the average marginal effect (with 90% confidence intervals) of *Legal Salience* across the observed range of *Conscientiousness* (using results from Model 4 in Table 18). It shows that the average marginal effect of legal salience is mostly flat across the range of *Conscientiousness*. That is, all justices are more likely to bargain in cases of greater legal importance; there is little increase in this effect among more conscientious justices. All we observe is that the confidence intervals get smaller among more conscientious justices. (Still, the results technically do reveal that increasingly conscientious justices are more likely to bargain in legally salient cases.)

The results suggest that *Political Salience* has a positive effect on a justice's willingness to bargain that increases as a function of *Conscientiousness*.

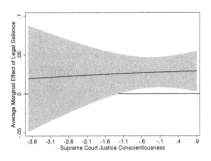
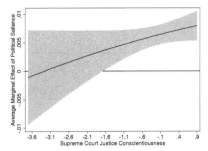

(a) Average Marginal Effect–Legal Salience   (b) Average Marginal Effect–Political Salience

FIGURE 44: *The conditional impact of Conscientiousness on Supreme Court justices' willingness to bargain with the majority opinion writer.* Panel (a) reports the average marginal effect (with 90% confidence intervals) of *Legal Salience* across the observed range of justice *Conscientiousness* using results from Model 4 in Table 18. Panel (b) reports the average marginal effect of *Political Salience* using results from Model 6 in Table 18.

Figure 44(b) shows that *Political Salience* exhibits a statistically significant impact on justices' proclivities to bargain among those scoring above −1.69 on the conscientiousness scale – representing more than 96 percent of the observations in the sample. And, this effect increases markedly among more conscientious justices.[16] Increasingly conscientious justices are, on average, less likely to bargain with the majority opinion author than less conscientious justices, but this relationship is mitigated in politically salient cases. In politically salient cases, conscientious justices appear *more likely* than less conscientious justices to bargain.

Types of Bargaining Responses
We now consider how *Conscientiousness* predicts *different types of individual bargaining responses*. Because our dependent variable here has multiple (non-ordinal) categories, we estimate a multinomial logistic regression model with robust standard errors. Table 19 reports the parameter estimates.[17] The baseline category represents a decision to join the majority opinion. That is, each column reports the predicted impact of a particular bargaining outcome *relative to joining* the majority opinion. Overall, the data establish that justices are more likely to join as a first response as they become increasingly

---

[16] It should be noted here that the differences between high and low conscientious justices is driven in large part by the steep decline in the probability of bargaining by high conscientious justices in low salient cases. They remain relatively constant in the bargaining behavior in highly salient cases.

[17] We retrieve different results for conscientiousness when specifying a bivariate model that does not account for other factors known to affect bargaining responses.

TABLE 19: *The Impact of Conscientiousness on the Type of Bargaining Response to the First Circulated Draft Opinion*

	Baseline Category: Join Majority Opinion Draft					
	Wait	Suggestion	Threat	Concur	Dissent	Will Write
Conscientiousness	−0.29*	0.13	0.04	−0.18*	−0.22*	0.004
	(0.10)	(0.09)	(0.11)	(0.06)	(0.09)	(0.09)
Openness	−0.31*	−0.05	−0.18*	−0.03	−0.08	−0.12
	(0.07)	(0.08)	(0.09)	(0.05)	(0.08)	(0.10)
Extraversion	0.15*	0.07	0.12	−0.16*	−0.02	0.24*
	(0.08)	(0.08)	(0.09)	(0.06)	(0.10)	(0.09)
Agreeableness	0.42*	−0.14*	−0.07	0.15*	−0.02	−0.11*
	(0.06)	(0.06)	(0.07)	(0.03)	(0.06)	(0.06)
Neuroticism	−0.04	0.19*	0.04	−0.01	−0.26*	−0.06
	(0.09)	(0.09)	(0.10)	(0.06)	(0.10)	(0.11)
Legal Salience	−0.16	0.18	−0.42*	0.44*	0.002	0.09
	(0.19)	(0.17)	(0.25)	(0.09)	(0.16)	(0.18)
Political Salience	0.07*	0.06*	0.04*	0.03*	0.02	0.04*
	(0.01)	(0.01)	(0.02)	(0.01)	(0.015)	(0.02)
Author Distance	0.02*	0.02*	0.04*	0.03*	0.02*	0.03*
	(0.004)	(0.004)	(0.005)	(0.002)	(0.004)	(0.004)
Coalition Distance	0.02*	−0.01	−0.02*	0.01*	0.04*	0.002
	(0.01)	(0.01)	(0.01)	(0.004)	(0.01)	(0.006)
Winning Margin	−0.12*	0.06	0.20*	0.01	−0.19*	−0.02
	(0.04)	(0.04)	(0.05)	(0.02)	(0.04)	(0.04)
Cooperation	−2.68*	−1.75*	−2.32*	−2.22*	−2.36*	−2.54*
	(0.54)	(0.57)	(0.83)	(0.38)	(0.57)	(0.64)
Case Complexity	−0.06	0.11*	0.01	0.10*	0.19*	−0.02
	(0.06)	(0.05)	(0.08)	(0.03)	(0.05)	(0.06)
End of Term	0.003*	0.003*	0.001	0.001	−0.001	0.005*
	(0.001)	(0.001)	(0.001)	(0.001)	(0.001)	(0.001)
Workload	0.02	0.01	0.001	0.002	−0.02	0.03*
	(0.015)	(0.01)	(0.02)	(0.01)	(0.013)	(0.015)
Chief Justice	−0.35	−0.88*	−0.51*	−0.22*	−0.48*	−0.16
	(0.23)	(0.24)	(0.28)	(0.12)	(0.22)	(0.24)
Freshman Author	−0.63*	0.11	−0.21	−0.06	−0.23	−0.37
	(0.28)	(0.21)	(0.28)	(0.13)	(0.21)	(0.27)
Expertise	−0.03	−0.05	0.16*	0.12*	0.001	0.07*
	(0.04)	(0.04)	(0.05)	(0.02)	(0.04)	(0.04)

(continued)

TABLE 19: (*continued*)

	Wait	Suggestion	Threat	Concur	Dissent	Will Write
	Baseline Category: Join Majority Opinion Draft					
Constant	-5.14^*	-4.11^*	-4.80^*	-3.55^*	-3.84^*	-4.82^*
	(0.29)	(0.25)	(0.32)	(0.15)	(0.24)	(0.29)
N	12,558					
χ^2	1117.02^*					

Note: Table entries are multinomial logistic regression coefficients with robust standard errors in parentheses; $^*p < .05$ (one-tailed). The dependent variable represents the type of bargaining response by a justice in the majority conference coalition to the first circulated draft opinion, 1969–1985. The baseline category represents a decision to join the majority opinion draft.

conscientious. This corroborates some of the results in the previous model. The least conscientious justice in the sample is 0.708 [0.652, 0.764] likely to join the majority opinion. This probability increases to 0.812 [0.797, 0.827] when viewing the most conscientious justice – a total expected increase of 0.104, or 15 percent.

Figure 45 displays the average marginal effect (with 90 percent confidence intervals) of *Conscientiousness* on each outcome while taking into account all relative odds among the categories. A conscientious justice is less likely to express a desire to wait, less likely to circulate a concurrence, and less likely to circulate a dissent. At the same time, conscientious justices are *more* likely to offer suggestions to the majority opinion writer.

Figure 46 reports the magnitude of these results, expressed as predicted probabilities. It shows that a min-to-max change in *Conscientiousness* exhibits a predicted decrease of 0.044 (68 percent) in the probability a justice will express a desire to wait, a 0.057 (46 percent) lower probability of circulating a concurrence, and a 0.03 (56 percent) lower probability of circulating a dissent. Conversely, the most conscientious justice has a 0.02 (114 percent) greater probability of making a suggestion to the opinion author compared to the least conscientious justice.

As we did previously, we next consider how legal and political salience condition this effect. Table 20 provides the regression results. For ease of interpretation, Figure 47 displays the average marginal effect (with 90 percent confidence intervals) of *Legal Salience* across the observed range of *Conscientiousness*, where each separate panel represents the predicted impact on a different bargaining outcome category. There is little evidence of an

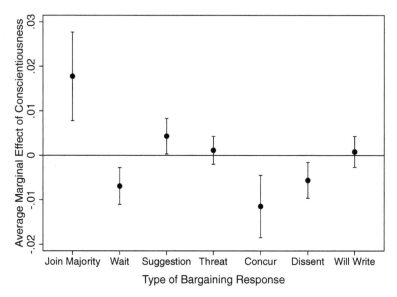

FIGURE 45: *The impact of Conscientiousness on the type of bargaining response to the first circulated draft opinion.* Estimates represent the average marginal effect (with 90 percent confidence intervals) of *Conscientiousness* on each bargaining response category using results from Table 19.

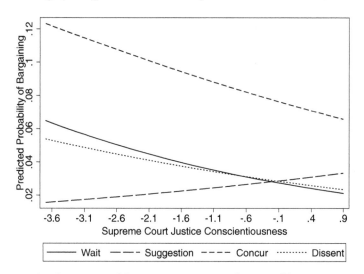

FIGURE 46: *The impact of Conscientiousness on the type of bargaining response to the first circulated draft opinion.* Panel (a) reports the predicted probability that a justice in the majority conference coalition will issue a particular bargaining response across the range of *Conscientiousness* using results from Table 19.

TABLE 20: *The Interactive Effect of Conscientiousness and Legal Salience on the Type of Bargaining Response to the First Circulated Draft Opinion*

	Baseline Category: Join Majority Opinion Draft					
	Wait	Suggestion	Threat	Concur	Dissent	Will Write
Conscientiousness	−0.28*	0.12	0.003	−0.18*	−0.22*	−0.005
	(0.10)	(0.10)	(0.11)	(0.06)	(0.09)	(0.10)
Legal Salience	−0.16	0.19	−0.32	0.45*	−0.01	0.11
	(0.19)	(0.17)	(0.26)	(0.10)	(0.17)	(0.18)
Conscientiousness ×	−0.06	0.04	−0.38*	0.02	−0.02	0.05
Legal Salience	(0.14)	(0.13)	(0.22)	(0.08)	(0.13)	(0.10)
Openness	−0.30*	−0.05	−0.18*	−0.03	−0.08	−0.12
	(0.07)	(0.08)	(0.09)	(0.05)	(0.08)	(0.10)
Extraversion	0.15*	0.07	0.12	−0.16*	−0.02	0.24*
	(0.09)	(0.07)	(0.09)	(0.06)	(0.10)	(0.09)
Agreeableness	0.42*	−0.14*	−0.08	0.15*	−0.02	−0.11*
	(0.06)	(0.06)	(0.07)	(0.03)	(0.06)	(0.06)
Neuroticism	−0.04	0.19*	0.04	−0.01	−0.26*	−0.06
	(0.09)	(0.09)	(0.10)	(0.06)	(0.10)	(0.11)
Political Salience	0.07*	0.06*	0.04*	0.03*	0.02	0.04*
	(0.01)	(0.01)	(0.02)	(0.01)	(0.015)	(0.02)
Author Distance	0.02*	0.02*	0.04*	0.03*	0.02*	0.03*
	(0.004)	(0.004)	(0.005)	(0.002)	(0.004)	(0.004)
Coalition Distance	0.02*	−0.01	−0.02*	0.01*	0.04*	0.002
	(0.01)	(0.01)	(0.01)	(0.004)	(0.01)	(0.006)
Winning Margin	−0.12*	0.06	0.20*	0.01	−0.19*	−0.02
	(0.04)	(0.04)	(0.05)	(0.02)	(0.04)	(0.04)
Cooperation	−2.68*	−1.75*	−2.32*	−2.22*	−2.36*	−2.54*
	(0.54)	(0.57)	(0.83)	(0.38)	(0.57)	(0.64)
Case Complexity	−0.06	0.11*	0.01	0.10*	0.19*	−0.02
	(0.06)	(0.05)	(0.08)	(0.03)	(0.05)	(0.06)
End of Term	0.003*	0.003*	0.001	0.001	−0.001	0.005*
	(0.001)	(0.001)	(0.001)	(0.001)	(0.001)	(0.001)
Workload	0.02	0.01	0.001	0.002	−0.02	0.03*
	(0.015)	(0.01)	(0.02)	(0.01)	(0.013)	(0.015)
Chief Justice	−0.35	−0.88*	−0.50*	−0.22*	−0.48*	−0.16
	(0.23)	(0.24)	(0.28)	(0.12)	(0.22)	(0.24)
Freshman Author	−0.63*	0.11	−0.21	−0.06	−0.23	−0.36
	(0.28)	(0.21)	(0.28)	(0.13)	(0.21)	(0.27)
Expertise	−0.03	−0.05	0.17*	0.12*	0.001	0.07*
	(0.04)	(0.04)	(0.05)	(0.02)	(0.04)	(0.04)

(continued)

TABLE 20: (*continued*)

	Baseline Category: Join Majority Opinion Draft					
	Wait	Suggestion	Threat	Concur	Dissent	Will Write
Constant	-5.14^*	-4.11^*	-4.80^*	-3.55^*	-3.84^*	-4.82^*
	(0.29)	(0.25)	(0.32)	(0.15)	(0.24)	(0.29)
N	12,558					
χ^2	1122.69^*					

Note: Table entries are multinomial logistic regression coefficients with robust standard errors in parentheses; $^*p < .05$ (one-tailed). The dependent variable represents the type of bargaining response by a justice in the majority conference coalition to the first circulated draft opinion, 1969–1985. The baseline category represents a decision to join the majority opinion draft.

interactive effect between *Conscientiousness* and *Legal Salience*. Six of the (seven) marginal effects plots show little meaningful change in the impact of legal salience as a function of conscientiousness. The one potential exception is that legal salience has no discernible impact on the probability of communicating a threat among the most conscientious justices in the sample, yet the least conscientious justice appears less likely to issue a threat in a legally salient (compared to nonsalient) case.

On the other hand, the analyses do uncover substantial evidence of an interactive effect between *Conscientiousness* and *Political Salience*. Table 21 reports these multinomial regression results. Figure 48 displays the average marginal effects of *Political Salience* across the range of *Conscientiousness* while accounting for all relative odds among the outcome categories. Three outcome categories stand out. First, Figure 47(a) shows that justices scoring above -1.71 on the conscientiousness scale – representing nearly 97 percent of the sample observations – are significantly less likely simply to join the opinion in cases with greater political salience. Second, the impact of *Political Salience* on the probability of making a suggestion increases significantly among more conscientious justices. Figure 47(c) shows that *Political Salience* begins to exhibit a statistically significant, positive impact on justices who score above -1.46 on the conscientiousness scale, which represents 97 percent of the total observations. Indeed, when viewing the most conscientious justice in the sample, a case with high political salience (compared to a low-salience case) can lead to as much as a 0.019 – or, 64 percent – increase in the probability that he or she offers a suggestion to the opinion writer. Third, the data indicate an interactive relationship between *Political Salience* and *Conscientiousness* on the likelihood of a justice indicating that he or she will write separately. Figure 47(g) shows that justices are more likely to express a

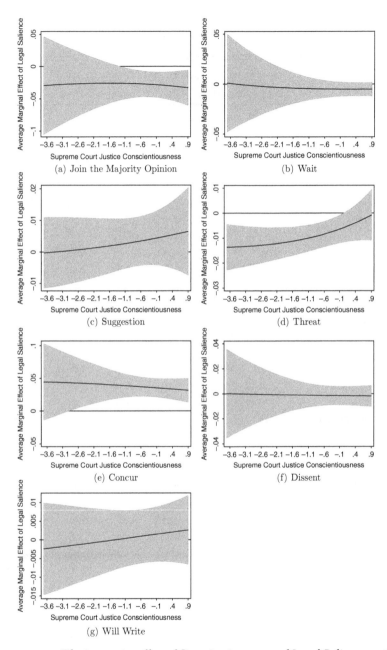

FIGURE 47: *The interactive effect of Conscientiousness and Legal Salience on the type of bargaining response.* Estimates represent the average marginal effect (with 90% confidence intervals) of *Legal Salience* across the observed range of justice *Conscientiousness* using results from Table 20. Each panel reports the result for a different type of bargaining response.

TABLE 21: *The Interactive Effect of Conscientiousness and Political Salience on the Type of Bargaining Response to the First Circulated Draft Opinion*

	Baseline Category: Join Majority Opinion Draft					
	Wait	Suggestion	Threat	Concur	Dissent	Will Write
Conscientiousness	−0.31*	0.11	0.02	−0.19*	−0.23*	−0.02
	(0.10)	(0.09)	(0.11)	(0.06)	(0.09)	(0.09)
Political Salience	0.07*	0.06*	0.04*	0.03*	0.022	0.05*
	(0.01)	(0.01)	(0.02)	(0.01)	(0.017)	(0.02)
Conscientiousness ×	0.02	0.015	0.01	0.01	0.006	0.02
Poli Salience	(0.015)	(0.013)	(0.02)	(0.01)	(0.02)	(0.014)
Openness	−0.31*	−0.05	−0.18*	−0.03	−0.08	−0.12
	(0.07)	(0.08)	(0.09)	(0.05)	(0.08)	(0.10)
Extraversion	0.15*	0.07	0.12	−0.17*	−0.02	0.23*
	(0.08)	(0.07)	(0.09)	(0.06)	(0.10)	(0.09)
Agreeableness	0.42*	−0.14*	−0.07	0.15*	−0.02	−0.11*
	(0.06)	(0.06)	(0.07)	(0.03)	(0.06)	(0.06)
Neuroticism	−0.05	0.19*	0.04	−0.02	−0.26*	−0.07
	(0.09)	(0.09)	(0.10)	(0.06)	(0.10)	(0.11)
Legal Salience	−0.16	0.18	−0.42*	0.44*	0.002	0.10
	(0.19)	(0.17)	(0.25)	(0.09)	(0.16)	(0.18)
Author Distance	0.02*	0.02*	0.04*	0.03*	0.02*	0.03*
	(0.004)	(0.004)	(0.005)	(0.002)	(0.004)	(0.004)
Coalition Distance	0.02*	−0.01	−0.02*	0.01*	0.04*	0.002
	(0.01)	(0.01)	(0.01)	(0.004)	(0.01)	(0.006)
Winning Margin	−0.12*	0.06	0.20*	0.01	−0.19*	−0.02
	(0.04)	(0.04)	(0.05)	(0.02)	(0.04)	(0.04)
Cooperation	−2.68*	−1.75*	−2.32*	−2.23*	−2.36*	−2.55*
	(0.54)	(0.57)	(0.83)	(0.38)	(0.57)	(0.64)
Case Complexity	−0.06	0.11*	0.01	0.10*	0.19*	−0.02
	(0.06)	(0.05)	(0.08)	(0.03)	(0.05)	(0.06)
End of Term	0.003*	0.003*	0.001	0.001	−0.001	0.005*
	(0.001)	(0.001)	(0.001)	(0.001)	(0.001)	(0.001)
Workload	0.025*	0.01	0.002	0.002	−0.02	0.03*
	(0.015)	(0.01)	(0.02)	(0.01)	(0.013)	(0.015)
Chief Justice	−0.35	−0.89*	−0.51*	−0.22*	−0.48*	−0.16
	(0.23)	(0.24)	(0.28)	(0.12)	(0.22)	(0.24)

(continued)

TABLE 21: (continued)

| | Baseline Category: Join Majority Opinion Draft | | | | | |
	Wait	Suggestion	Threat	Concur	Dissent	Will Write
Freshman Author	−0.63*	0.11	−0.21	−0.06	−0.23	−0.37
	(0.28)	(0.21)	(0.28)	(0.13)	(0.21)	(0.27)
Expertise	−0.03	−0.05	0.16*	0.12*	0.001	0.07*
	(0.04)	(0.04)	(0.05)	(0.02)	(0.04)	(0.04)
Constant	−5.15*	−4.12*	−4.81*	−3.56*	−3.84*	−4.83*
	(0.29)	(0.25)	(0.32)	(0.15)	(0.24)	(0.29)
N	12,558					
χ^2	1120.66*					

Note: Table entries are multinomial logistic regression coefficients with robust standard errors in parentheses; *p < .05 (one-tailed). The dependent variable represents the type of bargaining response by a justice in the majority conference coalition to the first circulated draft opinion, 1969–1985. The baseline category represents a decision to join the majority opinion draft.

desire to write separately in more politically salient cases and that this effect is greatest among the most conscientious justices. *Political Salience* exhibits a significant, positive relationship among justices scoring higher than −0.50 on the conscientious scale (or, 63 percent of the observations in the sample). And, the predicted difference in the probability of indicating "will write" when comparing a high versus low-salience case increases to as much as 0.011 at the high end of justice *Conscientiousness* – an expected increase of 50 percent.

These results confirm some of our expectations. Even though increasingly conscientious justices were not more likely to bargain than other justices (contrary to our expectations), when they did bargain, they responded largely as we expected. They were more likely to offer suggestions and less likely to issue wait statements, to dissent, and to concur. Moreover, in politically salient cases, they were more likely to issue will write statements and make suggestions.

8.5 CONCLUSION

Our central effort here was to determine whether conscientiousness influences how justices write opinions and how they bargain on the Court. Our results confirm that conscientiousness does in fact influence how justices behave during the opinion-writing process. Conscientious justices take longer to write opinions than less conscientious justices. They do so, we argue, to

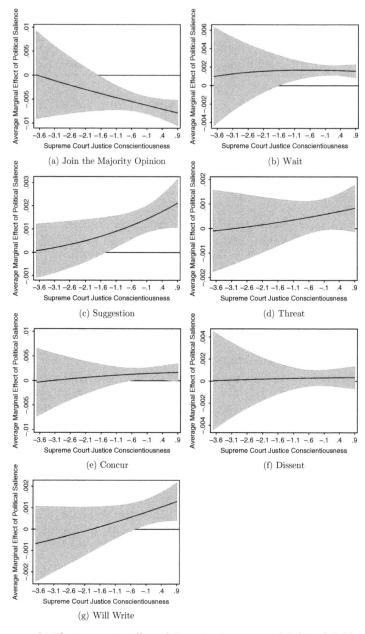

FIGURE 48: *The interactive effect of Conscientiousness and Political Salience on the type of bargaining response.* Estimates represent the average marginal effect (with 90 percent confidence intervals) of *Political Salience* across the observed range of justice *Conscientiousness* using results from Table 21. Each panel reports the result for a different type of bargaining response.

craft a better judicial product and to anticipate (and address) their colleagues' views. In this way, conscientious opinion writers exert a strong influence on the law.

We also found some admittedly less strong results when examining how conscientiousness influences justices' responses to opinion writers. Conscientious justices overall are less likely to bargain. But when it comes to salient cases, they bargain. What is more, conditional on them bargaining, conscientious justices are more likely to offer suggestions and less likely to wait, concur, or dissent. This is largely how we would expect the hardworking and rules-oriented justice to behave.

We should also note that these results are consistent with those we will present in the next chapter. There, we find that conscientious justices are more likely to write longer and more complex opinions. And so together, the results reveal that conscientious justices make their mark on opinion content. As such, let us turn to the next chapter.

8.6 APPENDIX

8.6.1 *Time-Varying Effects*

TABLE 22: *The Impact of the Conscientiousness Trait on Preemptive Accommodation by the Majority Opinion Writer – Time-Varying Effects (Only Conscientiousness)*

	Coefficient	Std. Error	Hazard Ratio
Main Covariates			
Conscientiousness	−1.00*	0.33	0.37
Openness	0.02	0.09	1.02
Extraversion	0.21*	0.09	1.24
Agreeableness	−0.17*	0.06	0.84
Neuroticism	−0.26*	0.11	0.77
Legal Salience	−0.14*	0.05	0.87
Political Salience	−0.02*	0.01	0.98
Conference Coalition Distance	0.01*	0.002	1.01
Conference Coalition Heterogeneity	−0.01*	0.003	0.99
Winning Margin	0.06*	0.01	1.06
Cooperation	−0.55	0.82	0.58
Case Complexity	−0.04*	0.02	0.96

(continued)

TABLE 22: (*Continued*)

	Coefficient	Std. Error	Hazard Ratio
End of Term	−0.005[*]	0.001	0.995
Workload	−0.10[*]	0.01	0.90
Chief Justice Author	−0.12	0.15	0.89
Freshman Author	−0.21[*]	0.12	0.81
Expertise	−0.01	0.03	0.99
Time-Varying Covariates			
Conscientiousness × Time (logged)	0.22[*]	0.08	1.25
N	2289		
χ^2	1178.49[*]		

Note: Table entries are Cox Proportional Hazard regression coefficients with robust standard errors (clustered on the majority opinion author) in parentheses; [*]$p < .05$ (one-tailed). The dependent variable represents, for each case, the number of days between the majority opinion assignment and circulation of the first majority opinion draft, 1969–1985.

TABLE 23: *The Impact of the Conscientiousness Trait on Preemptive Accommodation by the Majority Opinion Writer – Time-Varying Effects (All Assumption Violators)*

	Coefficient	Std. Error	Hazard Ratio
Main Covariates			
Conscientiousness	−1.07[*]	0.42	0.34
Openness	−0.72[*]	0.35	0.49
Extraversion	0.58	0.45	1.79
Agreeableness	−0.57[*]	0.27	0.57
Neuroticism	−0.85	0.55	0.43
Legal Salience	0.03	0.42	1.03
Political Salience	−0.02[*]	0.01	0.98
Conference Coalition Distance	0.02[*]	0.01	1.02
Conference Coalition Heterogeneity	−0.02	0.02	0.98
Winning Margin	0.06[*]	0.01	1.06
Cooperation	−2.49	3.75	0.08

(*continued*)

TABLE 23: (continued)

	Coefficient	Std. Error	Hazard Ratio
Case Complexity	−0.33*	0.14	0.72
End of Term	0.001	0.003	1.00
Workload	−0.36*	0.07	0.70
Chief Justice Author	0.49	0.79	1.64
Freshman Author	−0.19*	0.10	0.82
Expertise	−0.01	0.02	0.99
Time-Varying Covariates			
Conscientiousness × Time (logged)	0.25*	0.10	1.29
Openness × Time (logged)	0.20*	0.09	1.22
Extraversion × Time (logged)	−0.11	0.11	0.90
Agreeableness × Time (logged)	0.11*	0.06	1.11
Neuroticism × Time (logged)	0.16	0.13	1.17
Legal Salience × Time (logged)	−0.04	0.11	0.96
Conference Distance × Time (logged)	−0.004	0.003	1.00
Conference Heterogeneity × Time (logged)	0.003	0.005	1.00
Cooperation × Time (logged)	0.46	0.94	1.59
Case Complexity × Time (logged)	0.08*	0.04	1.08
End of Term × Time (logged)	−0.002*	0.001	0.998
Workload × Time (logged)	0.07*	0.02	1.07
Chief Justice Author × Time (logged)	−0.17	0.19	0.84
N	2289		
χ^2	299.55*		

Note: Table entries are Cox Proportional Hazard regression coefficients with robust standard errors (clustered on the majority opinion author) in parentheses; *$p < .05$ (one-tailed). The dependent variable represents, for each case, the number of days between the majority opinion assignment and circulation of the first majority opinion draft, 1969–1985.

8.6.2 Responsive Accommodation

In the main manuscript, we did not replicate Maltzman, Spriggs, and Wahlbeck's (2000) findings of responsive accommodation. We opted to not estimate those models because we have significant reservations over what, exactly, the dependent variable measures. The dependent variable is coded as 1 if a circulated draft was the final draft; 0 otherwise. As we (and they) are quick to acknowledge, this is a surrogate for a more direct measure of such accommodation. And it is not a particularly good one.

Nevertheless, for the interested reader, we replicate those models here. Following Maltzman, Spriggs, and Wahlbeck (2000), we estimate a random-effects cross-sectional time series probit regression model with robust standard errors (clustered on the case). Parameter estimates for the model appear in Table 24. Model 1 reports the unconditional results, while Models 2 and 3 specify an interaction with *Legal Salience* and *Political Salience*, respectively. As the table makes clear, the data exhibit no meaningful, unconditional relationship between a justice's conscientiousness and his or her level of responsive accommodation. And, as Figure 49(a) shows, the average marginal effect of *Legal Salience* does not vary significantly as a function of *Conscientiousness*. Yet, the data do suggest that justice conscientiousness interacts with *Political Salience* to affect the degree of responsive accommodation.

Consider Figure 49(b), which reports the average marginal effect of *Political Salience* across the range of *Conscientiousness*. An individual opinion draft is less likely to be the final circulation in cases with greater political salience, thereby suggesting greater accommodation on behalf of the majority opinion writer. But, this relationship exists exclusively among the most conscientious opinion authors in the sample. Specifically, *Political Salience* exhibits a statistically significant effect among justices scoring above −0.56 on the conscientious scale, representing 65 percent of the sample observations.

Figure 49(c) displays the magnitude of this effect, expressed as the predicted probability that an opinion draft is the final circulation across the range of *Conscientiousness*. The dashed line represents cases with high political salience (i.e., the 90th percentile) and the solid line represents low political salience (i.e., 10th percentile). The data indicate that the predicted difference between high versus low salience case is as much as 0.04 for the conscientious justice. That is, moving from a low to high salience case leads to an expected 11 percent decrease in the probability that an opinion draft is the final circulation. In other words, while the data suggest that the effect is modest on balance, the conscientious is meaningfully more likely to accommodate his or her colleagues through repeated opinion drafts in those cases that carry the greatest political implications.

Among the control predictors, opinion authors who are more open are less likely to accommodate their colleagues, while greater extraversion predicts more responsive accommodation. Similarly, when the majority opinion writer is more ideologically divergent from the nonjoiners or when there is greater preference heterogeneity among the coalition justices, he or she is more likely to circulate more opinion drafts to accommodate colleagues.

TABLE 24: *The Impact of Conscientiousness on Responsive Accommodation by the Majority Opinion Writer*

	Unconditional (1)	Legal Salience (2)	Political Salience (3)
Conscientiousness	−0.01	−0.01	0.01
	(0.03)	(0.03)	(0.03)
Openness	0.05*	0.05*	0.05*
	(0.03)	(0.03)	(0.03)
Extraversion	−0.13*	−0.13*	−0.13*
	(0.03)	(0.03)	(0.03)
Agreeableness	0.02	0.02	0.02
	(0.02)	(0.02)	(0.02)
Neuroticism	0.04	0.04	0.05
	(0.03)	(0.03)	(0.03)
Legal Salience	−0.06	−0.07	−0.06
	(0.06)	(0.06)	(0.06)
Conscientiousness × Legal Salience		−0.04	
		(0.06)	
Political Salience	−0.015*	−0.015*	−0.02*
	(0.006)	(0.006)	(0.01)
Conscientiousness × Political Salience			−0.012*
			(0.007)
Distance from Nonjoiners	−0.01*	−0.01*	−0.01*
	(0.001)	(0.001)	(0.001)
Heterogeneity of Nonjoiners	−0.02*	−0.02*	−0.02*
	(0.003)	(0.003)	(0.003)
Winning Margin	0.18*	0.18*	0.18*
	(0.01)	(0.01)	(0.01)
Cooperation of Nonjoiners	0.13	0.13	0.14
	(0.40)	(0.40)	(0.40)
Have Majority	0.83*	0.83*	0.82*
	(0.05)	(0.05)	(0.05)
Number of Suggestions	−0.47*	−0.47*	−0.47*
	(0.11)	(0.11)	(0.11)
Number of Waits	−0.47*	−0.47*	−0.48*
	(0.11)	(0.11)	(0.11)
Number of Will Writes	−0.41*	−0.41*	−0.41*
	(0.06)	(0.06)	(0.06)

(continued)

TABLE 24: *(continued)*

	Unconditional (1)	Legal Salience (2)	Political Salience (3)
First Drafts of SeparateOpinions	−0.16*	−0.16*	−0.16*
	(0.03)	(0.03)	(0.03)
Case Complexity	−0.05*	−0.05*	−0.05*
	(0.02)	(0.02)	(0.02)
End of Term	−0.004*	−0.004*	−0.004*
	(0.000)	(0.000)	(0.000)
Workload	−0.10*	−0.10*	−0.10*
	(0.01)	(0.01)	(0.01)
Chief Justice Author	−0.22*	−0.22*	−0.22*
	(0.07)	(0.07)	(0.07)
Freshman Author	0.03	0.03	0.03
	(0.07)	(0.07)	(0.07)
Expertise	0.02	0.02	0.02
	(0.02)	(0.02)	(0.02)
Constant	−1.17*	−1.17*	−1.16*
	(0.10)	(0.10)	(0.10)
N	6471	6471	6471
χ^2	1607.17*	1638.88*	1642.75*

Note: Table entries are random-effects cross-sectional time series probit regression coefficients with robust standard errors (clustered on the case) in parentheses; *$p < .05$ (one-tailed). The dependent variable represents whether a circulated majority opinion draft represents the final circulation, 1969–1985. The models include, but do not display, parameter estimates for five spline segments (Maltzman, Spriggs, and Wahlbeck 2000).

Next, coalitions with greater winning margins, or when the opinion author has already established a majority, lead to less responsive accommodation. Conversely, the data indicate that justices circulate more drafts when coalition members offer more suggestions, respond that they will wait, indicate an intent to write separately, and when circulating more first drafts of separate opinions. The majority opinion writer also exhibits more responsive accommodation in more complex cases, when there is more time before the end of the term, and when faced with a greater workload. Lastly, Chief Justice Burger was likely to circulate more opinion drafts than his colleagues on the Court.

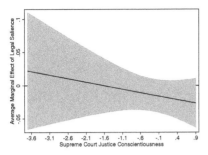

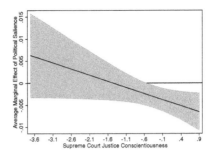

(a) Average Marginal Effect–Legal Salience   (b) Average Marginal Effect–Political Salience

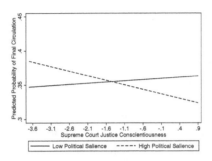

(c) Predicted Probability–Political Salience

FIGURE 49: *The conditional impact of the conscientiousness trait on whether a circulated majority opinion draft represents the final circulation.* Panel (a) reports the average marginal effect (with 90% confidence intervals) of *Legal Salience* across the observed range of justice *Conscientiousness* using results from Model 2 in Table 24. Panel (b) reports the average marginal effect of *Political Salience* using results from Model 3 in Table 24, and Panel (c) displays the corresponding predicted probabilities (the dashed line represents cases with high political salience [90th percentile] and the solid line represents low political salience [10th percentile]).

9

Conscientiousness and Supreme Court Opinion Content

In *United States* v. *Roy Lee Johnson* (2000), the Supreme Court faced a technical question about when a prisoner's period of supervised release begins.[1] A jury sentenced Roy Lee Johnson to 231 months of prison, plus 3 years of supervised release, for a series of drug and firearms crimes he committed. During his imprisonment, however, the Supreme Court struck down some of Johnson's sentence. As a result, Johnson wound up serving a longer prison sentence than he ought to have served. He wanted his "extra" time in prison to count toward his three-year supervised release period. The question the Court faced was whether 18 U.S.C. §3624, the relevant statute, counted that extra prison time toward Johnson's three-year supervised release period. If so, Johnson would face a minimal amount of time in supervised release. If not, he would still have to spend the next three years on supervised release.

A unanimous Supreme Court ruled against Johnson. Writing for the Court, Justice Kennedy focused on the text of the statute, the purpose of the statute, and the text of related statutes. According to Kennedy, the language of the statute did not allow Johnson to receive credit for his (extra) time served, regardless of the unwarranted prison time. More important for our present purposes, Kennedy's opinion was both cognitively complex and broad. It engaged multiple legal perspectives. Indeed, the opinion stands out as one of the most cognitively complex opinions in the Court's modern era. While we explain our measure of cognitive complexity below, Figure 50 illustrates the distribution of cognitive complexity of all majority opinions. *U.S.* v. *Roy Lee Johnson* sits at the tail of the distribution. In contrast, *United States* v. *Lashawn Banks* (2003), sits at the other end of the distribution. That case was a straightforward search and seizure dispute that turned on the question whether the fifteen- to twenty-second wait before forcible entry satisfied the Fourth

[1] *See United States* v. *Roy Lee Johnson*, 529 U.S. 53 (2000).

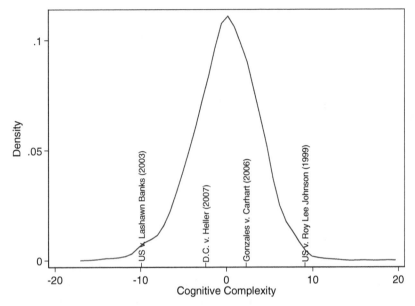

FIGURE 50: *The distribution of cognitive complexity in U.S. Supreme Court majority opinions.* The figure represents a kernel density plot of the distribution of the cognitive complexity of majority opinions.

Amendment. The short opinion, written by Justice David Souter, dealt with only a handful of legal points. For comparison purposes, we also display the cognitive complexity of two major and well known cases: *D.C.* v. *Heller* (2007) and *Gonzales* v. *Carhart* (2006). In *Heller*, the Court ruled that the Second Amendment protects an individual right to bear arms. In *Gonzales*, the Court upheld the Partial-Birth Abortion Ban Act of 2003.

Why did Kennedy and Souter write the opinions they did? Was their opinion language a function of the issue in the case? Did other contextual features, like the majority coalition size, influence their language? We suspect the answers to these questions are yes. But, we also suspect that their conscientiousness influenced their opinions. By our measures, Justice Kennedy scored high on the trait of conscientiousness while Justice Souter scored low.

We believe that conscientious justices write increasingly cognitively complex opinions that are longer, clearer, and contain more breadth than opinions written by less conscientious justices. Our results largely concur. The results reveal that conscientious justices are significantly more likely to write cognitively complex, legally broad opinions, and longer opinions, as we expect. A maximal increase in conscientiousness leads to a substantial increase in an opinion's cognitive complexity. It also correlates with a 10 percent increase in the breadth of the opinion, and a 21 percent increase in the number of words in an opinion. At the same time, such an increase in conscientiousness also leads to a substantial decrease in the rhetorical clarity of an opinion. All of this, we argue, stems from the conscientious justice's desire to be exhaustive, dutiful, and industrious.

We take no position on whether cognitively complex opinions are "worse" or "better" than less complex opinions. Nor do we presuppose that broader opinions are any better or worse. These are simply characteristics of opinions that we believe correspond to conscientiousness. And the data concur.

9.1 OPINION LANGUAGE AND THE SUPREME COURT

Justices and normative scholars frequently debate how broadly the Court should write its opinions. On the one hand, there are those who believe the Court should write narrow opinions – opinions that are limited to the facts of their cases. Generalist judges, they argue, lack expertise and should tread carefully for fear of delivering bad rulings. This view is captured by a perspective called "judicial minimalism" (Sunstein 1999). Judicial minimalism suggests that justices should stick to the facts at hand so as to avoid making errors that are hard to undo later (but see Schauer and Zeckhauser 2011). That is, because precedent binds courts, a wrong-headed decision today could lock in judges for years.[2] As a consequence, judicial minimalists argue that narrow holdings are better because they preserve the Court's flexibility in future cases. The Court can return to a dispute later, adapt to changed circumstances, and provide a more nuanced (and, presumably, a better) outcome (Sullivan 1992; Roberts 2006; Sunstein 1999). In some respects, this is an inherently conservative approach that recognizes the Court's institutional weaknesses and the fact that Supreme Court cases typically involves unique facts.

On the other hand, some scholars argue that the rule of law compels the Court to write broad opinions with more sweeping applications and that are not so narrowly tailored to the precise facts of individual cases (Scalia 1989). Why? Citizens deserve to know what actions are legally permissible *before* they carry them out. And when the Court takes a hyper-incremental approach

---

[2] To add to the Court's woes, justices lack the subpoena power of a legislature or the investigative power of an agency, further limiting judicial capability (see, e.g., Coan 2012).

(i.e., justices limit their decisions to the facts at hand), they fail to offer citizens guidelines on what actions are legally permissible (Korobkin 2000). Only opinions that deal fully and broadly with legal issues are predictable. A speed limit of sixty-five miles per hour is clearer and thus fairer to drivers than a requirement to not drive "too fast for conditions" (Scalia 1989). Broad opinions are much more informative, clear, and fair than narrow opinions.[3]

Kaiser Aluminum v. *Bonjorno* (1990) provides a good example of how this debate sometimes plays out in the Court's opinions. In *Kaiser*, a case regarding postjudgment interest rates in civil suits, the Supreme Court had to decide what version of a federal statute courts should apply – the statute in effect at the time of judgment, or the statute revised during the pendency of the appeal to the circuit court. The answer, according to Justice O'Connor and the majority, was the former – the law in effect at the time of the trial court judgment. Her opinion, however, was narrow and contained multiple exceptions. Courts could retrospectively apply law unless retrospective application would "result in manifest injustice to one of the parties or where there is clear congressional intent to the contrary."[4] Justice Scalia chafed at O'Connor's language. In a concurring opinion, he demanded a broad rule, stating simply: "the operation of nonpenal legislation is prospective only."[5] In part, the justices' disagreement was just as much about the breadth and clarity of the legal rule as it was about the legal rule itself.

As this discussion shows, opinion content matters. The breadth, complexity, clarity, and readability of opinions ... they all matter. But what leads justices to write certain kinds of opinions over others? Why do some justices go big while others pursue incremental change? We suspect that conscientiousness is a culprit.[6]

---

[3] In fact, many scholars took Justice O'Connor and other "judicial minimalists" to task for writing narrow opinions. For example, one scholar noted, "[O'Connor] often avoids adopting bright-line rules and opts instead for what has been termed contextual or individualized decision making" (Oakes 1992, 537). Her "narrow opinions have the effect of preserving her ability to change her mind in future cases ... [she] prefers vague standards to clear rules ... by [refusing] to commit herself to consistent principles, O'Connor forces the court and those who follow it to engage in a guessing game about her wishes in case after case" (Rosen June 3, 2001, 32).

[4] *See* 494 U.S. at 837.

[5] *See* 494 U.S. at 841 (Scalia, J., concurring).

[6] To be sure, court opinions contain a variety of empirical assessable elements, ranging from their linguistic attributes (Cross and Pennebaker 2014) to the cases they discuss (Hansford and Spriggs 2006).

9.2 A THEORY OF CONSCIENTIOUSNESS AND OPINION WRITING

We believe conscientious justices write cognitively complex, legally broader, longer, and rhetorically clearer opinions than less conscientious justices. These expectations are rooted in the fact that conscientious people strive to excel at their jobs, they are thorough, and they take care to produce the best work product possible.

Scholarship shows that conscientious individuals are more dutiful and responsible, and exhibit a higher desire to pursue goal-directed behavior than less conscientious individuals. Gul et al. (2004, 359) find that "[h]igh level conscientious scholars being very competent, disciplined and achievement striking are found to make extra efforts in database searching to get required information." In a study on how people search the Internet, Schmidt and Wolff (2016, 6) find that "[c]onscientious people have a high level of activity and an exhaustive exploitation of the search space," while less conscientious people use a search pattern aimed "at finding results fast but with little reflection" (see also Halder, Roy, and Chakraborty 2010). Conscientious people, in short, take more meticulous care of their work product than other people.

Scholarship also shows that conscientious people generally tend to consider more information in the process of decision making, which also leads us to believe that conscientious justices will write longer, more cognitively complex, and legally broader opinions. Recall Heinström (2003), who finds that conscientious people tend to seek out more information – and more complex information – to support their positions than less conscientious people. Heinstrom examined how graduate students sought out information to work on their research. The study investigated how students evaluated information, how they selected the documents they used for their research, and the effect of time pressure on their behavior. The results showed that conscientious people sought out thought-provoking documents instead of those that merely confirmed previous ideas. The conscientious students exhibited more engagement with the material and pushed themselves to consider more complex material. On the other hand, students with lower levels of conscientiousness tended to choose their information sources based on how easy it was to access.

As applied to judicial opinion writing, a dutiful judge surely believes it important to respond clearly to all legal arguments in a case. This, of course, would lead to a longer and legally denser opinion. Likewise, discussing multiple perspectives or dimensions associated with a case could lead to a more cognitively complex opinion – one that addresses multiple dimensions. What is more, a justice who incorporates more information is likely to write opinions that consider, and address, a greater diversity of legal viewpoints. This should lead to longer and more cognitively complex opinions. Furthermore, existing research argues that one hallmark of a quality opinion is a high degree of rhetorical clarity (Black, Owens, Wedeking, and Wohlfarth 2016b). Clearer opinions are better able to articulate doctrine in a way that audiences can understand and faithfully implement. Given that conscientious people seek to generate superior work products, we believe conscientious justices should seek to produce superior quality opinions. Consequently, they will seek to enhance their rhetorical clarity. In short, the written opinion represents a justice's primary, and most important, work product. As such, the conscientious justice should be most likely to expend the extra effort necessary to deliver the highest quality opinion possible. On balance, a model opinion is one that treats applicable law in a serious, thorough manner, considers multiple legal viewpoints and ideas, and does all of this as clearly as possible. As a result, the logic behind existing studies – and the likely role of conscientiousness on justices' opinion writing – lead us to propose four empirically testable hypotheses:

As a justice becomes more conscientious, she writes increasingly cognitively complex opinions.

As a justice becomes more conscientious, she writes legally broader opinions.

As a justice becomes more conscientious, she writes longer opinions.

As a justice becomes more conscientious, she writes rhetorically clearer opinions.

9.3 DATA AND MEASURES

To analyze our theoretical claims, we consider the impact of *Conscientiousness* on four indicators of Supreme Court majority opinion content: the degree of cognitive complexity, legal breadth, opinion length, and rhetorical clarity. To be crystal clear, we reiterate that we believe increasingly conscientious justices write majority opinions that exhibit greater cognitive complexity, more extensive legal breadth, greater length, and enhanced rhetorical clarity. Following Black, Owens, Wedeking, and Wohlfarth (2016b), we analyze the Court's majority opinions in all signed, orally argued decisions. We extend their analysis to include the 1947 to 2007 terms. The unit of analysis is the majority opinion associated with each case citation. We focus on four dependent variables – *Cognitive Complexity, Legal Breadth, Word Count,* and *Rhetorical Clarity.*[7]

Cognitive Complexity. Our first dependent variable measures the *Cognitive Complexity* of each majority opinion. We adopt, and extend, the measure constructed by Owens and Wedeking (2011) using the computer software program, Linguistic Inquiry and Word Count (LIWC).[8] LIWC captures different emotional and cognitive dimensions of speech by using a word-count strategy that searches for more than 2,300 words (or word stems) using specific dictionaries within a text file. LIWC tallies the percent of words in a document. The software covers more than seventy linguistic dimensions previously determined by independent judges (Pennebaker, Mehl, and Niederhoffer 2003).[9] Owens and Wedeking (2011) use a composite of ten LIWC indicators – six that were created explicitly to measure cognitive processes (causation, insight, discrepancy, inhibit, tentative, and certainty) and four linguistic indicators associated with cognitive processes (inclusiveness, exclusiveness, negations, and the percentage of words containing six or more letters).[10]

In a single dimensional scale, the cognitive complexity indicator taps into two elements: differentiation and integration. Individuals at the low end of the scale do not differentiate among perspectives or dimensions of an issue and, likewise, do not integrate multiple perspectives by making connections among the possible different perspectives. They see the world in black and white. Individuals in the middle of the scale differentiate between multiple perspectives but still do not make any connections or integrate those multiple perspectives. Individuals high in cognitive complexity show high levels of differentiation and also integration of multiple perspectives (for more details,

---

7   The pairwise correlations among these variables (with p-value and number of observations in parentheses) are: Cognitive Complexity-Legal Breadth 0.06 (p < 0.01, 6,717), Cognitive Complexity-Word Count 0.01 (p < 0.26, 6,695), Cognitive Complexity-Rhetorical Clarity 0.18 (p < 0.01, 6717), Legal Breadth-Word Count 0.55 (p < 0.01, 6,695), Legal Breadth-Rhetorical Clarity 0.04 (p < 0.01, 6,756), Word Count-Rhetorical Clarity −0.04 (p < 0.01, 6,695). The relatively low correlations suggests that they capture different elements of opinion writing.

8   The *cognitive complexity* estimate is generated with the formula: cognitive complexity = Zsixletter - Zcausation - Zinsight - Zdiscrepancy - Zinhibit - Ztentative - Zcertainty - Zinclusive - Zexclusive - Znegations. Each "Z" represents standardizing each LIWC indicator by converting them to Z scores (subtract off the mean, divide by the standard deviation). This is necessary because the LIWC indicators are looking for different numbers of words.

9   The use of percentages alleviates concerns about the length of the document being a confounding factor.

10 Moreover, including ten indicators of the concept increases the likelihood that the measure will represent all facets of the construct (i.e., possess strong content validity). See Owens and Wedeking (2011) for further details.

see Owens and Wedeking 2011).[11] The two cases at the opening of this chapter illustrate the differences in what the measure captures. Among the majority opinions in the sample, the distribution of *Cognitive Complexity*, as seen in Figure 50, approximates a normal distribution. It ranges from −16.45 to 19.06, with a mean value of −0.10 and standard deviation of 3.85.

Legal Breadth. Our second dependent variable taps into the majority opinion's legal breadth. We think of legal breadth as the amount of legal points the case makes. To measure legal breadth, we count the number of Headnotes that LexisNexis identifies in each opinion. Headnotes are written by LexisNexis legal editors to showcase the key legal points of a case. Headnotes are meant to help legal researchers identify the important points of an opinion and find other cases that raise similar legal issues, use similar terms of art, or apply closely matching language. Importantly, LexisNexis derives Headnotes directly from the opinion.

Our approach has several unique features that make it a useful proxy for legal breadth. First, Headnotes capture unique points of law in opinions. Second, LexisNexis is widely used among legal researchers, litigants, law clerks, and judges (Bermant 1999; Hellyer 2005), providing it with external validity. Finally, our measure comports with the theoretical definition of opinion breadth recently forwarded by Fox and Vanberg (2013) and has been used in similar contexts empirically (see Haire, Moyer, and Treier 2013).[12] Figure 51 shows the distribution of *Legal Breadth*. The distribution has a slight skew and ranges from zero to seventy-six headnotes, with a sample mean of 8.29 and standard deviation of 5.58. Several salient cases are listed as reference points of the distribution.

Word Count. Our third dependent variable measures opinion length by counting the total number of words in each majority opinion. Black and Spriggs (2008) highlight the importance of opinion length for the development of law and provide a detailed review of the scholarship on opinion length. Their review shows that previous scholars used opinion length as an indicator of workload, legal style, culture, quality, complexity, and the extent

---

[11] We use the 2001 LIWC dictionary to generate this measure. But the subsequent results are consistent when instead using the 2007 dictionary.

[12] In terms of face validity, we note that our measure captures the two case studies used by Fox and Vanberg (2013). They point to *Employment Division* v. *Smith* (1990) as illustrative of a broad opinion, whereas *City of Ontario* v. *Quon* (2010) typifies a narrow opinion. *Smith* had a total of twelve headnotes in it, whereas *Quon* had but only seven headnotes. As the average number of headnotes in an opinion is just over eight, we can confidently say that *Smith* is above average (z-score of about 0.67), whereas *Quon* is of below average breadth (z-score of roughly −0.18).

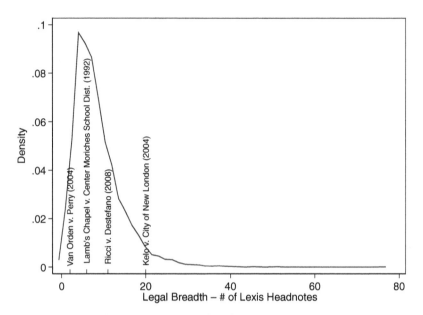

FIGURE 51: *The distribution of legal breadth in U.S. Supreme Court majority opinions.* The figure represents a kernel density plot of the distribution of legal breadth, measured as the number of Lexis headnotes.

to which an issue of the law is settled. Importantly, they illuminate the important normative debate surrounding opinion length and the potential negative consequences, such as time wasted, public disengagement, and lower court enforcement. Within our sample, *Word Count* has a mean of 4,638 total words and a standard deviation of 2,840. The shortest opinion has 108 total words while the longest opinion contains 35,190 words. The distribution has a similar shape and skew to the distribution for legal breadth.[13]

Rhetorical Clarity. Our fourth, and final, indicator of opinion content represents the rhetorical clarity of each majority opinion. To measure rhetorical clarity, we employ Black, Owens, Wedeking, and Wohlfarth's (2016*b*) measure of textual readability. This measure taps into the presentation of legal concepts in the opinion and "the clarity of [its] external communication as it is understood by others" (Black, Owens, Wedeking, and Wohlfarth 2016*a*, 711). We constructed the indicator using the single principal component representing the common variance in twenty-eight different textual readability measures. We scale this variable so that larger values reflect greater clarity.

---

[13] If we transform the word count by taking the natural log, the results remain the same.

Among the majority opinions in the sample, *Rhetorical Clarity* has a Gaussian distribution with a mean of −0.19 and a standard deviation of 4.22. Its range includes a minimum score of between −17.69 (very difficult to read) and +15.86 (very easy to read).

Conscientiousness. Our primary independent variable is *Conscientiousness*, which we described in Chapter 3. In this chapter, we measure *Conscientiousness* as the conscientiousness score of the majority opinion author.[14] Although all justices in a coalition may have a hand in shaping the majority opinion, we expect the author's personality predominantly shapes its content and character.

We expect positive relationships across each conscientiousness-dependent variable combination. We also control for the majority opinion author's scores on the four other personality traits – *Openness, Extraversion, Agreeableness,* and *Neuroticism.*

Intercircuit Uncertainty. We adopt Black, Owens, Wedeking, and Wohlfarth's (2016*b*) indicator of how scattered ideologically the circuit courts are each year. As the individual circuit courts become increasingly scattered – and thus more predisposed to exhibit conflict in their interpretation of federal law – justices may write less complex, less legally broad, shorter, and more rhetorically clear opinions to ensure greater harmony and uniformity among the circuits. Using the Judicial Common Space (JCS)[15], (Epstein, Martin, Segal, and Westerland 2007), *Intercircuit Uncertainty* represents the interdecile distance (i.e., between the 10th and 90th percentiles) among the circuit court median scores each year.[17] As Black, Owens, Wedeking, and Wohlfarth (2016*b*) explain, the interdecile distance seeks to balance the desire to capture the range of dispersion among the circuit medians

---

[14] We use the "majOpinWriter" variable in the Supreme Court Database to identify the majority opinion author.

[15] The JCS places Supreme Court justices (as measured by Martin and Quinn 2002) on the same ideological scale as federal circuit court judges, with scores ranging from negative (liberal) to positive (conservative). The Judicial Common Space uses the coding method suggested by Giles, Hettinger, and Peppers (2001), who argued when the norm of senatorial courtesy applies to a judge's appointment, that judge's ideal point estimate mirrors the home state senators' preferences. The estimate for such a judge is thus her home state senators' Poole and Rosenthal first-dimension Common Space scores.[16] If there are two home state senators from the president's party, the point estimate is the mean of the two; if only one senator hails from the president's party, the point estimate is that senator's score. When senatorial courtesy does not apply to the judge's appointment, the judge's ideal point estimate is the president's first dimension Common Space score.

[16] http://www.voteview.com/dwnomjoint.asp.

[17] In other words, we determine the JCS score of the median judge in each circuit year and then compute the distance between the 10th and 90th percentiles on the distribution of those circuit medians.

each year but without allowing the most aberrant outliers to distort the measure.[18]

Ideological Distance between the Supreme Court and the Circuit Courts. Our next control variable also follows Black, Owens, Wedeking, and Wohlfarth (2016*b*) and captures the general ideological distance between the Supreme Court and the circuit courts. Supreme Court justices may write less complex opinions and seek to enhance rhetorical clarity as the High Court and federal circuits become increasingly dissimilar ideologically. A clearer and less complex opinion may help the Court ensure greater compliance with its rulings among the circuits. Lower courts will find it harder to evade clearer and more concise opinions, and the public will be able to monitor lower courts more easily when the rulings are clear. *Ideological Distance* measures the distance between the average of the circuit court medians and the Supreme Court's median justice each term. That is, using the JCS scores, we compute the absolute value of the distance between (1) the mean of the circuit court medians each year and (2) the US Supreme Court's median justice.

Judicial Review. We next account for instances when the majority opinion strikes a federal or state law as unconstitutional. When taking the significant step of voiding the acts of elected branches, the Court's majority opinion author may seek to make his or her opinion less complex (and more clear) in order to direct future action to justify more clearly the Court's actions. We create two variables to capture these potential effects. *Federal Judicial Review* takes on a value of 1 when the Supreme Court Database indicates that the Court struck down an act of Congress; 0 otherwise. Similarly, *State Judicial Review* takes on a value of 1 when the Court nullified a state's law, regulation, or constitutional provision, as identified by the Supreme Court Database; 0 otherwise.[19]

Precedent Alteration. We control for whether the Court alters its own prior precedents, as these decisions may be inherently more complex and take longer to address the reasons why altering precedent is necessary. Alternatively, the opinion author may seek to write a less cognitively complex and legally broad opinion to facilitate compliance. *Precedent Alteration* takes on

---

[18] Nevertheless, all subsequent results are substantively consistent if measuring *Intercircuit Uncertainty* using either the full range or standard deviation of the circuit medians each year.

[19] We utilize the *declarationUncon* variable in the Supreme Court Database. Specifically, we assign a 1 to *Federal Judicial Review* and *State Judicial Review* when *declarationUncon* takes on a value of 2 and 3, respectively.

a value of 1 when the Supreme Court Database codes the Court as having formally altered an existing precedent; 0 otherwise.[20]

Amicus Participation. We account for the number of amicus curiae briefs in each case. Collins (2008) shows that greater amicus curiae participation corresponds with greater case complexity. To the extent that greater external interest signifies greater complexity (or salience), the majority opinion may naturally exhibit greater cognitive complexity, greater length and legal breadth, and more rhetorical clarity in cases with increased amicus involvement. We measure *Amicus Participation* by counting the number of amicus curiae briefs filed in each case using data from Collins (2008) (1953–2001 terms) and our own Lexis data collection (i.e., for the 1947–1952 and 2002–2007 Court terms).

Majority Coalition Controls. We include two control predictors to capture how differences across majority coalitions may lead the opinion author to write different opinions. First, *Coalition Heterogeneity* captures the majority coalition's ideological heterogeneity. To measure *Coalition Heterogeneity*, we identify the justices who are in the majority coalition and compute the standard deviation of their JCS scores. Second, *Majority Votes* represents the size of the majority coalition, as indicated by the number of justices in the coalition.[21]

Lower Court Dissent. We also control for whether, in each case the High Court decides, there was a dissent in the lower court that decided it. Cases in which a lower court judge dissents may be inherently more complicated. *Lower Court Dissent* receives a value of 1 in cases where a lower court judge dissented; 0 otherwise.

Separation of Powers Constraint. We account for the possibility that separation of powers considerations lead justices to write more ambiguous opinions. Owens, Wedeking, and Wohlfarth (2013) argue that justices write increasingly unclear opinions as they become more distant ideologically from Congress. We use the JCS scores to measure these possible separation of powers constraints. If the median justice falls between the House and Senate chamber medians – the median member of each chamber – *SOP Constraint* takes on a value of 0. Alternatively, when the median justice is more liberal or conservative than the median members of both the US House and Senate, *SOP*

---

[20] We utilize the *precedentAlteration* variable in the Supreme Court Database to identify decisions that formally altered prior precedent.

[21] We use the Supreme Court Database's "majority" indicator to identify the justices in each majority coalition and the *majVotes* variable to identify the size of the majority coalition.

Constraint equals the absolute value of the distance between that justice and the closest institutional median.

Prior Issue Decisions. In some areas of law, the Court has rendered a greater number of decisions. The Court's opinions may need to address all of those decisions. As a consequence, some opinions are likely to be longer and perhaps more muddled than others. We must account for that. We code *Prior Issue Decisions* as the number of cases the Court previously decided (since the 1946 term) in the issue area the present case involves.[22]

Infrequently Litigated Statute. Cases that involve infrequently litigated federal statutes may lead to opinions with more complex content. Thus, we create a dummy variable – *Infrequent Statute* – and assign a value of 1 to those cases the Supreme Court Database identifies as reviewing such statutes; 0 otherwise.[23]

Supreme Court Term. We account for variance in opinion content that might be due to deterministic shifts over time, given that the data exhibit evidence of long-term temporal changes in Supreme Court majority opinion content. Accordingly, *Supreme Court Term* represents the Court term associated with each majority opinion.

Issue Area Controls. Lastly, we account for differences in opinion content across issue areas by including fixed effects for the primary issue area within each case. We include a dummy variable for each broad issue area.[24]

9.4 METHODS AND RESULTS

We now turn to the results of the empirical models. Again, we consider four dependent variables: (Majority Opinion) *Cognitive Complexity, Legal Breadth, Word Count,* and *Rhetorical Clarity.* We estimate two regression models for each dependent variable: a baseline model that includes *Conscientiousness* (and the other four personality traits) and a second model that includes the full complement of controls.[25] Table 25 presents these results.

---

[22] We use the "issueArea" variable in the Supreme Court Database to identify the primary issue area within each case.

[23] The database identifies cases that involve infrequently litigated federal statutes with the "lawType" variable (i.e., when it takes on a value of 6).

[24] Specifically, we use the "issueArea" variable in the Database to identify the primary issue area within each case.

[25] The impact of *Conscientiousness* on all four opinion content dependent variables is also substantively consistent if we estimate bivariate models that include only *Conscientiousness* as a predictor (without controls).

	Cog. Complexity		Legal Breadth		Word Count		Rhetorical Clarity	
	(1)	(2)	(3)	(4)	(5)	(6)	(7)	(8)
Conscientiousness	0.17*	0.19*	0.04*	0.02*	0.04*	0.04*	−0.60*	−0.56*
	(0.07)	(0.07)	(0.01)	(0.01)	(0.01)	(0.01)	(0.07)	(0.07)
Openness	−0.42*	−0.38*	−0.00	0.00	0.05*	0.04*	−0.61*	−0.46*
	(0.04)	(0.04)	(0.01)	(0.01)	(0.01)	(0.01)	(0.05)	(0.04)
Extraversion	0.35*	0.30*	0.03*	0.01	−0.03*	−0.04*	0.45*	0.33*
	(0.06)	(0.06)	(0.01)	(0.01)	(0.01)	(0.01)	(0.06)	(0.06)
Agreeableness	−0.06	−0.09*	0.02*	0.02*	0.05*	0.06*	−0.08	−0.04
	(0.05)	(0.05)	(0.01)	(0.01)	(0.01)	(0.01)	(0.05)	(0.05)
Neuroticism	0.24*	0.22*	0.03*	0.01	0.04*	0.03*	0.07	0.02
	(0.05)	(0.05)	(0.01)	(0.01)	(0.01)	(0.01)	(0.06)	(0.06)
Intercircuit Uncertainty		−0.86*		−0.35*		−0.45*		2.09*
		(0.43)		(0.07)		(0.06)		(0.47)
Circuit Ideo Distance		0.26		0.11		−0.04		4.25*
		(0.51)		(0.08)		(0.08)		(0.55)
Federal Judicial Review		−0.20		0.17*		0.15*		−0.44
		(0.44)		(0.08)		(0.07)		(0.41)
State Judicial Review		0.59*		0.02		0.03		0.58*
		(0.20)		(0.03)		(0.03)		(0.25)
Precedent Alteration		0.48*		0.14*		0.26*		1.04*
		(0.29)		(0.05)		(0.05)		(0.31)
Amicus Participation		0.03*		0.02*		0.02*		0.02
		(0.01)		(0.002)		(0.002)		(0.01)
Coalition Heterogeneity		0.70		−0.02		0.07		−0.54
		(0.62)		(0.10)		(0.10)		(0.66)

(continued)

235

TABLE 25: (continued)

	Cog. Complexity		Legal Breadth		Word Count		Rhetorical Clarity	
	(1)	(2)	(3)	(4)	(5)	(6)	(7)	(8)
Majority Votes		0.15*		−0.03*		−0.08*		0.07*
		(0.04)		(0.01)		(0.01)		(0.04)
Lower Court Dissent		−0.18*		0.03*		0.07*		−0.21*
		(0.11)		(0.02)		(0.02)		(0.12)
SOP Constraint		−0.50		0.05		0.06		−4.85*
		(0.47)		(0.07)		(0.07)		(0.49)
Prior Issue Decisions		−0.002*		−0.001*		−0.00		−0.003*
		(0.001)		(0.000)		(0.00)		(0.001)
Infrequent Statute		0.34*		0.02		0.03		0.51*
		(0.13)		(0.02)		(0.02)		(0.13)
Supreme Court Term		0.03*		0.01*		0.01*		0.04*
		(0.004)		(0.001)		(0.001)		(0.004)
Constant	−0.01	−66.87*	2.12*	−25.28*	8.42*	−7.94*	−0.48*	−74.15*
	(0.07)	(8.07)	(0.01)	(1.30)	(0.01)	(1.27)	(0.08)	(8.65)
Issue Area Controls	No	Yes	No	Yes	No	Yes	No	Yes
N	6432	6288	6470	6326	6410	6270	6470	6326
F-Statistic	30.22*	21.69*	60.25*	1267.72*	166.07*	1436.52*	71.22*	29.80*
χ^2-Statistic	—	—	—	—	—	—	—	—

Note: Table entries are OLS (Models 1–2 and 7–8) or negative binomial (Model 3–6) regression coefficients with robust standard errors in parentheses. *p < 0.05 (one-tailed). The dependent variable represents the content indicator of each Supreme Court majority opinion (per curiam opinions excluded), 1947–2007, with larger values reflecting greater cognitive complexity, legal breadth, word count, and rhetorical clarity. Models 1, 3, 5, and 7 include, but do not display, fixed effects for the primary issue area of each case. Models 2, 4, 6, and 8 lose 140 observations due to missing data with the Amicus Participation variable. Models 2, 4, and 8 lose 4 more observations due to missing data on the Issue Area variable.

9.4.1 *Cognitive Complexity*

Our first set of models examines how conscientiousness influences the cognitive complexity of majority opinions. Because cognitive complexity is a continuous indicator, we estimate OLS regression models. We employ robust standard errors to account for the possibility of correlated errors, although all subsequent results (across all eight model specifications) for *Conscientiousness* are consistent if we alternatively fit the models with classical standard errors. Models 1 and 2 in Table 25 display these regression results. Across both model specifications, the data exhibit a statistically significant, positive relationship between *Conscientiousness* and *Cognitive Complexity*. That is, the results support the hypothesis that increasingly conscientious justices write majority opinions that exhibit greater cognitive complexity.

Figure 52 illustrates the magnitude of this effect, displayed as the predicted level of *Cognitive Complexity* across the observed range of *Conscientiousness* using the regression results from Model 2 in Table 25. For each set of predicted values, we hold all control variables constant at their mean (or, for binary variables, their modal) values. A justice exhibiting the minimum level of conscientiousness is likely to write a majority opinion that scores

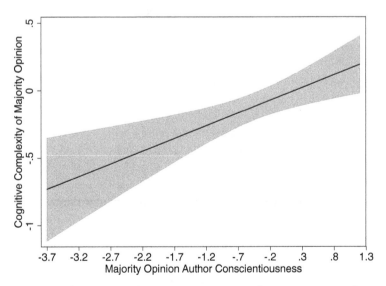

FIGURE 52: *The impact of conscientiousness on the cognitive complexity of Supreme Court majority opinions.* Estimates represent the predicted level of cognitive complexity (with 90 percent confidence intervals) across the range of *Conscientiousness* using results from Model 2 in Table 25.

a −0.731 [−1.184, −0.279] on the cognitive complexity scale. Conversely, a majority opinion author identified as having the maximum degree of conscientiousness is likely to write a majority opinion that scores an average of 0.193 [−0.059, 0.444]. Thus, having a more conscientious majority opinion author may, on average, lead to an opinion that is nearly one unit more complex on the cognitive complexity scale – a shift in *Cognitive Complexity* that represents roughly one-quarter of a standard deviation. Although this predicted effect appears modest on balance, it is substantively meaningful when one considers that the effect is on top of everything else we know about opinion writing. In fact, the impact of *Conscientiousness* exhibits a maximum predicted impact that exceeds nearly every other covariate in the regression model. In particular, it exceeds the expected effects of *State Judicial Review, Precedent Alteration, Majority Votes, Intercircuit Uncertainty, Prior Issue Decisions, Infrequently Litigated Statute, Lower Court Dissent,* and an increase in *Amicus Participation* from the minimum to the 99th percentile (i.e., zero to twenty-five amicus briefs).

Among the other personality traits, justices that score higher on the openness trait write less cognitively complex majority opinions. Similarly, the data suggest that opinion authors that are more agreeable also write less cognitively complex opinions. Extraverted and neurotic justices, on the other hand, appear to write more cognitively complex opinions.

Among our other controls, majority opinion authors write less cognitively complex opinions as the federal circuit courts become more ideologically scattered and therefore are more likely to generate legal conflicts. Also, cases that follow more frequent litigation within a given issue area, and decisions following dissent in the lower court, tend to be less cognitively complex. Cases that strike down an act of the elected branches at the state level, and majority opinions written with larger majorities, are more cognitively complex. Relatedly, when the Supreme Court formally alters its prior precedent or decides a case involving greater numbers of amicus participants, the majority opinions in those cases are more cognitively complex. Lastly, cases reviewing an infrequently litigated statute are more cognitively complex on balance, and the average majority opinion in more recent Supreme Court terms are more cognitively complex than earlier terms in the sample.

9.4.2 *Legal Breadth*

Our second set of models examines how *Conscientiousness* effects the *Legal Breadth* of an opinion, as indicated by the total number of LexisNexis Headnotes. Since *Legal Breadth* is an overdispersed count variable, we

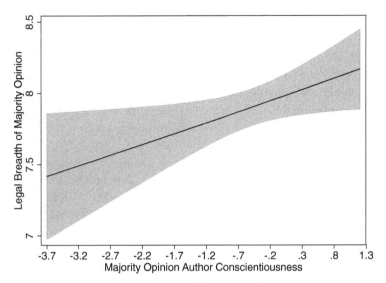

FIGURE 53: *The impact of conscientiousness on the legal breadth of Supreme Court majority opinions.* Estimates represent the predicted number of Lexis-Nexis Headnotes (with 90 percent confidence intervals) across the range of *Conscientiousness* using results from Model 4 in Table 25.

estimate negative binomial regression models with robust standard errors. (The results of a likelihood-ratio test indicate that we can reject the null hypothesis that the dispersion parameter (α) is zero [p < 0.001].) All results are substantively similar if we employ classical standard errors. Models 3 and 4 in Table 25 display the regression results. Across both model specifications, the data exhibit a statistically significant, positive relationship between *Conscientiousness* and *Legal Breadth*. That is, the data support the hypothesis that increasingly conscientious justices tend to write majority opinions with more extensive legal breadth.

Figure 53 shows the magnitude of this effect, displayed as the predicted count of Lexis Headnotes (i.e., degree of *Legal Breadth*) across the observed range of *Conscientiousness* using the regression results from Model 4 in Table 25. The least conscientious justice in the sample writes a majority opinion with an average of approximately seven identified LexisNexis Headnotes (predicted count = 7.417 [6.892, 7.942]). By contrast, the most conscientious author is likely to write a majority opinion with approximately eight Lexis Headnotes (predicted count = 8.167 [7.833, 8.500]). Thus, the data suggest that the observed variation in the majority opinion author's conscientiousness can yield an increase of nearly one additional LexisNexis Headnote on average, or an increase of more than 10 percent. While the magnitude of this predicted effect is modest, it is substantively significant when viewed in the context of the many alternative explanations for legal breadth borne out in the empirical model. What is more, this effect represents the predicted increase in legal breadth within a single case, on average. Since justices write many opinions over the duration of their careers, the total expected increase in legal breadth that conscientious justices contribute is far more substantial when viewed as an accumulation over decades of opinion writing.

Many of the control predictors also exhibit statistically significant relationships with *Legal Breadth*. Justices that score higher on the agreeableness trait write majority opinions with greater legal breadth. Majority opinion authors write narrower opinions as the federal circuit courts become more ideologically scattered. Cases that strike an act of the elected branches at the federal level are likely to exhibit greater legal breadth. Next, when the Supreme Court formally alters its prior precedent or decides a case involving more external amicus participants, the majority opinions in those cases are more legally broad. Also, cases that follow more frequent litigation within a given issue area tend to be less legally broad. Majority opinions written with larger majorities have less legal breadth. Decisions following dissent in the lower court tend to exhibit greater legal breadth. Lastly, the average majority opinion in more recent Supreme Court terms is increasingly broad legally.

9.4.3 *Word Count*

We now turn to our third indicator of Supreme Court opinion content – the length of the majority opinion. *Word Count* is an over-dispersed count, and thus we again estimate negative binomial regression models with robust standard errors.[26] Models 5 and 6 in Table 25 present these regression results. The results, in both the baseline and full model specifications, exhibit a statistically significant, positive relationship between *Conscientiousness* and *Word Count*. Majority opinion authors that score higher on the conscientiousness scale write opinions that employ more words.

Figure 54 displays the impact of justice conscientiousness on opinion length. It reports the predicted number of total words in the majority opinion across the observed range of *Conscientiousness* using the regression results

---

[26] The results of a likelihood-ratio test indicate that we can reject the null hypothesis that the dispersion parameter (α) is zero (p < 0.001). Results are similar if we employ classical standard errors.

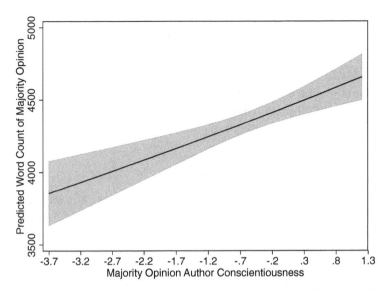

FIGURE 54: *The impact of conscientiousness on the length of Supreme Court majority opinions.* Estimates represent the predicted number of total words (with 90 percent confidence intervals) across the range of *Conscientiousness* using results from Model 6 in Table 25.

from Model 6 in Table 25. The results indicate that a justice with the lowest conscientiousness score in the sample writes a majority opinion with an average of approximately 3,850 words (predicted count = 3855.71 [3592.99, 4118.44]). Compare that to the most conscientious justice in the sample, who writes majority opinions with an average of roughly 4,650 words (predicted count = 4655.44 [4469.72, 4841.15]). This total predicted increase of 800 words – a 21 percent increase, or more than a quarter of a standard deviation – is both statistically significant and substantively meaningful. Thus, the results from this third opinion content indicator also comport with the previous two – conscientious justices appear more dutiful and thorough in communicating legal policy, as is evident through multiple indicators of an opinion's legal content.

Additionally, several control predictors exhibit statistically significant relationships with *Word Count*. Justices who score higher on the openness, agreeableness, and neuroticism traits write longer majority opinions, Conversely, more extraverted justices write shorter majority opinions. Next, similar to the empirical results from both the cognitive complexity and legal breadth models, majority opinion authors write shorter opinions as the federal circuit courts become more ideologically scattered. Similarly, opinions with larger majority coalitions contain fewer words. On the other hand, the data suggest that majority opinion authors tend to write longer opinions when striking a federal law, when the decision formally alters a prior Supreme Court precedent, when deciding a case involving more external amicus participants, and when reviewing a lower court decision with a dissent. Lastly, the Supreme Court's average majority opinion has been longer in more recent terms compared to earlier years in the sample.

9.4.4 Rhetorical Clarity

Our final indicator of majority opinion content reflects rhetorical clarity, scaled so that larger values represent greater rhetorical clarity. Because this dependent variable is a continuous indicator, we estimate OLS regression models (with robust standard errors).[27] Models 7 and 8 in Table 25 display these results. Both model specifications show a statistically significant, negative relationship between *Conscientiousness* and *Rhetorical Clarity*, suggesting that increasingly conscientious justices write less readable opinions.

Figure 55 illustrates the magnitude of *Conscientiousness*'s impact on rhetorical clarity. It reports the predicted level of *Rhetorical Clarity* across the observed range of *Conscientiousness* using the regression results from Model 8 in Table 25. A justice scoring at the minimum end of the conscientiousness distribution writes a majority opinion that scores an average of 1.52 [1.04, 2.00] on the readability scale. Conversely, a majority opinion author with the highest conscientiousness score in the sample writes a majority opinion that scores an average of −1.25 [−1.52, −0.97]. This minimum to maximum shift exhibits a total expected decrease in rhetorical clarity of 2.77 points – an expected decrease of roughly two-thirds of a standard deviation in rhetorical clarity.

This result is contrary to our expectation that increasingly conscientious justices will enhance their opinions' rhetorical clarity. Why this is the case, we cannot be sure. One possible explanation jumps out, however. Perhaps it is the case that conscientious justices, in the pursuit of performing their jobs in a thorough and dutiful manner, tend to write opinions that are more dense legally. The incorporation of additional legal reasoning may often carry the side effect of a more complex and messy textual presentation. This potential tradeoff between rhetorical clarity and legal clarity – or legal exhaustion – is worth further study.

---

[27] Results are similar if we employ classical standard errors.

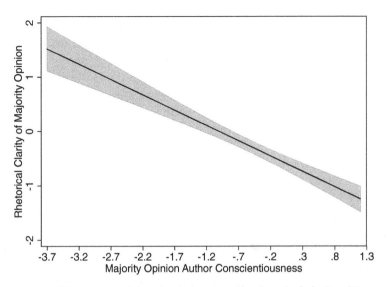

FIGURE 55: *The impact of conscientiousness on the rhetorical clarity of Supreme Court majority opinions.* Estimates represent the predicted level of textual readability (with 90 percent confidence intervals) across the range of *Conscientiousness* using results from Model 8 in Table 25.

Among the control predictors, we see that justices who score higher on the openness trait write less rhetorically clear opinions. Extraverted justices, by contrast, write opinions with greater clarity. Similarly, authors tend to write clearer opinions when the federal circuit courts are ideologically scattered, when there is greater ideological distance between the Supreme Court and the circuit courts, when striking a state government's laws, when the Court alters its precedent, when the majority coalition is larger, and when a case involves an infrequently litigated statute. Alternatively, justices write obfuscated opinions when they review a lower court decision that contained a dissent, when there is greater ideological distance between the Court and Congress, and in cases that follow more frequent litigation within a given issue area. Lastly, the Supreme Court's average majority opinion each term has exhibited greater rhetorical clarity over time.

9.5 CONCLUSION

We find support for our argument that justices' conscientiousness influences the kinds of opinions they write. We theorized that because conscientious justices are more dutiful, responsible, and exhibit more goal-directed behavior, they would write unique opinions. We examined four different indicators of Supreme Court opinion content – *cognitive complexity*, *legal breadth*, *opinion length*, and *rhetorical clarity* – and found considerable support for our argument. These findings suggest that conscientiousness is an important part of understanding why justices behave the way they do. Furthermore, the results suggest that conscientiousness meaningfully shapes the development of law, legal doctrine, and the communication of legal policy in the federal judiciary.

The results in this chapter illuminate our knowledge about the Court and justices. First, and most obviously, the results show just how important personality is for justices and the content of Supreme Court majority opinions. Second, the results suggest that conscientiousness can sometimes muddle the law.

Opinion content is relevant for other reasons as well. Broader and more cognitively complex opinions likely influence how lower courts comply (or fail to comply) with High Court precedent. When the Court writes vague opinions, it gives lower courts more deference: when it writes clearer opinions it gives them less deference. Broader and more cognitively complex opinions may also influence whether and how political actors respond to the Court's decisions. Black, Owens, Wedeking, and Wohlfarth (2016b) find that federal circuit courts are more likely to follow Supreme Court precedent when it is clear rather than ambiguous. Similarly, Corley and Wedeking (2014) show that lower courts are more likely to treat a Supreme Court precedent positively when the precedent expresses more certainty in its language.[28]

Establishing a personality-opinion content connection adds an important dimension to our overall view that justices' personalities are consequential – that they affect how they approach their jobs, the substance of judicial policy making, and thus how scholars should study judicial behavior and the US Supreme Court. In the next chapter, we push this inquiry further and consider how justices' conscientiousness affects their interpretation of precedent.

---

[28] On the flipside, Owens, Wedeking, and Wohlfarth (2013) find that when the Court becomes increasingly distant ideologically from Congress, justices alter the readability of their opinions in an effort to increase the costs on Congress to read and react to the Court's opinions.

10

Conscientiousness and the Treatment of Precedent

Valley Forge Christian College v. *Americans United for Separation of Church and State* (1982) is not a particularly well known case, at least to the general public.[1] Nevertheless, it is a highly consequential case because it defined and narrowed the conditions under which a large class of litigants could sue the federal government. Fourteen years before *Valley Forge*, in *Flast* v. *Cohen* (1968),[2] the Supreme Court held that taxpayers – even those who did not suffer any private, particularized injury – could sue the federal government over its taxing and spending programs. *Valley Forge*, however, narrowed that ruling considerably and made it nearly impossible for taxpayers to sue the federal government for generalized injuries. Justice Rehnquist's opinion held that taxpayers could sue the government – as taxpayers – only for congressionally authorized (not agency created) expenditures and only for violations of the Establishment Clause. Put simply, whereas *Flast* threw the door open for taxpayers to challenge federal expenditures, *Valley Forge* closed it. But not completely. Like a child afraid of the dark, the Court left the door open just a crack.

Some of the conservative justices wanted to slam that door shut in *Valley Forge* and emphatically overrule *Flast*. They could not convince their fellow conservatives, however. Justice Rehnquist, who wrote the opinion in *Valley Forge*, clearly wanted to overrule *Flast*. So too did Chief Justice Burger and Justice O'Connor. They believed Article III of the Constitution, which extends the judicial power only to cases or controversies, required litigants to have suffered a particularized injury in order to participate in federal court. And as far as they were concerned, generalized grievances over public expenditures did not suffice.

---

[1] See *Valley Forge Christian College* v. *Americans United for Separation of Church and State*, 454 U.S. 464 (1982).
[2] See *Flast* v. *Cohen*, 392 U.S. 83 (1968).

But their follow conservatives took a different approach. The otherwise conservative Justice Powell informed Rehnquist:

> I have noted with interest Sandra's suggestion that she is willing to go further and overrule *Flast* v. *Cohen*. I continue to think ... that *Flast* was an unsound opinion. Overruling it therefore has a good deal of appeal. Yet, I have some hesitation as to the desirability of doing this by a bare majority vote. (Wahlbeck, Spriggs, and Maltzman 2009*b*)

Powell would not go so far as to overrule *Flast*. And he was not alone. The mercurial but increasingly conservative Justice White likewise told Rehnquist: "I would not overrule *Flast*" (Wahlbeck, Spriggs, and Maltzman 2009*b*).

Why were some of the justices willing to overrule *Flast* while others were not? The conventional social science explanation suggests that justices treat precedent positively when they agree with it ideologically and treat it negatively when they disagree with it ideologically (Hansford and Spriggs 2006; Spaeth and Segal 1999). But even that explanation is incomplete. After all, in some cases, such as *Valley Forge*, some conservative justices vote to overrule precedent even while some of their conservative colleagues refuse. In some cases, some liberal justices vote to overrule precedent when other liberal justices do not. Clearly, non-ideological features strongly influence how justices treat precedent.

The question remains, though, what other features explain justices' treatment of precedent? While there likely are many – such as legal and public expectations (Zink, Spriggs, and Scott 2009; Schauer 1987; Knight and Epstein 1996), precedent age (Black and Spriggs 2013; Landes and Posner 1976), and coalition dynamics (Maltzman, Spriggs, and Wahlbeck 2000) – we argue that a justice's personality influences how he or she treats precedent. In particular, we believe (shocking, we know) that conscientiousness influences how justices treat precedent. Specifically, we believe that conscientious justices are less likely to overrule precedent than less conscientious justices, and that conscientiousness will mitigate the negative effects of ideological distance between the justices and the precedent at risk.

Overall, we find that increased conscientiousness leads justices to be more likely to treat precedent positively. It also makes them less likely to treat it strongly negatively. The results also show that conscientiousness mitigates the negative effects of ideological distance. Whereas less conscientious justices treat precedent positively or negatively as a function of their ideological distance from it, conscientious justices do not. The conscientious justice is less driven by ideological considerations when it comes to interpreting and applying precedent.

10.1 THE COURT'S TREATMENT OF PRECEDENT

Chief Justice Roberts made a number of memorable statements during his confirmation testimony before the Senate Judiciary Committee. Receiving the most attention, of course, was his remark that judges are like umpires who simply call balls and strikes. Perhaps more important, though, were his comments about the role of *stare decisis* and when justices should adhere to or overrule precedent.[3] With his disarming demeanor, Roberts stated that judges must have "the humility to recognize that they operate within a system of precedent shaped by other judges equally striving to live up to the judicial oath" (Roberts 2005). He then went on to discuss the "precedent on precedents." He described the purported conditions under which justices overrule precedent, such as whether the precedent has proven to be unworkable, whether subsequent legal developments have eroded the precedent, and whether there are few "settled expectations" surrounding the precedent.

What should be obvious to any reader is that these features (which come from the Court's doctrine) are remarkably vague and afford justices substantial discretion to apply or overrule a precedent. What does it mean to claim that a precedent has become "unworkable?" How much erosion must a precedent endure before enough is enough? How can justices even measure whether expectations surrounding a precedent are "settled?" These are messy questions that require observational data to answer.

Thankfully, scholars have scrutinized such empirical questions and generated a host of explanations for why justices treat precedent positively or negatively. One theory argues that justices create and revise precedent to achieve their policy goals. That is, liberals attack precedents that lead to conservative outcomes and conservatives attack precedents that lead to liberal outcomes. Another theory argues that justices follow precedent when other important actors expect them to. We explain each as follows.

10.1.1 Precedent as Policy

If there has been one belief on which most empirical legal scholars agreed, it is that justices treat precedent positively or negatively based on their ideological agreement with it (Brenner and Spaeth 1995; Segal and Spaeth 1996;

---

3 *Stare decisis* is Latin for "let the decision stand" (Collins and Ringhand 2013). It means judges should apply relevant legal rules from previously decided cases to the cases currently before them. As Black and Spriggs (2013, 326) state, precedents "defin[e] legal principles that indicate the relevance or importance of different factual circumstances for a legal dispute and [setting] forth legal consequences or tests that follow from particular sets of factual circumstances."

Wahlbeck 1997). The argument stems from the theory that justices use precedents to support their policy goals. That theory argues that justices decide how they want a case to come down and then find precedent to support that position (Segal and Spaeth 2002). (They are supposed to proceed in the opposite direction.) As if to prove the point, in one case, Chief Justice Warren told his law clerk, "This is the result. Write it up" (Peppers 2006, 150). According to this theory, if an existing precedent obstructs the justices' policy goals, they will circumvent it. Spaeth described the theory in his analysis of Justice Frankfurter's supposed judicial restraint, stating:

> Judicial restraint is thoroughly subordinated to the [policy] attitudes of the justices toward business and labor. The concept serves only to cloak the political character of the judicial process and thereby helps to preserve the traditional view that judges merely find and do not make law. Not only for Frankfurter, but for all the Warren Court justices, the concept of judicial restraint is an effective means of rationalizing response to policy-oriented values." (Spaeth 1964, 38)

Empirical analyses support the claim that precedents are forged in the kiln of justices' policy goals. For example, Spaeth and Segal (1999) examined whether justices in the minority in a precedent-setting case later switch their positions to support the original majority position in future, similar cases. They began by analyzing Supreme Court decisions in which at least one justice dissented. They then examined all "progeny" cases begotten by that original decision to determine whether the dissenting justice later followed his or her original dissenting position or voted in line with the newly created precedent. Their findings suggested that justices stubbornly cling to their original positions. Less than 12 percent of justices' votes followed precedent – and even those precedent-following votes came from only two justices.

The most exhaustive study of justices' treatment of precedent to date comes from Hansford and Spriggs (2006). The authors examined the conditions under which justices treat precedent positively (by applying it) or negatively (by distinguishing it or overruling it). They found that, all else being equal, justices are more likely to treat precedent negatively the farther away from it they are ideologically and more likely to treat it positively the closer they are to it. Perhaps more importantly, precedent vitality – the Court's past treatment of the precedent – conditions this behavior. (A case with high vitality is one that has received substantial support from the Court over time. A case with low vitality is one the justices have questioned and distinguished repeatedly.) Given two equally ideologically distant precedents, a justice is more likely to treat negatively the precedent with high vitality. Why? Because that precedent is doing the most policy "harm" to the justice. Similarly, given two equally ideologically close precedents, a justice is more likely to treat positively the one with low vitality, so as to "resuscitate" it. Precedent, according to this theory, is shaped and shuttered by justices' ideological goals, conditioned by its vitality.

10.1.2 Non-Ideological Explanations for the Treatment of Precedent

While the data suggest that justices' policy goals motivate a substantial amount of their behavior toward precedent, non-ideological considerations also appear to influence how they behave. This is because justices operate in an interdependent environment. The legislative and executive branch have expectations for how justices should use precedent (Collins and Ringhand 2013), as do members of the public and the legal community (Knight and Epstein 1996). To maintain the Court's legitimacy, and their own power, some have argued justices must therefore "play the part" that is expected of them by others and adhere to the norm of precedent. As Zink, Spriggs, and Scott (2009) state: "The Court must ... decide cases in a visibly independent and principled way; since its legitimacy is so closely identified with impartial adjudication, it must convince the public that legal outcomes result from the application of neutral decision-making criteria" (910).

Archival evidence indicates that justices know they are expected at least to make an effort to follow precedent. Knight and Epstein (1996) examined Justice Brennan's conference notes to determine, among other things, the extent to which justices referenced precedent in their private conferences. The authors' belief was that if precedent was merely a public tool justices used to cloak their policy goals, justices would not need to reference it in their private discussions, away from public consumption. But they did privately reference it. In fact, justices frequently discussed how precedent controlled the outcomes of cases. The authors argued that because the public and legal community believe in the role of *stare decisis*, justices must adhere to those expectations. And the conference records showed it.

Indeed, Zink, Spriggs, and Scott (2009) discover that the Court will likely lose legitimacy if it ignores precedent. The authors conducted an experiment in which they asked respondents whether they would support the Court or its opinions under various conditions. Some respondents were told that the Court overruled precedent while others were told the Court followed precedent. The results showed that respondents were more likely to support and accept Court decisions that were grounded in precedent.

In short, there is strong evidence to suggest that policy motivations influence how justices treat precedent. And there is evidence to suggest that external features can condition their behavior. But surely, as our example in *Valley Forge* suggested, other features matter as well. We believe justices' conscientiousness influences how they treat precedent.

10.2 A THEORY OF CONSCIENTIOUSNESS AND THE INTERPRETATION OF PRECEDENT

Conscientiousness, again, represents someone's desire to follow rules and norms, working within expectations, and behave dutifully. John and Srivastava (1999, 121) argue that conscientiousness touches on "impulse control that facilitates task- and goal-directed behavior, such as thinking before acting, delaying gratification, following norms and rules, and planning, organizing, and prioritizing tasks." Those who are less conscientious tend to be careless (McCrae and John 1992) and display disinhibition, with an orientation toward immediate gratification and impulsive behavior (Krueger and Markon 2014). Bogg and Roberts (2004) find that conscientious people are significantly less likely to engage in risky behaviors.

Given these findings, it seems intuitive to us that conscientious justices would be more respectful of precedent than less conscientious justices. As we suggested previously, the public expects justices to respect precedent. The legal community expects justices to follow precedent. If they fail to do so, the Court's legitimacy could suffer. This is something conscientious justices are likely to resist. And so they will be more careful with precedent than less conscientious justices.

Moreover, say what you will about the value of precedent as a tool for making policy; it does provide a coordinating function for justices and the legal community. It provides a sense of order, or structure, that defines the terms of the debate. Without requiring justices and parties to argue their cases within the confines of precedent, it is unclear how they would operate. Would litigants brief the Court entirely on policy grounds? Would they focus on what the elected branches want? Would they appeal to justices' social or religious backgrounds? Precedent offers a clear language that coordinates and channels the legal community. And as far as we can tell, the literature suggests that structure and coordination are things that clearly appeal to conscientious people who value rules and organization.

As a general matter, then, we expect increasingly conscientious justices to be more respectful of precedent. But what, exactly, does that mean? For starters, it means they will be more likely to treat precedent positively than their less conscientious colleagues. Because precedent is the currency with which most opinions and most justices operate, conscientious justices will treat it positively. Thus, we expect that *as a justice becomes more conscientious, she will be more likely to treat precedent positively.*

At the same time, justices cannot treat all precedents positively. Some treatments simply must be negative. This, of course, is largely a function of how we and others define "negative" treatment. The negative treatment of precedent can be either *distinguishing* it from the facts of the current case (a weak negative treatment) or *overruling* it altogether (a strong negative treatment). There are times when justices surely need to distinguish cases. It may matter, for example, that one case deals with the regulation of speech in a high school versus the regulation of speech in a university setting. The logic behind the First Amendment's protection may matter in one forum differently than in another. Distinguishing cases in this manner operates within the four walls of *stare decisis*. A justice who distinguishes a case still plays by the rules, so to speak. On the other hand, when a justice outright overrules an existing case, that is something altogether different. There, the justice sweeps aside the past decision. And while overrules may be necessary at times, they are considerably less conventional. As Joe Biden might say, "it's a big ... deal." As such, we expect that the dutiful, rules-following, conscientious justice will be more likely to engage in weak negative treatments (i.e., distinguishings) and less likely to engage in strong negative treatments (overrules). Stated more formally, we expect that *as a justice becomes increasingly conscientious, she will be more likely to treat a precedent weakly negatively, and less likely to treat it strongly negatively.*

Of course, we are under no illusion that conscientious justices are saints. Even the most conscientious justice will seek to further his or her policy goals, at least according to existing scholarship. But we suspect that conscientiousness will mitigate these effects. The policy behind precedent will matter, but will matter less to the conscientious justice. As such, we expect that *conscientiousness will mitigate the negative effects of ideological distance on justices' treatment of precedent.*

10.3 DATA AND MEASURES

To analyze our theoretical claims, we replicate the models from Hansford and Spriggs (2006) on the Supreme Court's interpretation of precedent from 1946 through 2001.[4] Their models treat every orally argued case (including

---

4 We thank Tom Hansford and Jim Spriggs for generously providing these data.

per curiam opinions and judgments of the Court) from 1946 to 1999 as a precedent that a future Supreme Court may interpret. That is, each precedent is at risk of overrule by a future Supreme Court. They then generate, for each precedent, an observation for each year, beginning with the year the Court established the precedent. For example, a precedent established in 1999 will have three interpretation observations in the data set (1999, 2000, and 2001). Thus, the unit of analysis is the precedent-interpretation year.[5] This data set consists of 6,363 Supreme Court decisions and more than 181,000 precedent-year observations.[6]

Dependent Variables. For each precedent, Hansford and Spriggs (2006) use *Shepard's Citations* to code (a) *whether* the Supreme Court interpreted the precedent, and (b) if so, the *nature* of that interpretation.[7] We employ three dependent variables: *Strong Negative Interpretation*, *Weak Negative Interpretation*, and *Positive Interpretation*. We distinguish between strong and weak negative interpretations because, as Hansford and Spriggs (2006, 50) state, "Distinguished may at times represent a somewhat weaker form of negative interpretation than the others because, while at a minimum it indicates that a case is inapplicable, it may not necessarily restrict the application of the precedent." Theoretically, we expect that more conscientious justices are less likely to undermine a precedent (i.e., a "strong" negative interpretation).[8]

Strong Negative Interpretation. A strong negative interpretation is one that *Shepard's* identifies as having "overruled," "criticized," "questioned," or "limited" an existing precedent. If Shepard's codes the precedent as having received such treatment, we assign a value of 1 to *Strong Negative Interpretation*; 0 otherwise.

---

5   Ideally, one would construct a data set at the level of the individual justice to create the closest match between justices' personalities and their decisions. We choose to keep this analysis at the case-level because of the inability to reliably determine the nature of dissenting justices' positions within each case. For instance, while we can easily determine if a justice dissented in, say, a decision that reflects a positive interpretation, we do not know definitively if that dissent reflects a preference for overturning that precedent, or merely distinguishing the interpretation case from the precedent, or some other disagreement with the majority decision that may not necessarily reflect negatively on the precedent.

6   Hansford and Spriggs (2006) exclude per curiam opinions that interpret precedents.

7   As Hansford and Spriggs (2006) explain, a mere citation to a precedent without interpreting its legal holding is insufficient to classify it as an interpretation of that precedent. There must be more to the interpretation. Experienced lawyers who work for LexisNexis (and *Shepard's*) read every Supreme Court decision to determine whether it interprets a precedent positively or negatively. It is worth noting that Hansford and Spriggs (2006) conduct a supplementary analysis which demonstrates the accuracy and validity of *Shepard's* as a tool to classify interpretations of precedent.

8   Hansford and Spriggs's (2006) data do indicate a small number of observations with multiple different interpretations in a single year.

Weak Negative Interpretation. A weak negative interpretation is one that *Shepard's* identifies as having "distinguished" a precedent. If Shepard's codes the precedent as having received such treatment, we assign a value of 1 to *Weak Negative Interpretation*; 0 otherwise.

Positive Interpretation. A positive interpretation is one that *Shepard's* identifies as having "followed" the precedent. If Shepard's codes the precedent as having received such treatment, we assign a value of 1 to *Positive Interpretation*; 0 otherwise.

Among the total number of precedent-year observations, we code 3,193 instances of positive interpretations, 3,360 weak negative interpretations, and 233 strong negative interpretations.

Conscientiousness. Our primary independent variable, again, is *Conscientiousness*. In this chapter, though, we modify the measure slightly. Because we necessarily must examine the treatment of precedent at the Court level, we aggregate the *Conscientiousness* measure to represent the median conscientiousness score on the Court each term. That is, for each term, we sort the sitting justices from the least-to-most conscientious, and select the median conscientiousness score. We use this score to predict the Court's precedent interpretation.[9] We also control for the median score of the four other personality traits – *Openness*, *Extraversion*, *Agreeableness*, and *Neuroticism*.

Next, we adopt as control predictors all of the variables from Hansford and Spriggs's (2006) original analysis of Supreme Court interpretations of precedent. We describe those control predictors below.

Ideological Distance. Hansford and Spriggs (2006) and others (e.g., Spaeth and Segal 1999) show that the Court's ideological distance from a precedent can influence how it interprets that precedent. All else being equal, the more distant the Court is ideologically from a precedent, the less likely it will be to interpret it positively (and the more likely it will be to interpret it negatively). As such, we control for each Court's ideological predisposition to treat a prior precedent-setting opinion positively (negatively). To do so, we adopt the Hansford and Spriggs (2006) indicator, reflecting the absolute value of the distance between the issue-specific policy position of the Court's median member each

---

[9] Since the Hansford and Spriggs (2006) treatment data are organized based on the calendar year, we match the term-specific *Conscientiousness Median* to the most proximate calendar year. For example, we use the median conscientiousness score among the justices sitting for the 1990 term to predict precedent interpretations in the 1991 calendar year. This results in twenty-five precedent interpretation observations (from 1946) that we must drop from Hansford and Spriggs's (2006) original analysis.

year and the issue-specific ideology of the median of the majority coalition in the original precedent case (see also Spriggs and Hansford 2001, 2002).

Precedent Vitality. How the Court interpreted a precedent in the past influences how it will treat the precedent today. Hansford and Spriggs (2006) measure *Precedent Vitality* as the number of previous positive interpretations minus the number of previous negative interpretations (up to but not including the year in which a treatment case was decided). Positive values correspond to precedents that are still considered to be good law. Negative values represents precedents viewed as being weak law.

Ideological Distance × *Vitality.* Hansford and Spriggs (2006) show how *Precedent Vitality* conditions the impact of *Ideological Distance* on the Court's interpretation of precedents. For instance, when looking at the probability the Court overrules precedent, they show that a precedent with greater vitality increases the effect of increasing ideological distance.

Concurring Opinions. The Court should be more likely to interpret precedents negatively that contained internal disagreement among the justices. We account for this internal disagreement by counting the number of special concurrences filed in the original precedent-setting case.

Vote Margin. As a second way to account for the degree of internal (dis)agreement on the precedent-setting Court, we look to the size of its majority coalition. Scholarship suggests that a Court will be more likely to interpret precedents negatively that were established by smaller coalitions of justices. We code *Vote Margin* as the number of justices joining the majority coalition in the precedent-setting case.

Total Prior Interpretations. The overall frequency with which the Court has already interpreted a precedent may also matter. We control for *Total Prior Interpretations*, which represents the total number of previous majority opinions that treated the precedent (up to and including the year prior to the observation).[10]

Court Agenda. We control for the Court's proclivity to interpret a precedent based on the composition of its docket. *Court Agenda* counts the total number of cases decided by the Court (in the given precedent-interpretation term) that share the precedent's issue area (Hansford and Spriggs 2006). In other words, for a criminal rights case, it examines how many criminal rights cases are on the Court's docket that term.

Precedent Complexity. The Court is likely to treat complex cases differently than easier cases. We capture this dynamic by employing a factor-analytic

---

[10] Hansford and Spriggs (2006) include positive, negative, and neutral treatments when generating this indicator.

score that combines the number of legal provisions and legal issues in the precedent-setting case.[11]

Amici Filings. Hansford and Spriggs (2006) include three control predictors that tap into a precedent's salience. They suggest that increasingly salient cases may be subject to a greater number of future interpretations. The first indicator – *Amici Filings* – is the total number of external amicus briefs that were submitted in the precedent-setting case. Cases with greater amicus participation signify more salient precedents.

Media Coverage. The second indicator of a precedent's salience reflects whether it received significant media coverage. Precedents with greater media coverage are more salient. We code *Media Coverage* as 1 when the precedent-setting case appeared on the front page of the *New York Times* the day after the Court decided it (Epstein and Segal 2000); 0 otherwise.

Per Curiam Precedent. The third control variable for precedent salience represents whether the precedent-setting opinion was a per curiam opinion. These are opinions that fail to identify an author and, instead, are written "for the Court." Such opinions tend to be less salient than the average case. We assign a value of 1 to precedents established via per curiam opinion; 0 otherwise.

Constitutional Precedent. The Court is likely to treat precedents decided on constitutional grounds differently than precedents decided on statutory grounds (Hansford and Spriggs 2006). *Constitutional Precedent* takes on a value of 1 if Hansford and Spriggs (2006) code the precedent-setting case as a constitutional precedent; 0 otherwise.

Overruled Precedent. We also suspect the Court will be significantly less likely to interpret a precedent if it has already been overruled. Following Hansford and Spriggs (2006), we include *Overruled Precedent*, which takes on a value of 1 if the Court already overruled the precedent; 0 otherwise.

Precedent Age. We also control for a precedent's age, which may affect the likelihood that a future Court will interpret a precedent positively or negatively. *Precedent Age* reflects the number of years between the precedent's adoption and the year of the current case.

Precedent Age Squared. Hansford and Spriggs (2006) show that a quadratic specification to control for precedent age is the most appropriate functional form. Thus, we also include the squared value of a precedent's age.

---

[11] This variable is Hansford and Spriggs's (2006) *Precedent Breadth* measure. We do not call it a "breadth" measure because we want to avoid confusion between this and our chapter that examines opinion breadth. At any rate, breadth is not the same thing as complexity.

10.4 METHODS AND RESULTS

With these data in hand, we first consider the unconditional impact of the conscientiousness trait on the Supreme Court's interpretation of precedent. Following Hansford and Spriggs's (2006) analyses, we estimate a separate model for each of our three dependent variables. For each dependent variable, we estimate two total models – a baseline model that includes only *Conscientiousness* (and the four other traits) and a second model that includes the full complement of covariates used by Hansford and Spriggs (2006).[12] We estimate logistic regressions due to the dichotomous dependent variable. We also estimate robust standard errors clustered on the precedent to account for the possibility of correlated errors.

The empirical results from Table 26 support our argument that conscientiousness influences how justices interpret precedent. Consider the impact of *Conscientiousness* on the Court's proclivity to interpret precedent strongly negatively, as reported in Models 1 and 2. The results show a negative and statistically significant relationship between the two variables. A more conscientious Court is less likely to issue decisions that strongly undermine, or outright overrule, precedent.[13] Figure 56(a) displays the magnitude of this effect (with 90 percent confidence intervals and using results from Model 2 in Table 26). When the median conscientiousness score on the Court is at its minimum, the Court is likely to produce a strong negative interpretation with a predicted probability of 0.0026 [0.0016, 0.0036]. By contrast, this probability decreases to 0.0006 [0.0004, 0.0009] when the median conscientiousness score is at its maximum level in the sample – a total expected change of 0.002, or a decrease of 77 percent. What is more, a more common shift of one standard deviation (0.312) above the mean level of conscientiousness yields an expected decrease of 0.0006 – a 44 percent decrease – in the probability the Court will interpret precedent in a strongly negative manner. In short, the results suggest that the justices' conscientiousness each year exhibits a rather large impact on whether the Court treats precedent in a strongly negative

---

[12] All empirical results are substantively consistent when specifying a baseline model that includes only conscientiousness (and no other personality trait indicators or control predictors).

[13] An additional modeling strategy would be to follow Hansford and Spriggs's (2006) analysis in Chapter 5, which employs a Cox proportional hazard model to estimate the Court's propensity to overturn precedent. A replication of this approach – with the addition of our personality median indicators – yields consistent results, showing how precedents are less at risk of being overturned when the Court is more conscientious. What is more, we retrieve similar results when estimating a penalized maximum likelihood logistic regression model (or, a rare events logistic regression), as a means to account for the relative (in)frequency, or rarity, in which we observe strong negative precedent interpretations in the sample data.

TABLE 26: *The Impact of Conscientiousness on Supreme Court Interpretation of Precedent*

	Strong Negative		Weak Negative		Positive	
	(1)	(2)	(3)	(4)	(5)	(6)
Conscientiousness	−1.84*	−1.85*	0.65*	0.42*	0.51*	0.24*
	(0.46)	(0.46)	(0.09)	(0.09)	(0.10)	(0.09)
Openness	0.41*	0.36*	0.17*	−0.02	0.16*	−0.04
	(0.14)	(0.15)	(0.05)	(0.05)	(0.05)	(0.05)
Extraversion	4.23*	4.16*	−0.07	−0.23	0.42	0.10
	(1.38)	(1.43)	(0.32)	(0.25)	(0.33)	(0.25)
Agreeableness	0.54*	0.52*	0.16*	0.18*	−0.08	0.04
	(0.19)	(0.19)	(0.05)	(0.04)	(0.05)	(0.04)
Neuroticism	0.68*	0.72*	−0.07	−0.28*	−0.87*	−1.19*
	(0.40)	(0.39)	(0.13)	(0.13)	(0.17)	(0.18)
Ideological Distance		0.03*		0.009*		−0.006*
		(0.01)		(0.002)		(0.003)
Precedent Vitality		−0.15		−0.09*		0.03
		(0.09)		(0.03)		(0.03)
Ideological Distance × Vitality		0.006*		0.004*		0.004*
		(0.003)		(0.002)		(0.002)
Concurring Opinions (precedent)		0.30*		0.07*		0.12*
		(0.13)		(0.03)		(0.03)
Vote Margin (precedent)		−0.16*		−0.013*		−0.02*
		(0.03)		(0.007)		(0.01)
Total Prior Interpretations		0.12*		0.15*		0.18*
		(0.02)		(0.01)		(0.02)
Court Agenda		0.014*		0.01*		0.012*
		(0.007)		(0.002)		(0.002)
Precedent Complexity		0.31*		0.19*		0.16*
		(0.12)		(0.04)		(0.05)
Amici Filings		0.10*		0.10*		0.11*
		(0.05)		(0.01)		(0.02)
Media Coverage		−0.10		0.26*		0.19*
		(0.20)		(0.05)		(0.06)
Per Curiam Precedent		−0.15		−0.98*		−1.43*
		(0.30)		(0.13)		(0.17)
Constitutional Precedent		0.16		0.54*		0.40*
		(0.16)		(0.04)		(0.05)

(continued)

TABLE 26: (*continued*)

	Strong Negative (1)	(2)	Weak Negative (3)	(4)	Positive (5)	(6)
Overruled Precedent		0.84* (0.38)		−0.95* (0.32)		−0.65* (0.35)
Precedent Age		0.01 (0.02)		−0.08* (0.01)		−0.10* (0.01)
Precedent Age Squared		−0.0007 (0.0005)		0.0004* (0.0002)		0.0007* (0.0002)
Constant	−7.38* (0.28)	−7.46* (0.39)	−3.82* (0.07)	−3.60* (0.09)	−3.67* (0.06)	−3.26* (0.09)
N	181,847	181,847	181,847	181,847	181,847	181,847
χ^2	19.59*	273.98*	301.49*	2050.92*	342.19*	2360.51*

Note: Table entries are logistic regression coefficients with robust standard errors (clustered on each precedent) in parentheses; *$p < .05$ (one-tailed). The dependent variable represents whether the Court majority interpreted a prior precedent in a strong negative, weak negative, or positive manner (1946–2001), among those precedents analyzed by Hansford and Spriggs (2006) (i.e., all orally argued cases, 1946–1999).

manner. And, we retrieve these results even after controlling for the full slate of predictors specified by Hansford and Spriggs (2006).

Next, consider the impact of *Conscientiousness* on the Court's proclivity to interpret precedent in a weakly negative manner. These results, in Models 3 and 4 in Table 26, suggest that an increasingly conscientious Court is more likely to interpret in a weakly negative manner. Figure 56(b) shows the predicted probability (with 90 percent confidence intervals) that the Court will interpret a precedent in a weakly negative manner across the observed range of *Conscientiousness* (using results from Model 4). A Court with the minimum conscientiousness exhibits a 0.016 [0.014, 0.017] probability of issuing a weakly negative interpretation while a Court with the maximum score has a probability of 0.021 [0.020, 0.023] – a predicted difference of 0.005, or a roughly 30 percent increase. A shift of one standard deviation above the mean conscientiousness score yields an expected increase of 0.0024 in the probability that the will interpret a precedent in a weakly negative manner. Thus, while *Conscientiousness* makes the Court less likely to adopt strong negative treatments, it makes it more likely to adopt weak negative treatments.

Finally, consider the impact of *Conscientiousness* on the Court's proclivity to interpret precedent positively. The regression results from Models 5 and

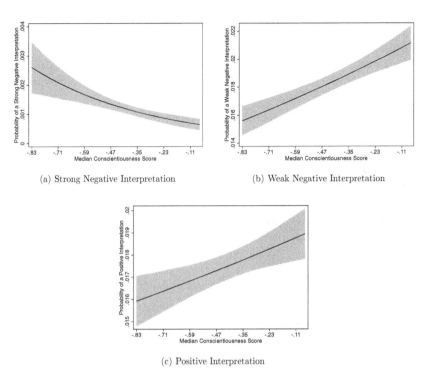

(a) Strong Negative Interpretation   (b) Weak Negative Interpretation

(c) Positive Interpretation

FIGURE 56: *The impact of conscientiousness on Supreme Court interpretation of precedent.* Panel (a) displays the predicted probability that the Court issues a strong negative interpretation of precedent (with 90 percent confidence intervals) across the range of *Conscientiousness* using results from Model 2 in Table 26. Panel (b) displays the probability that the Court issues a weak negative interpretation using results from Model 4. Panel (c) reports the probability that the Court issues a positive interpretation using results from Model 6.

6 in Table 26 show that *Conscientiousness* exerts a positive impact on the Court's proclivity to interpret precedent positively. The Court is significantly more likely to interpret a precedent positively when the justices are increasingly conscientious. Figure 56(c) displays the magnitude of this effect (using results from Model 6). The least conscientious Court in the sample will positively interpret a precedent with a probability of 0.016 [0.015, 0.017]. The most conscientiousness Court, however, will interpret a precedent positively with a probability of 0.019 [0.018, 0.020] – a total expected increase of 0.003, or approximately 20 percent. In short, the data offer considerable support for the argument that conscientiousness influences how justices treat precedent and, thus, the state of the law.

Among the control predictors, the results suggest that a Court with greater openness and extraversion is more likely to issue strong negative interpretations. Similarly, a more agreeable Court is more likely to interpret precedent in both a strongly and weakly negative manner. The neuroticism trait predicts a higher likelihood of strong negative treatments but a lower probability of weak negative and positive interpretations. The results for *Ideological Distance, Precedent Vitality*, and the interaction between the two predictors are consistent with those reported by Hansford and Spriggs (2006). That is, the Court is more likely to interpret precedent in a strongly, or weakly, negative manner when it is more predisposed to dislike it for ideological reasons. Similarly, greater ideological distance predicts fewer positive treatments. Yet, the data also suggest that these effects are conditional on precedent vitality. Greater vitality exacerbates the impact of ideological distance among both types of negative interpretations, but it attenuates its negative impact among positive treatments.

The other control predictors indicate the Court is more likely to interpret a precedent in any manner when there were more special concurrences or a smaller majority coalition in the precedent-setting case, when the given precedent has been interpreted more frequently by previous Courts, when the precedent's issue area is more prominent on the Court's agenda, when it is more legally complex (as indicated by the number of legal issues and provisions the precedent involves), and when there are more external amicus filers in the precedent-setting case. Similarly, precedents that originally appeared on the front page of the *New York Times* are more likely to lead to weak negative and positive interpretations. Alternatively, the Court is less likely to interpret a precedent in a weakly negative or positive manner if it was established with a per curiam opinion, and more likely to do so if it involved a constitutional issue. Precedents that have already been overruled in the past are more likely to generate strong negative interpretations but less likely to lead to weak negative or positive treatments. Lastly, among weak negative and positive treatments, the data confirm the existence of a quadratic relationship between a precedent's age and the Court's treatment of it.

10.4.1 *The Conditional Impact of Conscientiousness on the Interpretation of Precedent*

The previous section showed how *Conscientiousness* exhibits a substantial, unconditional impact on the Supreme Court's interpretation of precedent. Yet, conscientiousness may be particularly important as a modifier of (1) the ideological distance between the interpreting Court and the precedent;

and (2) a precedent's vitality. That is, *Conscientiousness* may work to mitigate the effect of *Ideological Distance* and accentuate the effect of *Precedent Vitality*. We consider the potential for these conditional relationships by adding two interaction terms to the models reported in Table 26: *Conscientiousness × Ideological Distance* and *Conscientiousness × Vitality*. Again, we estimate a baseline model without control variables (other than the personality traits) and a second model with the full complement of controls, for each of the three dependent variables. Table 27 reports these interactive results.

First, consider the interaction between conscientiousness and ideological distance. The left panel of Figure 57 displays the magnitude of this interactive effect, expressed as the predicted probability a Court will issue a strong negative interpretation. When ideological distance is low (i.e., the 10th percentile, or the solid line), the least conscientious Court is likely to treat a precedent in a strongly negative manner with a probability of 0.0016 [0.0009, 0.0024]. This predicted probability decreases to only 0.0006 [0.0003, 0.0009] when viewing the most conscientious Court. This change represents an expected 0.001 decrease in the probability of a strong negative treatment. Among situations of high ideological distance (i.e., the 90th percentile, or the dashed line), moving from the minimum to maximum *Conscientiousness* score exhibits an expected decrease in the probability of a strong negative interpretation from 0.0041 [0.0023, 0.0059] to 0.0007 [0.0004, 0.0010] – a decrease of 0.0034, or more than three times the impact of low ideological distance. In other words, the least conscientious Court is 150 percent more likely to issue a strong negative interpretation when it is predisposed to dislike the precedent than when the precedent is ideologically favorable. But, the difference between high versus low ideological distance disappears, statistically, among the most conscientious Courts (i.e., the top 42 percent of the distribution). This result indicates that the impact of conscientiousness on strong negative interpretations is quite substantial. Conscientiousness drives down the Court's probability of overruling and criticizing precedent.

The right panel of Figure 57 reports the average marginal effect of *Ideological Distance* (with 90 percent confidence intervals) across the observed range of *Conscientiousness Median*. It shows that the impact of ideological distance on the probability of a strong negative interpretation decreases markedly among more conscientious Courts. In fact, among the highly conscientious Courts – those whose medians are above −0.318 on the conscientiousness scale, representing 36 percent of the sample observations (or, 42 percent of the Court terms) – increasing ideological distance does nothing to the probability of the Court treating a precedent strongly negatively. When it comes

TABLE 27: *The Conditional Impact of Conscientiousness on Supreme Court Interpretation of Precedent*

	Strong Negative		Weak Negative		Positive	
	(1)	(2)	(3)	(4)	(5)	(6)
Conscientiousness	-1.54^*	-1.40^*	0.23^*	0.21^*	0.32^*	0.16
	(0.56)	(0.54)	(0.11)	(0.11)	(0.12)	(0.12)
Ideological Distance	0.021	0.00	0.02^*	0.02^*	0.005	-0.003
	(0.014)	(0.01)	(0.003)	(0.003)	(0.004)	(0.003)
Precedent Vitality	-0.46^*	-0.25^*	-0.001	-0.11^*	0.23^*	0.03
	(0.19)	(0.14)	(0.08)	(0.04)	(0.07)	(0.04)
Conscientiousness × Ideological Distance	$-0.03^{'}$	-0.04^*	0.04^*	0.02^*	0.02^*	0.008
	(0.02)	(0.02)	(0.01)	(0.01)	(0.01)	(0.007)
Conscientiousness × Vitality	-0.52^*	-0.19	-0.19^*	-0.02	-0.15^*	0.02
	(0.25)	(0.16)	(0.09)	(0.06)	(0.09)	(0.07)
Ideological Distance × Vitality	0.00	0.005	-0.002	0.005^*	-0.003	0.004^*
	(0.01)	(0.003)	(0.003)	(0.002)	(0.004)	(0.002)
Openness	0.49^*	0.36^*	0.18^*	-0.02	0.17^*	-0.04
	(0.15)	(0.15)	(0.05)	(0.05)	(0.05)	(0.05)
Extraversion	5.02^*	4.27^*	-0.05	-0.23	0.43	0.09
	(1.46)	(1.42)	(0.33)	(0.25)	(0.33)	(0.25)
Agreeableness	0.51^*	0.52^*	0.15^*	0.18^*	-0.05	0.04
	(0.19)	(0.19)	(0.05)	(0.04)	(0.05)	(0.04)
Neuroticism	0.74^*	0.71^*	-0.06	-0.28^*	-0.85^*	-1.19^*
	(0.40)	(0.39)	(0.13)	(0.13)	(0.17)	(0.18)
Concurring Opinions (precedent)		0.30^*		0.07^*		0.12^*
		(0.13)		(0.03)		(0.03)
Vote Margin (precedent)		-0.17^*		-0.013^*		-0.02^*
		(0.03)		(0.007)		(0.01)
Total Prior Interpretations		0.11^*		0.15^*		0.18^*
		(0.02)		(0.01)		(0.02)
Court Agenda		0.014^*		0.01^*		0.012^*
		(0.007)		(0.002)		(0.002)
Precedent Complexity		0.31^*		0.19^*		0.16^*
		(0.12)		(0.04)		(0.05)
Amici Filings		0.10^*		0.10^*		0.11^*
		(0.05)		(0.01)		(0.02)

(continued)

TABLE 27: (*continued*)

	Strong Negative (1)	(2)	Weak Negative (3)	(4)	Positive (5)	(6)
Media		−0.09		0.26*		0.18*
Coverage		(0.20)		(0.05)		(0.06)
Per Curiam		−0.16		−0.98*		−1.43*
Precedent		(0.30)		(0.13)		(0.17)
Constitutional		0.17		0.54*		0.40*
Precedent		(0.16)		(0.04)		(0.05)
Overruled		0.78*		−0.94*		−0.65*
Precedent		(0.39)		(0.32)		(0.35)
Precedent Age		0.01		−0.08*		−0.10*
		(0.02)		(0.01)		(0.01)
Precedent Age		−0.0007		0.0005*		0.0008*
Squared		(0.0005)		(0.0002)		(0.0002)
Constant	−7.67*	−7.18*	−4.09*	−3.68*	−3.74*	−3.29*
	(0.34)	(0.42)	(0.08)	(0.09)	(0.07)	(0.09)
N	181,847	181,847	181,847	181,847	181,847	181,847
χ^2	82.55*	304.05*	412.02*	2157.87*	495.08*	2379.15*

Note: Table entries are logistic regression coefficients with robust standard errors (clustered on each precedent) in parentheses; *$p < 0.05$ (one-tailed). The dependent variable represents whether the Court majority interpreted a prior precedent in a strong negative, weak negative, or positive manner (1946–2001), among those precedents analyzed by Hansford and Spriggs (2006) (all orally argued cases, 1946–1999).

to strong negative treatments of precedent, less conscientious Courts fall prey to the effects of ideological decision making, while increasingly conscientious Courts do not.

The left panel of Figure 58 reports the predicted probability that a Court will issue a weak negative interpretation across the range of *Conscientiousness* while holding constant *Ideological Distance* at high versus low values. When ideological distance is *low* (i.e., the 10th percentile, or the solid line), the most conscientious Court is likely to interpret a precedent in a weakly negative manner with a probability of 0.0183 [0.0167, 0.0199] . Conversely, the least conscientious Court is likely to interpret a precedent in a weakly negative manner with a probability of 0.0156 [0.0140, 0.0172] – or, 17 percent higher.

When, however, ideological distance is high (i.e., the 90th percentile, or the dashed line), moving from the minimum to maximum *Conscientiousness*

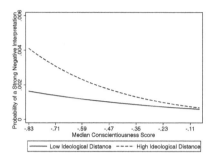
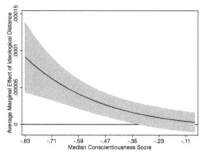

FIGURE 57: *The interactive effect of conscientiousness and ideological distance on the Supreme Court's strong negative interpretations of precedent.* The left panel displays the predicted probability that the Court issues a strong negative interpretation of precedent across the range of *Conscientiousness* using results from Model 2 in Table 27. The solid line reflects low *Ideological Distance* (10th percentile) while the dashed line represents high distance (90th percentile). The right panel displays the average marginal effect of *Ideological Distance* on the probability of a strong negative interpretation (with 90 percent confidence intervals) across the range of *Conscientiousness*.

score exhibits an expected increase in the probability of a weak negative interpretation from 0.0160 [0.0137, 0.0182] to 0.0266 [0.0238, 0.0294] – an increase of 0.0106. Thus, the most conscientious Court is more than 45 percent more likely to issue a weak negative interpretation of a precedent that it should dislike ideologically compared to one that is ideologically congruent. But, the impact of *Ideological Distance* is statistically indistinguishable from zero among the least conscientious Courts in the sample. This result suggests that a conscientious Court tends to exhibit more incremental changes to precedent, and does so when it is ideologically opportunistic.

The right panel of Figure 58 displays the interactive marginal effects in the weak negative model. It shows that increasingly conscientious Courts are more likely to interpret precedents in a weakly negative manner when they disagree ideologically with them. On the other hand, the least conscientious Courts exhibit no such inclination. Specifically, *Ideological Distance* exhibits no discernible impact on weak negative treatments below −0.64 on the conscientiousness scale, which represents 37 percent of the sample observations (or, 20 percent of the Court terms).

Now consider the positive treatment of precedent and ideological distance. The left panel in Figure 59 displays predicted probabilities that illustrate the magnitude of this interactive effect. The least conscientious Court is likely to interpret a precedent positively with a probability of 0.0173 [0.0154, 0.0192] when ideological distance is low (i.e., the 10th percentile, or the solid line).

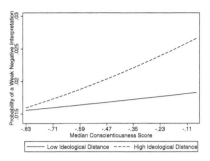 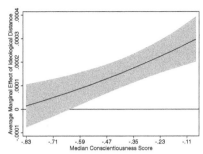

FIGURE 58: *The interactive effect of conscientiousness and ideological distance on the Supreme Court's weak negative interpretations of precedent.* The left panel displays the predicted probability that the Court issues a weak negative interpretation of precedent across the range of *Conscientiousness* using results from Model 4 in Table 27. The solid line reflects low *Ideological Distance* (10th percentile) while the dashed line represents high distance (90th percentile). The right panel displays the average marginal effect of *Ideological Distance* on the probability of a weak negative interpretation (with 90 percent confidence intervals) across the range of *Conscientiousness*.

This predicted probability increases to 0.0196 [0.0177, 0.0214] when looking at the most conscientious Court, resulting in an expected 0.0023 increase in the probability of a positive treatment. By contrast, when ideological distance is high (i.e., the 90th percentile, or the dashed line), moving from the minimum to maximum *Conscientiousness* score exhibits an expected increase in the probability of a positive interpretation from 0.0138 [0.0115, 0.0161] to 0.0182 [0.0160, 0.0204] – an increase of 0.0044, or nearly twice the impact of low ideological distance. Thus, the least conscientious Court is more than 20 percent less likely to interpret a precedent positively when it is ideologically unfavorable than when that Court should like the precedent.

The right panel in Figure 59 reports the average marginal effect of *Ideological Distance* on the probability of a positive precedent interpretation. Ideological distance exhibits a statistically significant, negative effect on positive interpretations among the least conscientious Court. Courts distant from precedent are less likely to treat precedent positively when they disagree with it ideologically. Yet, *Ideological Distance* exhibits a null effect among the most conscientious Courts – that is, those scoring above −0.245 on *Conscientiousness*. This represents more than 32 percent of the sample observations (or, 27 percent of the Court terms).

Next, consider the interactive effect with *Precedent Vitality*. Precedents with high vitality signify those that have been interpreted more favorably over time, and thus they exude greater legal authority. A conscientious Court, as a

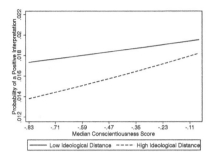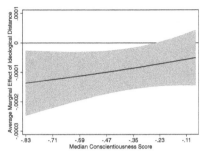

FIGURE 59: *The interactive effect of conscientiousness and ideological distance on the Supreme Court's positive interpretations of precedent.* The left panel displays the predicted probability that the Court issues a positive interpretation of precedent across the range of *Conscientiousness* using results from Model 6 in Table 27. The solid line reflects low *Ideological Distance* (10th percentile), while the dashed line represents high distance (90th percentile). The right panel displays the average marginal effect of *Ideological Distance* on the probability of a positive interpretation (with 90 percent confidence intervals) across the range of *Conscientiousness*.

result, should be more likely to respect precedents that have such authority. Figure 60 displays, for each dependent variable, the results of this interactive effect.

Figure 60(a) displays the average marginal effect (with 90 percent confidence intervals) of *Vitality* on strong negative interpretations, conditional on *Conscientiousness*. As the figure indicates, the impact of vitality does not vary meaningfully based on the level of conscientiousness.

Figure 60(b) shows the magnitude of the interactive relationship from the weak negative model, expressed as the predicted probability a Court will issue a weak negative interpretation across the range of *Conscientiousness* while holding *Precedent Vitality* at high and low values (i.e., values of 2 and −2). The most conscientious Court is 0.0039 less likely to issue a weak negative interpretation of a high-vitality precedent than a low vitality precedent (i.e., a probability of 0.0195 [0.0172, 0.0218] versus 0.0234 [0.0207, 0.0261]) − a decrease of 17 percent. Figure 60(c) displays the average marginal effect (with 90 percent confidence intervals) of *Precedent Vitality* on weak negative treatments across the range of *Conscientiousness*. It shows that the (negative) impact of vitality increases substantially among more conscientious Courts. Precedents with greater vitality are less likely to be interpreted in a weakly negative manner as the Court's degree of conscientiousness approaches its maximum. In fact, precedent vitality exhibits no discernible impact on weak negative treatments among the least conscientious Courts in the sample −

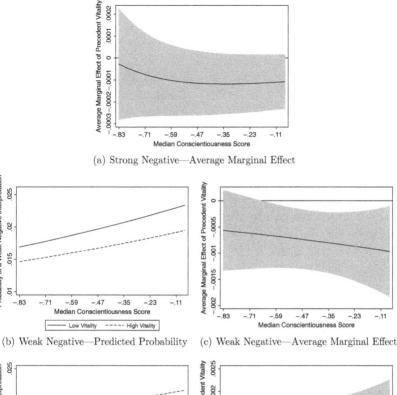

(a) Strong Negative—Average Marginal Effect

(b) Weak Negative—Predicted Probability   (c) Weak Negative—Average Marginal Effect

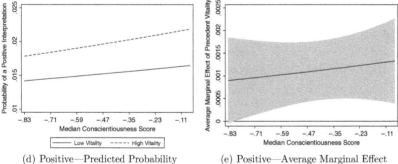

(d) Positive—Predicted Probability   (e) Positive—Average Marginal Effect

FIGURE 60: *The interactive effect of conscientiousness and precedent vitality on Supreme Court interpretation of precedent.* Panel (a) displays the average marginal effect of *Precedent Vitality* on the probability of a strong negative interpretation of precedent (with 90% confidence intervals) across the range of *Conscientiousness* using results from Model 2 in Table 27. Panel (b) displays the predicted probability that the Court issues a weak negative interpretation across the range of *Conscientiousness* using results from Model 4. The dashed line represents a high degree of *Precedent Vitality* while the solid line reflects a low value. Panel (c) reports the average marginal effect of *Precedent Vitality* on weak negative interpretations. Panels (d) and (e) display the interactive predicted probabilities and average marginal effect, respectively, from the positive interpretations analysis using results from Model 6.

those below −0.66 on the *Conscientiousness* scale, which includes 37 percent of the sample observations (or, 20 percent of the Court terms).

The Court's positive interpretations tell a similar story, albeit with a more muted effect. A conscientious Court is more likely to treat positively those precedents with high vitality than those with low vitality. Figure 60(d) shows that the least conscientious Court is 0.0036 more likely to issue a positive interpretation of a high-vitality precedent compared to one with low vitality (i.e., a probability of 0.0178 [0.0150, 0.0207] versus 0.0142 [0.0118, 0.0166]). Contrast this with the most conscientious Court in the sample, which is 0.0053 more likely to positively interpret a high-vitality precedent than one with low legal authority (i.e., a probability of 0.0218 [0.0188, 0.0249] versus 0.0165 [0.0143, 0.0186]). Thus, the impact of *Precedent Vitality* on positive interpretations is nearly 50 percent greater when comparing a high- to low-conscientious Court. Figure 60(e) displays the average marginal effect of *Precedent Vitality* on positive interpretations. It indicates that the (positive) impact of vitality on the probability of a positive treatment is higher among more conscientious Courts. Precedent vitality exhibits little impact on the least conscientious Courts in the sample.[14]

10.5 CONCLUSION

The results in this chapter highlight several important features of conscientiousness and its impact on law. First, conscientiousness leads to a Court that is, on balance, more likely to adhere to *stare decisis*. And, when the Court does alter precedent, the conscientious Court tends to do so in only an incremental fashion. Second, many scholars have documented how ideological congruence is a significant predictor of adherence to precedent. The conscientious Court, however, does not depart significantly from precedent for ideological concerns. Third, a precedent's legal authority exhibits its greatest impact on the conscientious Court. In short, conscientiousness matters when it comes to applying and overruling precedent.

These results speak to the stability of law on the High Court. The composition of the Court – more specifically, the traits of the justices on the Court – can have an important effect on the treatment of precedent. A Court composed of highly conscientious justices may maintain *stare decisis* and eschew large doctrinal changes.

---

[14] The impact of *Precedent Vitality* is marginally insignificant at the minimum score for the *Conscientiousness* (p = 0.057, one-tailed).

At the same time, these results speak to policy makers looking to effectuate legal change or to maintain the status quo. Want a Court that respects precedent? Appoint more conscientious justices. Want a Court that sees fit to ignore existing precedent? Appoint fewer conscientious justices. For example, Richard Nixon, hoping to undo liberal Warren Court decisions, might have had better luck by nominating someone other than Lewis Powell, a highly conscientious justice. The same could be said for Ronald Reagan and his selection of Anthony Kennedy. Future Democrat Presidents might similarly have more luck pulling back from Roberts era decisions by selecting less conscientious justices. These are, of course, policy decisions on which we take no position. Nevertheless, the results show relatively clearly that conscientious justices are more concerned about *stare decisis* than less conscientious justices.

We began this chapter discussing *Valley Forge Christian College* v. *Americans United for Separation of Church and State* (1982), a case in which the Court had to decide whether to expand, limit, or even overrule the taxpayer standing case, *Flast* v. *Cohen* (1968). Not surprisingly, the conservative justices on the Court disliked *Flast* and limited it. But some of the conservatives wanted to overrule it expressly. Justice Rehnquist was the most vocal critic of *Flast* and pushed for its overrule. Justices Powell and White, however, blocked the effort to overrule it formally – despite their jurisprudential and philosophical disagreements with it. Justices Powell and White, it should be noted, were among the most conscientious justices in our data.

Conscientiousness and Public Opinion

In *Swann* v. *Charlotte-Mecklenburg Board of Education* (1971),[1] Justice Brennan circulated a memo to his colleagues in which he observed: "[S]igns that opposition to *Brown* [v. *Board of Education of Topeka*] may at long last be crumbling in the South. The recent inaugural addresses of the new Governors of Georgia and South Carolina, and at least some of the newspaper surveys reported in the last month give concrete encouragement that this may be the case." This memo, displayed as Figure 61, shows that Brennan tried to make his colleagues aware of public opinion. He was not alone in that effort. In *Schneble* v. *Florida* (1972),[2] Justice Rehnquist sent a memo to his colleagues, stating, "I noticed in the Washington Post this morning a story to the effect that Governor Askew of Florida had granted a moratorium on all executions until January 1, 1973." In *First National Bank* v. *Bellotti* (1978),[3] Justice Stewart circulated a memo stating, "You will be interested in the enclosed copy of the lead editorial in this morning's *Wall Street Journal*, if you have not already seen it."[4]

These examples, and numerous others we could provide, show that Supreme Court justices pay attention to public opinion. The fact that they read newspapers and circulate them to their colleagues, often with comments, suggests that they follow the news, internalize and process public opinion, and perhaps even consider it when they decide cases.

A long train of scholarship suggests that justices follow public opinion when they decide cases (Owens and Wohlfarth 2019, 2017; Wedeking and Zilis 2018; Black, Owens, Wedeking, and Wohlfarth 2016b,a; Bryan and Kromphardt 2016; Casillas, Enns, and Wohlfarth 2011; Epstein and Martin 2011; Enns and Wohlfarth 2013; Giles, Blackstone, and Vining 2008; McGuire and Stimson

---

[1] *Swann* v. *Charlotte-Mecklenburg Board of Education*, 402 U.S. 1 (1971).
[2] *Schneble* v. *Florida*, 405 U.S. 427 (1972).
[3] *First National Bank* v. *Bellotti*, 435 U.S. 765 (1978).
[4] These memos come from Wahlbeck, Spriggs, and Maltzman (2009a).

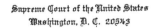

CHAMBERS OF
JUSTICE WM. J. BRENNAN, JR.

Supreme Court of the United States
Washington, D. C. 20543

March 8, 1971

RE: <u>Nos. 281 & 349 - Swann v. Charlotte-Mecklenburg</u>

Dear Chief:

At my request Potter gave me a copy of his revised memorandum in these cases which you have. After reading it and your third
circulation of March 4, I offer these comments.

Your circulation and Potter's draft reach the result of affirming
Judge McMillan's judgment, a result which I strongly support. But
the approaches of the two opinions differ significantly, and I hope we
may discuss the importance of the differences at the forthcoming
conference. For me, the matter of approach has assumed major
significance in light of signs that opposition to <u>Brown</u> may at long last
be crumbling in the South. The recent inaugural addresses of the new
Governors of Georgia and South Carolina, and at least some of the
newspaper surveys reported in the last month give concrete encouragement that this may be the case. Although affirmance of Judge McMillan's
judgment should of itself further the process, I nevertheless suggest
that our opinion should avoid saying anything that might be seized upon

FIGURE 61: *Image of internal Supreme Court memo from Justice Brennan to Chief Justice Burger in Swann v. Charlotte-Mecklenburg Board of
Education.*

2004; Flemming and Wood 1997; Stimson, Mackuen, and Erikson 1995; Mishler and Sheehan 1993, 1996; Murphy 1964). Still, these studies are limited
in their reach. Specifically, their theories tend to suggest that public opinion will influence *all* justices. But the fact of the matter is that some justices
seem to pay more attention to public opinion than others (see, e.g., Enns and
Wohlfarth 2013; Flemming and Wood 1997; Mishler and Sheehan 1996).

Why do some justices seem more concerned with – and even attuned to – public opinion than others? Having made it this far through the book, you undoubtedly expect the answer: conscientiousness. We believe conscientious justices are more likely to concern themselves with and follow public opinion than less conscientious justices. Conscientious people tend to be more exhaustive with their work, consider more alternatives, and pay greater attention to the consequences of their actions. Public opinion – and its impact on the political and legal worlds – relate to all these dynamics. And so we believe conscientious justices will be more likely to follow public opinion than less conscientious justices. The results support this claim. Increasing conscientiousness can raise the probability a justice follows public opinion by nearly 25 percent. What is more, we retrieve these results while controlling for all the other factors commonly believed to influence justices' votes.

11.1 PUBLIC OPINION AND THE COURT

Scholars have examined whether and why public opinion might influence Supreme Court justices.[5] The results tend to suggest that public opinion plays a role in how the justices decide, but scholars have proposed varying rationales to explain why it influences them (compare Owens and Wohlfarth 2019, 2017 *with* Casillas, Enns, and Wohlfarth 2011; Giles, Blackstone, and Vining 2008). There are, of course, weighty reasons for the Court generally to follow public opinion – or at least pay attention to it. Some scholars argue that justices look to public opinion for instrumental reasons, yet others believe they do so for reputational reasons, and still others believe their preferences change just like everyone else's.

Most scholars who argue that justices follow public opinion believe they do so for *instrumental* reasons. According to this argument, justices follow public opinion to protect the Court's legitimacy and, in turn, their own power. Justice Frankfurter once claimed, "The Court's authority ... rests on sustained public confidence in its moral sanction" (Caldeira 1986, 1209). So, justices follow public opinion because it is in their long term interests to do so; it reflects well on the Court, which, in turn, engenders more support and power.

But how can following public opinion enhance the Court's legitimacy? The Supreme Court lacks an electoral connection to voters. This dynamic, while enhancing judicial independence, also removes any connection to and benefit from popular sovereignty. Thus, the Court relies on public goodwill

---

5   See Enns and Wohlfarth (2017) for a detailed review of the literature examining public opinion's impact on the US Supreme Court.

for its institutional legitimacy. And so, "a series of wrong or imprudent judgments ... can undermine public faith in the [judiciary]" (Murphy 1964, 20). A consistent pattern of shirking public opinion could shake the public's confidence in the Court (Casillas, Enns, and Wohlfarth 2011). And when that confidence disappears, the Court suffers.

Empirical evidence supports the claim that the Court's legitimacy is a function of public support for its decisions. Bartels and Johnston (2013) suggest that ideologues who oppose specific Court decisions are more likely to challenge the Court's legitimacy than those who support its decisions (cf., Gibson and Nelson 2015). Caldeira (1986) finds, in part, that the Court's legitimacy decreases as it strikes more federal laws and sides with criminal defendants. Related work shows courts that a Court which systematically ignores *stare decisis* jeopardizes its institutional legitimacy (see, e.g., Zink, Spriggs, and Scott 2009; Bailey and Maltzman 2011). While the Court has a deep reservoir of diffuse support, frequent counter-majoritarian decisions could leave its legitimacy – and thus its power – at risk (Gibson, Caldeira, and Spence 2003, 365). Not to put too fine a point on it, but the Court's power goes so far as the public tolerates. Justices must therefore cultivate public support for the Court.

Other scholars who believe that justices follow public opinion argue they do so to ensure elected officials *implement* their opinions. When justices issue decisions that contradict public opinion, they risk inciting a negative reaction among elected officials. That is, although justices themselves do not face elections, those who implement their decisions do face elections. Consequently, even the most stubbornly independent justice may need to consider how the public will view the Court's decision. As McGuire and Stimson (2004, 1022) explain: "The Court requires the cooperation of legislative and executive officials, many of whom are themselves careful auditors of mass opinion. For that reason, the members of the Court must reflect on how well their preferred outcomes will be received and supported by implementers."

Other Court watchers take a different perspective, suggesting that justices concern themselves with public opinion for *reputational reasons*. Nearly all humans desire prestige, esteem, and acceptance (Baum 2006). As Bernheim (1994, 842) states, "most social scientists agree that individual behavior is motivated in large part by 'social' factors, such as the desire for prestige, esteem, popularity, or acceptance." The desire for acceptance is a strong human attribute, and pressure to seek it can be compelling. According to this theory, reputational concerns drive judges. As Baum (2006, 66) put it, judges "might respond to public opinion ... [because of] their interest in personal approval from the mass public." The theory's logic is simple. People want to be liked and respected. Judges are people. So, judges want to be liked and respected. Ruling against public opinion tends to make judges disliked and disrespected. And so judges will not often rule against public opinion.

While few scholars have tested this reputational theory empirically on the Supreme Court, there is at least some support for it as applied to lower court judges. Owens and Wohlfarth (2019) find that "native born" circuit court judges are more likely to follow public opinion in their circuits than other judges. That is, judges who were born, raised, and received their schooling in the state they represent in the circuit are more likely to follow that home state public opinion than a judge without such deep roots in the state. Their theory is that native born judges have a deeper connection to their states, and more concern for their reputation there, than other judges. The results agreed.

Still other scholars suggest a more mundane procedure is at work when justices appear to follow public opinion. They argue that justices' attitudes simply change along with the general public. The crux of the theory is that justices are like others in society who change over time (e.g., Giles, Blackstone, and Vining 2008). Just as the general public becomes more liberal or conservative on issues, so too do justices. As Justice Cardozo once stated, "The great tides and currents which engulf the rest of men do not turn aside in their course and pass the judges by" (Cardozo 1921, 168). To continue the metaphor, justices, like the rest of us, are like corks floating in a sea of public opinion, drifting whichever direction the tides take them.

All of these theories are plausible, but as we mentioned above, they are limited in some respects. With perhaps the exception of the reputational theory, they posit a constant and ubiquitous effect of public opinion on justices. That is, *all* justices should follow public opinion because *all* justices seek to maximize their power, the Court's legitimacy, ensure implementation, and protect their reputations. Or so the argument goes.

But these theories (with the exception of the reputational theory) suggest justices follow public opinion for reasons that are contextual or environmental, rather than physiological and psychological. Public opinion matters because the Court needs support from the public. It matters because justices must rely on political actors. It matters because external forces change justices' beliefs. There is little about the justices' own values that make public opinion more or less relevant. These features make existing theories of public opinion's role incomplete.

Moreover, not all justices respond the same way to public opinion. Some justices seem more interested in public opinion than others. Consider Justice Kennedy, who seemed much more interested in public opinion than many of his colleagues. Indeed, he often seemed to relish the role of the swing justice who tried to read the tea leaves of public opinion. Greenburg (2007, 159) provides this Kennedy quote before the Court released its opinion in the *Planned Parenthood* v. *Casey*[6] abortion decision:

> As [Kennedy] stood by the window in his office, looking at the protesters marching below, he told the reporter of his struggles. 'Sometimes you don't know if you're Caesar about to cross the Rubicon or Captain Queeg cutting your own tow line,' Kennedy said just before he went downstairs to the packed courtroom to announce the decision that would redefine him as a justice. (159)

Whereas Kennedy tried to understand public opinion, others did not. Consider Justice Douglas. He once ruled that trees could have legal personhood to establish standing to sue in Court.[7] In a time when divorce was frowned upon, Douglas had three (marrying four different women). And he stayed the execution of Julius and Ethel Rosenberg (Murphy 2003). All actions flew in the face of prevailing public opinion and norms. As Garrow (2003) writes, Douglas "did what he did in the open. He didn't give a damn what people thought of him."

If this book has shown anything so far, it is that conscientiousness matters. It influences all aspects of judicial behavior. We believe it also influences whether justices follow public opinion.

11.2 A THEORY OF CONSCIENTIOUSNESS AND PUBLIC OPINION

We discussed our theory of conscientiousness and judging in Chapter 2 but reiterate portions of it here. We believe conscientious justices are more likely to follow public opinion than less conscientious justices because they seek out, and incorporate, more information in the process of decision-making. They also are more attuned to their political environments and the Court's institutional standing because they value conventionality and desire to maintain good social environments (Mike et al. 2015).

As we have discussed repeatedly, the literature suggests that conscientious individuals work hard to achieve their goals. They are deliberate, self-disciplined, and well-organized. The more conscientious a person is, the more he or she is competent, dutiful, orderly, responsible and thorough (McCrae

---

[6] See *Planned Parenthood* v. *Casey*, 505 U.S. 833 (1992).
[7] See *Sierra Club* v. *Morton*, 405 U.S. 727 (1972).

and John 1992). At the same time, conscientiousness correlates positively with job performance. In fact, various studies have shown that conscientiousness is one of the best predictors of job performance across many different criteria and occupational groups (Mount and Barrick 1998; Salgado 1997). Barrick and Mount (1991) find that increased conscientiousness correlates with better job performance among professionals, police, managers, salespeople, and skilled/semi-skilled workers. Barrick, Mount, and Strauss (1993) find that sales representatives high in conscientiousness set higher goals and are more committed to those goals than those scoring low on this dimension. On a similar note, conscientious people tend to work well on teams because they are more dependable, thorough, persistent, and hardworking (Hough 1992; Mount, Barrick, and Stewart 1998). Put simply, conscientious people tend to perform their professional tasks more thoroughly than less conscientious people.

Along similar lines, Heinström (2003) finds that conscientious people tend to seek out more information to support their positions than less conscientious people. Heinstrom examines how graduate students seek out information to work on their research. The study investigates how students evaluate information, how they select the documents they use for their research, and the effect of time pressure on their information gathering. The results show that conscientious people seek out thought-provoking documents instead of documents that confirm previous ideas. The conscientious students appear to engage with the material more and push themselves to consider more complex material. On the other hand, less-conscientious students tend to choose their information sources based on how easy it is to access.

In a similar analysis, Gul et al. (2004, 359) find, "High level conscientious scholars being very competent, disciplined and achievement striking are found to make extra efforts in database searching to get required information." In a study on how people search the Internet, Schmidt and Wolff (2016, 6) find that "[c]onscientious people have a high level of activity and an exhaustive exploitation of the search space," while a less conscientious individual uses "a search pattern that aims at finding results fast but with little reflection." (see also Halder, Roy, and Chakraborty 2010).

One particularly notable aspect of conscientious people is their tendency to follow norms. As John and Srivastava (1999, 121) explain, conscientiousness "describes *socially prescribed impulse control* that facilitates task- and goal-directed behavior, such as . . . following norms and rules" (emphasis in original). What is more, as Mike et al. (2015, 659) state, conscientious people value conventionality and thus demonstrate an "inclination to support and follow the norms of society in order to maintain good social environments."

Applying these findings, we believe increasingly conscientious justices are more likely to follow public opinion than less conscientious justices. Of course, there is no rule of public opinion; justices are supposed to be independent and follow the rule of law.[8] Yet, justices do not make decisions in a political vacuum. Their decisions often have significant political consequences and can attract the attention of the news media, political elites, interest groups, and grassroots organizations. And, an accumulation of unpopular decisions that activates widespread scrutiny may be particularly damaging to the Court's reputation. Once the Court's reputation has been sullied, its legitimacy suffers, thereby jeopardizing the potency of future decisions. One may think of the winds of public opinion as an institutional norm that constrains justices' decision-making. Conscientious justices should be more keenly aware of, and thus receptive to, the prospect that decisions running afoul of societal norms may activate negative attention among the mass public.[9] Consequently, they should also be more likely to incorporate such information into their decision making based on an awareness of the potential consequences of significant public discord. In short, we expect that *as a justice becomes more conscientious, the justice will become increasingly likely to follow public opinion.*

11.3 DATA AND MEASURES

To examine whether conscientious justices are more likely to follow public opinion, we construct a data set of justices' individual votes in all orally argued

---

[8] One might argue that a conscientious justice may think it is improper to consider public opinion when making decisions. However, we argue that so long as justices are generally cognizant of their political environment – and the relevance of political constraints to the Court's institutional standing – then a conscientious justice should be the one most likely to view protecting the institution as a necessary duty of serving on the High Court.

[9] One might ask where justices find information on the current state of public opinion. As Enns and Wohlfarth (2017, 187) argue, "Public opinion moves systematically and predictably, and numerous indicators, such as election results, polls, and media reports, provide clues about the general state and direction of public opinion," as do amicus curiae briefs (e.g., Collins 2004). For instance, Justice Breyer has said, "Judges read newspapers, just like everybody else" (Farias 2015). Similarly, as Kingdon (1984, 153) argues, "People in and around government sense a national mood. They are comfortable discussing its content, and believe they know when the mood shifts."

Supreme Court merits decisions from the 1953 to 2013 terms.[10] Our unit of analysis is the justice-vote.

Dependent Variable. Our dependent variable, *Liberal Vote*, represents whether a justice cast a liberal or conservative vote in each case. We use the Supreme Court Database's "direction" variable to identify the ideological direction of each justice's vote. We code liberal votes as 1 and conservative votes as 0. We code votes as missing if the Database indicates that the ideological direction cannot be specified clearly, or if the justice did not participate in the particular case.

Conscientiousness. Our main covariate of interest is *Conscientiousness*, which we discuss in detail in Chapter 3. As with the other chapters of this book, we also include the other personality traits *Openness, Extraversion, Agreeableness,* and *Neuroticism.*

Public Mood. To capture the effect of national public opinion, we use the public mood indicator created by Stimson (1991).[11] Stimson's public mood measure is a longitudinal indicator of the public's general preference for more or less government over time. It is an aggregate, dynamic reflection of the general tenor of public opinion (and preference over desired public policy) on the standard liberal-conservative dimension (Stimson 1991). Scholars who examine public opinion in the courts use this measure frequently (e.g., Owens and Wohlfarth 2019, 2017; Black, Owens, Wedeking, and Wohlfarth 2016*a,b*; Enns and Wohlfarth 2013; Casillas, Enns, and Wohlfarth 2011; Epstein and Martin 2011; Giles, Blackstone, and Vining 2008; McGuire and Stimson 2004).[12]

Conscientiousness × Public Mood. We interact *Public Mood* with each justice's *Conscientiousness* to test whether the impact of public opinion is greater among more conscientious justices. We expect *Public Mood* to exhibit a positive relationship with justices' proclivity to vote liberally, and this positive impact should increase in magnitude among greater values of *Conscientiousness.*

Justice Ideology. We also account for each justice's ideological preferences. We use Segal and Cover's (1989) ideology scores to account for the

---

[10] To compile these data, we use the justice-centered Supreme Court Database organized by case citation, which is available at http://scdb.wustl.edu. We exclude those decisions that the Database identifies as a non-orally argued per curiam or a decree (i.e., "decisionType" = 2 or 4).

[11] We use updated estimates of public mood (May 2, 2016 data release) retrieved from: http://stimson.web.unc.edu/data/.

[12] Consistent with many prior studies, we match the public mood score each calendar year to the Supreme Court term (i.e., public mood in 2000 predicts Court decisions in the 2000 term), thereby creating a nine-month lag. This ensures that changes in public opinion temporally precede the Court's decisions.

likelihood that more liberal (conservative) justices are more likely to issue liberal (conservative) votes. The Segal-Cover scores were generated using content analyses of newspaper editorials, and thus offer indicators of the justices' ideological predispositions that are exogenous to their judicial votes. And, although these scores are most closely associated with justices' attitudes among civil liberties and civil rights, they represent the most suitable exogenous measure currently available to predict justices' votes. The scores range from 0 to 1, with larger (smaller) values signifying more liberal (conservative) attitudes.

Liberal SG. We also control for the ideological direction of the position taken by the Solicitor General when filing amicus curiae briefs and when participating as a party to a case. To measure these positions, we first identify all cases where the SG participated as amicus curiae or when the United States was a party to the case, consistent with our approach in Chapter 6.[13] We then code the ideological direction of each position by inferring it from the ideological direction of the lower court's decision and the litigant supported (represented) by the SG (United States).[14] For instance, a liberal position reflects one where the SG supported (or the United States was) the petitioner and the lower court issued a conservative decision. Conversely, we code the SG's position as conservative when the SG supported the petitioner following a liberal lower court decision. In sum, we assign a 1 to liberal SG/US positions, a 0 to those that are neutral (i.e., where the SG did not clearly support one litigant over the other, or where the SG did not participate in the case), and a −1 for conservative positions.[15] We expect that a justice will be more (less) likely to cast a liberal vote when the SG/US advocates a liberal (conservative) position.

Separation of Powers Controls. Following Epstein and Martin's (2011) analysis of public mood's impact on the US Supreme Court, we account for several

[13] To identify those cases where the SG filed a voluntary amicus brief, we rely on data from Wohlfarth (2009) and update it through the 2013 term. Next, we use the Supreme Court Database to identify all cases where the US government (or a federal agency) was a litigant and whether the government was the petitioner or respondent. This includes all cases where the Database identified the US government, Department of Justice, or a federal agency as a party, using the "petitioner" and "respondent" variables to identify the litigants.

[14] We use the Supreme Court Database's "lcDispositionDirection" variable to identify the ideological direction of the lower court's decision.

[15] Alternatively, one could specify multiple dummy variables to capture differential effects, thereby allowing the impact of liberal SG/US positions to be different from conservative positions and/or the impact of the SG as amicus curiae to differ from that of the United States as a party. Although we opt to simplify the specification by including a single SG/US position predictor as if it were continuous (see, e.g., Enns and Wohlfarth 2013), the results are substantively consistent if employing these alternative modeling approaches.

control variables related to the separation of powers. We include three predictors that capture the ideological predisposition of the president and the
median members of the House of Representatives and Senate – *President
Ideology*, *House Ideology*, and *Senate Ideology*, respectively. We use the Judicial Common Space (JCS) to generate these indicators each term (Epstein,
Martin, Segal, and Westerland 2007).[16] Larger JCS scores reflect more conservative policy preferences. We expect a negative relationship with these
predictors and justices' proclivity to vote liberally.

Lower Court Liberal. We also control for the ideological direction of the
lower court's decision (see, e.g., Epstein and Martin 2011). *Lower Court Liberal* takes on a value of 1 if the Supreme Court Database identified the
direction of the lower court's decision as liberal, and 0 if it was conservative.[17] Given the Supreme Court's well-known tendency to overturn the
lower court decision when granting cert and issuing a decision on the merits
(Black and Owens 2009a), we expect *Lower Court Liberal* to be negatively
related to a liberal vote. In other words, justices should be less (more)
likely to cast liberal votes when reviewing liberal (conservative) lower court
decisions.

Issue Area Controls. Lastly, we account for differences in behavior across
issue areas by including fixed effects for the primary issue area within
each case. We include a dummy variable for each broad issue area
(minus a baseline category) among those identified by the Supreme Court
Database.[18]

11.4 METHODS AND RESULTS

With these data in hand, we estimate a logistic regression model with robust
standard errors.[19] We estimate three total regression models: (1) a traits-only
baseline model that includes only the public mood-conscientiousness interaction and the four other personality trait measures; (2) a second model that

[16] The JCS scores are available at http://epstein.wustl.edu/research/JCS.
html.
[17] We use the Database's "lcDispositionDirection" variable to create this predictor. We drop
those few decisions where the Database indicates that the lower court decision did not exhibit
a clear ideological direction. The results are substantively consistent, however, if we create a
third category to capture these cases.
[18] We use the "issueArea" variable in the Database to identify the primary issue area within each
case.
[19] All subsequent results are substantively consistent if we instead estimate the model using
classical standard errors.

adds the justice ideology control predictor (but no other controls); and (3) a fully specified model with all control predictors.[20]

The empirical results from Table 28 support our hypothesis. Justices who score higher on *Conscientiousness* exhibit greater responsiveness to public mood. As public mood becomes more liberal, justices are more likely to issue liberal votes. Further, the magnitude of this effect increases significantly when looking at justices with greater conscientiousness.[21] This result is especially evident in Models 2 and 3, and it exists while controlling for multiple factors that are thought to shape justices' voting on the merits.[22]

Figure 62(a) shows the predicted probability a justice casts a liberal vote across the range of *Public Mood*. The dashed line in the figure represents a High Conscientiousness justice (at the 90th percentile [0.90]) on the *Conscientiousness* distribution, while the solid line represents a Low Conscientiousness justice (scoring at the 10th percentile [−1.72]). Clearly, a "Low Conscientiousness" justice exhibits no substantial (nor statistically significant) responsiveness to public opinion. By contrast, the most conscientious justice in the sample is likely to issue a liberal vote with a probability of 0.40 [0.38, 0.42] in the most conservative state of public opinion compared to a probability of 0.495 [0.48, 0.51] when public mood is at its most liberal – a shift of nearly 0.10, or approximately 25 percent. In short, the most conscientious justice exhibits a responsiveness to public opinion that is about two times greater than the justice of average conscientiousness, and nearly five times greater than the justice who exhibits the smallest (statistically significant) responsiveness.

Figure 62(b) tells a similar story. It reports the average marginal effect of *Public Mood* across the observed range of *Conscientiousness* using results from Model 3 in Table 28. Public opinion exhibits a statistically significant ($p < 0.05$, one-tailed), positive impact on justices scoring above −1.30 on

[20] All empirical results are substantively consistent when specifying a baseline model that does not include the other personality trait indicators (nor other control predictors).

[21] A model specification that does not include an interaction term between *Public Mood* and *Conscientiousness* confirms that public opinion also exhibits an unconditional and statistically significant, positive relationship with justices' decisions to vote liberally.

[22] The interactive effect of *Public Mood* and *Conscientiousness* in the baseline Model 1 is not as stark when compared to the other model specifications. As Model 2 shows, *Justice Ideology* is an important control predictor that further draws out the public mood-conscientiousness interactive effect. Nevertheless, when focusing on Model 1, the average marginal effect plot for *Public Mood* conditional on *Conscientiousness* (not displayed) shows an effect of public opinion on the most conscientious justice that is equivalent to the results from Models 2 and 3. The primary difference is that the least conscientious justice exhibits a responsiveness to public opinion that is greater in Model 1 (compared to the results from Models 2 and 3).

TABLE 28: *The Impact of Public Opinion and Justice Personality Traits on the US Supreme Court*

	(1)	(2)	(3)
Public Mood	0.027*	0.018*	0.015*
	(0.002)	(0.002)	(0.002)
Conscientiousness	−0.364*	−0.736*	−0.712*
	(0.120)	(0.125)	(0.133)
Public Mood × Conscientiousness	0.002	0.008*	0.008*
	(0.002)	(0.002)	(0.002)
Openness	−0.107*	−0.086*	−0.108*
	(0.007)	(0.007)	(0.008)
Extraversion	0.112*	0.093*	0.114*
	(0.011)	(0.011)	(0.012)
Agreeableness	−0.029*	−0.033*	−0.044*
	(0.008)	(0.009)	(0.009)
Neuroticism	−0.148*	−0.070*	−0.082*
	(0.010)	(0.010)	(0.011)
Justice Ideology		1.350*	1.308*
		(0.027)	(0.028)
SG/US Position			0.521*
			(0.014)
President Ideology			0.104*
			(0.025)
House Ideology			−0.181*
			(0.087)
Senate Ideology			−0.236*
			(0.130)
Lower Court Liberal			−0.585*
			(0.018)
Constant	−1.629*	−1.713*	−1.263*
	(0.132)	(0.134)	(0.142)
Issue Area Controls	No	No	Yes
N	58,054	58,054	57,512
χ^2	1070.78*	3517.66*	6474.07*

Note: Table entries are coefficients from a logistic regression model with robust standard errors in parentheses; *$p < 0.05$ (one-tailed). The dependent variable represents whether a justice cast a liberal vote, among all orally argued cases, 1953–2013. Model 3 includes, but does not display, fixed effects controls for the primary issue area in each case.

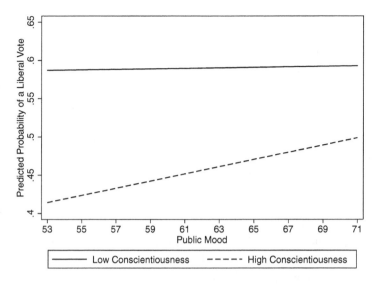

(a) Predicted Probability of a Liberal Vote

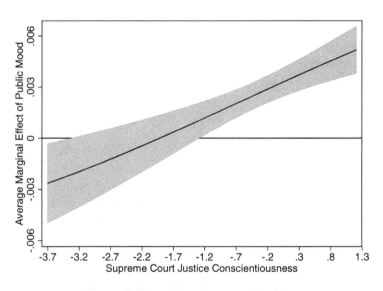

(b) Average Marginal Effect of Public Mood

FIGURE 62: *The moderating impact of conscientiousness on public opinion as a constraint on the US Supreme Court.* Panel (a) displays the predicted probability that a Supreme Court justice casts a liberal vote across the range of *Public Mood* using results from Model 3 in Table 28. The dashed line represents a (High Conscientiousness) justice at the 90th percentile (0.90) on the *Conscientiousness Trait* and the solid line represents a (Low Conscientiousness) justice at the 10th percentile (−1.72). Panel (b) reports the average marginal effect (with 90 percent confidence intervals) of *Public Mood* across the observed range of *Conscientiousness*.

Conscientiousness – representing 82.50 percent of the justice-vote observations, or twenty-seven (82 percent) of the thirty-three of the justices sitting on the Supreme Court during the sample period. Thus, public opinion exhibits a meaningful impact on most – though not all – of the justices in the sample.[23]

Among the control predictors, a justice's voting behavior is significantly affected by his or her ideological predisposition, as justices with more liberal (conservative) preferences are more likely to cast liberal (conservative) votes. Similarly, when the SG submits a liberal amicus brief, or the US government is a party advocating a liberal policy position, justices are more likely to cast liberal votes. Two of the three separation of powers predictors also exhibit the expected effects. Justices are less likely to cast liberal votes as the median member of the US Senate or the US House of Representatives becomes more conservative. The president ideology predictor, however, exhibits the unexpected result that justices are more likely to cast liberal votes as the president is more conservative. Consistent with prior research, the data confirm that justices are less likely to vote liberally when the Supreme Court reviews a liberal lower court decision. In terms of the other four traits, the results are largely useless, as the dependent variable is whether a justice cast a liberal vote. At any rate, the results reveal that extraverted justices are more likely to vote liberally, while more open, agreeable, and neurotic justices are less likely to vote liberally.

11.5 CONCLUSION

Scholars of judicial behavior have debated for decades over the potential rationale for why US Supreme Court justices might exhibit majoritarian tendencies in their decision making. And, among those scholars contending that public opinion is a relevant consideration on the Court, further debate exists around the extent of its impact. This chapter contributes to that extensive literature in a considerable way – Supreme Court justices exhibit heterogeneous responsiveness to public opinion that is due, at least in part, to their personalities. Thus, the Supreme Court-public opinion relationship might fundamentally be a function of the kinds of people who sit on the bench and their human, behavioral tendencies.

[23] The data also suggest that public mood has a significant, negative effect on justices at the very bottom of the conscientiousness scale – i.e., justices scoring below −3.30. This unexpected result, however, represents only 4.36 percent of the justice-vote observations, or one (3 percent) of the thirty-three sitting justices during the sample period.

The evidence presented here suggests that a justice's conscientiousness contributes to his or her tendency to steer the Court toward majoritarian decisions. The most conscientious justices (by our measures) in the modern era have exhibited considerable concern for public opinion when making decisions. By contrast, the least conscientious justices on the modern Supreme Court have exhibited no responsiveness to public opinion. This finding represents a new and novel source of heterogeneous decision making across justices. What is more, this chapter (alongside earlier chapters in this book) provides further evidence of the importance of justices' personalities – and conscientiousness in particular – in explaining majority outcomes on the Supreme Court.

Beyond scholarly and empirical debates over the Supreme Court–public opinion relationship, the results from this chapter also raise critical normative questions about the importance of justices' personalities in shaping the Court's role in the American political system. In particular, the findings suggest that a Supreme Court full of more conscientious personalities, for better or worse, is likely to represent a more majoritarian institution that is less likely to act as a countervailing force to the dynamics of public opinion in the United States. This raises noteworthy concerns regarding the Court's proclivity, or even desire, to act as a countermajoritarian institutional check on the elected branches in the American separation of powers framework.

These are, of course, normative questions that scholars can debate for years. There are other normative debates that involve conscientiousness as well. One of these considerations turns on recusal, and that topic is the focus of our next chapter.

12

Conscientiousness and Recusal

On January 8, 2010, a Justice Department Attorney reached out to Deputy Solicitor General Neal Katyal and revealed that the Obama administration was organizing a team "to get thinking about how to defend against inevitable challenges to the health care proposals that are pending." He asked if the SG's office would participate. Three minutes later, Katyal responded: "Absolutely right on. Let's crush them. I'll speak with [Solicitor General] Elena [Kagan] and designate someone." Katyal immediately emailed Kagan who, just a few minutes later, replied, "You should do it." A flurry of activity followed, with DOJ lawyers and the SG's office working to craft a winning legal strategy (Blackman 2013).

Now, fast forward two years. A maelstrom engulfs the Supreme Court as it decides the constitutionality of the Affordable Care Act. Solicitor General Kagan is now Justice Kagan. The SG's office seeks to protect the very law Kagan's office worked to defend. The Court receives a motion for Kagan to recuse herself from the case based on her previous involvement with it. The outcome of the case essentially hinges on Kagan's recusal decision. If she recuses, supporters of the Act lose what is sure to be a favorable vote, leaving the law in jeopardy. If she stays on, they have hope for success. What does Kagan do? She declines to recuse herself, hears the case, and votes to uphold the Act.[1]

Justice Kagan's failure to recuse was highly controversial. It triggered a significant amount of scholarship and journalism, not to mention handwringing. Conservatives howled in protest, arguing that Kagan ought to have recused. Some even suggested she should be impeached for staying on the case (Wolfe 2012). Liberals countered by questioning Justice Thomas's impartiality in light of his wife's anti-ACA lobbying at the conservative political action group, Liberty Central. They also reminded conservatives of previous cases in which

---

[1] *See National Federation of Independent Business* v. *Sebelius,* 567 U.S. 519 (2012).

Justice Scalia and then-Justice Rehnquist sat – cases where many people called on them to recuse.

While the normative aspects of recusal – and specific instances of failing to recuse – are important to examine, that is not the central theme of this chapter. We do not proscribe whether and when justices should recuse. There are legal arguments for strict and broad readings of recusal law. Instead, our goal is empirical in nature. We examine the conditions under which justices recuse and, more specifically, how conscientiousness influences those recusal decisions. We seek to uncover whether increasingly conscientious justices are more likely to recuse themselves than less conscientious justices. They are.

The results show that highly conscientious justices are 100 percent more likely to recuse themselves than less conscientious justices. Though the overall probability of recusal is small – as we would expect from justices on a court of last resort – this percent change is noteworthy. We also find evidence that less conscientious justices remain involved in cases where it might otherwise be appropriate for them to recuse. Perhaps, then, Court watchers should not have been surprised that Justice Kagan, who scores in the bottom 25 percent of justices in terms of conscientiousness, stayed on in *NFIB* v. *Sebelius*. These findings reveal, once again, that conscientiousness plays a significant role in justices' behavior.

12.1 FEDERAL RECUSAL LAW

We start by highlighting just what judicial recusal is. Simply put, recusal is: "the exclusion of a judge or justice from participating in an individual case" (Verilli 2016, xii). In other words, the judge has some conflict of interest – or appears to have one – and therefore does not preside in the case. A conventional case for recusal occurs where a judge's family member or former law partner is a party to a case, or where a recently appointed Supreme Court justice previously ruled on the case while serving as a judge on a federal court of appeals. In both scenarios, the judge will recuse.[2]

Recusal serves two major purposes. The first is to protect litigants from biased judges. Since courts mete out justice, judges must be neutral and

---

[2] This, however, was not always the case. During the first one hundred years of the Court's existence, the justices "rode circuit," which involved physically traveling to federal circuits and hearing cases with district court judges. As recounted by Giles (2015), although district court judges were prohibited from re-ruling on cases on which they had decided, no similar restriction applied to justices who could vote on a case as both a circuit court judge and Supreme Court justice.

unbiased. Equal justice is a fundamental tenet of the rule of law. Indeed, the phrase "Equal Justice Under Law" is carved into the front entrance of the Supreme Court building. The Constitution speaks of due process and the right to an impartial jury. The Declaration of Independence castigates King George III for meddling in the colonial judicial system and biasing judges against colonists. The Federalist Papers repeatedly discuss the importance of independent tribunals. Federalist Number 10 states, "No man is allowed to be a judge in his own cause, because his interest would certainly bias his judgment, and, not improbably, corrupt his integrity" (Madison 1961, 59). These and other foundational documents show that our system of law requires unbiased judges. And recusal is a mechanism used to remove the biased or potentially biased judge.

The second purpose of judicial recusal is to protect courts' legitimacy (Verilli 2016, xii). For courts to operate effectively, the public must perceive them to be neutral and legitimate. Unlike the other branches of the federal government, the judiciary lacks a direct electoral connection to the people. Those branches earn trust and legitimacy through popular sovereignty and the belief in majority rule. But federal judges are not elected by the people. They are appointed by the president and confirmed by the senate. They serve for life, barring impeachment and removal for treason, bribery, or other high crimes and misdemeanors. They are separated from direct public control. Consequently, given this lack of an electoral connection to the people, judges' major source of power is the public perception of fairness and integrity. Justice Frankfurter once claimed, "The Court's authority ... rests on sustained public confidence in its moral sanction" (Caldeira 1986, 1209). For the judicial branch to survive, people must trust judges. The public will not attack a judiciary it trusts. Opportunistic political demagogues will gain little traction from attacking a judiciary the public trusts. The law of recusal exists, in part, to secure the public's confidence and trust in our courts.

12.2 THE EVOLUTION OF FEDERAL RECUSAL LAW

Early in the Supreme Court's history, justices followed narrow common law standards on recusal (Flamm 2017). These standards were quite unlike the standards of today. Relying on Blackstone and Coke, judges recused when they carried a financial interest in the outcome of a case (Blackstone 2016). As Virelli (2011) states, "[u]nder English common law, only a direct pecuniary interest in the outcome of a case was grounds for recusal, and then only where another judge was able to hear the case in place of the recused judge, what later became known as the rule of necessity" (1195). (The rule of necessity holds that a judge who otherwise ought to be disqualified from a case may nevertheless hear and decide it if no other judge can do so.)

With this narrow recusal standard in mind, Chief Justice Marshall decided – and wrote the opinion in – *Marbury* v. *Madison* (1803), despite the fact that he was the Secretary of State who failed to deliver William Marbury's commission. (The reader will recall that Marbury sued then-Secretary of State James Madison to deliver his presidentially signed commission to be a justice of the peace after Marshall neglected to do so.) Similarly, Justice William Johnson heard cases involving the federal government despite the fact that he remained close with President Jefferson and maintained Court-related correspondences with him. These connections did not involve pecuniary interests and, therefore, the justices did not recuse themselves. On the other hand, Chief Justice Marshall recused himself in *Martin* v. *Hunter's Lessee* (1816) because he had a pecuniary interest in the outcome of the case, having purchased the land with disputed title in the case from Denny Martin, the petitioner. Pecuniary interests triggered recusal; little else did.

Federal recusal law has changed over time. No longer do justices remain in cases when they have such connections with parties. But this is a fairly recent development. It took time for the law to expand.

For most of its history, federal law focused exclusively on lower federal court judges and ignored the Supreme Court. In 1792, Congress passed its first judicial recusal statute, but it wrote the law so as to apply only to lower federal court judges. What is more, it required recusals only for pecuniary reasons or where the judge previously had been counsel for one of the parties (Virelli 2011, 1196). In 1821, Congress passed a law that required recusal when a lower federal court judge's relatives appeared before him (Verilli 2016, 5). In 1891, Congress required that federal circuit court judges recuse themselves from cases in which they had presided as trial court judges. And in 1911, Congress prohibited lower federal court judges from deciding cases in which they had been material witnesses (Id.). One can see in the evolution an expansion of the grounds for reversal. Still, these laws applied only to lower federal court judges. That would soon change.

Congress eventually, in 1948, adopted recusal legislation that applied to Supreme Court justices. The 1948 law "required recusal where a judge *or justice* had been a material witness, had been of counsel, or was related to an attorney or party in the case" or where the judge or justice had "substantial" financial interests in the case (Verilli 2016, 9, emphasis added). Later, in 1974, Congress revised the law to require justices to recuse where a reasonable person could reasonably question the justice's impartiality.

Today, 28 U.S.C. §455 governs most Supreme Court recusals. The first section, 28 U.S.C. §455(a), states that justices should recuse themselves when their impartiality might be questioned: "Any justice . . . shall disqualify himself in any proceeding in which his impartiality might reasonably be questioned." The second subsection, 28 U.S.C. §455(b), is more specific. It states that a judge or justice *shall* disqualify himself:

1. Where he has a personal bias or prejudice concerning a party, or personal knowledge of disputed evidentiary facts concerning the proceeding;
2. Where in private practice he served as lawyer in the matter in controversy, or a lawyer with whom he previously practiced law served during such association as a lawyer concerning the matter, or the judge or such lawyer has been a material witness concerning it;
3. Where he has served in governmental employment and in such capacity participated as counsel, adviser or material witness concerning the proceeding or expressed an opinion concerning the merits of the particular case in controversy;
4. He knows that he, individually or as a fiduciary, or his spouse or minor child residing in his household, has a financial interest in the subject matter in controversy or in a party to the proceeding, or any other interest that could be substantially affected by the outcome of the proceeding; or
5. He or his spouse, or a person within the third degree of relationship to either of them, or the spouse of such a person [has a connection to the case].

The due process clause also governs judicial recusal. In *Caperton* v. *A.T. Massey Coal Co.* (2009),[3] the Supreme Court recognized that the Due Process Clause of the Fourteenth Amendment (and, we suspect, the Fifth Amendment through reverse incorporation) governs judicial recusals.[4] The circumstances in *Caperton*, a West Virginia Supreme Court case, were shocking. The Harman Mining Company alleged that the A.T. Massey Coal Company wrongly cancelled its coal supply contract. At trial, the jury found in favor of Harman and awarded it $50 million in damages.

As the case made its way through the appeals process, however, Don Blankenship, the chief executive officer of A. T. Massey Coal Company,

---

3   See *Caperton* v. *A.T. Massey Coal Co.*, 556 U.S. 868 (2009).
4   See also *Tumey* v. *Ohio*, 273 U.S. 510 (1927) (where a judge's income from fines created an unlawful pecuniary interest).

sought to replace an incumbent justice on the High Court with one who might be more sympathetic to Massey Coal on appeal. (And yes, this was the same Don Blankenship who ran for US Senate in West Virginia in 2018, calling Senator Mitch McConnell "Cocaine Mitch" and railing against McConnell's connections to "Chinapeople.") Blankenship spent more than $3 million to elect Brent Benjamin and defeat sitting Justice Warren McGraw. Benjamin won the election, took his seat on the West Virginia Supreme Court, and went on to hear the appeal between Harman Mining and Massey Coal. Caperton, who was the president of Harman Mining, challenged Justice Benjamin's decision to stay on in the case. He believed Benjamin ought to have recused because he had a conflict of interest – the millions of dollars Blankenship spent to get him elected. Benjamin refused. The West Virginia Court went on to rule 3-2 in favor of Massey Coal, with Benjamin casting the deciding vote. Caperton then appealed to the US Supreme Court.

The High Court held that Benjamin's refusal to recuse violated the Fourteenth Amendment. Writing for a 5-4 majority, Justice Kennedy expressed:

> We conclude that there is serious risk of actual bias [and constitutional harm] – based on objective and reasonable perceptions – when a person with a personal stake in a particular case had a significant and disproportionate influence in placing the judge on the case by raising funds or directing the judge's election campaign when the case was pending or imminent. The inquiry centers on the contribution's relative size in comparison to the total amount of money contributed to the campaign, the total amount spent in the election, and the apparent effect such contribution had on the outcome of the election.[5]

As far as Kennedy and the other majority justices were concerned, there was simply too much personal interest to avoid recusal. "Blankenship's significant and disproportionate influence coupled with the temporal relationship between the election and the pending case" ought to have led Justice Benjamin to recuse.[6] The due process clause required recusal.

12.3 CURRENT RECUSAL PRACTICE

Still, these recusal rules – statutory and constitutional – do less to force Supreme Court justices to recuse than one might think. After all, §455

---

[5] See *Caperton* at 884.
[6] 556 U.S. at 886.

does not provide any guidance on the process justices should follow when determining whether to recuse. Nor does it offer any way to appeal a justice's refusal to recuse. Congress stated a general policy on the matter but then left it to justices to determine whether and when to recuse. The Court has described §455(a) as designed to "promote confidence in the judiciary by avoiding even the appearance of impropriety whenever possible." *Liljeberg* v. *Health Service Acquisition Corp.* (1988). Yet, *each justice* determines whether "a reasonable observer who is informed of all the surrounding facts and circumstances" would think he or she should recuse. Each justice, solely on his or her own, decides whether to recuse. As Chief Justice Roberts wrote in his 2011 Year End Report to Congress:

> [T]he individual Justices decide for themselves whether recusal is warranted under Section 455. They may consider recusal in response to a request from a party in a pending case, or on their own initiative. They may also examine precedent and scholarly publications, seek advice from the Court's Legal Office, consult colleagues, and even seek counsel from the Committee on Codes of Conduct … I have complete confidence in the capability of my colleagues to determine when recusal is warranted. They are jurists of exceptional integrity and experience whose character and fitness have been examined through a rigorous appointment and confirmation process. I know that they each give careful consideration to any recusal questions that arise in the course of their judicial duties. We are all deeply committed to the common interest in preserving the Court's vital role as an impartial tribunal governed by the rule of law (Roberts 2011, 8).

Illustrative of this practice is the Court's 1993 Statement of Recusal Policy (Verilli 2016, 30). There, seven of the nine justices signed on to a recusal policy that related to close relatives who practice law. The justices held that they would recuse when the relative took part in a case before the Court; conversely, if a relative was an associate at a firm that was involved in a case before the Court, but had not taken part in it at the Court or previously, the Justice would participate. What is important about the Statement – and that newly appointed justices continue to rely on it – is that the justices did not actually interpret §455. The justices "referenced the statute but employed few if any of the traditional tools of statutory interpretation" to adopt the Statement or guide their decisions to recuse (Verilli 2016, 33).

To be sure, 28 U.S.C. §455(b) is more specific in defining when justices should recuse. But even here, the law leaves it to the justices to determine when to recuse. And, perhaps just as importantly, as the Court of last resort, their decisions are final and unreviewable by any other court, or even by their colleagues on the Court.

Complicating matters further, justices strongly dislike recusal. They are inclined to hear all the cases they can. As Justice Ginsburg put it:

> [I]f one of us is out, that leaves eight, and the attendant risk that we will be unable to decide the case, that it will divide evenly ... When cases divide evenly, we affirm the decision below automatically. Because there's no substitute for a Supreme Court Justice, it is important that we not lightly recuse ourselves. (Ginsburg 2004)

This begs the question: Why do justices recuse? And under what conditions do they do so?

While there is considerable scholarship on recusals, most of it is normative or circumstantial (Flamm 2017; Henke 2013; Sample 2013; Verilli 2012; Bam 2011; McKeown 2011; Geyh 2010; Bassett 2005; Black and Epstein 2005; Frost 2005; Stempel 1987). Much of this is by necessity. Because the Court is so secretive, we hardly have enough data to paint a masterpiece. But neither are we forced to scribble in broad swaths with crayons. There is just enough data to make at least some sense of the justices' recusal decisions.

What little data exist on recusal offer some lessons (see, e.g., Hume 2014, 2017). For starters, the data suggest that justices are more likely to recuse when they have financial interests in the case. They are more likely to recuse when the petitioner and respondent are businesses, corporations, or financial institutions. As Hume tells us, when there are no such business interests in the case, the average justice has a 1.2 percent probability of recusing. But when both parties are business interests (and justices therefore are more likely to have stocks related to the case), that probability increases to 2.8 percent (Hume 2014, 643). These results accord with the statutory commands that justices recuse when their impartiality might be questioned and when they have financial connections to a case.

Additionally, recently appointed justices are much more likely to recuse than time-tested justices. A justice in his or her first year at the High Court tends to recuse in roughly 12.8 percent of cases. A veteran justice of ten years recuses in only 3.8 percent of cases (Hume 2014, 644). Justices who previously served as Solicitor General are more likely to recuse, as they have had direct experiences with many of the cases now coming to the Court. The more likely they are connected to a case, the more likely they are to recuse. It also appears that justices are more likely to recuse in statutory cases and when they are less concerned with clearing up conflict in the lower courts (Hume 2014, 646).

Finally, the literature suggests that justices near the median of the Court, and those on the extreme, are less likely to recuse than those a mild distance from the median. Hume (2014) suggests that justices near the median are less likely to recuse because their positions tend to win on the merits of cases. And justices on the extreme ends, he argues, are less likely to recuse because their participation "is needed for their attitudes to be represented" (646).

These results, however useful, tell us nothing about whether justices' personalities influence their decision to recuse. Consider two hypothetical justices. Both are liberals. Both previously served as circuit court judges. And both have the same financial investments. One recuses in a case; the other does not. Why? Our answer, at least in part, turns on their conscientiousness.

12.4 A THEORY OF CONSCIENTIOUSNESS AND RECUSAL

The connection between recusal and conscientiousness seems fairly evident. And by now, you've probably read enough descriptions of conscientiousness to be able to recite this from memory. As we discussed throughout the book, conscientiousness focuses in large part on a person's dutifulness and tendency to follow rules. Roberts et al. (2014, 1315) define it as a "propensity to be self-controlled, responsible to others, hardworking, orderly, and rule abiding." Others have argued that conscientiousness "describes socially prescribed impulse control" (John and Srivastava 1999, 121). It is the ability to put goals and work ahead of frivolity and personal interests.

Recusal thus seems bound up with conscientiousness. Hume's (2017) decision tree begins with the assessment of whether federal law demands recusal. Even at this initial stage, we can see a clear role for conscientiousness since following rules matters more to the highly conscientious justice than to the less conscientious justice. To the extent that ambiguity exists, a justice high on the conscientiousness trait would err on the side of recusing. Her low-conscientious colleague would not.

There are a number of additional instances in Hume's account where a justice needs to make similar judgment calls before deciding whether to participate or recuse. For example, justices must evaluate whether their non-participation would create an "institutional or policy hardship." As Hume notes, "when the institutional or policy hardships imposed by a recusal are likely to be small, a justice might choose to withdraw from a case to reinforce the impression that the Court is generally in compliance with the recusal statute" (2017, 40).[7] When weighing these considerations, we expect

---

7 This conjecture also accords with the research of Gibson and Caldeira (2012), who performed a series of survey experiments to examine the effects of a failure to recuse on judicial legitimacy

that the decision-making calculus of highly conscientious justices will place significantly greater weight on the importance of showing compliance with the law, which will increase the rates at which they recuse as compared to less conscientious justices.

This dynamic applies not only to the individual conflicts identified by the recusal statute, but also to the more general catch-all category of when a justice's impartiality could "reasonably be questioned." In this instance, according to Hume's theoretical model, a justice first must assess whether this statement is true. If yes, she performs the same assessment about the institutional or policy hardship that a recusal might create. Again, the connection with conscientiousness should be clear. Highly conscientious justices will be more likely to conclude that a possibility of bias exists. Furthermore, having answered yes to the bias inquiry, the justice ends up performing the same assessment with respect to the institutional or policy hardship.

Given this, we have a number of expectations for the effect of conscientiousness on a justice's recusal behavior. First, we expect that conscientiousness will exert an unconditional and positive effect on recusal. Rules matter more to the conscientious justice and so when evaluating whether participation will violate the law, the conscientious justice will be more likely to hew to a strict reading of the law. Empirically, this means we will observe a positive correlation between conscientiousness and the probability of recusal.

Second, conscientiousness should interact with the various statutory, institutional, and policy considerations that justices evaluate. That is, we expect statutory or institutional concerns will exacerbate the probability of recusal among highly conscientious justices. For example, financial conflicts are most likely to arise in cases involving businesses or corporations. If so, justices will be more likely to recuse in such cases. We expect, then, to observe a higher probability of recusal in such cases. But we also expect to see conscientiousness magnify the effect. A conscientious justice should be particularly responsive to the presence of multiple litigants who are financial entities (and might generate a financial conflict of interest).

At the same time, we also believe that conscientious justices may be more likely to stay involved in cases that call out for Supreme Court review. Like gravity, institutional reasons may pull a justice toward a case. For example, justices are more likely to vote to hear cases where the lower courts conflict over the interpretation of law or where a lower court judge dissented

among state court judges. The results strongly suggested that respondents held negative views of the court and the judge who refuses to recuse.

in the case. Most people believe the Court should step in to resolve legal conflict and legal ambiguity. If a justice recuses, however, the Court will be left with only eight justices to decide the matter. This departure creates the possibility of a 4-4 evenly divided court, which might prevent the Court from clarifying the law (but see Black and Bryan 2014). Given the Court's unique ability to clarify the law, a justice should be less likely to recuse when legal conflict and ambiguity are present. And we expect to observe an exacerbating effect of such institutional considerations among justices who are highly conscientious.

Unlike statutory or institutional factors, policy considerations uniformly push a justice to participate in a case when she otherwise, perhaps, should not (recall the example of Justice Kagan from the beginning of this chapter). That is, there is no circumstance where a justice's policy goals are better served by sitting out and giving up her ability to write, critique, or otherwise influence the Court's majority opinion. Accordingly, our expectation is that conscientiousness should have an attenuating effect on such policy variables. Whereas all justices see possible gains to be had, a justice who is highly conscientious discounts policy considerations in light of her desire to follow the rules and exercise self-restraint.

12.5 DATA AND MEASURES

Our underlying data come from Hume (2017), which provides the most systematic analysis to date of recusals by US Supreme Court justices. Hume's data cover the Court's 1946–2010 terms, representing more than 8,300 cases and 74,000 individual observations spread across 36 justices. We merge these data with our personality measures.

Dependent Variable. Our dependent variable, *Recuse*, comes directly from Hume's data and measures whether a justice recused in a case. If a justice recused, we code the variable as 1; 0 otherwise.[8] Hume removed cases where justices withdrew because of illness or because they came to the Court after oral arguments (2017, 49–50). The end result, then, is a measure that indicates when each justice discretionarily removed himself or herself from a case.

Figure 63 provides a descriptive snapshot of recusal practices across the sixty-five terms in the data. The x-axis of both the top and bottom panels

---

[8] To code it, Hume looked to the *Vote* variable in the Justice Centered version of the Supreme Court Database. When the entry for the justice included a "." it meant that the justice "was on the bench but did not participate" (638).

shows the Court's term. The y-axis in the top panel shows the proportion of justice-level recusals during a given term. Although the overall rate of recusal is about 1.6 percent, there is considerable term-to-term variation in recusal activity, with a handful of terms observing no discretionary recusals at all. The pronounced upward spike in 2010 corresponds to Justice Kagan's first term on the Court, where she recused in more than one-third of her observations in the data (i.e., twenty-nine out of eighty-five instances). Her high recusal rate is due to the fact that she was the US Solicitor General immediately prior to joining the Court and was therefore personally involved as an attorney with a number of the Court's cases. Thurgood Marshall also moved directly from SG to justice and, not surprisingly, he displayed a similar recusal pattern in his first year on the Court. He recused in almost 40 percent of his observations. His raw number of recusals (seventy-eight total) is nearly equal to the total number of participation opportunities associated with Justice Kagan (eighty-five total). (This, of course, shows how many more cases the Court heard during the 1960s than it does today.)

Although recusal is not especially common at the level of an individual justice, it is far more common as a Court-related phenomenon than many would anticipate. The bottom panel of Figure 63 displays these data. Here, the y-axis now reports the proportion of cases decided by the Court in a given term where at least one justice recused. Across our sixty-five terms of data, the overall average is about 12 percent. Thus, although recusal is not an everyday phenomenon, it occurs with some regularity.

Conscientiousness. Our main covariate of interest is *Conscientiousness*, which we discuss thoroughly in Chapter 3. We also control for justices' scores on the four other personality traits – *Openness, Extraversion, Agreeableness*, and *Neuroticism*.

The remainder of the independent variables come directly from Hume's (2017) replication data, which he most graciously (and promptly!) shared. We provide brief explanations of these covariates to offer readers with a full list of the ingredients that go into our statistical soup. We note within the parentheses after each variable name whether the factor is identified by Hume as being statutory, policy, or institutional.

Business Petitioner/Respondent (statutory). This variable accounts for whether the parties to the case represented business interests. We do so because justices are more likely to recuse when they have fiduciary connections to a case, and those connections are more likely to exist when business interests are involved. We code the variable as 2 if both parties are business interests, 1 if one of the parties is a business interest, and 0 if none of the parties are business interests.

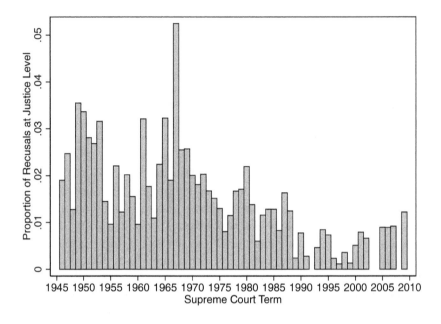

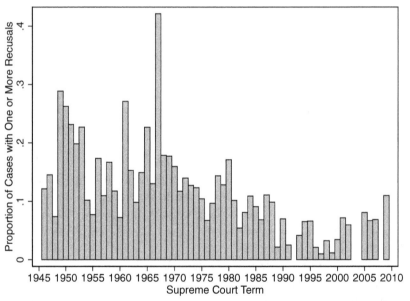

FIGURE 63: *Descriptive data on the relative frequency of discretionary recusals on the US Supreme Court.* The top panel presents the data at the level of the individual justice and the bottom panel displays the Court overall. These data come from Hume (2017).

Years of Service (statutory). This measure counts the numbers of years the justice served prior to the date the Court released its decision. Hume (2017) also includes the squared value of *Years of Service*. The intuition is that justices who have been appointed more recently will be more likely to have conflicts of interest from previous positions in the federal judiciary – conflicts that will lead them to recuse.

Solicitor General (statutory). This variable is a binary indicator that accounts for whether (=1) or not (=0) the justice previously served as US Solicitor General.

Solicitor General × *Years of Service* (statutory). This variable accounts for the fact that justices who are former SGs are more likely to recuse early in their career (while the cases on which they worked are still percolating) than later in their careers.

Federal Appellate Experience (statutory). This variable is a binary indicator that accounts for whether (=1) or not (=0) the justice previously served as a circuit court of appeals judge.

Federal Appellate Experience × *Years of Service* (statutory). This interaction accounts for the fact that justices who are former circuit court judges are more likely to recuse early in their career (while the cases over which they presided are still percolating) than later in their careers.

Conflict (institutional). This variable account for whether the justices noted, in their majority opinion, that they granted review to resolve a legal conflict among the lower courts. If so, the variable equals 1; 0 otherwise.

Dissent Below (institutional) The presence of a dissent in the lower court often sends a strong signal about the importance of a case, especially given that circuit court judges tend not to dissent. Their refusal is partly a function of time constraints (they hear so many cases per year that they cannot dissent often) and partly a function of norms against dissenting. Whatever the reason, it is clear that a dissent signals something important and needs to be taken into account. *Dissent Below* equals 1 when the Supreme Court Database records a lower court dissent in the case; 0 otherwise.

Case Salience (institutional). This measure of salience relies on the method employed by Epstein and Segal (2000). They examined whether a case made the front page of the *New York Times* the day after the Court released its decision. If so, we code the variable as 1; 0 otherwise.

Statutory Case (institutional). This variable accounts for whether the case involved a matter of statutory (as opposed to constitutional) interpretation. If so, it is coded as 1; 0 otherwise.

Median Ideological Distance (policy). This variable captures the ideological distance, using Martin-Quinn scores (Martin and Quinn 2002), between each individual justice and the median justice. Hume also includes *Median Ideological Distance Squared* and *Median Ideological Distance Cubed*. The expectation for these measures is that as a justice becomes distant from the median, she will be more likely to recuse because of her weakened ability to influence legal policy. Once a justice is sufficiently far from the median, however, the recusal probability is hypothesized to decrease again because the justice is now interested in recording a dissenting view.

Lower Court Ideological Distance (policy). This variable reports a justice's ideological (in)congruence with the direction of the lower court decision. To generate it, Hume multiplied the Martin-Quinn score of each justice with the ideological direction of the decision. Increasingly positive values correspond to agreement while increasingly negative values indicate disagreement.

Chief Justice (control). Hume included binary variables to account for each of the Chief Justices who served during the sample period. Different Chiefs might establish internal norms about the usage of recusals. Chief Justice Rehnquist, for instance, was a well-known believer in the duty-to-sit doctrine.

12.6 METHODS AND RESULTS

Given the dichotomous dependent variable, we estimate a series of logistic regression models. Parameter estimates for these models appear in Table 29.[9] Our particular focus, as it has been for the preceding pages, is how conscientiousness relates to recusal behavior. As expected, *we find a positive and statistically significant relationship between justice conscientiousness and the likelihood of recusal.* That is, conscientious justices are significantly more likely to recuse.

Figure 64 illustrates the magnitude of this effect. Along the x-axis we display the range of *Conscientiousness*. The y-axis shows the probability of recusal by a justice. For the least conscientious justices, we estimate a less than 1 percent chance of recusing. A justice with an average level of conscientiousness has a 1.5 percent chance of recusing – an increase of 50 percent. And, a highly conscientious justice has a 2 percent chance of recusing – a 100 percent increase from the minimum.

In absolute terms, these values are far from overwhelming. One might, then, discount the role conscientiousness plays in this aspect of judicial

---

9 The empirical results are consistent when specifying a bivariate model that includes only conscientiousness (and no control predictors).

TABLE 29: *The Impact of Supreme Court Justice Conscientiousness on Discretionary Recusal*

	Model 1 Coefficient	RSE	Model 2 Coefficient	RSE
Conscientiousness	0.239*	0.045	0.163*	0.050
Agreeableness	−0.034	0.027	0.022	0.031
Neuroticism	0.100*	0.035	0.253*	0.040
Openness	−0.021	0.023	−0.028	0.023
Extraversion	0.166*	0.036	0.156*	0.043
Statutory Considerations				
Business Petitioner/Respondent			0.409*	0.052
Years of Service			−0.183*	0.014
Squared Years of Service			0.005*	0.000
Solicitor General			2.106*	0.158
Solicitor General × Years of Service			−0.120*	0.020
Federal Appellate Experience			−0.332*	0.124
Federal App. Exp. × Years of Service			0.032*	0.010
Institutional Considerations				
Dissent Below			−0.103	0.086
Conflict			−0.658*	0.108
Case Salience			0.141	0.098
Case Statutory			0.433*	0.070
Policy Considerations				
Median Ideological Distance			−0.694*	0.114
Squared Median Ideo. Dist.			0.229*	0.045
Cubed Median Ideo. Dist.			−0.020*	0.005
Lower Court Ideological Distance			0.019	0.016
Vinson Court			0.238	0.151
Warren Court			0.191*	0.085
Rehnquist Court			−0.692*	0.139
Roberts Court			−1.067*	0.246
Constant	−4.066*	0.043	−3.306*	0.130
N	73811		73811	
χ^2	68.86*		1047.45*	

Note: Table entries for each model are coefficients from a logit regression model ("Coefficient") with clustered standard errors on the case ("RSE"). Model 1 includes only the personality trait measures. Model 2 adds the numerous variables from Hume's (2017) Model B. The Burger Court is the omitted baseline category with respect to the Chief Justice regime dummy variables. *$p < 0.05$ (two-tailed).

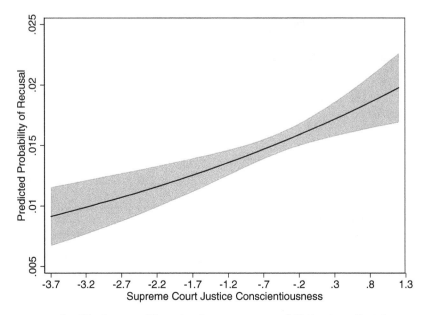

FIGURE 64: *The impact of Conscientiousness on recusal.* Estimates reflect the predicted probability (with 90% confidence intervals) of recusal across the observed range of *Conscientiousness* using results from Model 2 in Table 29. All other variables are held at their median values.

decision making. That would be misguided, however. The low percentages are driven not by the unimportance of conscientiousness but, rather, by the relatively rare occurrences of recusals. Recall the descriptive figures presented earlier, which show that although recusal occurs at the *case level* with some regularity (about 12 percent of all cases from 1946 to 2010), as a *justice-level* phenomenon it is (necessarily) less common. To wit, of the nearly 75,000 instances of participation we examine, a recusal occurs in only 1.6 percent (or, roughly 1,000) of them.

Moreover, the substantive magnitude of our result compares favorably with other factors that Hume (2017) identifies as correlating with recusals. The increase in recusal likelihood across the range of our conscientiousness measure is about 1.1 percentage points. This is twice as large as the impact of legal conflict (which reduces the probability of recusal) and more than twice as large as the impact of having a business litigant in a case (which increases the likelihood of a justice recusing). In short, recusal might be uncommon, but conscientiousness is a strong predictor of it when it occurs, and it compares favorably with other variables that influence recusal.

Looking at our controls, among the other four traits of the Big Five, we find no systematic relationship between a justice's recusal tendencies and either agreeableness or openness. The data suggest a positive relationship between both neuroticism and extraversion and the likelihood of recusal. All other controls perform as expected, besides *Dissent Below* and *Case Salience*, neither of which are statistically significant.

Beyond the unconditional effect just discussed, we also hypothesized that an interplay would exist between judicial conscientiousness and the statutory, institutional, and policy factors that affect the recusal decision. This stems mainly from our belief that justices might differentially weight such considerations depending on their level of conscientiousness. For instance, a justice who is less conscientious will find the pull of policy factors to be more important than a conscientious justice. Conversely, factors that counsel toward recusal will be more impactful for the highly conscientious justice. More generally, these interactions capture the close theoretical linkage between these variables and the foundational attributes of what it means for a justice to have high (or low) levels of conscientiousness.

To probe these expectations, we estimated a series of models in which we interacted conscientiousness with the statutory, institutional, and policy considerations identified by Hume and discussed previously. To keep things tractable, we did so iteratively, which is to say we estimated a model that interacted conscientiousness with the lower court disagreement variable and then a second model with the ideological distance from the median, and so on. Given the large number of constitutive variables we examined, we begin with Table 30, which provides a quick summary of the results we obtain for each of the interactions we evaluated. The columns in the table identify the type of consideration, which comes from Hume's classification, the specific variant of that consideration from the underlying model, and, finally, whether we recover the hypothesized interaction between that variable and our conscientiousness measure. A "✓" indicates that an interactive effect exists, whereas a "×" denotes that it does not. To be clear, the failure to recover an *interactive* effect does *not* mean that conscientiousness ceases to matter for the recusal decision. Rather, it indicates that although an unconditional effect exists, conscientiousness does not differentially activate the specific consideration being evaluated.

Overall, we find evidence of an interactive effect across all three consideration types. Starting with statutory considerations, we find that a justice's level of conscientiousness is associated with a differential response to the number of business or financial litigants involved in a case. Recall that this measure identifies the number of parties before the Court that represent business

TABLE 30: *Summary of Conscientiousness-Consideration Interactions*

Consideration	Variable	Result
Statutory	Business Pet./Resp.	✓
Statutory	Years of Service	✗
Statutory	Solicitor General Service	✗
Statutory	Federal Appellate Service	✓
Institutional	Dissent Below	✓
Institutional	Conflict	✗
Institutional	Case Salience	✗
Institutional	Case Statutory	✓
Policy	Median Ideological Dist.	✓
Policy	Lower Court Ideo. Dist.	✗
Norms	Chief Justice Regime	✓

interests, and takes on a value of 0, 1, or 2. We estimate a model that interacts *Conscientiousness* with the *Business Petitioner/Respondent* variable. Because there are only three possible values for this measure, we treat each one as its own distinct dichotomous measure for the purpose of the interaction. That is, we generate three exhaustive and mutually exclusive dummy variables for whether (1) neither party was a business, (2) only one party was a business, or (3) both parties were businesses. We select one of these (arbitrarily) as the omitted category to avoid perfect multicollinearity and then interact the other two with our conscientiousness measure. This allows us, substantively, to determine if *Conscientiousness* differentially impacts recusal when parties are businesses.

Results from this model appear in Figure 65. The x-axis shows the level of business involvement in a case. As in previous figure, the y-axis shows the likelihood a justice recuses. The plot type differentiates between a justice of low (circle) versus high (square) conscientiousness. Consistent with our initial, unconditional results, conscientious justices recuse with a higher probability than their less conscientious colleagues (i.e., the squares are all above the circles). And, consistent with Hume's original findings, there is a significant increase for both low and highly conscientious justices in the probability of recusal when one litigant is a business interest as compared to when none are.

The conditioning aspect of conscientiousness becomes apparent – albeit subtly – when looking at the effect of moving from only one party as a business interest to both parties as business interests (i.e., the middle to right-most points in the figure). When this happens, a justice who is high in conscientiousness responds with a modest, yet statistically significant, increase in her

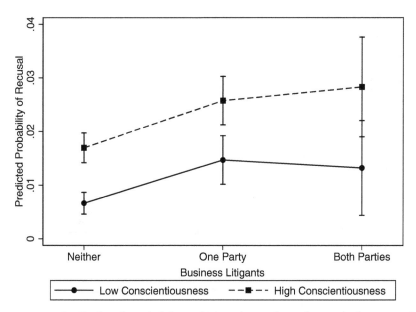

FIGURE 65: *Predicted probability of recusal, conditional on involvement of businesses as litigants in a case (x-axis) and the level of justice conscientiousness (different point shape and line type).* All other variables are held at their median values.

likelihood of recusing ($p < 0.05$, two-tailed test). Such is not the case for the less conscientious justice, however, who is no more (or less) likely to recuse when the number of business interests as parties increases to two. What is more, the low conscientious justice is no more or less likely to recuse when both parties are of business interest than she is when neither of the parties are ($p = 0.19$, two-tailed test).

We also find significant evidence of a statutory interaction with respect to whether a justice previously served as a federal court of appeals judge. To isolate this effect, we follow Hume's modeling strategy and examine whether conscientiousness conditions the interaction between the number of years a justice served and her previous experience on a federal court of appeals. The intuition is fairly straightforward: Justices who recently came from a US Court of Appeals to the High Court are, by virtue of having recently participated in circuit court cases, likely to have a large initial number of conflicts that remove them from a case. As time passes, however, cases with their previous participation will be "flushed" from the federal court system and so their recusal rates should reduce. To this argument, we simply add an examination of whether a justice's conscientiousness conditions this relationship.

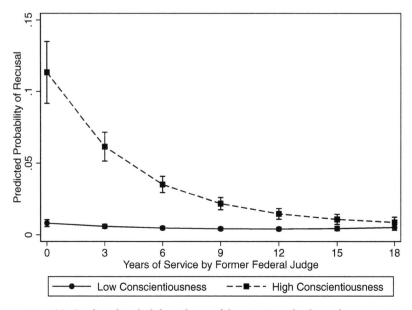

FIGURE 66: *Predicted probability of recusal for a justice who formerly was a circuit court judge, conditional on years of service on the Supreme Court (x-axis) and the level of justice conscientiousness (different point shape and line type).* All other variables are held at their median values.

Figure 66 plots the results of our analysis. The x-axis provides the number of years of *Supreme Court* service engaged in by a sitting justice who, prior to her appointment to the High Court, served as a circuit court judge. And, as before, the y-axis is the probability of recusal, with justice conscientiousness is denoted in the plot by the differential line/point types. As one can clearly see, the conditioning effect of conscientiousness is striking.

During a justice's first year on the Supreme Court, our results suggest that a highly conscientious justice has roughly 0.11 probability of recusing herself.[10] This probability drops off quickly as a justice's former experience becomes more distant. By contrast, a recently promoted former circuit court judge who is low in terms of her conscientiousness has just a 0.01 probability of recusing herself, all else equal. And, this non-recusal tendency remains essentially constant for the low-conscientious justice throughout her first eighteen years on the bench. Stated a bit differently, our results suggest that it is

---

[10] Note that for these hypotheticals, we define low versus high conscientiousness with respect to the actual observed values among former circuit court judges. Thus, we use values of −1.9 (low) and 0.9 (high), as opposed to full population values of −3.7 and 1.2.

only the most conscientious justices who opt to remove themselves from cases where they might have some conflict having been involved in the case in the lower court.

As suggested by the × marks in Table 30, we fail to find an interactive relationship between conscientiousness and either years of service or when a justice was previously the Solicitor General. This simply means that whether a justice is low or high with respect to conscientiousness does not significantly alter how either of these variables influences her propensity to recuse. As it turns out, service is negatively correlated with the probability of recusal and previously being the Solicitor General is positively related, but this effect itself is conditioned by the years of service as a justice (under a similar logic to the circuit court judge variable). For the sake of completeness, we provide graphs showing these results in Figure 71 (service) and Figure 72 (Solicitor General) in this chapter's appendix.

Consider, next, how conscientiousness conditions institutional factors. We hypothesized that highly conscientious justices would be more attuned to the importance of these factors and weigh them more heavily than justices low on the trait. We find supportive evidence for two such factors: *Dissent Below* and *Case Statutory*. Starting with the presence of a dissent below, Hume argues that justices will be less likely to recuse themselves when there is evidence from the lower courts that a case is controversial. This is true because such divisiveness might carry up to the Court and create a heightened risk of dead-lock. To assess this, we again interact our conscientiousness measure with whether a dissent was noted in the lower court's opinion. Figure 67 shows our substantive results.

Given the dichotomous nature of the presence of dissent, our presentational format has shifted slightly. In particular, we now put the level of conscientiousness on the x-axis and use the y-axis to indicate the marginal effect of moving from a hypothetical case with no dissent noted to one where there is dissent. To help put the marginal effect in perspective, note that the overall baseline probability of recusal across the entire data set is approximately 0.015.

As the figure illustrates, when viewing a low-conscientious justice, the point estimate for the marginal effect is actually positive – suggesting that she is more likely to recuse – though since the confidence interval contains zero, we cannot say it is statistically significant (p = 0.38, two-tailed). As a justice's conscientiousness increases, we see a gradual decrease in the estimated marginal effect. This indicates, substantively, that more conscientious justices are more likely to take seriously the risk of divisiveness with respect to their participation decision, which is consistent with our expectation that they will

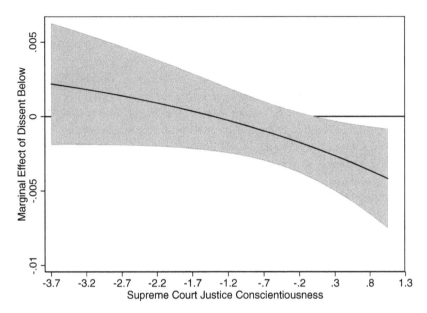

FIGURE 67: *Marginal effect of noted dissent in lower court on the probability of recusal, conditional on justice conscientiousness (x-axis).* All other variables are held at their median values.

respond more to institutional considerations. For values of conscientiousness above approximately −1.2, we estimate the marginal effect to be negative; for values of −0.2 or larger, the effect is statistically significant (p < 0.10, two-tailed). Although this appears to be limited to only the right-most region of the figure, it applies to fully 42 percent of the observations in our data.

The second institutional factor conditioned by conscientiousness is whether the case involves statutory, as opposed to constitutional, interpretation. Here, the expectation is that institutional considerations should make a justice more likely to recuse in statutory cases. As Hume argues, "In matters of constitutional interpretation, the justices are the final authorities, and this heightened institutional responsibility is likely to create incentives for justices to participate to clarify important questions of law" (2017, 47). Figure 68 provides the results of our interactive assessment of this argument. The figure is oriented in an identical manner to the previous one, which is to say it portrays the marginal effect of moving from a case being one of constitutional interpretation to that of statutory interpretation.

As a preliminary matter, we note that for all observed levels of justice conscientiousness, we find that a justice is more likely to recuse when the case poses a question statutory interpretation. This is manifested visually by the fact

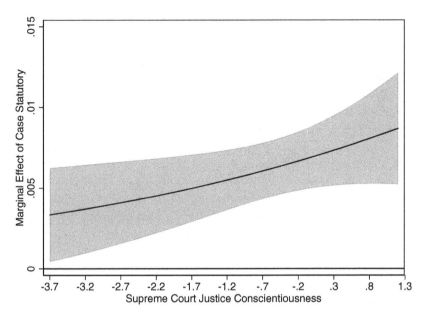

FIGURE 68: *Marginal effect of statutory interpretation case on the probability of recusal, conditional on justice conscientiousness (x-axis).* All other variables are held at their median values.

that the confidence interval for the marginal effect never crosses zero. But, as the plot reveals, we observe a modest positive slope to the marginal effect as the level of conscientiousness increases. That is, the presence of the statutory consideration matters more to a justice at the upper end of conscientiousness than it does to one who is lower on the trait. The marginal effect is about 2.6 times larger for the most conscientious justice in our data as compared to the least ($p = 0.11$).

There are also a couple of institutional considerations where we do not find a conditional effect with conscientiousness. Such is the case for both *Conflict* and *Case Salience*. In terms of the former, the results suggest that all justices are less likely to recuse when conflict is present in a case as opposed to when it is not. Unlike the statutory result just described, however, the magnitude of this effect is not appreciably different across the range of justice conscientiousness ($p = 0.44$, see Figure 73 in the appendix). As for the effect of *Case Salience*, we fail to find any significant relationship – regardless of conscientiousness – between the importance of a case and whether a justice participated in it. That is, the confidence interval for the marginal effect of salience always contains zero (see Figure 74).

Policy considerations, the third flavor of considerations we consider, are arguably the most controversial. Here, the justices' desire to retain influence on the Court's opinions lead them to participate in cases and refuse to recuse. We follow Hume and consider two varieties of this. First, we examine a justice's distance from the Court's median. The baseline expectation is that justices who are either very close or very distant from the median should be the least likely to recuse; those close to the median desire to influence the Court's majority opinion, while those who are distant have a similar appeal to make sure they can challenge the majority opinion – potentially by dissenting. As discussed previously, we hypothesize that conscientiousness should attenuate such policy-seeking relationships.

The two panels of Figure 69 show the results from this interactive model. The x-axes in both the top and bottom panels show a justice's ideological distance from the median. In the top panel, the y-axis displays the probability that a justice decides to recuse herself from a case. The solid line corresponds to a justice who is at the sample minimum on the conscientious scale. The dashed line, by contrast, is a justice who is at the sample maximum.

Consider the low-conscientious justice (the solid line). When that justice is at, or near, the median of the Court, she has well below a 1 percent chance of recusing. Why? Her absence would possibly deprive her of the opportunity to see her policy preferences etched into law. Her vote could be pivotal in the case. Her views would likely carry significant influence on the eventual opinion writer – assuming she was not the opinion writer herself. As we move this hypothetical justice farther from the median, however, her influence decreases, and so we observe a corresponding increase in her willingness to recuse. This effect plateaus when distance takes on a value in the 1.8 to 2.4 range, which is substantively equivalent to Justice Scalia's distance from Justice Kennedy in 2010 or Justice Stevens's distance from Justice Kennedy in 2008. As a justice becomes quite distant from the median, the probability of recusal gradually declines. Why? A justice this far from the median does not hope to influence the content of the majority but likely has in mind vocally dissenting, perhaps with a view toward keeping the majority coalition "honest" by poking and prodding it along. In other words, where control or voice matter least, less conscientious justices recuse. And where control or voice matter most, they stick around.

Now consider the highly conscientious justice (the dashed line). When that justice is at, or near, the median of the Court, she is much more likely to recuse than her less conscientious colleague. Indeed, *the conscientious justice is most likely to recuse precisely when she would have the most policy influence*. We estimate a greater than 3 percent chance that a highly conscientious

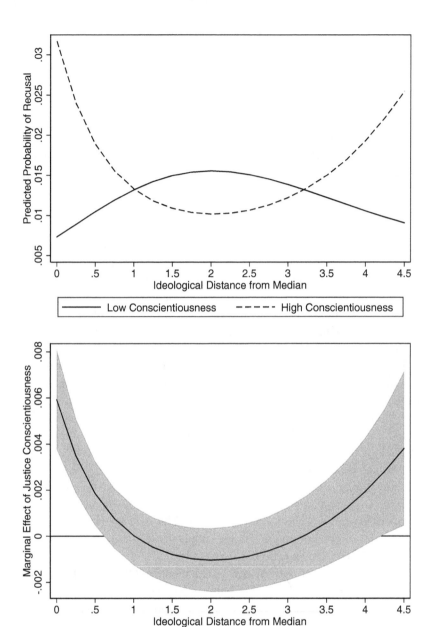

FIGURE 69: *Justice conscientiousness attenuates how ideological distance influences a justice's policy-motivated recusal behavior.* Whether a justice recuses when she is in an ideological position to exert influence (i.e., close to the median) depends upon her level of conscientiousness. The top panel presents the predicted probability of recusal, conditional on ideological distance (x-axis) and the level of justice conscientiousness (different line type). The bottom panel shows the marginal effect of a one-unit increase in justice conscientiousness, conditional on a justice's ideological distance from the median (x-axis). All other variables are held at their median values.

justice would recuse when she is at or near the median of the Court. This is more than *six times* the likelihood of the less conscientious justice. Moreover, a conscientious justice who is ideologically distant from the median recuses, even if that means losing her dissenting voice. The bottom panel of Figure 69 helps the interpretation. It presents the marginal effect of a one-unit increase in *Conscientiousness* conditional on a justice's ideological distance from the median. This plot is useful since the two lines in the top panel cross at two points and are reasonably close to each other for the middle range of ideological distance.

The bottom panel allows us to observe statistically meaningful effects for conscientiousness. If the shaded gray region (i.e., the 90 percent confidence interval) includes the dashed line, no difference exists between the high vs. low conscientious justice. As the panel makes clear, a difference does exist for two ranges of ideological distance: from 0 to roughly 0.6 and from around 4.2 to 4.5. Although these two ranges might seem relatively small on the figure, the left region actually includes nearly 35 percent of the observations in our analysis and the right-most region includes an additional 2 percent.

These results indicate that the policy-seeking motives of justices permeate into their recusal (and non-recusal) behavior. They also suggest, quite importantly, that conscientiousness substantially attenuates this behavior. Justices who value rules and norms are most likely to recuse precisely when they would have the most policy influence. Their less conscientious counterparts, by contrast, are the most likely to participate in these scenarios. Although we find strong support for the median ideological distance measure, we fail to find any similar effect for a justice's ideological distance from the lower court opinion. In particular, the results are consistent with those reported by Hume, who fails to recover a significant relationship. This does not change when we interact our conscientiousness measure with *Lower Court Ideological Distance* (see Figure 75 in the appendix).

Finally, we consider one last factor – the identity of the Chief Justice. We know that although the Chief has but a single vote, his leadership position allows him a considerable ability to shape the norms of the Court. The free-wheeling style of the Court's conference meetings under Chief Justice Burger, for instance, were quickly reined in under Chief Justice Rehnquist (Dickson 2001). Rehnquist was similarly known for being a stickler with respect to attorney's time limits at oral argument. Chief Justice Roberts, by contrast, provides attorneys additional time, particularly in important cases (Johnson and Black 2017). To the extent these are discretionary components, we might similarly expect to observe variation in recusal norms among different chiefs. This is all the more likely given that then-Associate Justice Rehnquist indicated his strong support for the duty-to-sit doctrine when he took the then unprecedented step of issuing a memorandum justifying his participation in *Laird* v. *Tatum* (1972).

The results of this analysis appear in the two panels of Figure 70. The top panel shows the results of a non-interactive model, which includes our traits measures but does not interact them with any of the Chief Justice indicators (i.e., Model 2 from Table 29 above). It provides some initial empirical evidence for the notion that the various chiefs have established different norms of behavior on their Courts. Although recusal rates were substantively the same under Chief Justices Vinson and Warren ($p = 0.73$), they nudged downward a bit under Chief Justice Burger ($p = 0.03$). This foreshadowed a significant drop under Chief Justice Rehnquist's leadership – the probability was essentially cut in half. Rehnquist's successor, Chief Justice Roberts, has shown a slight continuation of this tendency, with a recusal probability under his leadership that is marginally smaller than Rehnquist's ($p = 0.10$).

In the bottom panel of the figure, we now show the results of interacting justice conscientiousness with these Chief Justice regime indicators. For the tenures of Chief Justices Vinson, Warren, and Burger, we find that highly conscientious justices are, consistent with our earlier results, more likely to recuse than those lower on the trait. It is when we get to the Burger-Rehnquist transition that things get interesting (relatively speaking). Recall from just a moment ago that recusal probabilities shifted downward during the Rehnquist Court years. As the Chief, we suspect that Rehnquist established informal norms within the Court that counseled against recusing except when it was absolutely necessary. Such a position would be consistent with what we know about Rehnquist's beliefs regarding recusal. Interestingly, the data suggest that this policy shift was perceived, but only among highly conscientious justices. To wit, the probability that a high conscientious justice recuses drops from about 0.02 under Burger to just 0.006 under Rehnquist – a relative decrease of 70 percent that is statistically significant ($p < 0.01$). The Burger-Rehnquist change for a low conscientious justice, by contrast was in the opposite direction, though ultimately statistically insignificant ($p = 0.49$). This provides evidence that conscientiousness applies not just to well-defined rules or laws, but can also shape how a justice responds to broader aspects of institutional culture or norms.

12.7 CONCLUSION

In their work on the effects of recusal, Black and Epstein (2005) suggest that "it could be that certain kinds of justices, perhaps those who are pivotal in

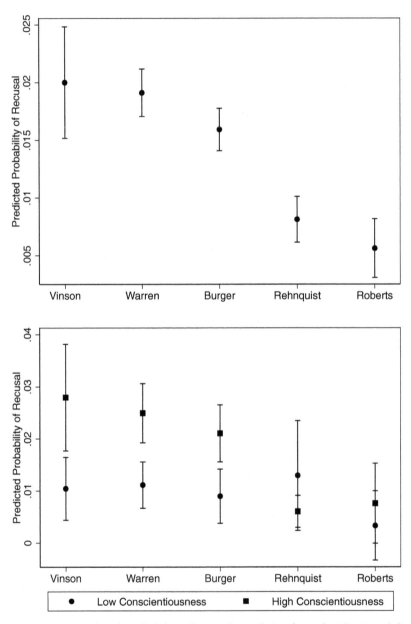

FIGURE 70: *Predicted probability of recusal, conditional on the identity of the Chief Justice.* The top panel comes from a non-interactive baseline model. The bottom panel shows the interaction between Chief Justice identity and individual justice conscientiousness. All other variables are held at their median values.

a particular area of law or who have been on the Court for some period of time" may be less likely to recuse. To their list of factors that could influence recusal, we add conscientiousness.

Recusal is an important normative topic that has received significant attention in recent years. In both the federal and, more often, the state judicial systems, scholars debate the merits of strong or weak recusal rules. Surprisingly, however, there is little empirical work on the conditions under which judges and justices recuse. Building off recent work by Hume, we address this issue.

We asked whether conscientiousness influences a justice's decision to recuse. We find a positive and statistically significant relationship between recusing and conscientiousness. Conscientious justices are twice as likely to recuse, all else equal, than non-conscientious justices. They do so, we believe, because they are more concerned with rules and obligations (and the appearance of legitimacy) than less conscientious justices. What is more, these conscientious justices recuse in precisely the circumstances when their less conscientious colleagues do not – when they otherwise would be tempted to stay in a case to obtain the policy they want. In short, conscientious justices are able to walk away from their policy preferences and recuse when their colleagues are not. We similarly find that conscientious justices are more sensitive to possible financial conflicts of interest and issues arising from cases that might have been involved with before joining the High Court. Taken together, these findings underscore the importance of justices' personalities to recusal practice and show that conscientiousness matters in yet another important empirical application of judicial behavior.

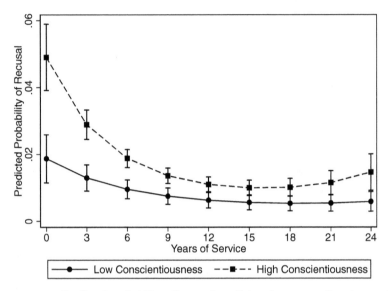

FIGURE 71: *Predicted probability of recusal conditional on years of service on the Supreme Court (x-axis) and the level of justice conscientiousness (different point shape and line type).* All other variables are held at their median values.

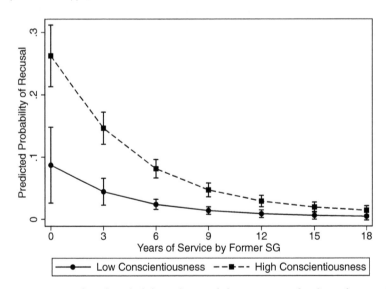

FIGURE 72: *Predicted probability of recusal for a justice who formerly was the Solicitor General, conditional on years of service on the Supreme Court (x-axis) and the level of justice conscientiousness (different point shape and line type).* All other variables are held at their median values.

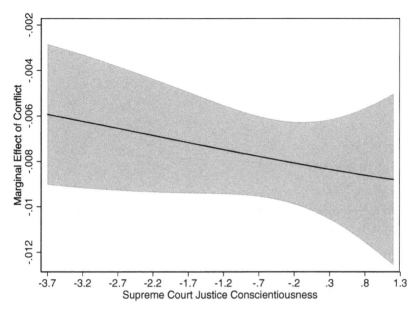

FIGURE 73: *Marginal effect of conflict on the probability of recusal, conditional on justice conscientiousness (x-axis).* All other variables are held at their median values.

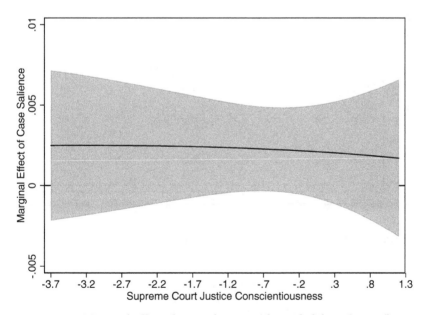

FIGURE 74: *Marginal effect of case salience on the probability of recusal, conditional on justice conscientiousness (x-axis).* All other variables are held at their median values.

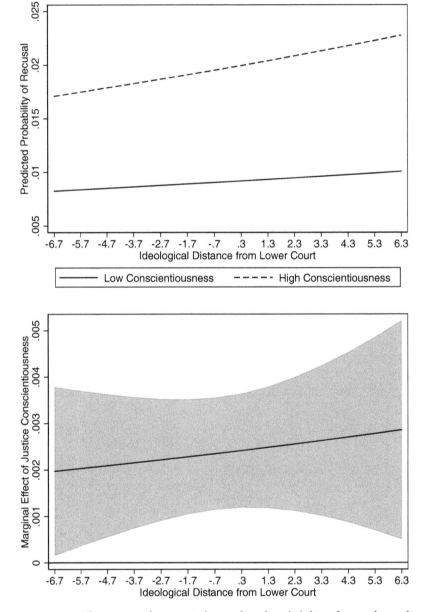

FIGURE 75: The top panel presents the predicted probability of recusal, conditional on ideological distance from the lower court (x-axis) and the level of justice conscientiousness (different line type). The effect of distance is insignificant for both low (p = 0.51) and high (p = 0.44) conscientiousness. The bottom panel shows the marginal effect of a one-unit increase in justice conscientiousness, conditional on a justice's ideological distance from the lower court (x-axis). The slope of this line is indistinguishable from zero (p = 0.67). All other variables are held at their median values.

13

Conclusion

Each March, more than fifty teams of mushers and sled dogs enter the Iditarod Trail Sled Dog Race in Alaska. The race is often said to commemorate the successful delivery of serum by sled dogs to Nome in 1925 when the town faced a diphtheria epidemic. This thousand-mile competition runs from Anchorage to Nome, through sparsely populated areas and with wind chills up to −100 degrees Fahrenheit. According to the rules, each musher must begin the race with 16 dogs on the towline – and end it with at least five.

To watch a highly trained team of sled dogs and their musher is to watch a finely tuned machine. When the musher commands the dogs to run, they run. When he yells "gee," they turn right. When he yells "yaw," they turn left. Sled, human, and canines appear as one, pulling across the snow. From a distance, they could almost be mistaken as a single polar creature, dashing across the tundra, with dusty white snow trailing their wake.

But though the team moves together in what appears to be near-perfect unison, certain dogs perform more of the work, and different work, than others. The two dogs at the front are the "lead dogs." They find and maintain the trail and set the pace for the other dogs to follow. Directly behind them are the "swing dogs." These dogs make sure the dogs behind them follow the trail when the lead dogs turn. (When the dogs in back see the lead dogs turn, they want to turn instantly, rather than continue on the trail a bit farther before turning.) The dogs immediately behind them are called "team dogs." They are responsible for carrying the heavy load of the sled and human. They run as fast as they can for as long as they can. They are the engines of the sled. Behind them, and immediately in front of the sled, are the "wheel dogs." These are often the biggest and strongest dogs because they are the first to pull the sled, either at the beginning of the race or up a hill (Cary and de Marcken 1999).

What in the world does dog sledding have to do with studying the Supreme Court? This: One cannot make inferences about all individuals within a group

by looking at the group as a whole. Team output can mask important differences among individuals on the team. Members may perform different
functions. They may have different attributes that are obscured by the collec-
tive effort. What looks like uniformity among the group is actually a function
of the pushing and pulling of different group members.

And so it is with our understanding of Supreme Court justices. Scholarship on justices and judicial behavior has largely treated justices as fungible.
They have been treated as actors with policy preferences that differ from one
another, but little else distinguishes them. They are seen as policy driven
actors in judicial robes. To be sure, some studies have looked at justices' social
backgrounds, their previous professional duties, and the like. But few studies
have examined how justices' differing personalities influence what we know
(or think we know) about judicial decision making.

This book shows that there is considerable variation in how justices behave
across many well-known features of the judicial process. Personality, and more
specifically, the trait of conscientiousness, influences how justices behave.
Justices' conscientiousness explains major gaps in much of the existing scholarship, and it provides us with a more complete picture of judicial behavior
on the US Supreme Court.

13.1 THE IMPORTANCE OF CONSCIENTIOUSNESS TO JUDGING

We mentioned in our introduction that empirical legal scholarship has
remained in "the clean and well-lit prison of one idea" (Chesterton 1908,
22). More specifically, it has focused almost exclusively on how policy preferences motivate justices. We do not take issue with the notion that policy
drives justices. Indeed, our analyses confirm that it does. Rather, we argue
that conscientiousness is also as important. The results concur. Personality, as
seen through the trait of conscientiousness, influences just about everything
justices do on the Court.

As we have shown, conscientiousness influences nearly every aspect of
judicial behavior. Chapter 4 showed that conscientiousness influences how
justices set the Court's agenda. Justices who are more conscientious are much
more likely to vote to grant review to cases with weak legal conflict than less
conscientious justices. This suggests that the conscientious justice is more
attuned to the Court's obligations to clarify law than his or her colleagues. We
also discovered that these highly conscientious justices are considerably less
likely to cast Join-3 votes – a weak form of a certiorari grant that many view
as "wishy washy." This, we argued, comes from the conscientious person's

deliberate behavior. Finally, the results showed that conscientious justices are less likely to cast forward-looking policy votes at the agenda stage, which indicates they are less concerned with how they can achieve their policy goals than their less conscientious colleagues. In short, traditional legal factors when "deciding to decide" are more likely to concern conscientious justices than the strategic pursuit of policy.

Chapter 5 revealed that conscientiousness often determines whether and how justices can be persuaded by legal counsel. The analyses showed that conscientious justices are more likely than their less conscientious colleagues to be influenced by strong legal arguments. As the amount of emotional content in a brief increases, the writer of that brief is less likely to capture the vote of conscientious justices. Such brief writers lose credibility and suffer dearly. Low conscientious justices did not reveal those same patterns of responsiveness. At the same time, highly conscientious justices are more likely to vote for attorneys who deliver strong oral arguments. Attorneys who make stronger oral arguments than their opposition are considerably more likely to capture the votes of conscientious justices. Less conscientious justices appear uninfluenced by the strength of oral argument. These findings provide important nuance to existing research on legal persuasion, brief writing, and oral argument.

Chapter 6 discovered that conscientious justices are more likely to follow the legal recommendations of the US Solicitor General's office than less conscientious justices. We believed that conscientious justices would be more likely to adopt the position recommended by the SG because they are more thorough and exhaustive in reaching decisions than their less conscientious colleagues. They are more likely to rely on objective information about the law, the Court's possible decisions, and the likely ramifications of them. Because conscientious justices value credible information – and the SG's office tends to provide it – conscientious justices are more likely to side with the SG. The analyses uncover that whether the SG acts as a party or amicus in a case, conscientious justices are more likely to adopt the SG's position. This suggests that one important foundation for the SG's status as the most esteemed litigator appearing before the Court is the degree of conscientiousness among the justices. As Court membership, and conscientiousness, changes, so too may the SG's track record.

In Chapter 7, we examined whether Chief Justices are more likely to assign opinions to conscientious justices. Chiefs have numerous motivations when assigning opinions, but surely among them is the desire to select someone who can craft a solid opinion. At the same time, modern Chiefs must assign opinions while keeping in mind the norm of equitable opinion assignment. The results reveal that in the average case, Chiefs are not any more likely to assign opinions to conscientious justices, which is what we would expect, given the Court's strong norm of opinion equity. The effects of conscientiousness, we argued, would be more nuanced. And they are. The Chief is considerably more likely to assign legally important opinions to conscientious justices than to less conscientious justices. Thus, the Chief Justice disproportionately looks to the conscientious justice when he or she requires the best work product among some of the Court's most legally important cases.

Chapter 8 showed that conscientiousness influences how and when justices bargain with each other. After an opinion writer circulates his or her opinion draft to the Court, conscientious justices behave differently than their less conscientious colleagues. They are more likely than their less conscientious justices to bargain with their colleagues in politically (but not legally) salient cases. In other words, in politically salient cases, conscientious justices are more likely than their less conscientious colleagues to exert effort to get the opinions correct – at least as they see it. What is more, conscientious justices are more likely than their colleagues to make suggestions to opinion authors to improve their opinions.

In Chapter 9, the results divulged that conscientiousness influences the language justices employ in their opinions. Conscientious justices are more likely to write cognitively complex opinions, legally broad opinions, longer opinions, and opinions with less textual readability. Conscientious justices seek to include more perspectives in their opinions, address more legal issues, and write longer opinions. These results, of course, are good and bad. On the one hand, conscientious justices seek to address and introduce as much legal content as possible – that is, to be thorough. On the other hand, in the process, they often create lengthy opinions that are perhaps more "lawyerly" and less accessible to the general public.

Chapter 10 revealed that justices' conscientiousness clearly effects the Court's treatment of precedent. A conscientious Court is significantly less likely to overrule or criticize a precedent than a less conscientious Court. Instead, a conscientious Court recognizes factual distinctions among precedents. Finally, conscientious justices are more likely to treat precedent positively than their less conscientious colleagues. Taken together, conscientious justices are more favorable to precedent, and conditional on them treating precedent negatively, they are more likely to make legal distinctions across successive cases instead of conspicuous repudiations of it. In short, conscientious justices are more likely than their colleagues to operate within the four walls of *stare decisis*.

Chapter 11 shows that conscientious justices are more likely to follow public opinion than their less conscientious colleagues. We argued that conscientious justices take more dynamics into account when deciding cases, including dynamics like their external environment. They look to more sources of information, investigate more options, and, apparently, look to a wider range of inputs than their less conscientious colleagues. Whereas less conscientious justices care little about public opinion, conscientious justices concern themselves with how the Court's decisions will play out with the general public. When the public becomes more liberal, conscientious justices vote more liberally. When the public becomes more conservative, conscientious justices vote more conservatively. They do so out of concern for the Court's institutional standing and to protect its legitimacy, which helps ensure the potency of the Court's future decisions.

Finally, we examined in Chapter 12 how conscientious justices treat recusal. As we argued throughout this book, conscientious individuals tend to be more dutiful and rule-following than less conscientious people. In the context of recusals, we expected conscientious justices to be more likely to recuse than their less conscientious colleagues. They are. What is more, the results show that conscientious justices are less likely to be tempted to stay in cases to accomplish their policy goals than are less conscientious justices. This suggests that conscientious justices are keenly aware of, and respond to, potential conflicts of interest in cases.

13.2 THE PAYOFF FOR UNDERSTANDING JUDICIAL CONSCIENTIOUSNESS

What's the payoff for having read this book? Readers should care about conscientiousness and judging for at least three reasons. First, knowing how conscientiousness influences justices can answer a number of current mysteries about justices and the Court. If justices vote to grant review for policy (or legal) reasons, why do ideologically similar justices not all vote the same way? Why do some justices vote to overrule precedent when their ideologically similar colleagues do not? Existing theories cannot answer these questions. Our results do answer these questions. We suspect that examining conscientiousness in other areas of judicial decision-making can unlock mysteries there as well. (More on that later.)

Second, readers should care about conscientiousness and the Court because conscientiousness influences every aspect of judicial behavior. As we showed in every empirical chapter throughout this book, Court action and the evolution of law are functions of conscientiousness. Anyone who

wants to understand the Court more fully must understand conscientiousness and the Court. Just as one cannot understand evolution without knowing
biology, one cannot understand judicial behavior without knowing about
conscientiousness.

Third, the importance of conscientiousness matters – or at least should
matter – to policy makers. Presidents who seek to influence the Court ought
to pay attention to the conscientiousness of those whom they select. Conscientiousness may make a justice more or less effective on the Court.
Conscientious justices may be more careful with (and respectful of) precedent. They may be more attentive to public opinion. They may be more
amenable to legal persuasion. Presidents looking to alter foundational precedents may beware the conscientious justice. Conversely, presidents seeking to
protect the status quo might seek out increasingly conscientious justices.

13.3 WHERE DO WE (AND YOU) GO FROM HERE?

Now that we have discovered conscientiousness matters, what do we (and
you) do next? The first thing we hope you do is **download our measures of
justices' personalities**. We have posted them on the website for this book as
well as on a Dataverse page.

The second thing we hope you do is think of other areas of research where
justices' personalities matter. There are numerous areas of judicial behavior
that we simply did not have the time (or space) to examine.

Although we surveyed an expansive portion of possible judicial behaviors,
we could not study everything. Our empirical inquiry is bookended by two of
the deciding to decide stages: picking cases (i.e., agenda setting) and assessing whether to participate in the decision-making process (i.e., recusal). Two
interesting and fairly easy to execute extensions of these topics could examine both the process by which justices join the Court and leave the Court.
In terms of the former, a burst of recent scholarship examines how nominees behave during confirmation hearings (Wedeking and Farganis 2010;
Farganis and Wedeking 2011; Collins and Ringhand 2013; Wedeking and
Farganis 2014). What kinds of answers do conscientious nominees offer? In
terms of retirement, are conscientious justices more or less likely to retire
strategically (Nelson and Ringsmuth 2009; Zigerell 2013)? Another interesting possibility could examine if conscientious opinion writers are more
likely to construct larger majority coalitions? This seems important given
that the size of the majority coalition is directly tied to how the media covers the Court (Zilis 2015). There is still more. One could examine which
traits of opinion writers are more responsiveness to court-curbing legislation

(Clark 2009; Mark and Zilis Forthcoming, 2018). The possibilities are numerous.

Further, the unit of analysis we generally used throughout this book was the behavior of individual justices in individual cases. We did so, of course, because personality is an individual-level phenomenon. But future studies might aggregate conscientiousness and look at Court level phenomena. From a substantive perspective, we believe it absolutely essential to assess how personality impacts law and legal policy, since that ultimately is the unique business of the Court. But since it is coalitions of justices who act to interpret precedent (as opposed to individuals), one might aggregate conscientiousness across the Court as a whole and look at things like docket size and overall collegiality.

If the existing psychology research on small groups is any indicator, we suspect those who do walk down this path will be well-rewarded. For starters, although there have been dozens of laboratory and field experiments examining personality composition in smaller work teams (Halfhill et al. 2005), none, so far as we are aware, have sought to examine how teams of political elites such as justices go about conducting their work. Furthermore, such efforts might bring some clarity to a literature that is rather muddled. Mohammed and Angell (2003) show that increased team conscientiousness is correlated with stronger performance in a multiweek group report-writing task. On the other hand, for more rapid-fire brainstorming tasks with ephemeral groups, Waung and Brice (1998) find that conscientious groups sometimes yield lower productivity than their less conscientious counterparts.

As to why this rather counterintuitive relationship might exist, Robert and Cheung (2010) suggest that "groups that are high in conscientiousness prefer to adopt systematic procedures for task completion, and become locked into their use even though such procedures are not always appropriate" (223). With a public rule manual in excess of eighty pages long (not to mention handbooks within each justice's chambers), it seems fairly obvious to us that the justices like such systematic procedures. Future work could assess how the overall personality profile of the Supreme Court influences objective things such as its output, as well as subjective things like how the public or political elites perceive it.

Future scholarship might devote more attention to other personality traits as well. We think conscientiousness is important – hence we wrote a book about it – but as a quick perusal of our regression table reveals, in controlling for the other four traits we also recover a number of statistically significant baseline relationships between a trait and aspects of judicial behavior. All of these remaining traits strike us as worthy of additional and in-depth scholarly inquiry. If we were to follow up with a sequel, we'd start with openness, which is related to how much an individual embraces new experiences and ideas. Looking back across our substantive chapters, we see a number of clear instances where we would expect openness to influence judicial behavior. But, as our treatment of conscientiousness illustrates, one needs to be sure that well-formed and logically coherent hypotheses drive the empirical tests.

Scholars should also consider how personalities influence behavior beyond the rarified territory of the US Supreme Court. The vast majority of appellate legal policy is created across the US Courts of Appeals, and so an incredibly important extension of our efforts here would be to apply the lens of personality to these courts. These efforts could examine not just judicial behavior within a circuit court, but also, of course, the important dynamics about how lower court judges interact with the High Court in terms of compliance with Supreme Court decision. One basic question, for instance, is whether conscientious lower court judges are more likely to comply with Supreme Court precedent.

Future efforts in this area could simultaneously examine how personality matters for lower court judges both as individual actors as we have (mostly) done here and also by looking at them from the small-group context. Circuit panels, both smaller in size and also rotating in terms of membership, provide an idealized environment for theory testing – an insight that only a small number of researches have embraced (e.g., Collins and Martinek 2011).

Switching institutions, we see no reason why, after generating valid estimates of personality, one could also not apply group-level insights into looking at how congressional committees or even Congress as a whole does (or does not) function. Ditto for aspects of executive politics, including the federal bureaucracy and decision-making in independent agencies.

* * *

During the Iditarod, mushers rarely enjoy straight shots across the snowy tundra. Instead, their paths twist and turn. They and their sled dogs must be able to navigate those turns. They win (and survive) by adapting when needed.

Scholarship on judicial behavior must follow that example and adapt. If we want our scholarship to remain relevant and as informative as it can be, we must update existing theories. The results from this entire book reveal that conscientiousness influences judicial behavior. Scholarship must now incorporate these findings.

References

Abraham, Henry J. 1999. *Justices, Presidents, and Senators: A History of the U.S. Supreme Court Appointments from Washington to Clinton*. Rowman & Littlefield.

Ackerman, Bruce A. 1974. "Book Review of Law and the Modern Mind, by Jerome Frank." *Daedalus* 103:119–130.

Aliotta, Jilda M. 1988. "Social Backgrounds, Social Motives and Participation on the U.S. Supreme Court." *Political Behavior* 10(3):267–284.

Alito, Samuel. 2017. "A Tribute to Justice Scalia." *Yale Law Journal* 126:1605–1608.

Aristotle, translated by Benjamin Jowett. 350 BCE. *Politics*. http://classics.mit.edu/Aristotle/politics.3.three.html.

Arnoux, Pierre-Hadrien, Anbang Xu, Neil Boyette, et al. 2017. "25 Tweets to Know You: A New Model to Predict Personality with Social Media." *AAAI Conference on Web and Social Media*, pp. 472–475. AAAI Publications.

Asuero, A.G., A. Sayago, and A.G. Gonzalez. 2006. "The Correlation Coefficient: An Overview." *Critical Reviews in Analytical Chemistry* 36:41–59.

Atkins, Burton, Lenore Alpert, and Robert Ziller. 1980. "Personality Theory and Judging: A Proposed Theory of Self-Esteem and Judicial Policy-Making." *Law and Policy Quarterly* 2(2):189–220.

Bailey, Michael, and Forrest Maltzman. 2011. *The Constrained Court: Law, Politics, and the Decisions Justices Make*. Princeton University Press.

Baker, Levi R., and James K. McNulty. 2011. "Self-Compassion and Relationship Maintenance: The Moderating Roles of Conscientiousness and Gender." *Journal of Personality and Social Psychology* 100(5):853.

Bam, Dmitry. 2011. "Making Appearances Matter: Recusal and the Appearance of Bias." *Brigham Young University Law Review* 2011:943–1002.

Barber, James David. 1965. *The Lawmakers*. Yale University Press.

Barber, James David. 1992. *The Presidential Character: Predicting Performance in the White House*. Prentice Hall.

Barrick, Murray R., and Michael K. Mount. 1991. "The Big Five Personality Dimensions and Job Performance: A Meta-Analysis." *Personnel Psychology* 44(1):1–26.

Barrick, Murray R., Michael K. Mount, and Judy P. Strauss. 1993. "Conscientiousness and Performance of Sales Representatives: Test of the Mediating Effects of Goal Setting." *Journal of Applied Psychology* 78(5):715–722.

Barrick, Murray R., Michael K. Mount, and Timothy A. Judge. 2001. "Personality and Performance at the Beginning of the New Millennium: What Do We Know and Where Do We Go Next?" *International Journal of Selection and Assessment* 9(1–2):9–30.

Bartels, Brandon L., and Andrew J. O'Geen. 2015. "The Nature of Legal Change on the US Supreme Court: Jurisprudential Regimes Theory and Its Alternatives." *American Journal of Political Science* 59(4):880–895.

Bartels, Brandon L., and Christopher D. Johnston. 2013. "On the Ideological Foundations of Supreme Court Legitimacy in the American Public." *American Journal of Political Science* 57(1):184–199.

Bassett, Debra Lynn. 2005. "Recusal and the Supreme Court." *Hastings Law Journal* 56:657–698.

Baum, Lawrence. 1997. *The Puzzle of Judicial Behavior*. University of Michigan Press.

Baum, Lawrence. 2006. *Judges and Their Audiences: A Perspective on Judicial Behavior*. Princeton University Press.

Baum, Lawrence. 2010. *The Psychology of Judicial Decision Making*. Oxford University Press. Chapter "Motivation and Judicial Behavior: Expanding the Scope of Inquiry," pp. 3–26.

Benesh, Sara C., Reginald S. Sheehan, and Harold J. Spaeth. 1999. "Equity in Supreme Court Opinion Assignment." *Jurimetrics* 39:377–389.

Benesh, Sara C., Saul Brenner, and Harold J. Spaeth. 2002. "Aggressive Grants by Affirm-Minded Justices." *American Politics Research* 30(3):219–234.

Benoit, Kenneth. 2018. "quanteda: Quantitative Analysis of Textual Data." R package version 0.99.22 (http://quanteda.io).

Bermant, Gordon. 1999. "Courting the Virtual: Federal Courts in an Age of Complete Inter-Connectedness." *Ohio Northern University Law Review* 25: 527–562.

Bernheim, B. Douglas. 1994. "A Theory of Conformity." *Journal of Political Economy* 102(5):841–877.

Black, Ryan, and Lee Epstein. 2005. "Recusal and the 'Problem' of an Equally Divided Supreme Court." *Journal of Appellate Practice and Process* 7(1):75–99.

Black, Ryan, and Ryan Owens. 2011b. "Consider the Source (and the Message): Supreme Court Justices and Strategic Audits of Lower Court Decisions." *Political Research Quarterly* 64(4):765–778.

Black, Ryan C., and Amanda C. Bryan. 2014. "Explaining the (Non)Occurrence of Evenly Divided Supreme Courts." *American Politics Research* 42(6):1077–1095.

Black, Ryan C., and Christina L. Boyd. 2012a. "The Role of Law Clerks in the U.S. Supreme Court's Agenda-Setting Process." *American Politics Research* 40(1):147–173.

Black, Ryan C., and Christina L. Boyd. 2012b. "US Supreme Court Agenda Setting and the Role of Litigant Status." *Journal of Law, Economics, & Organization* 28(1):286–312.

Black, Ryan C., and Christina L. Boyd. 2013. "Selecting the Select Few: The Discuss List and the U.S. Supreme Court's Agenda-Setting Process." *Social Science Quarterly* 94(4):1124–1144.

Black, Ryan C., and James F. Spriggs. 2013. "The Citation and Depreciation of U.S. Supreme Court Precedent." *Journal of Empirical Legal Studies* 10(2):325–358.

Black, Ryan C., and James F. Spriggs, II. 2008. "An Empirical Analysis of the Length of U.S. Supreme Court Opinions." *Houston Law Review* 45(3):621–683.

Black, Ryan C., Matthew E. K. Hall, Ryan J. Owens, and Eve Ringsmuth. 2016. "The Role of Emotional Language in Briefs before the U.S. Supreme Court." *Journal of Law and Courts* 4(2):377–407.

Black, Ryan C., and Ryan J. Owens. 2009a. "Agenda-Setting in the Supreme Court: The Collision of Policy and Jurisprudence." *Journal of Politics* 71(3):1062–1075.

Black, Ryan C., and Ryan J. Owens. 2009b. "Analyzing the Reliability of Supreme Court Justices' Agenda Setting Records." *Justice System Journal* 30(3):254–264.

Black, Ryan C., and Ryan J. Owens. 2011a. "Solicitor General Influence and Agenda Setting on the U.S. Supreme Court." *Political Research Quarterly* 64(4):765–778.

Black, Ryan C., and Ryan J. Owens. 2012a. "Looking Back to Move Forward: Quantifying Policy Predictions in Political Decision Making." *American Journal of Political Science* 56(4):802–816.

Black, Ryan C., and Ryan J. Owens. 2012b. *The Solicitor General and the United States Supreme Court: Executive Influence and Judicial Decisions.* Cambridge University Press.

Black, Ryan C., and Ryan J. Owens. 2012c. Supreme Court Agenda Setting: Policy Uncertainty and Legal Considerations. In *New Directions in Judicial Politics*, ed. Kevin T. McGuire, pp. 144–166. Routledge.

Black, Ryan C., and Ryan J. Owens. 2013. "A Built-In Advantage: The Office of the Solicitor General and the Supreme Court." *Political Research Quarterly* 66(2):451–463. Advanced online access available at http://prq.sagepub.com/content/early/2012/06/25/1065912912447995.abstract.

Black, Ryan C., and Ryan J. Owens. 2016. "Courting the President: How Circuit Court Judges Alter Their Behavior for Promotion to the Supreme Court." *American Journal of Political Science* 60(1):30–43.

Black, Ryan C., Ryan J. Owens, Justin Wedeking, and Patrick C. Wohlfarth. 2016a. "The Influence of Public Sentiment on Supreme Court Opinion Clarity." *Law & Society Review* 50(3):703–732.

Black, Ryan C., Ryan J. Owens, Justin Wedeking, and Patrick C. Wohlfarth. 2016b. *U.S. Supreme Court Opinions and Their Audiences.* Cambridge University Press.

Black, Ryan C., Ryan J. Owens, and Miles T. Armaly. 2016. "A Well-Traveled Lot: A Research Note on Judicial Travel by U.S. Supreme Court Justices." *Justice System Journal* 37(4):367–384.

Black, Ryan C., Sarah A. Treul, Timothy R. Johnson, and Jerry Goldman. 2011. "Emotions, Oral Arguments, and Supreme Court Decision Making." *Journal of Politics* 73(2):572–581.

Black, Ryan C., Timothy R. Johnson, and Justin P. Wedeking. 2012. *Oral Arguments and Coalition Formation on the U.S. Supreme Court: A Deliberate Dialogue.* University of Michigan Press.

Blackman, Josh. 2013. *Unprecedented: The Constitutional Challenge to Obamacare.* Public Affairs.

Blackstone, William. 2016. *The Oxford Edition of Blackstone's Commentaries on the Laws of England.* 1st ed. Oxford University Press.

Bleidorn, Wiebke, Christian Kandler, Rainer Riemann, Alois Angleitner, and Frank M. Spinath. 2009. "Patterns and Sources of Adult Personality Development: Growth Curve Analyses of the NEO PI-R Scales in a Longitudinal Twin Study." *Journal of Personality and Social Psychology* 97(1):142.

Bogg, Tim, and Brent W. Roberts. 2004. "Conscientiousness and Health-Related Behaviors: A Meta-Analysis of the Leading Behavioral Contributors to Mortality." *Psychological Bulletin* 130(6):887.

Boucher, Robert L., Jr., and Jeffrey A. Segal. 1995. "Supreme Court Justices as Strategic Decision Makers: Aggressive Grants and Defensive Denials on the Vinson Court." *Journal of Politics* 57(3):824–837.

Braman, Eileen. 2009. *Law, Politics, and Perception: How Policy Preferences Influence Legal Reasoning*. University of Virginia Press.

Braman, Eileen, and Thomas E. Nelson. 2007. "Mechanism of Motivated Reasoning?: Analogical Perception in Discrimination Disputes." *American Journal of Political Science* 51(4):940–956.

Brennan, William J., Jr. 1973. "The National Court of Appeals: Another Dissent." *University of Chicago Law Review* 40(3):473–485.

Brenner, Saul. 1979. "The New Certiorari Game." *Journal of Politics* 41(2):649–655.

Brenner, Saul, and Harold Spaeth. 1995. *Stare Indecisis: The Alteration of Precedent on the U.S. Supreme Court, 1946–1992*. Cambridge University Press.

Brenner, Saul, and Jan Palmer. 1988. "The Time Taken to Write Opinions as a Determinant of Opinion Assignments." *Judicature* 72:179–184.

Breyer, Stephen. 1992. "On the Uses of Legislative History in Interpreting Statutes." *Southern California Law Review* 65:845.

Bryan, Amanda C., and Christopher D. Kromphardt. 2016. "Public Opinion, Public Support, and Counter-Attitudinal Voting on the U.S. Supreme Court." *Justice System Journal* 37(4):298–317.

Buss, David M. 1992. "Manipulation in Close Relationships: Five Personality Factors in Interactional Context." *Journal of Personality* 60(2):477–499.

C-SPAN. 2009. "The Supreme Court: Home to America's Highest Court." Video documentary. Available online at http://supremecourt.c-span.org/Video/TVPrograms/SC_Week_Documentary.aspx (last accessed September 27, 2010).

Caldeira, Gregory A. 1986. "Neither the Purse Nor the Sword: Dynamics of Public Confidence in the Supreme Court." *American Political Science Review* 80(4): 1209–1226.

Caldeira, Gregory A., and John R. Wright. 1988. "Organized Interests and Agenda Setting in the U.S. Supreme Court." *American Political Science Review* 82(4): 1109–1127.

Caldeira, Gregory A., and John R. Wright. 1990. "The Discuss List: Agenda Building in the Supreme Court." *Law & Society Review* 24(3):807–836.

Caldeira, Gregory A., John R. Wright, and Christopher J. W. Zorn. 1999. "Sophisticated Voting and Gate-Keeping in the Supreme Court." *Journal of Law, Economics, & Organization* 15(3):549–572.

Caldwell, David F., and Jerry M. Burger. 1997. "Personality and Social Influence Strategies in the Workplace." *Personality and Social Psychology Bulletin* 23(10):1003–1012.

Caldwell, David F., and Jerry M. Burger. 1998. "Personality Characteristics of Job Applicants and Success in Screening Interviews." *Personnel Psychology* 51(1): 119–136.

Cameron, Charles M., Albert D. Cover, and Jeffrey A. Segal. 1990. "Senate Voting on Supreme Court Nominees: A Neoinstitutional Model." *American Political Science Review* 84(2):525–534.

Caplan, Lincoln. 1987. *The Tenth Justice: The Solicitor General and the Rule of Law*. New York: Vintage Books.

Cardozo, Benjamin N. 1921. *The Nature of the Judicial Process*. Yale University Press.

Carney, Dana R., John T. Jost, Samuel D. Gosling, and Jeff Potter. 2008. "The Secret Lives of Liberals and Conservatives: Personality Profiles, Interaction Styles, and the Things They Leave Behind." *Political Psychology* 29(6):807–840.

Cary, Bob, and Gail de Marcken. 1999. *Born to Pull: The Glory of Sled Dogs*. University of Minnesota Press.

Casillas, Christopher J., Peter K. Enns, and Patrick C. Wohlfarth. 2011. "How Public Opinion Constrains the U.S. Supreme Court." *American Journal of Political Science* 55(1):74–88.

Chamberlain, Ronald S. 1987. "Mixing Politics and Justice: The Office of the Solicitor General." *Journal of Law and Politics* 4:379–428.

Chapman, Benjamin P, Brent Roberts, and Paul Duberstein. 2011. "Personality and Longevity: Knowns, Unknowns, and Implications for Public Health and Personalized Medicine." *Journal of Aging Research* Article ID 759170.

Chesterton, G. K. 1908. *Orthodoxy*. John Lane the Bodley Head.

Cheung, Fanny M, Kwok Leung, Jian-Xin Zhang, Hai-Fa Sun, Yi-Qun Gan, Wei-Zhen Song, and Dong Xie. 2001. "Indigenous Chinese Personality Constructs: Is the Five-Factor Model Complete?" *Journal of Cross-Cultural Psychology* 32(4): 407–433.

Clark, Tom S. 2009. "The Separation of Powers, Court-Curbing and Judicial Legitimacy." *American Journal of Political Science* 53(4):971–989.

Coan, Andrew. 2012. "Judicial Capacity and the Substance of Constitutional Law." *Yale Law Journal* 122:422–458.

Coffin, Frank M. 1994. *On Appeal: Courts, Lawyering, and Judging*. W.W. Nortin and Company.

Collins, Jr., Paul M. 2004. "Friends of the Court: Examining the Influence of Amicus Curiae Participation in U.S. Supreme Court Litigation." *Law & Society Review* 38(4):807–832.

Collins, Jr., Paul M. 2007. "Lobbyists before the U.S. Supreme Court: Investigating the Influence of Amicus Curiae Briefs." *Political Research Quarterly* 60(1): 55–70.

Collins, Jr., Paul M. 2008. "Amici Curiae and Dissensus on the U.S. Supreme Court." *Journal of Empirical Legal Studies* 5(1):143–170.

Collins, Jr., Paul M., and Wendy L. Martinek. 2011. "The Small Group Context: Designated District Court Judges in the U.S. Courts of Appeals." *Journal of Empirical Legal Studies* 8(1):177–205.

Collins, Paul M. 2011. "Cognitive Dissonance on the U.S. Supreme Court." *Political Research Quarterly* 64(2):362–376.

Collins, Paul M., and Lori A. Ringhand. 2013. *Supreme Court Confirmation Hearings and Constitutional Change*. Cambridge University Press.

Collins, Todd A., and Christopher A. Cooper. 2012. "Case Salience and Media Coverage of Supreme Court Decisions: Toward a New Measure." *Political Research Quarterly* 20(10):1–12.

Cooper, James L. 1990. "The Solicitor General and the Evolution of Activism." *Indiana Law Journal* 65:675–696.

Cooper, Phillip J. 1995. *Battles on the Bench: Conflict Inside the Supreme Court*. University of Kansas Press.

Cordray, Margaret M., and Richard Cordray. 2008. "Strategy in Supreme Court Case Selection: The Relationship between Certiorari and the Merits." *Ohio State Law Journal* 69(1):1–51.

Corley, Pamela C. 2008. "The Supreme Court and Opinion Content: The Influence of Parties' Briefs." *Political Research Quarterly* 61(3):468–478.

Corley, Pamela C. 2010. *Concurring Opinion Writing on the U.S. Supreme Court.* SUNY Press.

Corley, Pamela C., and Justin Wedeking. 2014. "The (Dis)Advantage of Certainty: The Importance of Certainty in Language." *Law and Society Review* 48(1):35–62.

Corp., Stata. 2017. *Stata Multivariate Statistics Reference Manual.* Stata Press.

Crichlow, Scott. 2002. "Legislators' Personality Traits and Congressional Support for Free Trade." *Journal of Conflict Resolution* 46(5):693–711.

Cross, Frank B., and James W. Pennebaker. 2014. "The Language of the Roberts Court." *Michigan State Law Review* 2014:853–894.

Cross, Frank B., and Stefanie A. Lindquist. 2006. "The Decisional Significance of the Chief Justice." *University of Pennsylvania Law Review* 154:1665–1707.

Cushman, Barry. 2003. "Clerking for Scrooge (Reviewing *The Forgotten Memoir of John Knox: A Year in the Life of a Supreme Court Clerk in FDR's Washington*)." *University of Chicago Law Review* 70(2):721–749.

Danelski, David, and Artemus Ward, eds. 2016. *The Chief Justice: Appointment and Influence.* University of Michigan Press.

Danelski, David J. 1960. *American Court Systems: Readings in Judicial Process and Behavior.* W.H. Freeman.

Davis, Christopher M. 2011. "Invoking Cloture in the Senate." *Congressional Research Service Report,* RL32843.

Davis, Sue. 1990. "Rehnquist's Opinion Assignments." *Judicature* 74(2):66–72.

De Choudhury, Munmun, Scott Counts, and Eric Horvitz. 2013. "Predicting Postpartum Changes in Emotion and Behavior via Social Media." *Proceedings of the SIGCHI Conference on Human Factors in Computer,* pp. 3267–3276.

Dickson, Del, ed. 2001. *The Supreme Court in Conference (1940–1985): The Private Discussions Behind Nearly 300 Supreme Court Decisions.* Oxford University Press.

Dietrich, Bryce J., Scott Lasley, Jeffrey J. Mondak, Megan L. Remmel, and Joel Turner. 2012. "Personality and Legislative Politics: The Big Five Trait Dimensions among U.S. State Legislators." *Political Psychology* 33(2):195–210.

Dijkstra, Pieternel, and Dick PH Barelds. 2009. "Women's Well-Being: The Role of Individual Differences." *Scandinavian Journal of Psychology* 50(4):309–315.

Dudley, Nicole M., Karin A. Orvis, Justin E. Lebiecki, and Jose M. Cortina. 2006. "A Meta-Analytic Investigation of Conscientiousness in the Prediction of Job Performance: Examining the Intercorrelations and the Incremental Validity of Narrow Traits." *Journal of Applied Psychology* 91(1):40–57.

Enns, Peter K., and Patrick C. Wohlfarth. 2013. "The Swing Justice." *Journal of Politics* 75(4):1089–1107.

Enns, Peter K., and Patrick C. Wohlfarth. 2017. Making Sense of the Supreme Court-Public Opinion Relationship. In *Handbook of Judicial Behavior,* ed. Robert M. Howard, and Kirk Randazzo, pp. 180–195. Routledge Press.

Epps, Daniel. 2012. "What the 'Bailey' Case May Reveal about Supreme Court Ideology." *The Atlantic.* October 31.

Epstein, Lee, and Andrew D. Martin. 2011. *University of Pennsylvania Journal of Constitutional Law* 13:263–281.

Epstein, Lee, Andrew D. Martin, Jeffrey A. Segal, and Chad Westerland. 2007. "The Judicial Common Space." *Journal of Law, Economics, & Organization* 23(2): 303–325.

Epstein, Lee, and Jack Knight. 1998. *The Choices Justices Make*. CQ Press.

Epstein, Lee, and Jack Knight. 2013. "Reconsidering Judicial Preferences." *Annual Review of Political Science* 16:11–31.

Epstein, Lee, Jack Knight, and Andrew D. Martin. 2003. "The Norm of Prior Judicial Experience and Its Consequences for Career Diversity on the U.S. Supreme Court." *California Law Review* 91(4):903–966.

Epstein, Lee, and Jeffrey A. Segal. 2000. "Measuring Issue Salience." *American Journal of Political Science* 44(1):66–83.

Epstein, Lee, Jeffrey A. Segal, and Harold J. Spaeth. 2007. "Digital Archive of the Papers of Harry A. Blackmun." http://epstein.law.northwestern.edu/research/BlackmunArchive/.

Epstein, Lee, Jeffrey A. Segal, Harold J. Spaeth, and Thomas G. Walker. 2007. *The Supreme Court Compendium: Data, Decisions, and Developments*. 4th ed. CQ Press.

Epstein, Lee, Jeffrey A. Segal, Nancy Staudt, and Rene Lindstadt. 2005. "The Role of Qualifications in the Confirmation of Nominees to the U.S. Supreme Court." *Florida State University Law Review* 32:1145–1173.

Epstein, Lee, Jeffrey A. Segal, and Timothy Johnson. 1996. "The Claim of Issue Creation on the U.S. Supreme Court." *American Political Science Review* 90(4):845–852.

Epstein, Lee, and Joseph F. Kobylka. 1992. *The Supreme Court and Legal Change: Abortion and the Death Penalty*. University of North Carolina Press.

Epstein, Lee, and Thomas G. Walker. 2010. *Constitutional Law for a Changing America: Rights, Liberties, and Justice*. 7th ed. Congressional Quarterly Press.

Epstein, Lee, William M. Landes, and The Honorable Richard A. Posner. 2013. *The Behavior of Federal Judges: A Theoretical and Empirical Study of Rational Choice*. Harvard University Press.

Farganis, Dion, and Justin Wedeking. 2011. "'No Hints, No Forecasts, No Previews': An Empirical Analysis of Supreme Court Nominee Candor from Harlan to Kagan." *Law & Society Review* 45(3):525–559.

Farias, Cristian. 2015. "Comment on Ferguson? Not My Job, Says Justice Stephen Breyer." *New Republic. www.newrepublic.com/article/121294/stephen-breyer-dodges-noah-feldmans-question-about-ferguson*.

Flamm, Richard E. 2017. *Judicial Disqualification: Recusal and Disqualification of Judges*. 3rd ed. Banks and Jordan Law Publishing.

Flemming, Roy B., and B. Dan Wood. 1997. "The Public and the Supreme Court: Individual Justice Responsiveness to American Policy Moods." *American Journal of Political Science* 41(2):468–498.

Fox, Justin, and Georg Vanberg. 2013. "Narrow Versus Broad Judicial Decisions." *Journal of Theoretical Politics* 26(3):355–383.

Frank, Jerome. 1936. *Law and the Modern Mind*. Tudor Publishing Company: New York.

Friedman, Howard S., Joan S. Tucker, Carol Tomlinson-Keasey, Joseph E. Schwartz, Deborah L. Wingard, and Michael H. Criqui. 1993. "Does Childhood Personality Predict Longevity?" *Journal of Personality and Social Psychology* 65(1): 176–185.

Frost, Amanda. 2005. "Keeping Up with Appearances: A Process-Oriented Approach to Judicial Recusal." *Kansas Law Review* 53:531–593.

Garrow, David J. 2003. "The Tragedy of William O. Douglas." *The Nation*, April 14, 2003, https://www.thenation.com/article/tragedy-william-o-douglas/.

George, Alexander L., and Juliette L. George. 1964. *Woodrow Wilson and Colonel House: A Personality Study*. Courier Corporation.

George, Linda G., Ravenna Helson, and Oliver P. John. 2011. "The 'CEO' of Women's Work Lives: How Big Five Conscientiousness, Extraversion, and Openness Predict 50 Years of Work Experience in a Changing Sociocultural Context." *Journal of Personality and Social Psychology* 101(4):812–830.

Gerber, Alan S., Gregory A. Huber, David Doherty, et al. 2010. "Personality and Political Attitudes: Relationships across Issue Domains and Political Contexts." *American Political Science Review* 104(1):111–133.

Geyh, Charles G. 2010. *Judicial Disqualification: An Analysis of Federal Law*. Federal Judicial Center.

Gibson, James L. 1981. "Personality and Elite Political Behavior: The Influence of Self Esteem on Judicial Decision Making." *Journal of Politics* 43(1):104–125.

Gibson, James L., and Gregory A. Caldeira. 2009. *Citizens, Courts, and Confirmations: Positivity Theory and the Judgments of the American People*. Princeton University Press.

Gibson, James L., and Gregory A. Caldeira. 2011. "Has Legal Realism Damaged the Legitimacy of the U.S. Supreme Court?" *Law and Society Review* 45(1):195–219.

Gibson, James L., and Gregory A. Caldeira. 2012. "Campaign Support, Conflicts of Interest, and Judicial Impartiality: Can Recusals Rescue the Legitimacy of Courts?" *Journal of Politics* 74(1):18–34.

Gibson, James L., Gregory A. Caldeira, and Lester Kenyatta Spence. 2003. "The Supreme Court and the U.S. Presidential Election of 2000: Wounds, Self-Inflicted or Otherwise?" *British Journal of Political Science* 33(4):535–556.

Gibson, James L., Gregory A. Caldeira, and Vanessa A. Baird. 1998. "On the Legitimacy of National High Courts." *American Political Science Review* 92(2):343–358.

Gibson, James L., and Michael J. Nelson. 2015. "Is the U.S. Supreme Court's Legitimacy Grounded in Performance Satisfaction and Ideology?" *American Journal of Political Science* 59(1):162–174.

Giles, Michael W., Bethany Blackstone, and Richard L. Vining. 2008. "The Supreme Court in American Democracy: Unraveling the Linkages between Public Opinion and Judicial Decision Making." *Journal of Politics* 70(2):293–306.

Giles, Michael W., Virginia A. Hettinger, and Todd Peppers. 2001. "Picking Federal Judges: A Note on Policy and Partisan Selection Agendas." *Political Research Quarterly* 54(3):623–641.

Giles, Wil. 2015. "Affirmation Bias? Supreme Court Decision-Making in the Circuit Riding Century." *University of Chicago Undergraduate Law Review* 4(3):106–133.

Ginsburg, Ruth Bader. 2003. "Workways of the Supreme Court." *Thomas Jefferson Law Review* 25:517–528.

Ginsburg, Ruth Bader. 2004. "An Open Discussion with Justice Ruth Bader Ginsburg." *Connecticut Law Review* 36:1033.

Goldman, Sheldon. 1966. "Voting Behavior on the United States Court of Appeals, 1961–1964." *American Political Science Review* 60(2):374–383.

Gosling, Samuel D., Peter J. Rentfrow, and William B. Swann Jr. 2003. "A Very Brief Measure of the Big-Five Personality Domains." *Journal of Research in Personality* 37(6):504–528.

Graetz, Michael J., and Linda Greenhouse. 2016. *The Burger Court and the Rise of the Judicial Right*. Simon & Schuster.

Greenburg, Jan Crawford. 2007. *Supreme Conflict: The Inside Story of the Struggle for Control of the United States Supreme Court*. Penguin Books.

Greenhouse, Linda. 1989. "Oblique Clash between 2 Justices Mirrors Tensions about Abortion." *New York Times*. November 30, 1989. www.nytimes.com/1989/11/30/us/oblique-clash-between-2-justices-mirrors-tensions-about-abortion.html.

Greenhouse, Linda. 2005. *Becoming Justice Blackmun: Harry Blackmun's Supreme Court Journey*. New York: Times Books.

Greenstein, Fred I. 1969. *Personality and Politics: Problems of Evidence, Inference, and Conceptualization*. Princeton University Press.

Gruenfeld, Deborah H. 1995. "Status, Ideology, and Integrative Complexity on the U.S. Supreme Court: Rethinking the Politics of Political Decision Making." *Journal of Personality and Social Psychology* 68:5–20.

Gul, Sumeer, Iram Mukhtar Mahajan, Tariq Ahmad Shah, and Nahida Tun-Nisa. 2004. "Influence of Personality Traits on Information Seeking Behaviour: A Case Study of Research Scholars in the field of Botany." In *Innovative Ideas, Technologies and Services*, ed. Sanjeev Kumar, Nandni Dutta, Tariq Ashraf, and Naheed Mohsini. Indira Gahdhi National Centre for the Arts, New Delhi, India: Pragun Publication. International Conference on the Convergence of Libraries, Archives and Museums (ICLAM 2015).

Haire, Susan, Laura Moyer, and Shawn Treier. 2013. "Diversity, Deliberations, and Judicial Opinion Writing." *Journal of Law and Courts* 1(2):303–330.

Halder, Santoshi, Anjali Roy, and P. K. Chakraborty. 2010. "The Influence of Personality Traits on Information Seeking Behaviour of Students." *Malaysian Journal of Library & Information Science* 15(1):41–53.

Halfhill, Terry, Eric Sundstrom, Jessica Lahner, Wilma Calderone, and Tjai M. Nielsen. 2005. "Group Personality Composition and Group Effectiveness: An Integrative Review of Empirical Research." *Small Group Research* 36(1): 83–105.

Hall, Matthew E. K. 2018. *What Justices Want: Goals and Personality on the US Supreme Court*. New York: Cambridge University Press.

Hampson, Sarah E., Lewis R. Goldberg, Thomas M. Vogt, and Joan P. Dubanoski. 2007. "Mechanisms by Which Childhood Personality Traits Influence Adult Health Status: Educational Attainment and Healthy Behaviors." *Health Psychology* 26(1):121–125.

Hanmer, Michael, and Kerem Ozan Kalkan. 2013. "Behind the Curve: Clarifying the Best Approach to Calculating Predicted Probabilities and Marginal Effects from Limited Dependent Variable Models." *American Journal of Political Science* 57:263–277.

Hansford, Thomas G., and James F. Spriggs, II. 2006. *The Politics of Precedent on the U.S. Supreme Court.* Princeton: Princeton University Press.

Harvey, Anna, and Michael Woodruff. 2013. "Confirmation Bias in the United States Supreme Court Judicial Database." *Journal Law, Economics, and Organization* 29(2):414–460.

Heinström, Jannica. 2003. "Five Personality Dimensions and Their Influence on Information Behaviour." *Information Research* 9(1):9–1.

Heller, Daniel, David Watson, and Remus Ilies. 2004. "The Role of Person Versus Situation in Life Satisfaction: A Critical Examination." *Psychological Bulletin* 130(4):574–600.

Hellyer, Paul. 2005. "Assessing the Influence of Computer-Assisted Legal Research: A Study of California Supreme Court Opinions." *William and Mary Law School Scholarship Repository.*

Helson, Ravenna, Constance Jones, and Virginia S. Y. Kwan. 2002. "Personality Change Over 40 Years of Adulthood: Hierarchical Linear Modeling Analyses of Two Longitudinal Samples." *Journal of Personality and Social Psychology* 83(3):752.

Henke, Kristen L. 2013. "If It's Not Broke, Don't Fix It: Ignoring Criticisms of Supreme Court Recusals." *Saint Louis University Law Journal* 57:521–546.

Hermann, Margaret G. 1977. *A Psychological Examination of Political Leaders.* Free Press.

Hermann, Margaret G. 1984. *Foreign Policy Decision Making: Perceptions, Cognition, and Artificial Intelligence.* Praeger.

Ho, Daniel E., and Kevin M Quinn. 2010. "Did a Switch in Time Save Nine?" *Journal of Legal Analysis* 2(1):69–113.

Hough, Leatta M. 1992. "The 'Big Five' Personality Variables–Construct Confusion: Description Versus Prediction." *Human Performance* 5(1–2):139–155.

Hume, Robert J. 2014. "Deciding Not to Decide: The Politics of Recusals on the U.S. Supreme Court." *Law and Society Review* 48(3):621–655.

Hume, Robert J. 2017. *Ethics and Accountability on the U.S. Supreme Court.* SUNY Press.

Hurtz, Gregory M., and John J. Donovan. 2000. "Personality and Job Performance: The Big Five Revisited." *Journal of Applied Psychology* 85(6):869–879.

Hurwitz, Mark S., and Oseph V. Stefko. 2004. "Acclimation and Attitudes: 'Newcomer' Justices and Precedent Conformance on the Supreme Court." *Political Research Quarterly* 57(1):121–129.

IBM. 2017. "The Science behind the Service." IBM Watson Personality Insight Documentation.

Jackson, Joshua J., and Brent W. Roberts. 2017. Conscientiousness. In *The Oxford Handbook of the Five Factor Model,* ed. Thomas A. Widiger. New York: Oxford University Press.

Jackson, Joshua J, Tim Bogg, Kate E Walton, et al. 2009. "Not All Conscientiousness Scales Change Alike: A Multimethod, Multisample Study of Age Differences in the Facets of Conscientiousness." *Journal of Personality and Social Psychology* 96(2):446.

James, William. 1890. *The Principles of Psychology.* Holt and Company.

Jenkins, John A. 1983. "The Solicitor General's Winning Ways." *American Bar Association Journal* 69:734.

John, Oliver P, and Sanjay Srivastava. 1999. "The Big Five Trait Taxonomy: History, Measurement, and Theoretical Perspectives." *Handbook of Personality: Theory and Research* 2(1999):102–138.

Johnson, Timothy, James F. Spriggs II, and Paul J. Wahlbeck. 2007. "Oral Advocacy before the United State Supreme Court: Does It Affect the Justices' Decisions?" *Washington University Law Review* 85:457–527.

Johnson, Timothy R. 2003. "The Supreme Court, the Solicitor General, and the Separation of Powers." *American Politics Research* 31(4):426–451.

Johnson, Timothy R. 2004. *Oral Arguments and Decision Making on the United States Supreme Court*. Albany, NY: SUNY Press.

Johnson, Timothy R. 2009. "The Digital Archives of Justices Blackmun and Powell Oral Argument Notes." www.polisci.umn.edu/ tjohnson/oanotes.php.

Johnson, Timothy R., Paul J. Wahlbeck, and James F. Spriggs II. 2006. "The Influence of Oral Argumentation before the U.S. Supreme Court." *American Political Science Review* 100(1):99–113.

Johnson, Timothy R., and Ryan C. Black. 2017. "The Roberts Court and Oral Argument: A First Decade Retrospective." *Washington University Journal of Law and Policy* 54:137–148.

Johnson, Timothy R., Ryan C. Black, Jerry Goldman, and Sarah A. Treul. 2009. "Inquiring Minds Want to Know: Do Justices Tip Their Hands with Their Questions at Oral Arguments in the U.S. Supreme Court?" *Washington University Journal of Law & Policy* 29:241–261.

Jokela, Markus, Alexandra Alvergne, Thomas V. Pollet, and Virpi Lummaa. 2011. "Reproductive Behavior and Personality Traits of the Five Factor Model." *European Journal of Personality* 25(6):487–500.

Judge, Timothy A., Chad A. Higgins, Carl J. Thorensen, and Murray R. Barrick. 1999. "The Big Five Personality Traits, General Mental Ability, and Career Success across the Lifespan." *Personnel Psychology* 52(3):621–652.

Judge, Timothy A., Joseph J. Martocchio, and Carl J. Thorensen. 1997. "Five-Factor Model of Personality and Employee Absence." *Journal of Applied Psychology* 82(5):745–755.

Kapust, Daniel. 2011. "Cicero on Decorum and the Morality of Rhetoric." *European Journal of Political Theory* 10(1):92–112.

Keller, Jonathan W., and Dennis M. Foster. 2012. "Presidential Leadership Style and the Political Use of Force." *Political Psychology* 33(5):581–598.

Kennedy, George A. 2007. *Aristotle on Rhetoric*. Oxford University Press.

Kern, Margaret L., and Howard S. Friedman. 2008. "Do Conscientious Individuals Live Longer? A Quantitative Review." *Health Psychology* 27(5):505–512.

Kimball, Bruce A. 2006. "The Proliferation of Case Method Teaching in American Law Schools: Mr. Langdell's Emblematic Abomination, 1890–1915." *History of Education Quarterly* 46(2):192–247.

Kingdon, John W. 1984. *Agendas, Alternatives, and Public Policies*. Boston: Little-Brown.

Kirman, Igor. 1995. "Standing Apart to Be a Part: The Precedential Value of Supreme Court Concurring Opinions." *Columbia Law Review* 95(8):2083–2119.

Klein, David, and Gregory Mitchell. 2010. *The Psychology of Judicial Decision Making*. Oxford University Press.

Knight, Jack, and Lee Epstein. 1996. "The Norm of Stare Decisis." *American Journal of Political Science* 40(4):1018–1035.

Knox, John. 2002. *The Forgotten Memoir of John Knox.* University of Chicago Press.

Korobkin, Russell B. 2000. "Behavioral Analysis and Legal Form: Rules vs. Standards Revisited." *Oregon Law Review* 79:23.

Kosma, Montgomery N. 1998. "Measuring the Influence of Supreme Court Justices." *Journal of Legal Studies* 27:333–372.

Krewson, Christopher N. 2018. "Save This Honorable Court: Shaping Public Perceptions of the Supreme Court off the Bench." *Political Research Quarterly.* DOI: 1065912918801563.

Krueger, Robert F., and Kristian E. Markon. 2014. "The Role of the DSM-5 Personality Trait Model in Moving toward a Quantitative and Empirically Based Approach to Classifying Personality and Psychopathology." *Annual Review of Clinical Psychology* 10:477–501.

Krueger, Robert F., and Wendy Johnson. 2008. "Behavioral Genetics and Personality." *Handbook of Personality: Theory and Research*, pp. 287–310. Guilford Press.

Kunda, Ziva. 1990. "The Case for Motivated Reasoning." *Psychological Bulletin* 108(3):335–358.

Landes, William M., and Richard A. Posner. 1976. "Legal Precedent: A Theoretical and Empirical Analysis." *Journal of Law and Economics* 19(2):249–307. DOI: 10.1093/acrefore/9780190228637.013.91.

Lane, Elizabeth A., and Ryan C. Black. 2017. "Agenda Setting and Case Selection on the U.S. Supreme Court." *Oxford Research Encyclopedia of Politics.*

Langdell, Christopher Columbus. 1871. *A Selection of Cases on the Law of Contracts: With References and Citations.* Little, Brown.

Larsen, Randy J., and David M. Buss. 2014. *Personality Psychology: Domains of Knowledge about Human Nature.* 5th ed. McGraw-Hill.

Laswell, Harold D. 1930. *Psychology and Politics.* University of Chicago Press.

Lazarus, Edward. 2005. *Closed Chambers: The Rise, Fall, and Future of the Modern Supreme Court.* Reissue edition. New York: Penguin Books.

Leiman, Joan Maisel. 1957. "The Rule of Four." *Columbia Law Review* 57(7):975–992.

Liu, Zhe, Yi Wang, Jalal Mahmud, Rama Akkiraju, Jerald Schoudt, Anbang Xu, and Bryan Donovan. 2016. "To Buy or Not to Buy? Understanding the Role of Personality Traits in Predicting Consumer Behaviors." *Part II Lecture Notes in Computer Science* 10047:337–346.

Madison, James. 1961. Number 10. In *The Federalist*, ed. Jacob Cooke. Wesleyan University Press.

Mairesse, Fancois, Marilyn A. Walker, Matthias R. Mehl, and Roger K. Moore. 2007. "Using Linguistic Cues for the Automatic Recognition of Personality in Conversation and Text." *Journal of Artificial Intelligence Research* 30:457–500.

Malouff, John M, Einar B Thorsteinsson, Nicola S Schutte, Navjot Bhullar, and Sally E Rooke. 2010. "The Five-Factor Model of Personality and Relationship Satisfaction of Intimate Partners: A Meta-Analysis." *Journal of Research in Personality* 44(1):124–127.

Maltzman, Forrest, James F. Spriggs II, and Paul J. Wahlbeck. 2000. *Crafting Law on the Supreme Court: The Collegial Game.* New York: Cambridge University Press.

Maltzman, Forrest, and Paul J. Wahlbeck. 1996. "May It Please the Chief? Opinion Assignments in the Rehnquist Court." *American Journal of Political Science* 40(2):421–433.

Maltzman, Forrest, and Paul J. Wahlbeck. 2004. "A Conditional Model of Opinion Assignment on the Supreme Court." *Political Research Quarterly* 57(4): 551–563.

Mark, Alyx, and Michael A Zilis. 2018. "Restraining the Court: Assessing Accounts of Congressional Attempts to Limit Supreme Court Authority." *Legislative Studies Quarterly* 43(1):141–169.

Mark, Alyx, and Michael A Zilis. Forthcoming. "The Conditional Effectiveness of Legislative Threats: How Court Curbing Alters the Behavior of (Some) Supreme Court Justices." *Political Research Quarterly*.

Martin, Andrew D., and Kevin M. Quinn. 2002. "Dynamic Ideal Point Estimation via Markov Chain Monte Carlo for the U.S. Supreme Court, 1953–1999." *Political Analysis* 10(2):134–153.

Martin, Andrew D., and Kevin M. Quinn. 2005. "Can Ideal Point Estimates Be Used as Explanatory Variables?" Unpublished manuscript, available at http://adm.wustl.edu/supct/resnote.pdf.

Martineau, Robert J., Kent Sinclaie, Michael E. Solomine, and Randy J. Holland. 2005. *Appellate Practice and Procedure*. Thomson.

Mason, Alpheus Thomas. 1964. *William Howard Taft: Chief Justice*. Oldbourne.

Masood, Ali S, Benjamin J Kassow, and Donald R Songer. 2017. "Supreme Court Precedent in a Judicial Hierarchy." *American Politics Research* 45(3):403–434.

McAdams, Dan P. 1992. "The Five-Factor Model in Personality: A Critical Appraisal." *Journal of Personality* 60(2):329–361.

McCann, Stewart J. H. 2005. "Longevity, Big Five Personality Factors, and Health Behaviors: Presidents from Washington to Nixon." *The Journal of Psychology* 139(3):273–288.

McCrae, Robert R., and Oliver P. John. 1992. "An Introduction to the Five-Factor Model and Its Applications." *Journal of Personality* 60(2):175–215.

McCrae, Robert R., and Paul T. Costa. 1987. "Validation of the Five-Factor Model of Personality Across Instruments and Observers." *Journal of Personality and Social Psychology* 52(1):81–90.

McCrae, Robert R., and Paul T. Costa Jr. 1997. "Personality Trait Structure as a Human Universal." *American Psychologist* 52(5):509.

McCrae, Robert R., and Paul T. Costa Jr. 2003. *Personality in Adulthood*. Guilford Press.

McGuire, Kevin T. 1993. "Lawyers and the U.S. Supreme Court: The Washington Community and Legal Elites." *American Journal of Political Science* 37(2): 365–390.

McGuire, Kevin T. 1995. "Repeat Players in the Supreme Court: The Role of Experienced Lawyers in Litigation Success." *Journal of Politics* 57(1):187–196.

McGuire, Kevin T., and James A. Stimson. 2004. "The Least Dangerous Branch Revisited: New Evidence on Supreme Court Responsiveness to Public Preferences." *Journal of Politics* 66(4):1018–1035.

McKeown, M. Margaret. 2011. "To Judge or Not to Judge: Transparency and Recusal in the Federal System." *The Review of Litigation* 30:653–669.

Mike, Anissa, Kelci Harris, Brent W. Roberts, and Joshua J. Jackson. 2015. Conscientiousness. In *International Encyclopedia of the Social and Behavioral Sciences*, 2nd ed., Vol. 4., ed. J. Wright, pp. 658–665. Elsevier.

Mishler, William, and Reginald S. Sheehan. 1993. "The Supreme Court as a Countermajoritarian Institution? The Impact of Public Opinion on Supreme Court Decisions." *American Political Science Review* 87:87–101.

Mishler, William, and Reginald S. Sheehan. 1996. "Public Opinion, the Attitudinal Model, and Supreme Court Decision Making: A Micro-Analytic Perspective." *The Journal of Politics* 58:169–200.

Mohammed, Susan, and Linda C. Angell. 2003. "Personality Heterogeneity in Teams: Which Differences Make Difference for Team Performance?" *Small Group Research* 34(6):651–677.

Mondak, Jeffrey J. 2010. *Personality and the Foundation of Political Behavior*. Cambridge University Press.

Mondak, Jeffrey J., and Karen D. Halperin. 2008. "A Framework for the Study of Personality and Political Behavior." *British Journal of Political Behavior* 38:335–362.

Mondak, Jeffrey J., Matthew V. Hibbing, Damarys Canache, Mitchell A. Seligson, and Mary R. Anderson. 2010. "Personality and Civic Engagement: An Integrative Framework for the Study of Trait Effects on Political Behavior." *American Political Science Review* 104(1):85–110.

Mount, Michael K., and Murray R. Barrick. 1998. "Five Reasons Why the "Big Five" Article Has Been Frequently Cited." *Personnel Psychology* 51(4):849–857.

Mount, Michael K., Murray R. Barrick, and Greg L. Stewart. 1998. "Five-Factor Model of Personality and Performance in Jobs Involving Interpersonal Interactions." *Human Performance* 11(2–3):145–165.

Moyer, Laura. 2012. "The Role of Case Complexity in Judicial Decision Making." *Law and Policy* 34(3):291–312.

Murphy, Bruce Allen. 2003. *Wild Bill: The Legend and Life of William O. Douglas*. Random House.

Murphy, Walter F. 1964. *Elements of Judicial Strategy*. Chicago: University of Chicago Press.

Nelson, Kjersten R., and Eve M. Ringsmuth. 2009. "Departures From the Court: The Political Landscape and Institutional Constraints." *American Politics Research* 37(3):486–507.

Nickerson, Raymond S. 1998. "Confirmation Bias: A Ubiquitous Phenomenon in Many Guises." *Review of General Psychology* 2(2):175–220.

Nunn, Clyde A., Harry J. Crockett, and J. Allen Williams. 1978. *Tolerance for Nonconformity*. San Francisco: Jossey-Bass.

Oakes, James L. 1992. "Keynote Address-Conference on Compelling Government Interests: Introduction by Hon. James L. Oakes." *Albany Law Review* 55(3):535–538.

O'Brien, David M. 1997. "Join-3 Votes, the Rule of Four, the Cert. Pool, and the Supreme Court's Shrinking Plenary Docket." *Journal of Law and Politics* 13:779–808.

O'Brien, David M. 2005. *Storm Center: The Supreme Court in American Politics*. 7th ed. New York: W.W. Norton.

O'Brien, Tim. 2009. *A Good Quarrel: America's Top Legal Reporters Share Stories from Inside the Supreme Court*. University of Michigan Press.

Ochs, Donovan J. 1989. "Cicero and Philosophic Inventio." *Rhetoric Society Quarterly* 19(3):217–227.

Owens, Ryan. 2010*a*. "The Separation of Powers and Supreme Court Agenda Setting." *American Journal of Political Science* 54(2):412–427.

Owens, Ryan. 2010*b*. "The Separation of Powers and Supreme Court Agenda Setting." *American Journal of Political Science* 54(2):412–427.

Owens, Ryan J., and David A. Simon. 2012. "Explaining the Supreme Court's Docket Size." *William and Mary Law Review*.

Owens, Ryan J., and Justin P. Wedeking. 2011. "Justices and Legal Clarity: Analyzing the Complexity of Supreme Court Opinions." *Law and Society Review* 45(4):1027–1061.

Owens, Ryan J., Justin P. Wedeking, and Patrick C. Wohlfarth. 2013. "How the Supreme Court Alters Opinion Language to Evade Congressional Review." *Journal of Law and Courts* 1(1):35–59.

Owens, Ryan J., and Justin Wedeking. 2012. "Predicting Drift on Politically Insulated Institutions: A Study of Ideological Drift on the U.S. Supreme Court." *Journal of Politics* 74:487–500.

Owens, Ryan J., and Lee Epstein. 2005. "Amici Curiae during the Rehnquist Years." *Judicature* 89(3):127–133.

Owens, Ryan J., and Patrick C. Wohlfarth. 2014. "State Solicitors General, Appellate Expertise, and State Success before the U.S. Supreme Court." *Law and Society Review* 48(3):657–685.

Owens, Ryan J., and Patrick C. Wohlfarth. 2017. "Public Mood, Previous Electoral Experience, and Responsiveness Among Federal Circuit Court Judges." *American Politics Research* 45(6):1003–1031.

Owens, Ryan J., and Patrick C. Wohlfarth. 2019. "The Influence of Home-State Reputation and Public Opinion on Federal Circuit Court Judges." *Journal of Law and Courts*: Forthcoming. DOI: https://doi.org/10.1086/703066.

Palmer, Jan. 1982. "An Econometric Analysis of the U.S. Supreme Court's Certiorari Decisions." *Public Choice* 39:387–98.

Pang, Xun, Barry Friedman, Andrew Martin, and Kevin Quinn. 2012. "Endogenous Jurisprudential Regimes." *Political Analysis* 20:417–436.

Pearson, Lionel. 1975. "The Virtuoso Passages in Demosthenes' Speeches." *Phoenix* 29(3):214–230.

Pennebaker, James W., and Laura A. King. 1999. "Linguistic Styles: Language Use as an Individual Difference." *Journal of Personality and Social Psychology* 77:1296–1312.

Pennebaker, James W., Mattias R. Mehl, and Kate G. Niederhoffer. 2003. "Psychological Aspects of Natural Language Use: Our Words, Our Selves." *Annual Review of Psychology* 54:547–577.

Pennebaker, James W., Ryan L. Boyd, Kayla Jordan, and Kate Blackburn. 2015. "The Development and Psychometric Properties of LIWC2015." Technical report available online at www.liwc.net.

Pennington, Jeffrey, Richard Socher, and Christopher D. Manning. 2014. "GloVe: Global Vectors for Word Representation." www.aclweb.org/anthology/D14-1162.

Peppers, Todd C. 2006. *Courtiers of the Marble Palace: The Rise and Influence of the Supreme Court Law Clerk*. Stanford University Press.

Perry, Jr., H. W. 1991. *Deciding to Decide: Agenda Setting in the United States Supreme Court*. Harvard University Press.

Pervin, Lawrence A. 1994. "A Critical Analysis of Current Trait Theory." *Psychological Inquiry* 5(2):103–113.

Posner, Richard A. 1993. "What Do Judges and Justices Maximize? (The Same Thing Everybody Else Does)." *Supreme Court Economic Review* 3:1–41.

Posner, Richard A. 2008. *How Judges Think*. Harvard University Press.

Pritchett, C. Herman. 1941. "Divisions of Opinion among Justices of the U.S. Supreme Court, 1939–1941." *American Political Science Review* 35:890–898.

Pritchett, C. Herman. 1969. "The Development of Judicial Research." In *Frontiers of Judicial Research*, ed. Joel Grossman, and Joseph Tanenhaus, pp. 27–42. Wiley.

Provine, Doris Marie. 1980. *Case Selection in the United States Supreme Court*. University of Chicago Press.

Ramey, Adam J., Jonathan D. Klinger, and Gary E. Hollibaugh Jr. 2017. *More Than a Feeling: Personality, Polarization, and the Transformation of the U.S. Congress*. University of Chicago Press.

Ramey, Adam J., Jonathan D. Klinger, and Gary E. Hollibaugh Jr. 2019. "Measuring Elite Personality Using Speech." *Political Science Research and Methods* 7: 163–184.

Ray, Laura Krugman. 1990. "The Justices Write Separately: Uses of the Concurrence by the Rehnquist Court." *University of California Davis Law Review* 23:777–831.

Rehnquist, William H. 1977. "Sunshine in the Third Branch." *Washburn Law Journal* 16:559–570.

Rehnquist, William H. 2001. *The Supreme Court*. Revised and updated edition. Vintage Books.

Richards, Mark J., and Herbert M. Kritzer. 2002. "Jurisprudential Regimes in Supreme Court Decision Making." *American Political Science Review* 96(2):305–320.

Robert, Christopher, and Yu Ha Cheung. 2010. "An Examination of the Relationship between Conscientiousness and Group Performance on a Creative Task." *Journal of Research in Personality* 44(2):222–231.

Roberts, Brent W., Carl Lejuez, Robert F., Krueger, Jessica M., Richards, and Patrick L. Hill. 2014. "What Is Conscientiousness and How Can It Be Assessed?" *Developmental Psychology* 50(5):1315–1330.

Roberts, Brent W., and Daniel Mroczek. 2008. "Personality Trait Change in Adulthood." *Current Directions in Psychological Science* 17(1):31–35.

Roberts, Brent W., Joshua J. Jackson, Jennifer V. Fayard, Grant Edmonds, and Jenna Meints. 2009. "Conscientiousness." In *Handbook of Individual Differences in Social Behavior*, ed. Mark R. Leary, and Rick H. Hoyle, pp. 369–381. The Guilford Press.

Roberts, Brent W., Joshua J., Jackson, Jessica Burger, and Ulrich Trautwein. 2009. "Conscientiousness and Externalizing Psychopathology: Overlap, Developmental Patterns, and Etiology of Two Related Constructs." *Development and Psychopathology* 21(3):871–888.

Roberts, Brent W., Kate E., Walton, and Wolfgang Viechtbauer. 2006. "Patterns of Mean-Level Change in Personality Traits across the Life Course: A Meta-analysis of Longitudinal Studies." *Psychological Bulletin* 132(1):1.

Roberts, Brent W., Nathan R. Kuncel, Rebecca Shiner, Avshalom Caspi, and Lewis R. Goldberg. 2007. "The Power of Personality: The Comparative Validity of Personality Traits, Socioeconomic Status, and Cognitive Ability for Predicting Important Life Outcomes." *Perspectives on Psychological Science* 2(4): 313–345.

Roberts, Brent W., Tim Bogg, Kate E. Walton, Oleksandr S. Chernyshenko, and Stephen E. Stark. 2004. "A Lexical Investigation of the Lower-Order Structure of Conscientiousness." *Journal of Research in Personality* 38(2): 164–178.

Roberts, Brent W., and Timothy Bogg. 2004. "A Longitudinal Study of the Relationships between Conscientiousness and Social-Environmental Factors and Substance-Use Behaviors That Influence Health." *Journal of Personality* 72(2): 325–354.

Roberts, John G. 2005. "Testimony before the Senate Judiciary Committee." www .judiciary.senate.gov/imo/media/doc/GPO-CHRG-ROBERTS.pdf.

Roberts, John G. 2006. "Chief Justice Roberts 2006 Commencement Address to Georgetown Law School." http://apps.law.georgetown .edu/webcasts/eventDetail.cfm?eventID=144.

Roberts, Roxanne. 2016. "Time Off the Bench: The Social Lives of Supreme Court Justices." *Washington Post*. March 1.

Rohde, David W. 1972. "Policy Goals, Strategic, Choice and Majority Opinion Assignments in the U.S. Supreme Court." *Midwest Journal of Political Science* 16(4):652–682.

Rosen, Jeffrey. 2001. "A Majority of One." *The New York Times*. June 3. Section 6: Column 1:32.

Rosen, Jeffrey. 2007. *The Supreme Court: The Personalities and Rivalries That Defined America*. Holt Paperbacks.

Rubenzer, Steven J., Thomas R. Faschingbauer, and Deniz S. Ones. 2000. "Assessing the U.S. Presidents Using the Revised NEO Personality Inventory." *Assessment* 7(4):403–419.

Ruger, Theodore W. 2006. "The Chief Justice's Special Authority and the Norms of Judicial Power." *University of Pennsylvania Law Review* 154:1551–1574.

Salgado, Jesus F. 1997. "The Five Factor Model of Personality and Job Performance in the European Community." *Journal of Applied Psychology* 82(1):30.

Salokar, Rebecca Mae. 1992. *The Solicitor General: The Politics of Law*. Temple University Press.

Sample, James. 2013. "Supreme Court Recusals from Marbury to the Modern Day." *Georgetown Journal of Legal Ethics* 26:95–151.

Scalia, Antonin. 1994. "Dissenting Opinions." *Journal of Supreme Court History* 1994:33–44.

Scalia, Antonin, and Bryan A. Garner. 2008. *Making Your Case: The Art of Persuading Judges*. Thomson.

Scalia, Antonin S. 1989. "The Rule of Law as a Law of Rules." *University of Chicago Law Review* 56:1175–1181.

Schauer, Frederick. 1987. "Precedent." *Stanford Law Review* 39:571–605.

Schauer, Frederick. 2000. "Incentives, Reputation, and the Inglorious Determinants of Judicial Behavior." *University of Cincinnatiati Law Review* 68:615–636.

Schauer, Frederick, and Richard Zeckhauser. 2011. *Litigation versus Regulation*. University of Chicago Press.

Schmidt, Thomas, and Christian Wolff. 2016. "Personality and Information Behavior in Web Search." *Proceedings of the Association for Information Science and Technology* 53(1):1–6.

Schwartz, Bernard. 1990. *The Ascent of Pragmatism: The Burger Court in Action.* Addison-Wesley.

Schwartz, Bernard. 1995. "Supreme Court Superstars: The Ten Greatest Justices." *Tulsa Law Journal* 31(1):93–159.

Schwartz, H. Andrew, Johannes C. Eichstaedt, Margaret L. Kern, et al. 2013. "Personality, Gender, and Age in the Language of Social Media: The Open Vocabulary Approach." *PLOS One* 8(9):1–15.

Scigliano, Robert. 1971. *The Supreme Court and the Presidency.* Free Press.

Scollon, Christie Napa, and Ed Diener. 2006. "Love, Work, and Changes in Extraversion and Neuroticism Over Time." *Journal of Personality and Social Psychology* 91(6):1152.

Scott, Kevin M. 2006. "Understanding Judicial Hierarchy: Reversals and the Behavior of Intermediate Appellate Judges." *Law and Society Review* 40(1):163–191.

Segal, Jeffrey A., and Albert D. Cover. 1989. "Ideological Values and the Votes of Supreme Court Justices." *American Political Science Review* 83(2):557–565.

Segal, Jeffrey A., and Harold J. Spaeth. 1996. "The Influence of Stare Decisis on the Votes of United States Supreme Court Justices." *American Journal of Political Science* 40(4):971–1003.

Segal, Jeffrey A., and Harold J. Spaeth. 2002. *The Supreme Court and the Attitudinal Model Revisited.* Cambridge University Press.

Slotnick, Elliot E. 1979a. "Judicial Career Patterns and Majority Opinion Assignment on the Supreme Court." *Journal of Politics* 41(2):640–648.

Slotnick, Elliot E. 1979b. "Who Speaks for the Court? Majority Opinion Assignment from Taft to Burger." *American Journal of Political Science* 23(1):60–77.

Smelcer, Susan Navarro, Amy Steigerwalt, and Richard L. Vining. 2013. "Bias and the Bar: Evaluating the ABA Ratings of Federal Judicial Nominees." *Political Research Quarterly* 66(4):827–840. Working Paper.

Snyder, Mark. 1994. "Traits and Motives in the Psychology of Personality." *Psychological Inquiry* 5(2):162–166.

Sokol, Ronald P. 1967. *Language and Litigation: A Portrait of the Appellate Brief.* The Michie Company.

Solomon, Brittany C., and Joshua J. Jackson. 2014. "Why Do Personality Traits Predict Divorce? Multiple Pathways through Satisfaction." *Journal of Personality and Social Psychology* 106(6):978–996.

Songer, Donald R. 1979. "Concern for Policy Outputs as a Cue for Supreme Court Decisions of Certiorari." *Journal of Politics* 41(4):1185–1194.

Soto, Christopher J. 2015. "The Little Six Personality Dimensions from Early Childhood to Early Adulthood: Mean-Level Age and Gender Differences in Parents' Reports." *Journal of personality* 84(4):1–14.

Spaeth, Harold J. 1964. "The Judicial Restraint of Mr. Justice Frankfurter–Myth or Reality." *Midwest Journal of Political Science* 8(1):22–38.

Spaeth, Harold J. 2001. *The Burger Court Judicial Database: 1969–1985 Terms.* Michigan State University Press.

Spaeth, Harold, and Jeffrey Segal. 1999. *Majority Rule or Minority Will: Adherence to Precedent on the U.S. Supreme Court.* Cambridge University Press.

Spain, Seth M, Peter Harms, and James M LeBreton. 2014. "The Dark Side of Personality at Work." *Journal of Organizational Behavior* 35(S1):S41–S60.

Spriggs, II, James F., and Thomas G. Hansford. 2001. "Explaining the Overruling of U.S. Supreme Court Precedent." *Journal of Politics* 63(4):1091–1111.

Spriggs, II, James F., and Thomas G. Hansford. 2002. "The U.S. Supreme Court's Incorporation and Interpretation of Precedent." *Law & Society Review* 36(1):139–160.

Staudt, Nancy, Lee Epstein, and Peter Wiedenbeck. 2006. "The Ideological Component of Judging in the Taxation Context." *Washington University Law Review* 84:1797–1821.

Stempel, Jeffrey W. 1987. "Rehnquist, Recusal, and Reform." *Brooklyn Law Review* 53:589–667.

Stern, Robert L., Eugene Gressman, Stephen M. Shapiro, and Kenneth S. Geller. 2002. *Supreme Court Practice.* 8th ed. The Bureau of National Affairs.

Stimson, James A. 1991. *Public Opinion in America: Moods, Cycles, and Swings.* Boulder: Westview Press.

Stimson, James A., Michael B. Mackuen, and Robert S. Erikson. 1995. "Dynamic Representation." *American Political Science Review* 89(3):543–565.

Sullivan, John L., James Piereson, and George E. Marcus. 1979. "An Alternative Conceptualization of Political Tolerance: Illusory Increases 1950s–1970s." *American Political Science Review* 73(3): 781–794.

Sullivan, Kathleen M. 1992. "The Justices of Rules and Standards." *Harvard Law Review* 106:22–123.

Sunstein, Cass R. 1999. *One Case at a Time: Judicial Minimalism on the Supreme Court.* Harvard University Press.

Tanenhaus, Joseph, Marvin Schick, and David Rosen. 1963. "The Supreme Court's Certiorari Jurisdiction: Cue Theory." In *Judicial Decision-Making*, ed. Glendon A. Schubert, pp. 111–132. Free Press.

Tausczik, Yla R., and James W. Pennebaker. 2010. "The Psychological Meaning of Words: LIWC and Computerized Text Analysis Methods." *Journal of Language and Social Psychology* 29:24–54.

Tellegen, Auke. 1988. "The Analysis of Consistency in Personality Assessment." *Journal of Personality* 56(3):621–663.

Teply, Larry L. 1990. *Legal Writing, Analysis, and Oral Argument.* WEST.

Tetlock, Philip E., Jane Bernzweig, and Jack L. Gallant. 1985. "Supreme Court Decision Making: Cognitive Style as a Predictor of Ideological Consistency of Voting." *Journal of Personality and Social Psychology* 48:1227–1239.

Ulmer, S. Sidney. 1984. "The Supreme Court's Certiorari Decisions: Conflict as a Predictive Variable." *The American Political Science Review* 78(4):901–911.

Ulmer, S. Sidney, William Hintz, and Louise Kirklosky. 1972. "The Decision to Grant or Deny Certiorari: Further Considerations of Cue Theory." *Law & Society Review* 6(4):637–644.

Ura, Joseph Daniel. 2014. "Backlash and Legitimation: Macro Political Responses to Supreme Court Decisions." *American Journal of Political Science* 58:110–126.

Verilli, Louis J. 2012. "Congress, the Constitution, and Supreme Court Recusal." *Washington and Lee Law Review* 69:1535–1606.

Verilli, Louis J. 2016. *Disqualifying the Supreme Court: Supreme Court Recusal and the Constitution*. University Press of Kansas.

Virelli, Louis J. 2011. "The (Un)Constitutionality of Supreme Court Recusal Standards." *Wisconsin Law Review* 2011:1181–1234.

Wahlbeck, Paul J. 1997. "The Life of the Law: Judicial Politics and Legal Change." *Journal of Politics* 59(3):778–802.

Wahlbeck, Paul J. 2006. "Strategy and Constraints on Supreme Court Opinion Assignment." *University of Pennsylvania Law Review* 154(6):1729–1755.

Wahlbeck, Paul J., and Forrest Maltzman. 2005. "Opinion Assignment on the Rehnquist Court." *Judicature* 89(3):121–126.

Wahlbeck, Paul J., James F. Spriggs, and Forrest Maltzman. 2009a. "The Burger Court Opinion Writing Database." http://supremecourtopinions.wustl.edu/.

Wahlbeck, Paul J., James F. Spriggs, II, and Forrest Maltzman. 2009b. "The Burger Court Opinion Writing Database." First Release. Data file and codebook dated August 6, 2009 and downloaded from http://home.gwu.edu/wahlbeck/index_files/Page365.htm.

Waller, Niels G., and Joe D Zavala. 1993. "Evaluating the Big Five." *Psychological Inquiry* 4(2):131–134.

Ward, Artemus, and David L. Weiden. 2006. *Sorcerers' Apprentices: 100 Years of Law Clerks at the United States Supreme Court*. New York: New York University Press.

Waung, Marie, and Thomas S. Brice. 1998. "The Effects of Conscientiousness and Opportunity to Caucus on Group Performance." *Small Group Research* 29(5):624–634.

Wedeking, Justin, and Dion Farganis. 2010. "The Candor Factor: Does Nominee Evasiveness Affect Judiciary Committee Support for Supreme Court Nominees." *Hofstra Law Review* 39(2):329–368.

Wedeking, Justin, and Dion Farganis. 2014. *Supreme Court Confirmation Hearings in the U.S.Senate: Reconsidering the Charade*. University of Michigan Press.

Wedeking, Justin, and Michael A. Zilis. 2018. "Disagreeable Rhetoric and the Prospect of Public Opposition: Opinion Moderation on the U.S. Supreme Court." *Political Research Quarterly* 71(2):380–394.

Wedeking, Justin P. 2010. "Supreme Court Litigants and Strategic Framing." *American Journal of Political Science* 54(3):617–631.

Winter, David G. 1987. "Leader Appeal, Leader Performance, and the Motive Profiles of Leaders: A Study of American Presidents and Elections." *Journal of Personality and Social Psychology* 52(1):196–202.

Winter, David G. 2003. *The Psychological Assessment of Political Leaders*. University of Michigan Press.

Winter, David G., Oliver P. John, Abigail J. Stewart, Eva C. Klohnen, and Lauren E. Duncan. 1998. "Traits and Motives: Toward an Integration of Two Traditions in Personality Research." *Psychological Review* 105(2):230–250.

Witt, L.A., Lisa A. Burke, Murray R. Barrick, and Michael K. Mount. 2002. "The Interactive Effects of Conscientiousness and Agreeableness on Job Performance." *Journal of Applied Psychology* 87(1):164–169.

Wohlfarth, Patrick C. 2009. "The Tenth Justice? Consequences of Politicization in the Solicitor General's Office." *Journal of Politics* 70(1):224–237.

Wolfe, Sarah. 2012. "Rep. Louie Gohmert Suggests Impeachment of Kagan over Health Care Ruling." www.pri.org/stories/2012-06-28/rep-louie-gohmert-suggests-impeachment-kagan-over-health-care-ruling-video.

Wood, Sandra L., Linda Camp Keith, Drew Noble Lanier, and Ayo Ogundele. 2000. "Opinion Assignment and the Chief Justice: 1888–1940." *Social Science Quarterly* 81(3):798–809.

Woodward, Bob, and Scott Armstrong. 1979. *The Brethren: Inside the Supreme Court.* Simon & Schuster.

Wrightsman, Lawrence S. 2006. *The Psychology of the Supreme Court.* Oxford University Press.

Zigerell, L. J. 2013. "Justice Has Served: U.S. Supreme Court Retirement Strategies." *Justice System Journal* 34(2):208–227.

Zilis, Michael. 2015. *The Limits of Legitimacy: Dissenting Opinions, Media Coverage, and Public Responses to Supreme Court Decisions.* University of Michigan Press.

Zink, James R., James F. Spriggs II, and John T. Scott. 2009. "Courting the Public: The Influence of Decision Attributes on Individuals' Views of Court Opinions." *Journal of Politics* 71(3):909–925.

Index

1993 Statement of Recusal Policy, 292
20,000 *Leagues Under the Sea*, 32

A.T. Massey Coal Company, 290, 291n
Abraham, Henry J., 1
actuaries, 29
Affordable Care Act, 286n
Affordable Care Act cases, *See National Federation of Independent Business* v. *Sebelius*
agenda setting, 82–85, *See also* call for the views of the Solicitor General
  amicus briefs, 97, 105, 110
  case importance, 85, 88
  cert pool, 79n, 79, 83–84
  cert pool memos, 79n, 80, 83–84, 86–87, 90–92
  conference voting, 84–85, 94
  conscientiousness, *See* conscientiousness
  discuss list, 84, 84n, 86, 93, 94n
  granting review, 85–88
  "Join-3" votes, 7, 79–81, 84–85, 93, 94, 137
  judicial review, 85, 87–88, 97
  legal conflict, 79, 85–86, 94–96, 109
  petition for the writ of certiorari, 82
  policy considerations, 85–87, 92, 97–98, 102, 154
  Solicitor General's influence, 96, 109–110
  Supreme Court Rule 10, 79, 85, 89
agreeableness, 4
  agenda setting, 101
  definition of, 4, 22
  estimates of, 41, 44

ideology, 77
job satisfaction, 77
"Join-3" votes, 104
judicial behavior, 5, 74n
longevity, 71
love, 74
marriage, 72
measurement of, 37, 60, 67
merits briefs, 131
number of children, 71
Office of the Solicitor General, 152
oral argument, 134
policy-based strategic votes, 109
validity of measure, 69–70
workplace performance, 74–77
Akkiraju, Jerald Schoudt, 38n
Aliotta, Jilda M., 3, 17–18, 32, 189
Alito, Samuel A., 2, 79n, 83, 112
Alpert, Lenore, 6, 17
American Bar Association, 5, 53
Angell, Linda C., 325
Angleitner, Alois, 21
Argentine Republic v. *Amerada Hess Shipping Corp.* (1989), 92
Aristotle, 11, 113–114
Ark of the Covenant, 29
Armaly, Miles T., 43
Armstrong, Scott, 2, 93, 94n, 172n
Arnoux, Pierre-Hadrien, 38n
Askew, Reubin, 270
Assize of Measures, 29
Asuero, A.G., 65, 67
Atkins, Burton, 6, 17

attitudinal model, *See also* judicial decision making and ideology, *See also* judicial decision making and policy preferences, 3, 12, 14

Bailey, Michael, 16, 273
Bailey v. U.S. (2013), 112–113
Baker, Levi R., 25
Baldus, David, 161
Bam, Dmitry, 293
Barber, James David, 16n
Barelds, Dick P.H., 47
Barrick, Murray R., 22–23, 120, 191, 276n
Bartels Brandon L., 15, 273
Bassett, Debra L., 293
Baum, Lawrence, 3, 15, 33n, 273n
Benesh, Sarah C., 87, 168
Benjamin, Brent, 291n
Benoit, Kenneth, 39
Bermant, Gordon, 229
Bernheim, B. Douglas, 273
Bernzweig, Jane, 3, 16
Biden, Joe, 251
"Big Five" traits, *See also* agreeableness; conscientiousness; extraversion; neuroticism; openness, 4, 5, 18–19, 21n, 21, 22, 25, 53, 303
   structure of, 20
Black, Hugo, 2, 31, 40–41
Black, Ryan C., 7, 8, 33, 43, 79n, 79, 84–88, 90, 93, 94n, 94–97, 106, 114–116, 118, 119, 121n, 121–124, 126, 130–131, 139, 140, 143, 147, 152–153, 153n, 153, 157, 227, 229, 230n, 232n, 244, 246, 247, 271, 278, 280, 293, 296, 312, 313
Blackman, Josh, 286
Blackmun, Harry, 1–2, 80–82, 87, 92, 95n, 137–138, 141, 155, 164, 172n, 180, 183, 187
   digital archives, 7, 79, 93, 94, 124, 153
Blackstone, William, 288n
Blackstone, Bethany, 271, 272, 274, 278
Blankenship, Don, 290, 291n
Bleidorn, Wiebke, 21
Bogg, Tim, 25n, 47, 49, 51–53, 250
Boucher, Jr., Robert L., 87
Bowers v. Hardwick (1986), 185–187
Bowsher v. Synar (1986), 186
Boyd, Christina L., 84, 94, 123
Boyette, Neil, 38n
Braman, Eileen, 17
Brandeis Louis, 1

Brennan, William J., 83, 85, 93n, 94, 163, 172, 173, 249, 270n
Brenner, Saul, 85–87, 170n, 170, 248
Breyer, Stephen A., 43, 112, 277
Brice, Thomas S., 325
Brown v. Board of Education of Topeka (1954), 270
Bryan, Amanda C., 271, 296
Burger, Jerry M., 24n, 24
Burger, Jessica, 144n
Burger, Warren E., 19, 34n, 43, 166–168n, 172n, 173, 180, 186, 196, 204, 220, 245, 312, 313n, 313
Burger Court Opinion Writing Database, 183, 193–197
Burney, David, 161n
Burton, Harold, 53
Bush v. Gore (2000), 88, 119n
Buss, David M., 3, 20, 24n, 24, 117

Caesar, Julius, 275
Caldeira, Gregory A., 12, 85–88, 94, 97, 119, 140, 272, 288, 294
Caldwell, David F., 24n, 24
Callicles, 113
Cameron, Charles M., 53n
Caperton v. A.T. Massey Coal Co. (2009), 290n
Caplan, Lincoln, 140, 143
Cardozo, Benjamin N., 274n
Carey, Bob, 319
Carney, Dana R., 54, 76, 77
case-method approach, *See* legal theory model
Casillas, Christopher J., 147, 271–273, 278
certiorari, *See* agenda setting
Chamberlain, Ronald S., 139n, 140
Chapman, Benjamin P., 71
Chakraborty, P.K., 24, 226, 276
Charlie and the Chocolate Factory, 32
Cheung, Yu Ha, 325
Chesterton, G.K., 3, 320
Chrichlow, Scott, 16n
Cicero, 113
City of Ontario v. Quon (2010), 229n
Civil Rights Act of 1964, 78
Clark, Tom S., 325
Coan, Andrew, 224
Code of Conduct for United States Judges, 11n, 11
Coffin, Frank M., 115
cognitive dissonance theory, 17

cognitive rigidity, 17
Coleman-Liau Index, 123
Collins, Jr., Paul M., 3, 17, 123, 233n, 247, 249, 277, 324, 326
Collins, Todd A., 78
Committee on Codes of Conduct, 292
Common Space Scores, *See also* Judicial Common Space, 231
concurring opinions, 58, 59n, 61, 65, 69
    accommodation of other justices, 65
    joined, 65–67, 67n
    majority opinions, 59–61
    mixed, 61
    regular, 61–65
    riding shotgun, 112
    solo, 65–67, 67n
    special, 61–65
confirmation bias, 46
conscientiousness, 3–5, 7
    agenda setting, 6–7, 88–89, 98–102, 110, 320, 324
    definition of, 4–5, 22–23, 89, 117, 142, 142n, 144n
    emotional language and credibility, 8, 26, 113, 114, 117–118, 126–131, 135
    estimates of, 41–43
    health, 25n
    ideology, 54
    job satisfaction, 51–54
    "Join-3" votes, 7, 91–93, 102–104, 110
    judicial behavior, 5–6, 12, 26–28, 67
    judicial selection, 6, 33
    learning, 23–24
    legal arguments, 7–8, 26, 120, 321
    legal conflict, 7, 26, 81–82, 89–91, 93, 98–101, 110
    legislators, 25, 25n, 30
    logic, 113
    longevity, 46–48, 70
    love, 49–51, 74
    marriage, 49–50
    measurement of, 7, 36, 37n, 37, 60
    merits briefs, *See also* emotional language and credibility, 121, 126–131, 135
    number of children, 47n, 47–49
    Office of the Solicitor General, 6, 8, 27, 138–139, 142, 144, 148–153, 157–160, 321
    opinion assignment, 6, 8, 162, 171, 172n, 178n, 321
    opinion bargaining, 8–9, 184, 189, 191n, 198, 201, 202, 204, 207, 213, 322

opinion content, 9, 223, 226, 227, 237, 239, 240, 242, 322
opinion writing, 8–9, 27
oral argument, 114, 120–121, 131–135
policy-based strategic votes, 93, 105, 106n, 108–110
policymakers, 6
precedent, 6, 9, 26, 246, 251, 256, 258, 261, 268, 322
preparedness, 24
public opinion, 6, 9, 27, 272, 275, 281, 284, 323
quality of argument, 8, 26
recusal, 9–11, 26, 287, 295, 300, 302, 310, 315, 323, 324
social environment, 24–25, 92
validity of measure, 46, 69–70
voting, 27, 54–56
workplace performance, 23, 51n, 51, 52, 91, 120
work productivity, 51–53, 53n
Constitution, United States, 32
Cooper, Christopher A., 78
Cooper, James L., 140
Cooper, Phillip J., 10
Cordray, Margaret M., 91
Cordray, Richard, 91
Corley, Pamela C., 58, 115, 116, 244
Costa, Jr., Paul T., 4, 21n, 21, 144n
Counts, Scott, 31
Court packing plan, *See also* "Switch in Time That Saved Nine", 13–14
Court's Legal Office, 292
Cover, Albert D., 51, 53n, 54, 124, 146, 278
Cox, Archibald, 147n
criterion validity, 7, 45–47, 49, 51, 56, 57, 69
Cross, Frank B., 162, 225
cubits, 29, 29n
Cushman, Barry, 1

Dahl, Roald, 32
Danelski, David J., 162n
Davis, Christopher N., 43
Davis, Sue, 166
D.C. v. *Heller* (2007), 223
De Choudhury, Munmun, 31
de Marcken, Gail, 319
Demosthenes, 113
Dickson, Del, 312
Diener, Ed, 21
Dietrich, Bryce J., 25n

Digital Equipment Corp v. *Desktop Direct Inc.* (1994), 86, 95
Dijkstra, Pieternel, 47, 72
Dixie Furniture Store, 161n
Donovan, John J., 51, 75, 77n, 77
Douglas, William O., 41, 43, 49, 54n, 54, 62, 66, 77, 172n, 275n
Duberstein, Paul, 71
Dudley, Nicole M., 51
Dupree, Bernard, 161n

Edmonds, Grant, 20
Eight Amendment, 183n
Eli Lilly v. *Medtronic, Inc.* (1990), 88
Elman, Philip, 10
Employee Retirement Income Security Act of 1974, 137
Employment Division v. *Smith* (1990), 229n
Enns, Peter K., 147, 271n, 272, 273, 277, 278n, 279
Epps, Daniel, 112
Epstein, Lee, 3, 12, 14, 15, 31, 34, 53n, 83n, 93, 98, 115, 116, 139, 140, 146–147, 153, 180, 187, 231, 249, 255, 271, 278–280, 293, 299, 313
Erickson, Robert S., 271
extraversion, 4
    definition of, 4, 22
    estimates of, 43–45
    ideology, 77
    job satisfaction, 77
    "Join-3" votes, 104
    love, 74
    marriage, 73
    measurement of, 37
    merits briefs, 131, 135
    Office of the Solicitor General, 151–152
    oral argument, 134
    policy-based strategic votes, 109
    validity of measure, 69–70
    workplace performance, 74–77

Farganis, Dion, 324n
Farias, Cristian, 277
Faschingbauer, Thomas R., 161n
Fayard, Jennifer V., 20
Federalist 10, 288
Federalist 78, 12
Federalist Papers, The, 288
Fifth Amendment, 290
First National Bank v. *Bellotti* (1978), 270

"Fixer Upper", 27
Flamm, Richard E., 288, 293
Flast v. *Cohen* (1968), 245, 246n, 269n
Flemming, Roy B., 271
Florence County School District v. *Carter* (1993), 141
Foster, Dennis M., 7, 30
Fourteenth Amendment, 290, 291
    Due Process Clause, 290
Fourth Amendment, 112, 223
Fox, Justin, 229n
Frank, Jerome, 12
Frankfurter, Felix, 10, 32, 248n, 272, 288
Franklin v. *Gwinett County Public Schools* (1992), 87n
Freeman v. *Pitts* (1992), 87n, 87
Friedman, Howard S., 25n, 46
Frost, Amanda, 293

Gallant, Jack L., 3, 16
Gambino v. *United States* (1997), 86
Gardiner v. *Sea-Land Services, Inc.* (1986), 95, 95n
Garner, Bryan A., 114, 116–118
Garrow, David J., 275
George, Alexander L., 161n
George III, King of England, 288
George, Juliette L., 161n
George, Linda G., 51
Gerber, Alan S., 54, 76, 77
Geyh, Charles G., 293
Gibson, James L., 12, 17n, 119, 273, 294
Giles, Michael W., 98, 147, 231, 271, 272, 274, 278
Giles, Wil, 287
Gill v. *Whitford* (2018), 168n
Ginsburg, Ruth Bader, 91, 293n
Global Vectors for Word Representation, 35
GloVe, *See* Global Vectors for Word Representation
Goldberg, Arthur, 66
Goldman, Sheldon, 16
Gonzales, A.G., 65, 67
Gonzales v. *Carhart* (2006), 223
Gorgias, 113
Gorsuch, Neil M., 31n, 49, 53, 79n, 83
Gosling, Samuel D., 76, 77
Graetz, Michael J., 33, 34n, 172
Greenburg, Jan Crawford, 275
Greenhouse, Linda, 33, 34n, 119, 172n, 172
Greenstein, Fred I., 3

Gruenfeld, Deborah H., 3, 16
Gul, Sumeer, 24, 142n, 226, 276

Hadley v. *U.S.* (1992), 2
Haire, Susan, 229
Halder, Santoshi, 24, 226, 276
Halfhill, Terry, 325
Hall, Matthew E.K., 3, 7, 8, 18–19, 30, 35, 37n,
    58–59, 62, 65, 67, 69, 114, 116, 118, 121n,
    121–124, 126, 130–131
    agenda setting, 18, 88–89
    "Big Five", 18
    intra-Court bargaining, 18
    limitations of approach, 18–19, 30, 57–58,
        61–65, 69, 88–89
    merits voting, 18
    opinion assignment, 18, 170, 171n
    opinion bargaining, 192, 193n
    opinion writing, 18
    SCIPE measures, 56–57, 57n, 58, 61–65, 67,
        69, 192
Halperin, Karen D., 16n
Hamilton, Alexander, 12
Hampson, Sarah E., 25n
Hansford, Thomas G., 15, 225, 251n, 255n,
    256n, 246–260
Harlan II, John Marshall, 32
Harman Mining Company, 290, 291n
Harms, Peter D., 21n
Harry Potter series, 32
Harvey, Anna, 46
Hawthorne effect, 38
Heinstrom, Jannica, 23, 142, 226, 276
Heller, Daniel, 49, 73–76
Hellyer, Paul, 229
Helson, Ravenna, 21, 51
Henke, Kristen L., 293
Hermann, Margaret G., 16n
Hettinger, Virginia A., 98, 147, 231
Hicks, Melvin, 78, 164n
Hintz, William, 85
Ho, Daniel E., 13
Horvitz Eric, 31
Hough, Leatta M., 23, 191, 276
Hollibaugh, Jr., Gary E., 16n, 25, 30, 35, 58n
Hume, Robert J., 293–296n, 299, 300n, 302,
    303n, 304, 305, 307, 308, 310, 312
Hurtz, Gregory M., 51, 75, 77n, 77
Hurwitz, Mark S., 15

IBM Watson Personality Insights, *See* Watson
    Personality Insights program
ideological drift, 17
Iditarod Trail Sled Dog Race, 319, 326
Industrial Society and Its Future, 32
Ingraham v. *Wright* (1977), 183, 184n
Ilies, Remus, 49, 73, 74

J.E.B. v. *T.B.* (1994), 164
Jackson, Joshua J., 20, 21n, 49, 72–73, 75, 144n
Jagger, Mick, 47n, 49n
James, William, 20, 21n
Japan Whaling Association v. *American
    Cetacean Society* (1986), 185
J.C.S., *See* Judicial Common Space
Jefferson, Thomas, 289
Jenkins, John A., 139, 140
John, Oliver P., 20–23, 51, 89, 117, 189, 191, 250,
    276, 294
Johnson, Timothy R., 1, 2, 8, 114, 115, 119–120,
    123–126, 140, 157, 312
Johnson, Roy Lee, 222n
Johnson, Wendy, 20
Johnson, Christopher D., 273
Johnson, William, 289
Jokela, Markus, 47n, 72
Jones, Constance, 21
Jones, Indiana, 29n
Jowett, Benjamin, 11
Judge, Timothy A., 23, 47n, 51, 71–72, 74–77,
    120
Judicial Common Space, 98, 106, 146, 153,
    231n, 233n, 280
judicial decision making
    credibility, 114
    dissents, 14
    ideology, 3, 12–15, 33
    law, 11–13, 16
    logic, 114
    motivation, 15, 80
    personality, *See* judicial personality and
        decision making
    policy preferences, 14, 27
    precedent, 15–16
judicial minimalism, 224, 225n
judicial personality
    data used to measure, 33n, 31–34, 38
    decision making, 17
    judicial behavior, 3, 11–12, 15, 16n, 16, 17, 27
    measurement of traits, 29–31, 33n, 33, 38–41,
        59–68

motives, 17–18
self-esteem, 17
utility maximization, 18
validation of estimates, 43–46
judicial recusal
28 U.S.C. §455, 290n, 292
definition of, 287
purposes, 287, 288
jurisprudential regimes, 15

Kagan, Elena, 31, 47, 49, 286n, 287, 296, 297n
Kaiser Aluminum v. *Bonjorno* (1990), 225
Kandler, Christian, 21
Kapust, Daniel, 113
Kassow, Benjamin J., 16
Katyal, Neal, 286n
Kavanaugh, Brett M., 31n, 49
Keller, Jonathan W., 7
Kennedy, Anthony M., 2, 53, 119, 137–138, 156,
    164, 222, 223n, 269, 274, 275n, 291n, 310
Kennedy, George A., 113–114
Kern, Margaret L., 46
Kimball, Bruce A., 13
King, Laura A., 121
King v. *Burwell* (2014), 2
Kingdon, John W., 277
Kirklosky, Louise, 85
Klein, David, 3
Klinger, Jonathan D., 16n, 25, 30, 35, 58n
Knight, Jack, 3, 12, 14, 15, 31, 187, 246, 249
Knox, John, 1
Kobylka, Joseph F., 116
Korobkin, Russel B., 225
Kosma, Montgomery N., 53
Krewson, Christopher N., 43
Kritzer, Herbert M., 15
Krueger, Robert F., 20, 23, 250
Kunda, Ziva, 46
Kwan, Virginia S.Y., 21

Labor Management Relations Act, 137
Laird v. *Tatum* (1972), 313
Landes, William M., 34, 246
Lane, Elizabeth A., 79n
Langdell, Christopher Columbus, 13
Larsen, Randy J., 3, 20
Lasley, Scott, 25
Laswell, Harold D., 16n
Lazarus, Edward, 1, 93n, 94
LeBreton, James M., 21n
Lee, Rex, 139

legal realism, *See also* attitudinal model, 13,
    15, 86
legal theory model, 12–14
LEGO, 110, 181
    Hogwarts Express, 110
    Millennium Falcon, 110
Leiman, Joan Maisel, 80n
LexisNexis, 252
    Headnotes, 229n, 238, 239n
Liberty Central, 286
Liljeberg v. *Health Service Acquisition Corp.*
    (1988), 292
Linguistic Inquiry and Word Count program,
    35–36, 36–38n, 121–122, 228, 229n
Lindquist, Stephanie A., 162
Liu, Zhe, 30
LIWC, *See* Linguistic Inquiry and Word
    Count program
Local 144 Nursing Home Pension
    Fund v. *Demisay* (1993), 137–138
Longfellow, Henry Wadsworth, 112

Mackuen, Michael B., 271
Madison, James, 287, 289
Malouff, John M., 73–74
Mairesse, Fancois, 35, 36, 37n, 37, 58n
Maltzman, Forrest, 16, 162n, 166–169n, 169,
    170n, 172n, 172, 175n, 185n, 187, 189, 190n,
    193n, 193, 196, 197n, 198, 217, 218n, 246n,
    246, 270, 273
Manning, Christopher D., 35
Marbury v. *Madison* (1803), 289
Marbury, William, 289
Mark, Alyx, 325
Markon, Kristian E., 23, 250
Marshall, John, 289n
Marshall, Thurgood, 41, 83, 93n, 94, 172, 173,
    186, 297
Martin, Andrew D., 31, 33, 98, 106, 124,
    146–147, 231, 271, 278–280, 299
Martin, Denny, 289
Martin-Quinn scores, 54, 55, 57n, 75–77,
    124–125, 299, 300n
Martin, Steve, 47n, 49n
Martin v. *Hunter's Lessee* (1816), 289
Martineau, Robert J., 115
Martinek, Wendy L., 326
Martocchio, Joseph J., 47n, 71–72
Mason, Alpheus Thomas, 1
Masood, Ali S., 16
McAdams, Dan P., 21n

McCann, Stewart J.H., 71
McConnell, Mitch, 291
    as "Cocaine Mitch", 291
McCleskey, Warren, 161, 162n
McCrae, Robert R., 4, 20, 21n, 21, 23, 89, 117,
    144n, 250, 276
McGraw, Warren, 291
McGuire, Kevin T., 120, 123, 126, 147, 271, 273,
    278
McKeown, M. Margaret, 293
McNulty, James K., 25
McReynolds, James, 1–2, 10
Meachum v. *Fano* (1976), 184
Mehl, Mattias R., 228
Meints, Jenna, 20
merits briefs, 114–116
    conscientiousness, *See* conscientiousness
    credibility, 114, 116–117
    emotional language, 114, 116–117, 121
    framing of argument, 115–116
    justice ideology, 124
    litigant influence, 114
Mertens v. *Hewitt Associates* (1993), 90, 155,
    156
Mike, Anissa, 144, 275, 277
Mishler, William, 271n
Mitchell, Gregory, 3
Mohammed, Susa, 325
Monaghan, Henry, 184
Mondak, Jeffrey J., 4, 16n, 22, 25n, 190
motivated reasoning, 46
Mount, Michael K., 22–23, 120, 191, 276n, 276
Moyer, Laura, 17, 229
Mroczek, Daniel, 21
Murphy, Bruce Allen, 54n, 275
Murphy, Frank, 49, 51
Murphy, Walter F., 271, 273

National Advertising Company v. *Raleigh*
    (1988), 87n, 141
*National Federation of Independent
    Business* v. *Sebelius* (2012), 88, 119n, 286,
    287
Nelson, Michael J., 273, 324
Nelson, Thomas E., 17
neuroticism, 4
    definition of, 4, 22
    estimates of, 41, 44
    ideology, 77
    job satisfaction, 77
    longevity, 71

    love, 74
    marriage, 72
    measurement of, 37n, 37, 59, 60, 67
    merits briefs, 131, 135
    number of children, 72
    oral argument, 134
    validity of measure, 69–70
    workplace performance, 74–77
New Deal, 13–14
New York v. *Eastway Corporation* (1987), 95n
New York Times, 255, 260, 299
Nickerson, Raymond S., 46
Niederhoffer, Kate G., 228
Nixon, Richard M., 34n, 269
NLRB v. *Food Store Employees Union* (1974),
    2
non-response bias, 38
Nunn, Clyde A., 29

Oakes, James L., 225
Obamacare cases, *See National Federation of
    Independent Business* v. *Sebelius*
Obergefell v. *Hodges* (2015), 2
O'Brien, David M., 92, 114n, 119
Ochs, Donovan J., 113
O'Connor, Sandra Day, 2, 155, 162, 164, 225n,
    245, 246n
O'Geen, Andrew J., 15
O'Melveny & Myers v. *FDIC* (1994), 86
Office of the Solicitor General, 8, 27, 88,
    122–123, 123n, 125, 139–140
    agenda setting, 139, 139n, 144, 145n, 152–153
    amicus briefs, 139, 144, 145, 147n
    call for the views of the Solicitor General,
        84n, 84, 94, 137, 139, 145n, 153n, 155–156,
        159
    conscientiousness, *See* conscientiousness
    Deputy Solicitor General, 140
    influence on justices, 141–142
    justice ideology, 146, 150–152, 152n
    merits success, 144
    as policy setter, 139
    politicization, 147n
    professionalism, 143, 160
    quality legal representation, 140
    relationship with the justices, 143–144
    success at the Supreme Court, 140
    Supreme Court Rule 37, 139
    "Tenth Justice", 143
Old Testament, 29
Ones, Deniz S., 16n

openness, 4
  agenda setting, 101
  definition of, 4, 22
  estimates of, 41, 44
  ideology, 77
  job satisfaction, 77
  judicial behavior, 5
  longevity, 71
  love, 74
  marriage, 72
  measurement of, 36, 37n, 36–59
  merits briefs, 131, 135
  number of children, 72
  Office of the Solicitor General, 152, 159
  oral argument, 134
  policy-based strategic votes, 109
  validity of measure, 69–70
  workplace performance, 74–77
opinion bargaining
  circulate, 187
  joinder, 185
  suggestions, 185
  threaten, 186
  wait, 186
  will write, 187
oral argument, 118–120
  Blackmun's grading of, 124
  conscientiousness, *See* conscientiousness
  credibility, 114n
  information collection, 119–120
  interruptions, 119
  justice ideology, 124–125
  legitimacy, 119
  policy preferences, 120
  strength of argument, 114, 120, 124
Owens, Ryan J., 7, 8, 17, 31, 33, 43, 79, 84–88,
  92, 93, 94n, 94–97, 106, 114–116, 118, 121n,
  121–124, 126, 130–131, 139, 140, 143, 147,
  152–153, 153n, 153, 157, 168, 227, 228n,
  230n, 232n, 233, 244, 271, 272, 274, 278n,
  280

Palmer, Jan, 87, 170
Pang, Xun, 15
Partial-Birth Abortion Ban Act of 2003, 223
Paul v. *Davis* (1976), 184
Pearson, Lionel, 113
Pennebaker, James W., 30, 121, 225, 228
Pennington, Jeffrey, 35
Pennsylvania v. *Ritchie* (1987), 2
Peppers, Todd C., 98, 147, 184, 231, 248

Perry, H.W., 85, 88, 92, 140, 143
personality
  absence of, 39–40
  "Big Five" traits, *See* "Big Five" traits
  definition of, 3–4, 17–18, 20
  estimation of, 7
  measurement of, 29–30, 33, 34
  motives, 17n
  profile, 4
  surveys, 38, 39
  traits, *See* traits
  words, 30
Personality Recognizer, 37, 38n, 59, 62, 67, 69
  how it works, 38n, 58n, 35–58
persuasion, 113–114
  credibility, 113–114
  dispositio, 113
  inventio, 113
  logic, 113–114
  pathos, 113
Pervin, Lawrence A., 20, 21n
Pink Floyd, 181
Planned Parenthood v. *Casey* (1992), 275
Plato, 113
Poole, Keith, 231
Posner, Richard A., 3, 15, 34, 246
Powell, Lewis F., 53, 119, 161, 162n, 180, 183,
  184n, 185, 246n, 269n, 269
Pritchett, C. Herman, 14–16, 27
Provine, Doris Marie, 140
psychoeconomic model of decision-making,
  See also Hall, Matthew E.K., 18
public mood, 147, 147n, 152n

quanteda, 39
Queeg, Captain, 275
Quinn, Kevin M., 13, 33, 106, 124, 231, 299

Ramey, Adam J., 16n, 25, 30, 35, 37n, 58n
rational choice model, *See* strategic model
Ratzlaf v. *United States* (1994), 164
Ray, Laura Krugman, 58
Reagan, Ronald, 269
Rehnquist Court, 46
Rehnquist, William, 79, 80, 85, 92, 115, 155,
  162–164n, 167, 168n, 170, 173, 183, 184n,
  245, 246n, 269, 270, 287, 300, 312, 313n
Remmel, Megan L., 25
Rentfrow, Peter J., 77
Richard the Lionheart, 29
Richards, Mark J., 15

Riemann, Rainer, 21
Ringhand, Lori A., 247, 249, 324
Ringsmuth, Eve, 8, 114, 116, 118, 121n, 121–124, 126, 130–131, 324
Robert, Christopher, 325
Roberts, Brent W., 17n, 17, 20n, 20, 21n, 21, 22, 23n, 25n, 47, 49, 51–53, 71, 89, 117, 142, 144n, 144, 250, 294
Roberts, John G., 11–13, 57n, 168n, 224, 247n, 269, 292n, 312, 313
Roberts, Owen, 13
Roberts, Roxanne, 45–46
Roe v. Wade (1973), 172
Rohde, David W., 162
Roosevelt, Franklin Delano, 13–14
Rosen, David, 85
Rosen, Jeffrey, 6, 225
Rosenberg, Ethel, 275
Rosenberg, Julius, 275
Rosenthal, Howard L., 231
Rowling, J.K., 32
Roy, Anjali, 24, 226, 276
Rubenzer, Steven J., 16n
Ruger, Theodore, 162

Saint Mary's Honor Center v. Hicks (1993), 78–83, 92, 164–165
Salgado, Jesus F., 23, 276
Salokar, Rebecca Mae, 140, 143
Sample, James, 293
Sayago, A., 65, 67
Scalia, Antonin, 2, 41, 49, 61–62, 65, 79n, 79, 80, 112–114, 116–118, 156, 162, 164n, 164, 169, 224, 225n, 225, 287, 310
Schauer, Frederick, 3, 224, 246
Schick, Marvin, 85
Schlatt, Frank, 161n
Schmidt, Thomas, 24, 226, 276
Schneble v. Florida (1972), 270
Schwartz, Bernard, 53, 180
Schwartz, H. Andrew, 36–38, 38n
Scigliano, Robert, 140, 143
SCIPE measures, *See* Hall, Matthew E.K.
Scott, John T., 246, 249n, 273
Scott, Kevin M., 15
Second Amendment, 223
Securities Industry Association v. Board of Governors of the Federal Reserve (1984), 141
Segal-Cover scores, 51n, 51–53, 53n, 53–56, 74, 124, 146, 279

Segal, Jeffrey A., 3, 14, 33n, 33, 51, 53n, 54, 87, 93, 98, 115, 124, 140, 146, 153, 231, 246, 248, 253, 255, 278, 280, 299
Shah, Tariq Ahmad, 17
Sheehan, Reginald S., 168, 271n
Shepard's Citations, 252, 253n
Simon, David A., 91, 168
Sinhah, Vibha, 38n
Slotnick, Elliot E., 168n
Smelcer, Susan Navarro, 53
Snyder, Mark, 4
Socher, Richard, 35
social desirability effect, 38
Socrates, 113
Sokol, Ronald P., 116
Solicitor General, *See* Office of the Solicitor General
Solomon, Brittany C., 49, 72–73, 75
Songer, Donald R., 16, 85, 87
Soto, Christopher J., 21n
Sotomayor, Sonia, 49
Souter, David H., 32, 41, 80, 223n, 223
Spaeth, Harold J., 3, 14, 33n, 33, 87, 93, 94, 140, 153, 168, 246, 248, 253
Spain, Seth M., 21n
Spence, Lester Kenyatta, 273
Spinath, Frank M., 21
Spriggs, Jr., James F., 8, 15, 114, 120, 124–126, 140, 162, 172, 185n, 185, 187, 189, 190n, 193n, 193, 196, 197n, 198, 218n, 246n, 249n, 251n, 255n, 256n, 217–273
Srivastava, Sanjay, 20–22, 89, 189, 191, 250, 276, 294
stare decisis, 249, 251, 268, 269, 273, 322
definition of, 247n
Stata Corporation, 65
Staudt, Nancy, 180
Stefko, Oseph V., 15
Steigerwalt, Amy, 53
Stempel, Jeffrey W., 293
Stern, Robert L., 88, 91
Stevens, John Paul, 83, 137–138, 155, 164, 186, 310
Stewart, Abigail J., 20, 23, 191
Stewart, Potter, 183, 270
Stimson, James A., 147, 147, 271n, 273, 278n
Stone, Harlan, 1
strategic model, 3, 12, 14–15
Strauss, Judy P., 23, 276
Sullivan, John L., 29
Sullivan, Kathleen M., 224

Sunstein, Cass R., 224n
Supreme Court clerks, 83–84
Supreme Court Clerk's Office, 82
Supreme Court Database, 46, 59, 123, 144,
    145n, 145, 146, 148n, 171n, 231, 232n, 234n,
    279n, 280n, 278–296
Supreme Court Individual Personality
    Estimates, 171
Swann, Jr., William B., 77
*Swann v. Charlotte-Mecklenburg Board of
    Education* (1971), 270
"Switch in Time That Saved Nine", *See also*
    Court packing plan, 13

Taft, William Howard, 168
Tanenhaus, Joseph, 85
Tausczik, Yla R., 121
Telecommunications Policy, Office of, 169
Tellegen, Auke, 20
Tennessee v. Middlebrooks (1993), 164
Teply, Larry L., 116
Tetlock, Philip E., 3, 16
Thomas, Clarence, 5, 43–45, 59, 112, 156, 164n,
    286
Thorensen, Carl J., 47n, 71–72
traits, 3–4, 17–18, 20, 22, *See also*
    agreeableness; conscientiousness;
    extraversion; neuroticism; openness
    and "Big Five", *See* "Big Five" traits
    and "Big Seven", 21
    bright, 21n
    dark, 21n
    definition of, 20
    heritability of, 20–21
    influence of environment, 20–21
    legislators, 30
    motives, 20
    six factor model, 21
    stability of, 20–21
    Supreme Court justices, *See* judicial
        personality and traits
Trautwein, Ulrich, 144n
Treier, Shawn, 229
Tumey v. Ohio (1927), 290
Turner, Joel, 25
Tun-Nisa, Nahida, 17

Ulmer, S. Sidney, 85, 86
Unibomber, 32
United States v. Lashawn Banks (2003), 222
United States v. Roy Lee Johnson (2000), 222n

Ura, Joseph Daniel, 119
U.S. Law Week, 97, 102, 110

*Valley Forge Christian College v. Americans
    United for Separation of Church and
    State* (1982), 245, 246n, 250, 269
Vanberg, Georg, 229n
Verilli, Louis J., 287, 288, 289n, 292, 293
Verne, Jules, 32
Viechtbauer, Wolfgang, 21n
Vining, Richard L., 53, 271, 272, 274, 278
Vinson, Fred, 10, 32n, 43, 313
Voting Rights Act, 83n

Wahlbeck, Paul M., 8, 114, 120, 124–126, 140,
    162n, 166, 167n, 169n, 169, 170n, 172,
    172n, 175n, 185n, 185, 189, 190n, 193n, 193,
    196, 197n, 198, 218n, 246n, 217–270
Walker, Thomas G., 83n, 140
Waller, Niels G., 21n
Wall Street Journal, 270
Walton, Kate E., 21n
Wang, Jalal Mahmud, 38n
Ward, Artemus, 83, 162, 184
Warren, Earl, 34n, 41, 167, 168, 173n, 248n,
    269, 313
Warren Court, 46
Washington Post, 270
Watson, David, 49, 73, 74
Watson Personality Insights program, 7, 34, 57
    how it works, 34–35, 69
    performance compared to Personality
        Recognizer, 35–38, 38n
    standardization of judicial personality
        estimates, 40–41, 69
Waung, Marie, 325
Weaver v. Massachusetts (2017), 59
Webster v. Reproductive Health Services
    (1988), 2
Wedeking, Justin P., 17, 31, 43, 116, 119, 147,
    227, 228n, 230n, 232n, 233, 244, 271n, 278,
    324n
Weiden, David L., 83, 184
West Coast Hotel v. Parrish (1937), 13
Westerland, Chad, 98, 146, 231, 280
White, Byron R., 32n, 32, 79, 82, 91, 137–138,
    155, 164, 185–187, 269
Whittaker, Charles E., 32
Wiedenbeck, Peter, 180
Wikipedia, 35, 46
Winter, David G., 7, 16n, 17, 20n, 30

Witt, L.A., 23, 110, 120
Wohlfarth, Patrick, 8, 43, 96, 140n, 143, 145,
    147n, 147, 227, 230n, 232n, 233, 244, 271,
    272n, 272–274, 277, 278n, 279
Wolfe, Sarah, 286
Wolff, Christian, 24, 226, 276
Wood, B. Dan, 271n
Wood, Sandra L., 168, 170
Woodruff, Michael, 46
Woodward, Bob, 2, 93, 94n, 172n
Wright, Ben, 161n
Wright, John R., 85–88, 94, 97, 140

Wrightsman, Lawrence S., 3, 16

Xu, Anbang, 38n

Zavala, Joe D., 21n
Zeckhauser, Richard, 224
Zigerell, L. J., 324
Zilis, Michael A., 278, 324, 325n
Ziller, Robert, 6, 17
Zink, James R., 246, 249n, 273
Zorn, Christopher J.W., 85, 87–88

CPSIA information can be obtained
at www.ICGtesting.com
Printed in the USA
LVHW011807091222
734912LV00003B/878

9 781316 618004